EDUCATION TODAY

THE FOUNDATIONS
OF A PROFESSION

Also available with **Education Today: The Foundations of a Profession**

Instructor's Resource Manual, by Janis Fine (Loyola University of Chicago) and Thomas Mott, consisting of Part I (Instructional Aids), Part II (Test-Item File), and Part III (Sampler of Transparency Masters). ISBN: 0-312-04696-0.

Transparency Masters—approximately 40 two-color transparencies, half from the text and half original. ISBN: 0-312-09207-5.

Computerized Test-Item File—available in three versions:

IBM 3.5″ disk (ISBN: 0-312-09209-1)
IBM 5.25″ disk (ISBN: 0-312-09210-5)
Macintosh (ISBN: 0-312-09208-3)

Video: Produced specifically for *Education Today*, this video features a panel of experienced and novice teachers discussing strategies for teaching and learning from the text as well as footage of actual classroom situations. ISBN: 0-312-10733-1.

To order any of the above items, contact your St. Martin's sales representative or call 1-800-446-8923.

EDUCATION TODAY

THE FOUNDATIONS OF A PROFESSION

Joan K. Smith
Loyola University of Chicago

L. Glenn Smith
Northern Illinois University

St. Martin's Press/New York

Acquisitions Editor: Naomi Silverman
Development Editor: Bob Weber
Project Editor: Richard Steins
Production Manager: Pat Ollague
Art Director: Sheree Goodman
Text Design: Proof Positive/Farrowlyne Associates, Inc.
Text Art: Fine Line, Inc.
Cover: Joseph DePinho
Cover Art: © Jonathan Bumas 1993
Photo Editor: Inge King

Library of Congress Catalog Card Number: 92–50029

Manufactured in the United States of America.

8 7 6 5 4

f e d c b a

For information, write:

St. Martin's Press, Inc.
175 Fifth Avenue
New York, NY 10010

ISBN: 0–312–04695–2

Acknowledgments

Chapter-opening Photographs

Chapter 1, page 3: Lawrence Migdale/Stock, Boston; **Chapter 2, page 27:** National Education Association; **Chapter 3, page 49:** Bob Daemmrich/The Image Works; **Chapter 4, page 83:** Seth Resnick/Stock, Boston; **Chapter 5, page 111:** Tony Freeman/PhotoEdit; **Chapter 6, page 141:** The Image Works; **Chapter 7, page 167:** Paul Conklin/PhotoEdit; **Chapter 8, page 201:** Bettmann; **Chapter 9, page 231:** North Wind Picture Archives; **Chapter 10, page 261:** Mark Antman/The Image Works; **Chapter 11, page 297:** Bob Daemmrich/The Image Works; **Chapter 12, page 321:** Bob Daemmrich/The Image Works; **Chapter 13, page 343:** NASA.

Acknowledgments and copyrights continue at the back of the book, on page 367, which constitutes an extension of the copyright page.

For our Parents—
Mildred, Elenor, and Raymond;
and
Frank and Letha

And for all parents who start the educational process
with their children
and maintain educational and caring roles
throughout the parental life span

About the Authors

■

 **Joan K. Smith** is Associate Dean of the Graduate School of Loyola University, Chicago, where she holds a joint appointment as professor in the Department of Educational Leadership and Policy Studies and in the Department of History. Currently she is president of the Society of Professors of Education, is serving a second term on the Board of Examiners for the National Council for Accreditation of Teacher Education (NCATE), and is a member of the International Standing Conference on the History of Education; she has also been president of the International Society of Educational Biography and editor of *Educational Studies.* Before joining Loyola University, Smith taught at Iowa State and at Illinois State universities, as well as at the community college level. She was a teacher in the public schools of Illinois and Iowa before completing a Ph.D. in educational foundations at Iowa State University.

 **L. Glenn Smith** is a professor in the Department of Leadership and Educational Policy Studies, Northern Illinois University, where he also chairs the department and is curator of the Blackwell History of Educational Research Collection. He has edited *Educational Studies* and *Vitae Scholasticae* and has been president of the International Society of Educational Biography and of the Council of Learned Societies in Education. Smith has taught in both public and parochial schools and at four universities (Oklahoma, Iowa State, Houston, and Northern Illinois); he also has served on two boards of the National Council for Accreditation of Teacher Education (NCATE), and he acts as a consultant to the Schul Museum in Nürnberg, Germany, in developing an exhibit about multicultural education in America.

PREFACE

DESIGN AND PURPOSE OF TEXT

Education Today is an introduction to the foundations of education for people who are thinking about becoming—or have decided to become—educators. It is designed for use either in introduction to education courses or in upper-level foundations-type courses. For introductory courses the text assumes no previous knowledge of the field of education, and it presents a complete overview of the discipline. For upper-level or postbaccalaureate courses the book is based on current research and original source materials and documents that provide an in-depth study. In using the term *foundations* we mean the comprehensive study of educational theories, practices, and issues in relation to the general fields of sociology, psychology, history, philosophy, and law. This approach lets us link educational policies to the broader social policies and context in which they exist.

Foundations and introductory education textbooks are often regarded as being dry and dull, as lacking in style, and as being exhaustive—yet shallow—in their coverage of material. We have aimed to overcome such defects by providing an organization, focus, and narrative that allow readers to grasp the "big picture" while also closely examining the educational establishment of the late twentieth century. We intend to take readers on a journey through the vast terrain of education in order to provide a comprehensive overview of its foundations. For the most part the trip will be fast-paced, but at times we will slow down to get a better view of a particular educational scene or to contemplate its human dimensions.

Many Americans are quite sophisticated about schools and about their expectations concerning public education. Most of us think we understand our schools, because we have spent a lot of time in them and because we hear about education almost daily in the media. But sometimes we think our experiences have made us education experts. We don't make this mistake with other professions. For example, we hire experts to care for our health and to tend to our legal needs, and we don't conclude that we have expert knowledge of medicine or law. We seem to know that our medical and legal opinions are simply the result of personal experiences. But when it comes to education, we often mistake opinions for facts.

As professional educators we have been involved actively and intimately in the theory, research, and practice of education for over thirty years. Together we have over sixty years' experience at all levels of schooling. We respect the field as a complicated and culturally sensitive enterprise; we see education as a barometer of the country's social, psychological, political, and legal atmosphere. We are not blind to the shortcomings of our profession, and we care deeply about its present and future conditions. Primarily, then, we hope that *Education Today* will help readers develop a more realistic, more meaningful understanding of teaching and schooling than might be attained through personal experience.

ORGANIZATION AND CONTENT OF TEXT

Education Today consists of thirteen chapters that explore three main themes: the past, the present, and the future.

Part I, "Today," includes five chapters that investigate current aspects of education. Chapter 1 ("Today's Teacher") takes a look at who goes into teaching, and why; Chapter 2 ("Teaching as a Profession") compares the evolution of teaching with the development of other professions; and Chapter 3 ("Managing Schools") describes the people who manage our schools. Chapters 4 and 5 ("Social Class and Education" and "Education for Equity and Diversity") then explore the social foundations of education by looking closely at the demographic characteristics of American students and the mission of the public schools to equalize educational opportunities for all.

Part II, "Yesterday and Today," contains five chapters that offer insights into present educational conditions by examining the past to provide psychological, historical, and philosophical contexts. Chapter 6 ("Learning") and Chapter 7 ("Curricula and Learning") present the psychological foundations of education by describing theoretical and applied developments related to teaching and learning. Chapter 8 ("European Backgrounds") and Chapter 9 ("American Developments") provide a historical framework in which to view contemporary education; together they present the historical foundations of education. Chapter 10 ("Philosophy and Education") explores the philosophical foundations of American education.

Part III, "Today and Tomorrow," comprises three chapters that look closely at the issues affecting today's schools and at the issues that are likely to be significant as we enter a new century. Chapter 11 ("Education and the Courts") describes how the legal system affects education by focusing especially on First Amendment rights, issues of church and state, segregation, and school board issues. Chapter 12 ("Issues in Education") looks at broader social and educational issues and the challenges they pose to our schools. Finally, Chapter 13 ("Education in the Twenty-first Century") looks into the "crystal ball" to forecast some of the social, technological, and environmental trends that are likely to affect future education; the chapter emphasizes global interdependency and its effects on American education.

SPECIAL FEATURES OF TEXT

Education Today incorporates numerous pedagogical features to orient and guide students through each chapter of the text. Before describing them, however, let us emphasize four special features that are designed to engage students' attention and help them relate the material to their personal experiences:

- Each chapter begins with a **vignette** that makes content relevant by bringing it to life in case-study form. The vignette provides an excellent starting point for classroom discussions.

- Each chapter includes a brief biographical profile called **Yesterday's Professional** that focuses on the life and educational contributions of a particular person; again, the purpose is to personalize the chapter's content and to help students connect the present with the past.

- Throughout each chapter **Research Says . . . for Tomorrow's Education** prods students' curiosity and provides opportunities for in-depth study of recent research into specific areas; these boxed displays also encourage students to evaluate educational research.

- In each chapter **Comparative Perspective on Today's Issues** poses a question and briefly outlines two opposing positions about an educational issue that is central to the chapter's content. This encourages students to develop a personal point of view about the issue, based on material in the chapter.

Besides these special features, each chapter of *Education Today* includes the following pedagogical aids:

An **epigraph and color photo** introduce the chapter's content and main theme.

A list of **Advanced Organizers**—focus statements—highlight the chapter's main topics, in sequence, and provide a structure for supplemental activities.

The **Chapter Outline** lists the main headings to give students a preview of content and its organization.

Throughout the chapter **Key Terms** appear in bold type where they are defined, and they are listed at the end of the chapter; all terms also appear in the **Glossary**.

Numerous **tables**, **drawings**, **and photographs**—most appearing in color—illustrate important material throughout the text.

Footnotes are positioned to the side of the text they cite, providing easy access to original and primary sources.

A **Conclusions** section ends each chapter by summarizing its main ideas and viewpoint.

An annotated list of **Suggested Readings** steers students to significant sources of information about the chapter's content.

ANCILLARY PACKAGE

The following ancillary materials are available from the publisher for use with *Education Today.*

An **Instructor's Resource Manual** includes an instructional section (Part I) consisting of chapter outlines and overviews, discussion questions, activities, small-group break-outs, and evaluation worksheets; test questions (Part II); and a sampler of transparencies from the complete transparency package available to adopters of the text.

A **computerized test-item file** consists of questions from the Instructor's Resource Manual available in three disk formats (IBM 3.5 and 5.25, and Macintosh).

A **transparency package** consists of some 40 two-color transparency masters, about half from the book and half original.

A **video** was produced specifically to accompany the text. It showcases a panel of experienced and novice teachers who model good teaching by discussing strategies for teaching and learning from *Education Today*. Also included is footage of actual classroom situations used to illustrate the issues, concepts, and methods presented.

The computerized test-item file, transparency package, and video are available to adopters of the text.

ACKNOWLEDGMENTS

We want to acknowledge and express appreciation for the contributions of several colleagues. Special thanks go to Rob Cooper, Northern Illinois University, and to Max Bailey, Loyola University of Chicago, for carefully reading and reviewing Chapter 11, ''Education and the Courts.'' We are also deeply grateful to Martha Tevis, University of Texas, Pan American, and to Janis Fine, Loyola University, for reviewing early drafts of the manuscript and making many helpful suggestions. Along with Thomas Mott, Chicago Public Schools, Dr. Fine prepared the Instructor's Resource Manual and the Test-Item File, which are major aids for teachers who use this textbook. Among the many reviewers whose advice helped shape the manuscript we thank Leo W. Anglin, Kent State University; Donald L. Barnes, Ball State University; Joseph L. DeVitis, State University of New York, Binghamton; and Fred D. Kierstead, University of Houston, Clear Lake.

Out gratitude goes as well to Quaing Lee, whose artistic talent lies behind many of the drawings and transparency masters, and to Mary Jo Long, who helped prepare the Glossary. Special thanks go also to Caryn Rudy, Northern Illinois University, and to Cynthia Hasemeier, formerly of Loyola, who typed early drafts of the manuscript; and to Kim Williams, Loyola University, who marshaled countless clerical details during the book's production.

For St. Martin's Press Richard Steins was invaluable in helping develop the book into its final form; and words fall short in expressing gratitude to Bob Weber, Development Editor, for his encouragement and skillful editing throughout the book's progress to publication. Finally, we are grateful to two acquisitions editors at St. Martin's: Kathleen Keller, who helped shape the project during its inception and drafting, and Naomi Silverman, who steered all these efforts to completion.

Joan K. Smith
L. Glenn Smith

CONTENTS

■

II YESTERDAY AND TODAY   139

III   TODAY AND TOMORROW   295

TO THE STUDENT

We have written *Education Today* with you in mind. As former students ourselves, we remember that textbooks sometimes were dreary and lifeless compendiums of material that seemed irrelevant to our own goals and needs. For that reason we have tried to make this textbook as lively and readable as possible, so that your interest in the subject of education will continue to grow and develop.

This book is designed to introduce you to the field of education and to help you make informed decisions about teaching as a career or about the schooling of your children. Although the book covers many scientific aspects of education and some material is developed in depth, we have not written in a scientific or scholarly style. We have concentrated, instead, on the narrative— on the story line—so that the material will be both relevant and interesting to you.

This introductory text is based on what we call the "foundations" of education: the social, psychological, historical, philosophical, and legal aspects of education. Together, all these frameworks will provide a potent lens through which we can view the broader social problems that are related to educational theories, practices, and issues in America. In other words, education is based on and reflects many kinds of human endeavor; in turn, the study of education also illuminates many other areas of our lives.

The book includes thirteen chapters that are grouped into three parts: Part I, "Today"; Part II, "Yesterday and Today"; and Part III, "Today and Tomorrow." Yes, we will begin with the present, but then we will relate it to the past and, finally, to the future. We firmly believe that it is impossible to understand American education today without having a firm grasp on the past developments that shaped it. If you think a minute about one of your best friends, you will realize that you know quite a bit about her or him. You know where your friend was born and grew up, and you know some of the significant experiences that shaped your friend's life. You probably could even make some predictions about your friend's future, based on what you already know.

We believe that the same kind of learning process applies to the study of a discipline, such as education: To understand it well, we need to know something about its past; and to anticipate where it might be headed, we need to know where it has been. Otherwise, we will be stuck in the present, like someone with amnesia. When we know about the past, we can better understand the present—and we can better anticipate the future, perhaps even avoiding past mistakes.

We have included a variety of features in the text to guide you through it and to help you relate it to your own life. First, here's a list of the study aids that appear in every chapter (listed in order of appearance):

The chapter's title page includes an **epigraph and color photo** to announce the topic and introduce the main theme.

Advanced Organizers (topic statements) tell you what you will learn, in what order, and the **Chapter Outline** gives you a list of the main headings.

The text begins with a **vignette**, a real-life example of the chapter's content, to set the scene.

Throughout the chapter **Key Terms** are shown in bold type, and they are listed at the end of the chapter as well as in the **Glossary** at the end of the book.

Footnotes are directly to the side of the text, where you can check them at a glance.

Many **tables**, **drawings**, **and photographs**—often in color—emphasize important points; use them to look ahead and to review the material.

The last section, **Conclusions**, briefly summarizes the chapter's main points and its point of view.

Following the list of Key Terms is an annotated list of **Suggested Readings**; these will guide you to good sources of information about major topics that interest you.

Besides these study aids, every chapter includes the following special features:

■ **Research Says . . . for Tomorrow's Education**   These boxed displays call your attention to some of the latest educational research and guide you to sources so that you can evaluate it.

■ **Comparative Perspective on Today's Issues**   These pose a question about some current issue and give you two opposing points of view about it; consider what your own position might be, based on your reading of the chapter.

■ **Yesterday's Professional**   This is a biographical profile of an educator whose career and contributions advanced the subject under discussion.

Your impressions of the education system and your assessment of it are based on your experiences as a student. Now, by reading *Education Today*, you can broaden your knowledge and sharpen your insights into the complex enterprise known as American education. Having taught at every level and having engaged in educational research for many years, we know that the system has many blemishes, and we have included them for your consideration. Even so, we remain committed to education and are optimistic about future developments. We hope that this book will help you to find a professional role in education so that you can help to shape its future.

EDUCATION TODAY

THE FOUNDATIONS OF A PROFESSION

What if teaching and school management should come to be looked upon as a profession, not less to be protected from the unqualified nor less to be rewarded and conditioned to the highest possible performance than the priesthood, law, or medicine?

—*Henry Holmes* Atlantic Monthly *(January 1940)*

I

TODAY

Because Americans have experienced some form of schooling for a good portion of their lives, most people tend to think that their opinions about education are quite informed and well founded—almost expert, at times. And since taxes support our system of public education, Americans are especially outspoken in criticizing schools. For both these reasons education is often described in terms of negative stereotypes, but—as with any profession or institutional enterprise—not all the criticism is valid.

The five chapters in Part I of *Education Today* describe the educational enterprise as it now exists, situating it within its professional, social, historical, and political contexts. Throughout this section we include profiles and descriptions of today's teachers, their students, and the administrators who manage our schools. The hope is that accurate information will both dispel distorted ideas about education and reinforce correct ideas. We also hope that these chapters will give readers insight into what it means to be a teacher in America today.

Chapter 1 presents a portrait of the people who enter the teaching profession. Besides describing their traditional preparation and qualifications, we look at some trends and alternative approaches to teacher training. Then we examine teachers' salaries, their social status, and the satisfactions (and dissatisfactions) they experience.

Chapter 2 outlines the evolution of teaching as a profession, from earliest times to today's collective bargaining. We explore whether or not teachers are truly professionals like doctors and lawyers by examining the essential characteristics of a profession and by presenting an ongoing comparison of the fields of teaching, medicine, and the law.

Chapter 3 examines the management of American schools by describing today's administrators: principals, superintendents, and boards of education. We also take a close look at how our school systems are financed—and the educational issues that relate to school funding.

Chapters 4 and 5 shift the discussion to consider the demographic characteristics of today's students and their families—the social foundations of American education. Chapter 4 surveys the social-class structure of the United States and how it influences the educational achievement of various groups of students. Issues of social inequality are addressed by examining various studies of how genetic and environmental factors may influence students' intelligence.

Finally, Chapter 5 extends the discussion of demographic issues by describing the evolution of ethnic and cultural diversity in America. What should be the goals of education in a multicultural society? How should they be advanced? The chapter explores both historical and current issues relating to the education of minority students and female students.

Today's Teacher

Late in the last century . . . there were three equally disreputable professions: medicine, law and education.
Doctors and hospitals . . . were the people and places associated with death. . . . Lawyers . . . were
despicable. The profession appeared to be run by the greedy and the conservative. . . . It was also true . . .
that teachers were simply persons who were unfit for the rigors of farm, factory or commercial life.

—David C. Berliner, "Knowledge Is Power," Equity and Excellence, *24 (Winter 1989) 2: 4–5*

Today's Teacher

ADVANCED ORGANIZERS

In this chapter you will learn

Who goes into the teaching profession, and how they compare with students who are pursuing other careers

How teacher candidates are prepared and certified for their professional careers

Who today's teachers are, and how they differ from teachers in the past

What today's teachers are paid, and what their professional status is, compared with yesterday's teachers

Whether or not teachers are satisfied with their profession and career choices

CHAPTER OUTLINE

DEMOGRAPHIC PROFILE OF TEACHER CANDIDATES
  Education Majors vs. Noneducation Majors
  Training and Certification of Teachers

TEACHING IN PERSPECTIVE
  Teaching Today
  Teaching in the Past

SELECTED CHARACTERISTICS OF TEACHING
  Teachers' Pay
  Teachers' Status
  Ascribed Status and Earned Status

EDUCATION AS A CAREER: THE BALANCE SHEET
  Satisfactions of Teaching
  Dissatisfactions of Teaching

CONCLUSIONS

indy Brown and Bob Jones have just graduated from state university, having earned their first professional degrees. Approximately half the students in this program were female, and they will find employment opportunities that are equal to males in their field. Cindy grew up in a middle-class suburb, whereas Bob came from a working-class family and lived near a large city. Both graduated with B/B+ averages from high schools that offered strong college preparatory programs. Cindy plans to seek employment in the suburbs, and Bob wants to work in the city. Both have said that they chose their field because it would give them a sense of personal achievement and satisfaction.

So far this description could fit graduates from a variety of disciplines, including law, business, and medicine (although the proportion of females in M.D. programs is closer to one-third than to one-half).[1] These profiles, however, are intended to characterize typical males and females who have chosen careers as secondary and elementary teachers, respectively. The fact that both Cindy and Bob are white is also typical of education majors—and of the general college population, whose minority members are declining.[2] Following is a more detailed description of today's graduates in teacher education.

DEMOGRAPHIC PROFILE OF TEACHER CANDIDATES

■

EDUCATION MAJORS VS. NONEDUCATION MAJORS

Recent research indicates that education majors match the performance of non-education majors on college entrance examinations. Several comparative studies were prompted by a 1982 report that depicted teacher candidates as scoring lower than students who chose other majors in college. But current research paints a brighter picture. For example, today's teacher candidates are described as having completed solid college preparatory programs with B to high-B grade-point averages and as having scored as well as noneducation majors on the Scholastic Aptitude Test (SAT) and the American College Test (ACT). Both groups have engaged in similar extracurricular activities in high school, and both have come from relatively large families. Most of their mothers and two-thirds of their fathers have earned some college credit.

The future educators, however, are not exactly like their noneducation counterparts. For one thing, a higher percentage of noneducation majors grew up in homes where the combined income in 1985–86 was greater than $50,000. Another difference is that a larger portion of teacher candidates reported that

[1]Cassandra L. Book and Donald J. Freeman, "Differences in Entry Characteristics of Elementary and Secondary Teacher Candidates," *Journal of Teacher Education* 37 (March–April 1986): 47–51. For descriptions and personal accounts of the fields of medicine and law see Dr. X, *Intern* (New York: Harper & Row, 1965); and Dan C. Lortie, "Laymen to Lawmen: Law School, Careers, and Professional Socialization," *Harvard Educational Review* 29 (Fall 1959): 352–369. Although these sources are dated, they remain accurate.

[2]Educational Testing Service, "Teaching," *ETS Policy Notes* 3 (Spring 1991): 1–10; Edmund J. Farrell, "On the Growing Shortage of Black and Hispanic Teachers," *English Journal* 79 (January 1990): 39–46; Nancy L. Zimpher and Suzan Yessayan, "Recruitment and Selection of Minority Populations into Teaching," *Metropolitan Education* 5 (Fall 1987): 57–71; and Mary E. Dilworth, "Black Teachers: A Vanishing Tradition," *Urban League Review* 11 (Summer–Winter 1987–88): 54–58.

RESEARCH SAYS

For Tomorrow's Education . . .

Education majors at Michigan State University compare favorably with noneducation majors on tests measuring scholastic aptitude. Mean scores for education majors on the Scholastic Aptitude Test (SAT) fall in the 60th percentile (verbal) and 58th percentile (math) for all MSU students, and their mean scores on the American College Test (ACT) fall into the 47th percentile for all MSU students. These findings are part of the growing body of research that contradicts earlier studies stating that education majors scored lower on the SAT. See Cassandra L. Book et al., "Comparing Academic Backgrounds of Education and Non Education Majors," (July 1984), ED 256 755. Also see "Differences in Entry Characteristics of Elementary and Secondary Teacher Candidates," *Journal of Teacher Education* 27 (March–April 1986): 47–51. More recent studies support the MSU findings. See "Teaching," *ETS Policy Notes* 3 (Princeton, N.J.: Educational Testing Service, Spring 1991): 1–10.

they read for pleasure, and more of them were elected to the National Honor Society. They also expressed greater interest in helping others and in working with children, and they were less concerned about salaries than were noneducation students.[3]

TRAINING AND CERTIFICATION OF TEACHERS

Each state in some way *certifies* that teacher candidates are qualified for positions in its schools. In general, this means that the candidate has met the state's standards of quality and is eligible for its teaching license. But the teaching profession has tended to blur the distinction that is often made between licensing and certification in other fields, such as medicine. Strictly put, **licensing** is really the "process by which an agency or government *grants permission* to an individual to engage in a given occupation upon finding that the applicant has attained the minimal degree of competency required to ensure that the public health, safety, and welfare will be reasonably well protected." In contrast, **certification** is the "process by which a government or non governmental agency *grants recognition* to an individual who has met certain predetermined qualifications set by a credentializing agency."[4] Usually, to be certified by a state, a teacher candidate needs a bachelor's degree representing a specific number of education courses from a state-approved college or university.

Most teacher preparation programs in the United States include three basic components. They begin with a *liberal arts and sciences* body of coursework that dominates the first two years of study. Next, a secondary teacher candidate focuses on a *specialized subject field*, or major block of coursework in the subject that the candidate intends to teach. (Elementary teacher candidates usually take a series of courses in elementary subjects, and some states require them to be

[3]Jeffrey A. Owings, "National Education Longitudinal Study of 1988: First Follow-up" (Washington, D.C.: National Center for Education Statistics, U.S. Department of Education, 1990); Book and Freeman, "Differences in Entry Characteristics of Elementary and Secondary Teacher Candidates"; Cassandra L. Book et al., "Comparing Academic Backgrounds and Career Aspirations of Education and Noneducation Majors" (July 1984), ED 265 755; *AACTE Briefs* 5 (April 1984): 13; and 5 (June 1984): 2; and V. S. Vance and P. C. Schlechty, "The Distribution of Academic Ability in the Teaching Force: Policy Implications," *Phi Delta Kappan* 63 (September 1982): 22–27.

[4]Stephen L. Murray, "Synthesizing Teacher Testing Policy" (Portland, Ore.: Northwest Regional Educational Laboratory, October 1986), ED 295 926, 6.

liberal arts majors as well.) Finally, teacher candidates take a *professional education sequence* designed to orient them to the profession and to train them in the science and art of teaching. This part of the program usually culminates in practice teaching.

Most teachers, when asked to evaluate their training programs, rate practice teaching as the most valuable component. Having a successful and beneficial experience as a student teacher seems to depend on two things: (1) the skill and competency of the cooperating teacher in the school system and (2) developing rapport both with the cooperating teacher and with the candidate's supervising teacher at the university or college. Teacher candidates often single out their interaction with experienced teachers and other student teachers as providing the most valuable input and feedback. Because candidates rank their practice teaching so highly, it is increasingly common for preparatory programs to include additional on-the-job, field, or clinical experiences. Such work is usually part of the professional education sequence.[5]

Most four-year training programs devote the last two years to the professional education sequence and to specialized courses in the candidate's subject field. Some colleges and universities offer a five-year program that includes graduate work and culminates in a master's degree; this sometimes allows additional time for practice teaching. The state of Oregon is an example. It requires teacher candidates to complete a bachelor's degree before entering an elementary or a secondary teacher training program. In some of Oregon's programs candidates

Most teachers rate practice teaching as the most valuable part of their training—so valuable, that many preparatory programs have increased the time a candidate spends in the field, usually during the professional education sequence. —Mary Kate Denny/PhotoEdit

[5]Mary C. Ellwein, M. Elizabeth Grane, and Ronald E. Comfon, "Talking about Instruction: Student Teachers' Reflections on Success and Failure in the Classroom," *Journal of Teacher Education* 41 (November–December 1990): 3–14.

can earn their master's degree along with the Basic Certificate in Elementary Education (kindergarten through ninth grade) or the Basic Certificate in Secondary Education (fifth grade through twelfth grade). Such a program usually requires additional coursework and some type of research project.[6]

When training is complete and a degree has been earned, prospective teachers are ready to apply for certification in the state where they plan to teach. Certificates are granted either for subject areas or for grade levels to be taught. In the past a candidate's academic record or work in appropriate education courses—along with evidence of sound moral character—have been normal requirements for certification. Today, however, many states require candidates to complete a competency test; in fact, most state laws now require teachers who are seeking certification to complete some form of competency measure.

The certification process varies greatly from state to state, regardless of a movement to standardize it. For example, the National Council for the Accred-

[6]See, for example, a description of the Graduate Teacher Education Program (GTEP) offered at Portland (Oregon) State University, in the Portland State *Bulletin 1991–1992* (Portland State University, 1991).

Comparative Perspective on Today's Issues . . .

◆ ARE TESTS OF TEACHERS' KNOWLEDGE FAIR?

The Issue   Teacher testing became part of most states' educational reforms during the 1980s. In general, states have used testing as a certification requirement; however, Texas and Arkansas have gone a step farther by requiring competency measures for all teachers in their systems.

YES   National opinion surveys have revealed strong public support for requiring satisfactory test performance as an entry-level condition for teaching. Tests of teachers' knowledge can play an important role in the certification and licensing process. They can confirm that a prospective teacher has (1) basic knowledge of subjects in the field he or she will teach, (2) a minimal level of pedagogical theory and skills, and (3) competencies in language and communication. With proper test construction, validation, and norming, tests of teachers' knowledge can function as they do in such professions as law and medicine, where basic knowledge of the field must be demonstrated in order to gain state licensure.

NO   Although most states require testing to enter the teaching profession, the tests do not enhance the professionalism of the occupation, as legal and medical examinations for licensure do. The reason for this shortcoming is that tests of teachers' knowledge are not developed and controlled by the profession. In addition, there is no common baseline of knowledge that all candidates must demonstrate for entry. Instead, pass rates are based on cutoff scores that fluctuate with each pool of testing candidates. These circumstances can hardly raise the selectivity standards of the profession. Finally, existing tests, such as the National Teacher Examination, do not adequately reflect the knowledge base for which prospective teachers should be held accountable.

Source: Based on James Wm. Noll, ed., *Taking Sides: Clashing Views on Controversial Educational Issues*, 5th ed. (Guilford, Conn.: Dushkin, 1989), 332–341.

Beginning teachers are often left alone once they enter the classroom, but some districts have mentoring programs in which the first-year intern is assigned to an experienced teacher who guides, counsels, and befriends the newcomer. —*Jim Pickerell/Stock, Boston*

itation of Teacher Education (NCATE) has been concerned with certification issues and has hoped to avoid inbred, provincial procedures by providing better regulation over standards. Similarly, the National Association of State Directors of Teacher Education Certification (NASDTEC) has endorsed a broad set of certification requirements, and many states have adhered to them. Most professional educators hope that such measures will lead to more uniform certification approaches among the states. At present states vary even in the duration of their teaching certificates; some issue them for life, while others require that they be renewed every three to five years.

During periods of teacher shortages, alternative approaches to certification may arise. These usually involve some form of field supervision and coursework during a teacher's first few years. Such alternatives concern many educators, however, who think they will erode the standards and quality of teaching.

Once they enter the classroom, beginning teachers are usually left alone to manage and instruct their students. But recently some districts have begun to provide supervised classroom experiences for beginning teachers. Such an arrangement is generally known as a **mentoring program**; in a typical situation the first-year teacher, or intern, is assigned to an experienced teacher who guides and counsels the intern. The Los Angeles Unified School District has published vignettes or case studies based on real-life classroom experiences in its mentoring program (see *Mentor Teacher Casebook* and *Intern Teacher Casebook*, available from Far West Laboratory in San Francisco).[7]

[7]"Tales from Mentors and Interns," *American Teacher* 73 (March 1989): 3; and Ellwein, Grane, and Comfon, "Talking about Instruction."

TEACHING IN PERSPECTIVE

■

TEACHING TODAY

Cindy and Bob will fit well among the teachers whose ranks they will soon join. Half their colleagues in both elementary and secondary schools will have at least fourteen years of teaching experience. Almost all will have completed some graduate courses, and more than half will have earned masters' degrees. Nationally, fewer than 10 percent of these teachers will be Asian-American, Hispanic, African-American, or Native American; yet at least 20 percent of their students will be from these ethnic groups, with the proportion increasing to half or more in large urban settings.

RESEARCH SAYS

For Tomorrow's Education . . .

Because the ranks of minority teachers are small and getting smaller, different strategies are needed to provide incentives for entering the profession. Current examples include the earning for minorities of more college credits at the high school level (Syracuse University's Project Advance) and the subsidizing of minority teachers' college education in return for service in the public schools. Unfortunately, such programs have not made a significant difference in the number of minority students entering teaching or even college. See the National Education Association report cited in "U.S. Classrooms Short of Men and Minorities," *Chicago Tribune,* 7 July 1992, p. 5; and Nancy L. Zimpher and Suzan Yessayan, "Recruitment and Selection of Minority Populations into Teaching," *Metropolitan Education* 5 (Fall 1987): 57–71.

[8]"U.S. Classrooms Short of Men and Minorities," *Chicago Tribune,* 7 July 1992, p. 5; Mary E. Dilworth, "Motivation, Rewards, and Incentives," Trends and Issues Paper No. 3 (Washington, D.C.: ERIC Clearinghouse on Teacher Education, 1991), ED 330 692; E. D. Tabs, *Selected Characteristics of Public and Private School Teachers: 1987–88* (Washington, D.C.: National Center for Education Statistics, U.S. Department of Education, 1990); National Center for Education Statistics, "Background and Experience Characteristics of Public and Private School Teachers: 1984–85 and 1985–86 Respectively" (Survey Report), ED 301 561; Robert Knoop, "Causes of Job Dissatisfaction Among Teachers" (paper presented at the Annual Meeting of the Canadian Society for Studies in Education, Hamilton, Ontario, Canada, 31 May–3 June 1987), ED 284 355; Roger R. Hock, "Professional Burnout Among Public School Teachers," *Public Personnel Management* 17 (Summer 1988): 180; U.S. Department of Commerce, Bureau of the Census, *The Statistical Abstract of the United States, 1989,* tab. 222; and Richard L. Flander, "A Systems Approach to Management Effectiveness Training" (paper presented at the Annual Meeting of the American Association of School Administrators, Dallas, March 1985), ED 277 085.

Bob will likely find an equal number of male and female teachers at his high school, although the percentage of male teachers is declining; men make up only about one-third of the entire teaching force. In general, male teachers have working-class backgrounds, and the choice of teaching as a profession allows them to change their social status and become more middle class. Bob will also find that those colleagues who have taught longer than five years are, for the most part, happy with their career choice. They may complain about their salaries, but they enjoy having summers free, and they are fulfilled by working with and serving others.

Cindy's experienced colleagues in the elementary grades will also have backgrounds like hers, and she will find that they enjoy teaching for many of the same reasons given by secondary teachers. But since the vast majority of her peers will be female (about 88 percent), another satisfaction of teaching comes to the fore: Many females value the ease with which they can combine a teaching career and family responsibilities. Unlike male secondary teachers, most of Cindy's female elementary colleagues will have middle-class backgrounds.[8]

TEACHING IN THE PAST

Compared with the professionalism demanded of teachers today, training in the past was more flexible and far less rigorous. One result was that a teacher's social standing was less clear. During colonial times, for example, a potential teacher merely needed the approval of the local minister or town official, who asked little more than whether the person could read and write. (Colonial schools gave students only the most rudimentary instruction.) Some accounts of the time vividly describe the colonial teacher as a ''town drunk,'' an indentured servant, or a ''ne'er-do-well'' who was much given to absenteeism and even running away. Other accounts report that teachers were well respected and honored in the community. Both pictures probably have truth, for the situation varied not only from colony to colony but also from town to town.

Often college students—from Harvard or Yale, for example—would engage in ''keeping school'' to earn extra money; or colonial housewives might take youngsters into their homes to teach them reading and writing as the women did their chores. In the second case the school was called a **dame school**, and the woman was often paid in crops. To prepare for college, students went either to grammar schools or to academies, where the masters themselves were usually college graduates. Latin and the classics were the usual requirements for matriculation into one of the few colleges.

By the mid-nineteenth century, as teaching became more feminized, professional preparation became more standardized. Training institutions, called **normal schools**, were founded; the first tax-supported one was established in Lexington, Massachusetts, in 1839. Training programs consisted of mastering the common or elementary school subjects and then moving on to psychology, philosophy, history of education, methods of teaching, observation in classrooms, and practice teaching. The early training programs ranged from two to four years, after which a diploma was awarded. Entrance requirements involved little more than having the ability to read and write, but by the twentieth century a secondary school education was becoming standard. To train secondary teachers, institutions added courses in pedagogy to their philosophy or psychology departments. Late in the nineteenth century, states established departments of education, and certification procedures were formulated. At first, graduation from a normal school or completion of specialized education courses was the minimum requirement for teacher certification.

During the first half of the twentieth century the normal schools that survived were gradually transformed into teacher colleges and then into state universities with degree-granting authority. In addition, many institutions added departments and schools of education to train elementary teachers and to provide the professional education sequence for secondary teachers. In many respects the development and growth of the teaching profession have paralleled the professionalization of medicine and law.

As late as the end of the nineteenth century, for example, medical practitioners were regarded as charlatans in whom the public had little confidence. Doctors practicing during the Civil War believed that pus was a natural part of healing and that using maggots was the best way to clean a wound (because they

Francis Wayland Parker
1837–1902

Known as the "Father of Progressive Education," Parker was born near Manchester, New Hampshire. His father died when he seven, and—as was the custom of the time—the boy was apprenticed to a neighboring farmer who could teach him a livelihood in the absence of his father. He attended school when he could, and at sixteen he began teaching in local country schools. After six years, in 1859, he was called to Carrollton, Illinois, to head its district school, but the Civil War brought his tenure to a close as Carrollton's pro-South sentiment grew. Parker returned to New Hampshire and in 1862 joined the Union Army, eventually advancing to the rank of colonel—a title that remained with him for the rest of his life.

After the war and a period of convalescence (he had been hit in the neck by a small cannon ball), Parker returned to his home town and accepted the position of head teacher. Dissatisfied with educational practices there, he went to teach in Dayton, Ohio, where he thought schooling approaches would be less rigid. He began reading the works of contemporary educational theorists and, upon the death of an aunt, decided to travel to Europe to study education. There he encountered the ideas of the Swiss theorist Johann Heinrich Pestalozzi, and German educators Friedrich Froebel, and Johann Herbart.

After 2½ years of study abroad, Parker returned to the United States with the resolve to put his new knowledge into practice. In 1873 he was appointed superintendent of schools in Quincy, Massachusetts, where he abolished rote-memory teaching practices in favor of methods that took into account students' interests and needs—an approach that came to be known as the Quincy Method. After a brief stint as superintendent in Boston, Parker moved to Chicago in 1883 to head the Cook County Normal school.

Yesterday's Professional

By now the Quincy Method was widely known if not universally accepted. At Cook County Normal, Parker's approach caught the attention of Joseph Mayer Rice, a journalist and educational reformer who wrote a series of newspaper articles pointing to Parker's work as a bright light on a generally bleak educational landscape. His work was also discovered by Anita McCormick Blaine, daughter of International Harvester founder Cyrus McCormick and a member of the University of Chicago's board of trustees. She convinced Parker to bring his ideas and best faculty members to the University of Chicago, where they became its school of education. Parker was also given an endowment to start a laboratory school; he did so in 1898, and by the end of the century it had opened within the university.

Unfortunately, Parker's wife and partner in education died, and his own health and spirits began to decline. He left Chicago to recuperate in the South, where he died in the spring of 1902. His faculty and lab school at the University of Chicago were merged into the department of education, which then was headed by John Dewey. Parker's contribution to education was his ability to train teachers scientifically, teaching them to foster students' intellectual, moral, and physical development at a time when rote memorization was the norm.

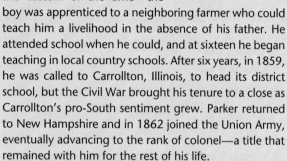

only ate diseased tissue). Most American physicians scoffed at vital knowledge that was derived from the biological sciences and used in Europe. Their medical training consisted of eight months of didactic lectures, and there was no gradation or sequencing of courses. To receive a medical degree, candidates merely passed a set of brief and perfunctory oral questions, and there was no state licensing.

Then, during the first decades of the twentieth century, the medical profession was transformed. Many explanations for this have been offered, in such sources as Abraham Flexner's *Medical Education in the United States and Canada* and George Stevens's *Structure of American Medical Practice, 1875–1941.* But it is enough for us to note that the transformation did occur and hinged on the efforts of the American Medical Association, on university acceptance of scientific medicine, and on large endowments for hospital building. Thus today's medical profession has become the archetype and displays the characteristics that other occupations must have in order to be considered a profession.

The legal profession also was transformed early in this century, although some practitioners are still regarded as "ambulance chasers" and people of unethical and unsavory character. In our modern, complex, and bureaucratic society, it is attorneys who possess the knowledge needed to open legal doors in the institutions of business, commerce, health, education, and government.[9]

TABLE 1.1 Teachers' Average Salaries by State, 1991–92

State	Average Salary	State	Average Salary
Connecticut	$47,510	Florida	$31,070
Alaska	43,800	Kentucky	30,880
New York	43,335	Wyoming	30,425
New Jersey	41,027	Maine	30,097
Michigan	40,700	Texas	29,719
California	40,425	Georgia	29,539
D.C.	39,673	North Carolina	29,334
Rhode Island	39,397	Iowa	29,196
Maryland	39,073	Kansas	29,101
Pennsylvania	38,715	Missouri	28,923
Massachusetts	37,256	Tennessee	28,621
Nevada	36,989	South Carolina	28,209
Illinois	36,528	Montana	27,590
Wisconsin	35,227	West Virginia	27,366
Washington	34,880	Nebraska	27,231
Delaware	34,548	Arkansas	27,168
Hawaii	34,488	Alabama	26,954
Indiana	34,247	Utah	26,524
Oregon	34,101	Oklahoma	26,514
Minnesota	33,700	Louisiana	26,411
Vermont	33,200	Idaho	26,345
Ohio	33,198	New Mexico	26,244
New Hampshire	33,170	North Dakota	24,495
Colorado	33,072	Mississippi	24,368
Virginia	32,243	South Dakota	23,291
Arizona	31,176		

Source: AFT Local Teachers Salary Survey, American Federation of Teachers, Washington, D.C.

[9]Willard S. Elsbree, *The American Teacher: Evaluation of a Profession in a Democracy* (New York: American Book Company, 1939), 109–117, 336–340; and David C. Berliner, "Knowledge Is Power," *Equity and Excellence* 24 (Winter 1989) 2: 4–19.

SELECTED CHARACTERISTICS OF TEACHING

■

TEACHERS' PAY

A major difference among the professions is seen in the pay and prestige of teachers compared with doctors and lawyers. If Cindy or Bob takes a first job in one of the fourteen better-paying states, their beginning salary will likely exceed $22,000 for nine to ten months of teaching. But if they start in North Dakota, South Dakota, Louisiana, Utah, or Idaho, they are likely to earn less than $18,000. In some wealthier districts and in a few private schools, their starting salary would be above $32,000. Most districts' highest salaries are about twice the entry-level pay. Table 1.1 on page 13 presents teachers' *average* salaries in 1991.

If Cindy or Bob finds a job in the country's highest-paying districts—usually in affluent suburbs—they can look forward to a maximum salary of $60,000 to $75,000. And if they are interested in moving into administrative jobs after a few years in teaching, they can anticipate even higher pay. Elementary principals, for example, tend to earn about 155 percent of the average teacher's salary in a district.[10] Superintendents average well over $70,000, and most receive additional allowances for travel, insurance, retirement, and sometimes housing. Many large cities and a growing number of affluent smaller districts pay their chief school officers well over $100,000 annually. Table 1.2 shows average salaries for various positions in the school system.

From the early 1970s until the mid-1980s, educators' average salary increases lagged behind inflation. But beginning in 1986—after more than a decade of losing net purchasing power—educators' pay raises began to outpace

TABLE 1.2   Average Salaries in Public School Systems

Position	1989	1992
Superintendents (contract)	$71,190	$83,342
Assistant superintendents	59,655	69,315
Subject-area supervisors	43,555	50,580
Principals:		
Elementary school	45,909	53,856
Middle school	49,427	57,504
High school	52,987	61,768
Assistant principals:		
Elementary school	38,360	45,558
Middle school	42,292	48,956
High school	44,002	51,318
Classroom teachers	29,608	34,565

Source: Data for 1989 and 1992 are from the National Survey of Salaries and Wages in Public Schools conducted annually by the Educational Research Service. These data were also reported by Glen Robinson and Melinda Brown in the "Research Supplement" section of the *Principal.* See "School Salaries, 1988–89" (May 1989): 49; and "Principals, Salaries, and Benefits, 1991–92," 72 (May 1992): 51.

[10]Principals work an average of 221 days per year, compared with 186 days per year for teachers. Calculated on a daily basis, the salary of elementary principals is 31 percent greater than the salary of teachers. The average salary of high school principals is a little higher than the average salary of elementary principals. Gene E. Robinson and Melinda H. Brown, "Principals' Salaries and Benefits, 1991–92," *Principal* 71 (May 1992): 51, 56.

inflation; they continue to do so, even though most workers' pay is not quite keeping up with inflation.[11] This improved trend in teachers' pay is likely to continue during this century, since the education work force is retiring and the number of jobs will almost certainly exceed the pool of qualified applicants.

TEACHERS' STATUS

Relative **status**, or relative rank in a hierarchy of prestige, is one way that social scientists describe and compare occupations. They do this by asking people to rank-order a list of occupations, rating each according to how they perceive its importance or value. The results of such surveys tend to oversimplify a complex topic, but they do give some idea of how a cross-section of the population views various occupations. As shown in Figure 1.1, people tend to rank teachers positively, although not as high as physicians, lawyers, or bankers. On the other hand, most people rate teachers ahead of farmers, salespeople, funeral directors, realtors, local political officers, plumbers, electricians, carpenters, and many other occupations that are socially essential, that may offer pleasant working conditions, or that may provide higher incomes.

Another piece of information derived from such status surveys is that the rather positive image of teaching as a profession has been stable over time. Many colonial teachers—whether grammar masters or dame school teachers—seem to have been accorded a good deal of respect, although less than people gave to ministers and major officials. Even on the American frontier, teachers enjoyed considerable prestige. And in this century the amount of status associated with

[11]E. D. Tabs, *Selected Characteristics of Public and Private School Teachers: 1987–88;* "Teachers: Pay Rising Little Past Inflation," *Atlanta Journal and Constitution,* 22 July 1989, p. A-5; and Mark Memmott, "Workers' Pay and Benefits Lag Behind Inflation," *USA Today,* 26 July 1989, p. B-1.

FIGURE 1.1   U.S. Public's Rating of Eleven Occupations

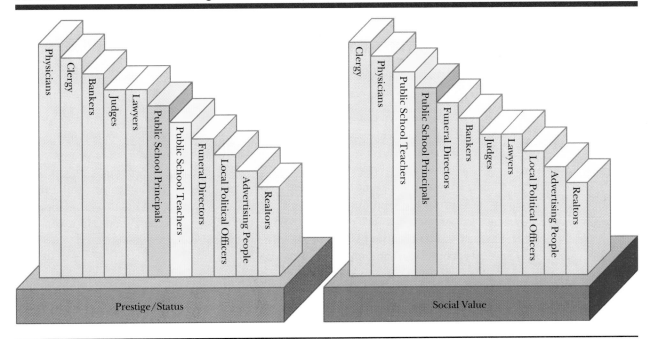

Source: Stanley M. Elam, "The Second Gallup/Phi Delta Kappa Poll of Teachers' Attitudes toward the Public Schools," *Phi Delta Kappan* 70 (June 1989): 792.

teaching has been positive and constant.[12] The phenomenon appears to be worldwide: Whether in Thailand, England, India, or the United States, teachers enjoy substantial status, though not the highest. Not all occupations are so consistently appreciated. For example, in the late 1960s "businessman" ranked high in some countries but was quite far down the list in others.[13]

The amount of general status associated with education is one of several factors that a potential teacher must consider, and the perception of status is, of course, an individual matter. Many people find that teaching is held in sufficient esteem to be satisfying. Others may enjoy teaching but think they need greater prestige in order to feel accomplished. If this occurs, teachers either must change their feelings about the need for higher status or must leave teaching for a more prestigious career; otherwise they will live in conflict.

Complicating the relationship between work and status is the wide variation of status *within* an occupation. For example, most people are more in awe of heart surgeons or psychiatrists than they are of physicians in family practice. Similarly, even among teachers in the same school, individual status varies widely. Thus the head basketball coach in a small midwestern high school is likely to feel much stronger approval (or disapproval) than do regular teachers in the same school. In general, high school teachers rate a little more highly than do elementary teachers, and the job of heading up a school connotes greater status than teaching in one. College teachers, however, rank above school administrators in many people's opinions.

Individual teachers, counselors, and administrators may become especially popular with students, parents, colleagues, or members of the community, and thus they experience greater esteem than their colleagues do. Whether a specific educator feels adequately appreciated depends on several factors, including his or her personal values. Each person brings a set of expectations to the educational enterprise. Some people's experiences and family traditions predispose them to see teaching as an occupation of sufficiently high status, while other people view things differently and feel they need a career with greater prestige.

ASCRIBED STATUS AND EARNED STATUS

So far we have looked at teachers' **ascribed status**, or the degree of respect that the public generally grants to educators. But most people don't make lasting career decisions based on random encounters with the feelings of strangers and acquaintances. More influential in choosing teaching as a career is the way one's friends, fellow students, parents, colleagues, supervisors, and influential members of the community regard the profession. Teachers can shape the views of these people more directly than they can of the public in general. In short, they can attain **earned status** by performing in a way that commands the respect of people who see them in action every day.

Another variable in the status equation is the kind of community and school in which one works. Some communities take strong interest in their schools, participating extensively in school activities and providing constant support. In such a setting teachers feel they are in partnership with parents, students, and the community at large; they are much more likely to feel valued than they would

[12]George A. Kanzaki, "Fifty Years (1925–1975) of Stability in the Social Status of Occupations," *Vocational Guidance Quarterly* (December 1976): 101–105; and John A. Fossum and Michael L. Moore, "The Stability of Longitudinal and Cross-sectional Occupational Prestige Rankings," *Journal of Vocational Behavior* 7 (1975): 305–311.

[13]Marion Edman, *A Self-Image of Primary School Teachers: A Cross Cultural Study of Their Role and Status in Twelve Cities* (Detroit: Wayne State University Press, 1968), 147–158.

in a community that takes little interest in its schools. In looking for a teaching position, then, it is well worth the trouble to learn how a community regards its schools and how it treats its educators. How much status does the community ascribe to teachers, and how much status do teachers have to earn through un-usual efforts? Experienced teachers know that the balance between these two kinds of status is a significant factor in how well they like their jobs as time passes.

EDUCATION AS A CAREER: THE BALANCE SHEET

Descriptions of "average" conditions in a field as large, various, and complex as education fall short of telling the whole story. Do such facts that teachers enjoy relatively high status and that their average salaries are increasing mean that a particular teacher will have an acceptable standard of living and will continue to be happy with teaching as a career choice? For many people the answer will be yes, but for others teaching will not be the right choice. To help you consider the situation, let's look more closely at what teachers say they like and don't like about the profession.

RESEARCH SAYS

For Tomorrow's Education . . .

The high levels of stress and burnout that were reported in the literature during the late 1970s and early 1980s were "overstated." Milstein and Farkas conclude that "education as a field is not nearly so marked by the littered casualties of distress that are envisioned in the literature." See "More Teachers Satisfied with Job," *USA Today*, 7 July 1992, p. 1D; Jan Zulich, "Why Teach? Contemporary Answers to an Old Question," *Delta Kappa Gamma Bulletin* 57 (Fall 1990) 1: 24–26; and Mike Milstein and James Farkas, "The Over-stated Case of Educator Stress," *Journal of Educational Administration* 26 (July 1988): 232–249.

Again, some social science concepts will be helpful. In discussing how peo-ple respond to their jobs, social scientists sometimes speak of "satisfiers" and "dissatisfiers." Although the terms are not the most elegant, they *are* useful. A **satisfier** is any aspect of a job that appeals positively—that makes the job worth-while—to a person. In contrast, a **dissatisfier** is something about the job that the person feels is a definite liability. In either case the person must feel strongly enough about the item to consider keeping or leaving the job because of it.

For example, every day John spends an hour driving to and from work—an hour each way. He really likes his job and has made good friends among his coworkers, and he probably can't match his salary anywhere else. But rush-hour traffic is so fatiguing—and the two-hour time loss is so annoying—that John is thinking seriously about looking for a job closer to home. Commuting has become a dissatisfier for John. What should he do? Should he give up his job, or are there other solutions to his problem? Well, suppose John finds a train that he can take to and from work. Although the commute still takes time and costs money, now John can use the time reading and relaxing. His effort in getting to and from work is no longer a serious annoyance. Although the commute may not have become a satisfier, at least it is no longer a dissatisfier. John can stop thinking about changing jobs.

Because an individual's perceptions are the basis for satisfaction or dissatisfaction, employees differ about what they like and dislike about a job. A wage of $20 per hour may be a satisfier for someone who now earns $15, but it may be a dissatisfier for a person who was just laid off from a job paying $25 per hour. The same factor—$20 per hour—is perceived differently by different individuals. This points to another dimension of satisfaction that is worth noting. Because people are multifaceted and life is complex, it is not unusual for some aspect of a job to be both satisfying *and* dissatisfying. Delores, for example, is a twenty-nine-year-old buyer for a major department store. Each year she makes several trips to exotic cities throughout the world, staying in luxury hotels, eating in four-star restaurants, and meeting many interesting people. These are the exciting, satisfying aspects of her job. But Delores has a six-month-old daughter whom she adores—and who can't go on the trips with her. The hassles and expense of finding good child care and the emotional strain of being separated from her daughter are so dissatisfying that Delores is thinking about leaving her job. The very things that make the job satisfying to Delores are also what make it dissatisfying.

These examples make the point that each person is unique, and so are teachers. We all go through a process of development and change throughout life, which makes it difficult to say what satisfies and dissatisfies any one of us at any one time. Surveys indicate that the percentage of educators who said that they would still choose the same career declined between the early 1970s and 1984, but since then the trend has been reversed.[14] A similar indicator is the public's response to this question: "Would you like to have a child of yours take up teaching in the public schools as a career?" Table 1.3 summarizes parents' responses at five different points over twenty years.

Of course, asking teachers whether they would still choose their careers is not the same as asking them how much satisfaction they have found as educators. (Among the general population only 39 percent of Americans expect to have the same job five years from now, and 31 percent are planning to leave their present work.[15]) One recent sophisticated study assessed the satisfaction of educators from seventeen school districts in Ontario by having them complete Hoppock's job dissatisfaction inventory. The results, based on responses from 1,865 elementary and secondary educators, are reported in Table 1.4.

Although there is no comparable study of U.S. educators, other cross-national research suggests that they and Canadian educators feel remarkably alike.[16] For example, a 1987 survey of six hundred teachers, principals, and counselors in Ohio showed only 5.2 percent with "very little" or "low" job satisfac-

[14]"More Teachers Satisfied with Job," *USA Today*, 7 July 1992, p. 1D; and U.S. Department of Commerce, Bureau of the Census, *The Statistical Abstract of the United States, 1989*, tab. 222.

[15]Louis Harris, *Inside America* (New York: Vintage Books, 1987), 51.

[16]Edman, *A Self-Image of Primary School Teachers*, 147–158.

TABLE 1.3   Parents Who Would, or Would Not, Like Child
to Take Up Teaching as a Career (Percent)

	1969	1980	1983	1988	1990
Yes*	75	48	45	58	51
No	15	40	33	31	38
Uncertain	10	12	22	11	11

*Parents who had children in public schools reacted more positively than did parents who did not (62 percent vs. 56 percent).

Sources: Alec M. Gallup and Stanley Elam, "The 20th Annual Gallup Poll of the Public's Attitudes toward the Public Schools," *Phi Delta Kappan* 70 (September 1988): 43; and "The 22nd Annual Gallup Poll of the Public's Attitudes toward the Public Schools," *Phi Delta Kappan* 72 (September 1990): 47. This question was dropped from the poll after 1990.

tion. The remaining 94.8 percent reported "moderate" (40.3 percent) or "great" (54.5 percent) satisfaction.[17] Similarly, a survey of teachers in San Diego in 1988 found "very little burnout and relative[ly high] satisfaction with most aspects of their profession."[18] Recently the school board in Cobb County, Geor-

TABLE 1.4   Summary of Canadian Educators' Responses
to Hoppock's Job Dissatisfaction Survey

	Percent (N = 1,865)
1 I never feel satisfied with my job; I hate it and would quit at once if I could; no one dislikes his/her job more than I dislike mine.	0.0
2 I seldom feel satisfied with my job; I dislike it and would take almost any other job in which I could earn as much as I am earning now; I dislike my job much more than most people dislike theirs.	0.3
3 I occasionally feel satisfied with my job; I don't like it and would like to change both my job and my occupation; I dislike my job more than most people dislike theirs.	1.8
4 I feel satisfied with my job about half the time; I am indifferent to it and would like to exchange my present job for another one; I like my job as well as most people like theirs.	6.1
5 I feel satisfied with my job a good deal of the time; I like it and I am not eager to change my job, but I would do so if I could get a better job; I like my job better than most people like theirs.	30.0
6 I feel satisfied with my job most of the time; I am enthusiastic about it and cannot think of any job for which I would exchange it; I like my job much better than most people like theirs.	52.3
7 I feel satisfied with my job all the time; I love it and would not exchange my job for any other; no one likes his/her job better than I like mine.	9.5

Source: Robert Knoop, "Causes of Job Dissatisfaction Among Teachers" (paper presented at the Annual Meeting of the Canadian Society for Studies in Education, Hamilton, Ontario, Canada, 31 May–3 June 1987), ED 284 335.

[17]Ernest M. Shuttenberg, Frank L. O'Dell, and Caroline M. Kaczala, "Vocational Personality Types and Sex-Role Perceptions of Educational Administrators, Counselors, and Teachers" (paper presented at the Annual Meeting of the American Educational Research Association, 20–24 April 1987), ED 286 270.

[18]Hock, "Professional Burnout," 180.

gia, began surveying all teachers who leave their jobs and found that "most of our departing teachers [about two hundred annually] are retiring or relocating because their spouses (many of whom work for major corporations in nearby Atlanta) are being transferred to another state."[19] Finally, a survey conducted by the National Education Association revealed that 59 percent of its members would still choose teaching if they had to make a career decision today. These educators were satisfied with their jobs because (1) pay was better, (2) work conditions were improving, and (3) recent reforms had given them a voice in managing and operating schools. Other recent studies also indicate that most teachers and educators are much happier with their vocational choices than was suggested by earlier press reports.[20] Educators are also more satisfied with their jobs than are workers in other jobs (see Figure 1.2).

SATISFACTIONS OF TEACHING

Given the extensive negative publicity about education during the early 1980s, why are so many teachers satisfied with their vocation? Although the answer is not simple, a consistent picture emerges both from research studies and from teachers' personal accounts. Part of the answer lies in the three reasons cited above: better pay, better conditions, and an increased voice in school management. But much of the answer reflects the nature of teaching as work and the reasons why people choose it in the first place.

Teachers' descriptions of what they like most about their work tend to center on the *process* of teaching itself—on the series of highly personalized interactions combined with responsibility for ongoing, dynamic group situations. "The very best thing I like," says teacher Gary Nuernberger, "is watching the lights go on—working with a kid who just can't catch on and is struggling and struggling." It's the challenge of *not* turning students off, he adds, of *not* "making

[19]Mike Tenoschok, "When Teachers Resign, Ask Why—And Then Learn from What They Tell You," *American School Board Journal* 175 (September 1988): 26–27.

[20]"More Teachers Satisfied with Job," *USA Today*, 7 July 1992, p. 1D. Also see Harris, *Inside America*, 52; and Mike Milstein and James Farkas, "The Over-stated Case of Educator Stress," *Journal of Educational Administration* 26 (July 1988): 232–249: "We believe . . . that education as a field is not nearly so marked by the littered casualties of distress that are envisioned in the literature."

FIGURE 1.2   Percentages of Workers Very Satisfied with Work

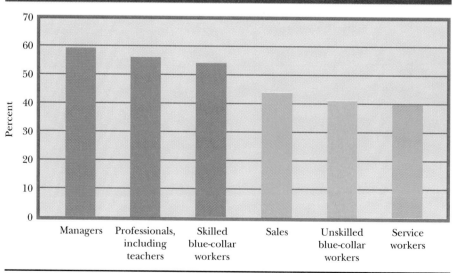

Source: Louis Harris, *Inside America*, 52.

them feel like they're dumb or stupid." It's "getting them over the hump [until they say] 'oh, that's easy!' "[21]

RESEARCH SAYS

For Tomorrow's Education . . .

Factors relating to a teacher's burnout include the imposition of measurable goal achievement by administrators, inadequate trust in teachers' professional adequacy, a disagreeable school culture or physical environment, desire for greater personal accomplishment, and a limited ability to promote students' development. See Isaac A. Friedman, "High- and Low-Burnout Schools: School Culture Aspects of Teacher Burnout," *Journal of Educational Research* 84 (July–August 1991) 6: 325–333; Judith Haymore Sandholtz, "Demands, Rewards, and Effort: A Balancing Act for Teachers," ED 338 591; and Victoria Cadavid and Fred Lunenburg, "Pupil Control Ideology and Dimensions of Teacher Burnout" (paper presented at the Annual Meeting of the American Educational Research Association, Chicago, 3–7 April 1991), ED 333 560.

When teachers describe specific frustrations or dissatisfiers, they rarely complain about teaching; they talk instead about work conditions. High among their complaints are such issues as struggles with school boards for adequate pay; hours spent on recordkeeping; lunchroom, playground, and hallway supervision; the absence of parental support for childrens' learning; and arbitrary supervision by administrators (especially those who fail to spell out their expectations or criteria for evaluation or who do not take into account teachers' expert knowledge and experience when setting policies and regulations). "Some parents . . . you work very well with, but there are some that just don't give a damn about their kids," said Nuernberger when we asked him what he dislikes about being a teacher. "I guess, tied with that, I don't like administrators who . . . just will not let you teach and have to parentally administer teachers. I think I hate that the most."[22]

When asked in an opinion poll how satisfying their chosen work is, teachers must try to balance the (satisfying) thrill of helping learners break through barriers against the (dissatisfying) frustrations of working in a bureaucracy. Any individual teachers' answers might differ from May to October, or from the first to the fourth to the twentieth year of teaching. Over the course of their careers most teachers ask themselves many times whether or not to continue in their calling.

Workers in general certainly ask themselves similar questions. Most people spend the majority of their adult lives in some kind of full-time employment. The nature of industrial and postindustrial work is such that forecasters predict several changes of job and work locations for the majority of the work force. Furthermore, many people will also change their occupations at least once and perhaps as many as four or five times during their work lives.[23] The transitory,

[21]Interview with Gary Nuernberger, fall 1990.

[22]Ibid.

[23]"Career Hopping in a Brave New Corporate World," *Chicago Tribune,* 27 August 1989, sec. 8, p. 1; reprinted from the *Los Angeles Daily News.*

peripheral nature of some work is very difficult to integrate with the rest of one's life, as author Robert Bellah notes:

> With the coming of large-scale industrial society it became more difficult to see work as a contribution to the whole and easier to view it as a segmented, self-interested activity. But though the idea of a calling has become attenuated and the largely private "job" and "career" have taken its place, something of the notion of calling lingers on, not necessarily opposed to, but in addition to job and career.[24]

Educator William Ayers thinks this description "perfectly fits many fine teachers," including four whom he investigated in detail:

> These teachers continue to find in their work a vital link between private and public worlds, between personal fulfillment and social responsibility. They bring to their work a sense of commitment, of connectedness to other people and to shared traditions, and of the collective good will. They seem to reject the calculation and contingency that pervades so much work today, embodying instead a sense of work closely tied to a sense of self, a view that work is not merely what one does, but who one is. And they accomplish all this as an act of affirmation in a social and cultural surrounding that devalues their contribution and rewards them sparingly.[25]

People don't choose teaching because they expect to make a lot of money, become famous, or wield much political power. Sure, they usually hope for an

[24]Robert N. Bellah et al., *Habits of the Heart* (New York: Harper & Row, 1985), 66.
[25]William Ayers, "Teaching and Being: Connecting Teachers' Accounts of Their Lives with Classroom Practice" (paper presented at the Annual Meeting of the American Educational Research Association, 5–9 April 1988, New Orleans), ED 294 841.

For most teachers, it's not just a j-o-b: "I like to be surrounded by children. My happiest memories are when we've done something and are all giving to something that's going on—there probably isn't a greater job satisfaction than that." —Bob Kramer/The Picture Cube

adequate livelihood while at the same time making an "act of affirmation." But the literature suggests that most people who choose teaching want an ennobling sense of self; they have a calling to feel useful, to help people grow, develop, and learn.[26] When teachers say what they like about their work, they report having attained goals like these.

A few years ago researchers interviewed secondary teachers in eight "disadvantaged" schools (that is, in working-class, economically depressed neighborhoods)—four schools in Yorkshire, England, and four in Michigan. The researchers assumed that teachers in such schools faced especially difficult circumstances and lacked what we have called "satisfiers." But when they asked what it was like to be a classroom teacher, they got the following responses:

Teachers must balance the thrill of helping learners break through barriers against the frustrations of working in a bureaucracy—and do it "in a social and cultural surrounding that devalues their contribution and rewards them sparingly." —Mary Kate Denny/PhotoEdit

[26]See, for example, Dilworth, "Motivation, Rewards, and Incentives"; Thomas J. DeLong, "Teachers and Their Careers: Why Do They Choose Teaching?" *Journal of Career Development* 14 (Winter 1987): 118–125; and Book and Freeman, "Differences in Entry Characteristics," 47–51. Louis Harris (*Inside America*, 54) reports that 48 percent of Americans list as their primary job requirement that "work be important and give you a real feeling of accomplishment"; only 18 percent singled out high pay as their chief criterion.

I like the stimulation, the activity. I'm never bored. I still get fun when you can really teach and not have to discipline.   (USA)

It's magic! It's the whole thing of putting on a performance . . . like when I go into the classroom or when I walk out of the staffroom—it's like going on the stage.   (UK)

I enjoy the physical activity of teaching.   (USA)

I like to be surrounded by children. My happiest memories are when we've done something and you are all giving to something that's going on—there probably isn't a greater job satisfaction than that.   (UK)

I love kids, I really do like being around them—in a non-professional term they crack me up, they really do.   (USA)

It's the continuous creative activity which is both a strain and a reward in itself. Because every day it's up to you. You don't come and sit at the desk and do the same thing day after day. Every day is different and what you do during that day is mainly up to you.   (UK)[27]

Because teaching conditions are not equal in all schools or all communities, the general level of satisfaction among teachers may vary from one school to another. Yet teachers satisfaction does *not* appear to depend on their students' social class, ethnicity, or financial backgrounds.

While a small percentage of educators always say they are satisfied, and an even smaller percentage never or rarely admits to being satisfied, experience suggests that most teachers find themselves somewhere between these extremes.

[27]Pam Poppleton et al., "The Experience of Teaching in 'Disadvantaged' Areas in the United Kingdom and the USA," *Comparative Education* 23 (1987): 309.

What teachers like most is the process of teaching, the interactions and responsibility for group situations. Most people who choose teaching as a career feel a calling to help others grow, develop, and learn. —Bill Bachmann/PhotoEdit

"Teaching is pain and humor, joy and anger, dreariness and epiphany," William Ayers reminds us.[28] Or, as one teacher says, "There are some extremely gratifying moments in this business but they are flashes—like in a kaleidoscope; they aren't a constant—neither are the frustrations, but there are more of those."[29]

Frustration, anxiety, and self-doubt are inevitable aspects of growing and developing as a teacher. Indeed, every new teacher experiences some of the doubt that Susan Hubbuch recalls from her first teaching experience:

> Basically, I was scared to death. Barely older than the students sitting in front of me, I was preoccupied with maintaining my authority in the classroom. It was imperative that those students never realize that, deep in my heart, I felt I had little right to stand before them as an expert.[30]

DISSATISFACTIONS OF TEACHING

William Ayers defined teaching as "a way of being in the world that breaks through the boundaries of the traditional job and redefines all of life and teaching itself in the process.[31] To the extent that one achieves this, teaching is likely to be a satisfying—though not necessarily an easy—way of life. Because teaching is hard work, involves a personal investment, and so readily interacts with how teachers feel about themselves, levels of satisfaction and dissatisfaction tend to correlate highly with how successful people feel as teachers.

A number of external forces can either aid or hinder a teacher's success. Cooperative parents, appreciative students, supportive administrators, adequate facilities and supplies, manageable class sizes, shared decision-making power over curricula, texts, schedules—all these contribute to teachers' feelings of success. When these external factors are inadequate or missing, educators find it far more difficult to be or feel successful.

Internal forces also have an impact on teachers' feelings of success. Those who understand and accept themselves, who have positive attitudes about life, who have good knowledge bases in their subjects, and who have learned personal and group interaction skills are likely to be and feel successful. The evidence is convincing that many teachers who feel most dissatisfied about their jobs also feel dissatisfied about life in general and have low self-esteem.[32] Less extremely, when teachers set unrealistic standards for themselves and students, their resulting disappointment can be a dissatisfier. "I used to judge my ability as a teacher by the ability of my students to produce error-free, entertaining, insightful essays in a short period of time," writes Susan Hubbuch. "For each student who failed to reach this mark, I put a large F in my gradebook of myself as a teacher."[33]

CONCLUSIONS

People who choose teaching as a career today are academically able and are at least as well educated as in the past; their scores on college entrance exams match

[28]Ayers, "Teaching and Being," 13.
[29]Poppleton et al., "The Experience of Teaching in 'Disadvantaged' Areas," 308.
[30]Susan M. Hubbuch, "The Anatomy of a Sea Change," *The Writing Instructor* (Fall 1984): 33.
[31]Ayers, "Teaching and Being," 15.
[32]Sharon L. Barkdoll, "The Relationship Between Life Affirming Constructs and Teachers' Coping with Job Related Stress and Job Satisfaction" (paper presented at the Society of Behavioral Medicine Scientific Sessions, Washington, D.C., 20–23 March 1991), ED 333 322. Also see Knoop, "Causes of Job Dissatisfaction," 10–14.
[33]Hubbuch, "Anatomy of a Sea Change," 35–36.

the scores of noneducation majors. Teacher candidates come from baccalaureate programs that prepare them for state certification, and they are entering a job market in which demand exceeds supply. Their salaries are rising faster than the rate of inflation, and this is likely to continue throughout the 1990s. The same is true for other educators, including administrators, counselors, researchers, and university teachers. Educators are more satisfied with their career choices than some press reports in the 1980s indicated; the levels of stress and burnout that they experience are also lower, although the picture is not uniformly positive.

Although teachers' status and pay are not likely to increase enough to become significant satisfiers, they need not be dissatisfiers. Many people continue to feel "called" to education—viewing it as more than simply a job and finding satisfaction by influencing and improving students' lives. Anyone who seeks challenging work that offers opportunities for personal growth along with social significance would do well to consider a career in education.

KEY TERMS

licensing	status
certification	ascribed status
mentoring program	earned status
dame school	satisfier
normal school	dissatisfier

SUGGESTED READINGS

William Ayers, "Teaching and Being: Connecting Teachers' Accounts of Their Lives with Classroom Practice" (paper presented at the Annual Meeting of the American Educational Research Association, New Orleans, 5–9 April 1988), ED 294 841. This paper presents first-hand perspectives from teachers as they reflect on their professional and personal lives.

Jamie Escalante. The autobiography of the high school teacher made famous in the 1988 movie *Stand and Deliver* tells of his success in teaching calculus to a group of minority students in Los Angeles.

Ann Lieberman and Lynne Miller, *Teachers, Their World and Their Work* (Alexandria, Va.: Association for Supervision and Curriculum Development, 1984). Lieberman and Miller explore and describe the affective world of teachers.

Dan C. Lortie, *Schoolteacher: A Sociological Study* (Chicago: University of Chicago Press, 1975). A classic study of the nation's public schools that uses historical, ethnographic, and empirical methodologies to describe sociological aspects of the teaching profession.

Teaching as a Profession

2

All the professions begin as unions seeking to control the market. . . . The difference between a union and a profession is not in function, but in legitimacy. . . . Unions become professions when people forget that they are unions.

—James H. Sutton, *"The Ideological Basis of Teacher Organization,"* ED 275 634

We in education are haunted by the public's erroneous belief that someone can walk in off the street and deliver a curriculum to 30 or so children. Raising any number of children and having gone to school for a number of years does not make an expert teacher. I believe we are on the threshold of creating a scientific basis for the art of teaching that will be acceptable to the general public as truly specialized knowledge.

—David C. Berliner, *"Knowledge Is Power,"* Equity and Excellence, 24 (Winter 1989) 2: 6

2

Teaching as a Profession

ADVANCED ORGANIZERS

In this chapter you will learn

How the concepts of unionism and professionalism evolved

Why and how teachers unionized

What it means to be a professional today

Whether or not teachers are regarded as professionals

CHAPTER OUTLINE

EVOLUTION OF TEACHING PROFESSIONALISM
   Phase 1: Noblesse Oblige
   Phase 2: Individual Professionals
   Phase 3: Organized Pre-Unions
   Phase 4: Unionized Semiprofessionals

PROFESSIONALISM AND THE PUBLIC SCHOOL TEACHER
   A Recognized, Exclusive Body of Knowledge
   Application of Knowledge for Clients' Welfare
   Autonomy of Teachers
   Collegiality Among Teaching Professionals

CONCLUSIONS

ane Wells, a young African-American teacher in Detroit's elementary school system, faced a busy day. Her sixth-grade classes were starting an important unit on American government, which Jane particularly enjoyed teaching since she had minored in political science. She had spent long hours outside the classroom planning the unit so that students' learning would be maximized—especially because many pupils in the class were achieving below grade level.

As Jane took a last sip of coffee and prepared to leave her apartment for school, she paused to watch a local television newscast covering a recent conflict between the Detroit Federation of Teachers (DFT) and the school board. As usual, Jane thought, the reporter's word choices and phrasing favored the board's position: "According to a board spokesperson, the teachers are refusing to implement a new reading-record folder that will better monitor the reading progress of Detroit's elementary school students."

As the report concluded, Jane sighed: "Here we go again. The media are giving the impression that we aren't truly professional in our commitment to serving students. People will think that teachers are preoccupied with their work conditions and are not concerned enough with students' learning."

Three years of teaching gave Jane a different point of view. As a member of the DFT (an affiliate of the American Federation of Teachers), Jane knew what effects the proposed policy would have on her daily routine. The reading-record folder had more than 475 entries that she would have to fill out for each of her thirty-five sixth-graders. Teachers would have to do this within their already-busy schedules, without any extra help.

"If this policy is implemented," Jane thought, "I'll be spending my free hours outside the classroom on records management, not on professional activities that improve my teaching and lesson planning." Since the DFT had entered into arbitration hearings with the board, Jane hoped that the policy would not become a reality—at least in its present form.

The DFT had enthusiastic support from elementary school teachers, who agreed that the reading-record folder represents "needless, duplicative and redundant paper work for teachers and substantially increases the noninstructional functions of the classroom teacher and takes substantially from the time a teacher needs to spend working with or preparing for his/her students."[1]

EVOLUTION OF TEACHING PROFESSIONALISM

Although Chapter 1 made it clear that most teachers are pleased with their choice of careers, this does not mean that they are happy with everything about their work. The chief satisfactions come from interacting with students and making a positive contribution to students' lives and society in general. But at one or more points in their careers a significant number of teachers experience problems with salary, class size, their relations with administrators, and the lack of support from some parents and the community at large.

[1]John Elliot, "Teachers in Revolt," *Detroit Teacher*, 11 November 1988, p. 2.

While each teacher finds some personal way of dealing with such issues, usually the most effective way to address teachers' career problems is through professional organizations. In the United States most teachers are members of two organizations: their state or local affiliate of the National Education Association (NEA) or a local affiliate of the American Federation of Teachers (AFT). Today most countries—especially highly industrialized ones—have similar professional organizations for elementary and secondary teachers. But in the long history of teaching, this is a recent development.

To understand the role of today's professional organizations, a short history of their development is in order. We will briefly examine four phases: (1) noblesse oblige, (2) individual professionals, (3) organized pre-unions, and (4) unionized semiprofessionals. After describing the evolution of teaching, we will evaluate it as a profession today.

PHASE 1: NOBLESSE OBLIGE

Human beings have been showing each other how to do things since earliest prehistory. As specialized roles and activities developed—warrior, priest, artisan—someone had to teach the next generation how to perform their duties. At first, everyone learned special designated skills from senior members of the society, who considered it their "noble obligation" (*noblesse oblige*) to instruct the young. The elders did this not as their primary activity but on a part-time basis, out of a sense of civic duty. It did not occur to anyone to earn a living by teaching.

RESEARCH SAYS

For Tomorrow's Education . . .

The gradually diminishing number of minority teachers is cause for much concern because the erosion is happening at a time when the percentage of minority students is increasing. See "Welcoming Minority Teachers," *Harvard Education Letter* 5 (May–June 1989): 6.

With the development of written language, around 3000 B.C., the knowledge and skill needed to convey literacy became so complex that there developed a class of teachers who devoted full time to the craft of instructing.[2] Among these were aristocrats, whose independent wealth allowed them to instruct free of charge; but eventually other people came to support themselves by teaching for a fee.

PHASE 2: INDIVIDUAL PROFESSIONALS

The Greek philosopher Protagoras, in the fifth century B.C., was the first person to offer a clear defense of teaching for a livelihood.[3] Starting life as a humble porter, he gradually acquired such skill and fame as a teacher that he became wealthy from the tuition his pupils paid. His younger contemporary Socrates,

[2]Christopher J. Lucas, "The Scribal Tablet-House in Ancient Mesopotamia," *History of Education Quarterly* 19 (Fall 1979): 305–352.

[3]Plato, *Protagoras, Great Books of the Western World* (Chicago: University of Chicago Press, 1952).

Teaching as a livelihood began in Greece, and for nearly 2,000 years each teacher personally negotiated pay and work issues. Socrates and Plato, shown in the School of Athens by Renaissance painter Raphael, were early teaching professionals.   —Scala/Art Resource, NY

who was destined for even greater fame, criticized Protagoras for charging fees to teach. To this day the debate continues between those who see teaching as primarily a noble duty and those who view it as a social service worthy of pay.

For centuries people who earned their livings as teachers did so strictly as individuals. From the days when Augustine (later sainted) in fourth-century Africa to the time when Sarah Gillespie sought her first job in 1883 in Iowa, each teacher personally negotiated his or her salary and other conditions of work. If employers failed to keep their side of the agreement (as Charlestown, Massachusetts, did with Ezekiel Cheever during the seventeenth century), the basic solution was to move to another town (Boston, in Cheever's case).[4] University teachers were an exception. Beginning in the thirteenth century, teachers of what we now call "higher" education incorporated themselves in order to gain control over their work conditions. Although only university teachers were involved in this development, a university's curriculum at the time included liberal arts, math, and science courses that now are taught in secondary schools.

PHASE 3: ORGANIZED PRE-UNIONS

During the early nineteenth century several local teacher associations developed in America. By the 1830s a number of New England educators organized a re-

[4]L. Glenn Smith and Henry Hornbeck, "The Price of a Teacher: A History of Income and Status in American Education," in *The Social Role and Evolution of the Teaching Profession in Historical Context: Social Conditions and Prestige of Teachers in Different Countries—Regions,* ed. Simo Seppo, 5 vols. (Juensuu, Finland: Bulletin No. 25 of the Faculty of Education, University of Juensuu, 1988) 3: 27–32.

gional association for the purpose of discussing educational questions.[5] As more and more settlers pushed well beyond the area of the original colonies, some teachers felt the need for a national organization. In August 1857, in Philadelphia, forty-one men and two women met to form the National Teachers Association (NTA). Although the NTA's charter claimed to include "all practical teachers" in the country, women could only be honorary members; they could write papers but had to listen to "gentlemen members" read and discuss their ideas. In 1866 female teachers forced the group to substitute the word *person* for *gentleman* in the membership article of its constitution.[6]

In 1870 the NTA changed its name to the National Education Association as three other organizations merged with it. By the 1880s attendance at the group's annual summer conventions was running into the thousands. "Practical teachers" covered their own expenses to hear noted speakers discuss matters of pedagogical interest. But many attendees were administrators or book-company representatives whose school districts or firms paid their way to the convention. The annual meeting thus became the place where school superintendents and normal school presidents who had political aspirations could see and be seen, hear and be heard. In 1906 the organization received a congressional charter as the **National Education Association (NEA)**.

By the early 1900s the NEA was thriving from the dues of thousands of teachers—a majority of them women—while its governance and management were concentrated in the hands of a small "inner circle" revolving around Columbia University's president, Nicholas Murray Butler. At the 1910 annual meeting, however, a dramatic floor fight resulted in the election of Dr. Ella Flagg Young as the first female president of the NEA. One year earlier Young had been named general superintendent of Chicago's schools, becoming the first woman to head a large city school system. For a time in later years the NEA followed a policy of alternating its presidency between males and females, and recently Mary Futrell was president for three consecutive terms (from 1986–87 to 1988–89).

Despite the surge of reform that swept through the NEA as part of Young's election, the organization and most state and local affiliates shied away from confronting school districts over salary or work conditions until the 1960s. Only after the rival and more openly militant American Federation of Teachers seemed to be outgaining it did the NEA begin to advocate "withholding professional services" as a way of forcing districts to deal with educators' concerns. In the mid-1960s superintendents and principals left the NEA to form their own professional organizations, and then this largest teacher organization dropped its opposition to being regarded as a union.

PHASE 4: UNIONIZED SEMIPROFESSIONALS

The fact that most turn-of-the-century teachers were in elementary schools and were female meant that America's public school teaching force was not only professionally disenfranchised but also politically voiceless. The first impulses to correct the professional part of this situation were felt in Chicago in 1897, when a group of teachers formed the Chicago Teachers Federation (CTF). Under the forceful leadership of former elementary teachers Margaret A. Haley and

[5]Marshall O. Donley, Jr., "The American Schoolteacher: From Obedient Servant to Militant Professional," in *Collective Bargaining Techniques in Education*, ed. J. Donald Herring and Joseph A. Sarthory (Austin, Tex.: Mesa Publications, 1980), 45–56.

[6]L. Glenn Smith, "The Changing of the Guard: William Torrey Harris and the Passing of the Old Order in the NEA," *Texas Tech Journal of Education* 8 (Winter 1981): 27–43. For a discussion of these nineteenth-century and early twentieth-century developments see also Joan K. Smith, "The Changing of the Guard: Margaret A. Haley and the Rise of Democracy in the NEA," *Texas Tech Journal of Education* 8 (Winter 1981): 5–25.

Margaret A.
Haley

1861–1939

Unionism was a major factor in
the development of teaching as
a professional endeavor, and
Chicago's Margaret Haley was
among the key figures in forming teacher unions. Born near
Joliet, Illinois, on November 15, 1861, "Maggie was the
second of eight children born to Irish Catholic parents
whose families had immigrated for better working conditions and educational opportunities. Her father was a
self-educated man who owned two stone quarries and
who had strong beliefs in the democratic process, moral
justice, and social reform—values which he passed on to
Margaret. When his quarry was closed because he refused to become involved in shady corporate dealings,
Maggie supported his decision by giving up her dream
of going to college and by becoming a teacher at the
age of sixteen."*

Haley prepared for teaching by completing a normal
course during the summer, and she accepted her first
position, in a country school, before her seventeenth
birthday. She was about five feet tall and weighed about
one hundred pounds—characteristics that led her students to mistake her for one of their classmates on the
first day of school.

After teaching in country schools for the next few
years, Haley eventually received a sixth-grade teaching
appointment in Chicago, in 1884. She also attended
classes at the Cook County Normal School, under the
direction of Colonel Francis Wayland Parker (see "Yesterday's Professional" in Chapter 1). During the early
1890s Haley and other female elementary school teachers had decided to band together to protest their low
pay and the lack of a retirement pension. By 1895 they
had succeeded in bringing a pension plan to passage,
and they were developing salary guidelines. In 1897,
however, the pension plan was threatened by its actu-
arial schedule; at a meeting to correct this, the Chicago
Teachers Federation (CTF) was formed.

By 1899 Haley was Vice-President of the CTF and—
like her father—was interested in justice and reform is-

sues. One strong concern at the time was that Chicago's
board of education had not paid teachers the approved
salary increases that the CTF had fought for. Haley and
CTF President Catharine Goggin discovered that the
board's treasury was short of revenues because many
corporations had not paid taxes on property valued at
over $100 million. When they talked to attorney and for

Yesterday's Professional

mer governor John P. Altgeld about securing these
taxes,he told them that they were right in what they
wanted to do but that they would not win against these
powerful businesses. Their responses revealed their motivations for proceeding with the tax fight: Goggin said,
"I don't care whether we win or lose if we are right"; and
Haley said, "I do not see why we should not win if we
are right."[†]

They won their case in the courts in 1902, and
$600,000 in back-taxes was paid to the board's treasury.
But it was 1906 before the board voted to use the money
to pay teachers their back-salary increases. During this
time the CTF had affiliated with 200,000 voting men in
the Chicago Federation of Labor, and the group had
hired two attorneys: Isaiah T. Greenacre and his new assistant, Clarence Darrow. It also hired Haley and Goggin
to pursue their reform work full time on behalf of Chicago's public school teachers.

Haley continued to be the CTF's business representative—a paid position—for the next twenty-nine years,
until she retired in 1935. During that time she helped
lobby for the first teacher tenure law (passed in 1917)
and worked doggedly to ease the Depression's economic
effects on Chicago's teachers. She summed up her work
this way: "The teachers' fight has been a fight in the
general cause of liberty . . . for a time-honored institution, the free public schools . . . it began to run amuck
whenever it disturbed a papered interest."[‡]

Haley retired to California, where she died of a heart
attack in 1939.

*Based on Joan K. Smith, Ella Flagg Young: Portrait of a Leader (Ames, Iowa: Iowa
State University Research Foundation/Educational Studies Press, 1979), 121–143; and
L. Glenn Smith and Joan K. Smith et al., Lives in Education: People and Ideas in the
Development of Teaching (Ames, Iowa: Educational Studies Press, 1984), 282–287.

[†]Ibid., 128.

[‡]Ibid., 284.

Catharine Goggin, the CTF was instrumental in bringing about much-needed and long-promised salary increases. In fact, Chicago's elementary teachers had received no raise for twenty years (from 1886 to 1906); the school board had approved increases but then rescinded them, lacking the needed money. The CTF itself brought additional revenues into the school budget by forcing Chicago's corporate structure to comply with tax laws, thereby creating more money for schools.

From 1906 to 1917 the CTF pressed for legal assurances that gave public school teachers the right to a pension system, a salary schedule, and **tenure**, or a guaranteed term of office after one completed a period of probation. Tenure aimed to protect teachers from being summarily dismissed without cause.

In all these areas the CTF was successful, but not without help. As early as October 1902 it affiliated with a local union, the Chicago Federation of Labor (CF of L), in order to get the support of a politically franchised and occupationally forceful group of men. However, in its last battle—to gain tenure for Chicago's teachers—the CTF had to agree to resign membership from the CF of L; only if it did so would the school board give its much-needed support for a tenure protection law.

Before the CTF disaffiliated from the CF of L, it joined seven other teacher organizations to form the **American Federation of Teachers (AFT)**, on 15 April 1916. The number of local unions needed to obtain a national charter from the American Federation of Labor (AF of L) was eight, and the CTF (Local 1) became the heart of this new teacher union. Two other Chicago unions—the Federation of Men Teachers (Local 2) and the Federation of Women High School Teachers (Local 3)—were among the seven locals. The others were teacher organizations from Gary, Indiana (Local 4); New York City (Local 5); Washington, D.C. (Local 6); Scranton, Pennsylvania (Local 7); and Oklahoma City (Local 8).

Chicago was not the only city where teacher unions were politically active during the first decades of this century. A group of teachers in San Antonio, Texas, joined the AF of L in September 1902. Unions were becoming the professional voice of teachers who sought to improve their work conditions and to participate in decision making that formulated the aims, methods, and materials of public education.[7]

As membership in the NEA grew during the 1920s, the AFT went into decline. It rose again during the 1930s and 1940s, as teachers faced payless paydays during the Depression and struggled with salaries that fell behind inflation after World War II. In 1937 Chicago's locals united and took the CTF's place as Local 1. New York City's United Federation of Teachers (UFT) became Local 2 and successfully competed against its older rival (Local 5). By the 1960s the UFT was the major organizational force for teachers in New York.

As unionism spread, an attitude of militancy arose, even among teachers. The new locals were ready to use "the Weapon" of labor—the strike—in order to survive the sledgehammer of inflation that hit teachers so hard after World War II. Before the war teachers earned an average of 12 percent more than other workers, but by 1951 they were earning 4 percent *less*. Yet a strike was something that most teachers had never considered before, even during the Great Depres-

[7]For accounts of the CTF and AFT, see Mary J. Herrick, *The Chicago Schools: A Social and Political History* (Beverly Hills: Sage Publications, 1971); Joan K. Smith, *Ella Flagg Young: Portrait of a Leader* (Ames, Iowa: Educational Studies Press, Iowa State University Research Foundation, 1979); Wayne J. Urban, *Why Teachers Organized* (Detroit: Wayne State University Press, 1982); and Margaret A. Haley, *Battleground: The Autobiography of Margaret A. Haley*, ed. Robert L. Reid (Urbana: University of Illinois Press, 1982).

As unionized semiprofessionals, teachers fought for collective bargaining—the legal right to negotiate as a group to improve their salary and work conditions. In the 1940s and 1950s teachers adopted "the Weapon" of labor: the strike. —Northern Illinois University

sion, when some cities—including Chicago—failed to pay teachers for months at a time.[8]

It is against this backdrop during the 1940s and 1950s that teachers' militancy came to the forefront. The period from 1942 to 1968 witnessed more than a hundred strikes—at a time when the courts held that strikes by teachers were illegal. The walkouts involved some twenty thousand teachers belonging to three types of groups: local unions affiliated with the AFT, associations affiliated with the NEA and state associations, and independent organizations.

Economic conditions were at the heart of most strikes. For example, in 1949 the Minneapolis teacher union closed the schools after being told that teachers would work four fewer weeks and would have to take a 10-percent salary cut. That same year teachers in Avoca, Pennsylvania, struck when they failed to receive 3½ months of back salary.

Some strikes during this period went beyond teachers' salary needs and focused on the right to bargain legally for better economic and work conditions. This right to negotiate with an employer for better wages, hours, and work conditions is called **collective bargaining**. In 1946 the teacher association in Norwalk, Connecticut, closed the schools until the board recognized it as the sole bargaining agent for the system. By far the most well-known strike of this period occurred in New York City in 1960, when five thousand UFT members struck the system to force the board to concede the legitimacy of collective bargaining. After one day the board agreed, and the teachers voted (by more than 3 to 1) for collective bargaining; soon after this, they chose the UFT as their sole bargaining agent.[9]

[8]For an account of Depression conditions in Chicago see Herrick, *Chicago Schools;* and Haley, *Battleground,* 227–276. See also Joan K. Smith, "Social Reconstruction and Teacher Unionism: Chicago's Response to the Great Depression," *Illinois Schools Journal* (Special Issue).

[9]Donley, "The American Schoolteacher."

During the 1960s and 1970s teachers throughout the country struck their systems to earn the right to bargain with their employers for specific conditions of employment. By 1972 some 1,445,329 instructional employees were covered by bargained contracts.[10]

COLLECTIVE BARGAINING   Private-sector employees won the right to bargain for wages and work conditions earlier than did teachers and others in the public sphere. From the 1940s to the 1970s, however, public opinion—and therefore legislation and legal interpretations—generally became much more favorable to unions and bargaining. Today most teachers, police officers, firefighters, postal workers, and ther public employees are covered by contracts that periodically (usually annually) are agreed upon through conversations between management and union representatives.[11] Most teachers favor this development.[12] A majority of states have now adopted comprehensive public-employee collective bargaining statutes.[13] Even in states that have not authorized collective bargaining, most of its features are commonplace.

The following five characteristics define collective bargaining as it is practiced in educational settings today:

1. Districtwide bargaining units

2. Periodic negotiation of comprehensive contracts lasting for a specific period of time

3. A requirement of "good faith" negotiation restricted to "bread-and-butter" issues

4. Multistep grievance procedures to resolve disputes that arise during the life of the contract

5. Binding arbitration as a final solution to any disagreements that cannot otherwise be resolved

In states where legislatures have not enacted collective bargaining laws, negotiations are usually legal under "meet and discuss" regulations. Such arrangements, however, often lack provisions for grievances or for arbitration of unresolvable disagreements.

What does unionized bargaining mean for America's communities and schools? Answers vary widely, depending on the traditions and conditions in each of the country's fifteen thousand school districts. A small percentage seem to have difficulty in negotiations almost every year; strikes or strike threats loom frequently, and teachers, administrators, students, and parents often experience heightened tension. But each year a far greater number of districts reach contract agreement with no disruption and little acrimony. Strikes make dramatic news, and so they tend to be emphasized by the media.

What about teachers? How does collective bargaining affect them? To some extent the answer again depends partly on the kind of district and community involved. But significant variables are also introduced by each teacher's personality and preferences. A relatively small percentage of teachers ignore all professional organizations—whether local, state, or national. The majority, however, join at least their local bargaining unit, and they participate in some meetings and organizational activities. Another relatively small but significant percentage

[10]Ibid.

[11]John E. Owen, "The U.S. Labor Union Movement: Its History and Current Problems," in *Collective Bargaining Techniques in Education,* 3–10; and Abraham L. Gitlow, "Public Employee Unionism in the United States: Growth and Outlook," ibid., 11–26.

[12]"Whither Collective Bargaining?" *VEA News* (May 1989): 3; Charles E. Bolden, "Collective Bargaining—An Opinion," *WV School Journal* 117 (March 1989) 1: 2; and "Professional Negotiations: Collective Bargaining," *The Update* (September 1988): 11.

[13]Robert W. Sauter, "Lessons to Be Learned from the Ohio Experience: A Union Perspective," *Journal of Law and Education,* 18 (Spring 1989): 289–312.

of teachers are quite active professionally; they serve as representatives of their school or district, hold office, and attend state or national meetings. From this group a small number of teachers even leave their classrooms to work full time for local, state, or national organizations.

REFINING COLLECTIVE BARGAINING   Because collective bargaining in public education is relatively new, courts are constantly interpreting and refining laws, regulations, and policies through litigation. Also, when states approve collective bargaining through legislation, they usually create labor relations boards that interpret laws and regulations and rule on some disputed points that end up being grieved.

Among the areas of potential disagreement over collective bargaining that courts continue to address are "bread-and-butter" issues, or what is and is not negotiable. In general, courts have tried to reserve "policy issues" to administrators and school boards while holding that school districts *must* bargain about educators' salaries and work conditions. But the two kinds of issues often overlap. For example, is class size basically a matter of policy, or is it really an aspect of work conditions? It's both, of course, and courts generally find it to be negotiable. Yet school districts are not obliged to accede to the bargaining unit's demands in order to be acting in "good faith" (the phrase found in most bargaining clauses).[14]

Courts usually apply a three-part test in deciding whether or not an item is negotiable, holding that it is bargainable only if it

- "intimately affects work and welfare of public employees
- "has not been preempted by statute or regulation
- "is a matter on which negotiated agreement would not significantly interfere with the exercise of inherent management prerogatives pertaining to determination of government policy."[15]

Although few things are ever final in case law, the following generalizations can be drawn from recent decisions:

1. Teachers cannot be required to join a union, but the automatic withholding of dues from a teacher's salary is legal, and nonmembers may be required to pay that portion of dues which the union spends on contract negotiations.[16]

2. The number of days per year that teachers will work is subject to bargaining, but the beginning and ending dates of work, and any makeup days required by unanticipated school closings, are not negotiable.[17]

3. School boards may not bargain away their responsibility to evaluate teachers; they may—but are not required to—negotiate about the procedures and details of evaluation.[18]

4. Decisions about curricula, including the addition and deletion of areas of study, are reserved to management, which may elect to "consult" with teachers.[19]

5. The size of the teaching staff and support staff is a management decision, but "reduction in force" *procedures* are negotiable under some

[14]*West's Educational Law Digest*, 178.

[15]Ibid.; and Decatur Bd. of Educ., Dist. No. 61 v. Illinois Educ. Labor Relations Bd., 129 Ill.Dec. 693, 536 N.E.2d 743.

[16]Shinn v. Illinois Educ. Labor Relations Bd., 132 Ill.Dec. 284, 539 N.E.2d 847; Cumero v. Public Employment Relations Bd., 262 Cal.Rptr. 46; Hudson v. Chicago Teachers Union, Local No. 1, 699 F.Supp. 1334; and Lowary v. Lexington Local Bd. of Educ., 704 F.Supp. 1430, on reconsideration in part 704 F.Supp. 1476.

[17]Halley v. Board of School Trustees of Blackford County School Corp., 531 N.E.2d 1182; Public Employee Relations Bd. v. Washington Teachers' Union Local 6, AFT, 556 A.2d 206; and Montgomery County Educ. Ass'n, Inc. v. Board of Educ. of Montgomery County, 534 A.2d 980, 311 Md. 303.

[18]Sweet Home Cent. School Dist. of Amherst and Tonawanda v. Sweet Home Service Employees Ass'n, 522 N.Y.S.2d 58, 134 A.D.2d 892; Board of School Trustees of Gary Community School Corp. v. Indiana Educ. Employment Relations Bd., 543 N.E.2d 662; and Wethersfield Bd. of Educ. v. Connecticut State Bd. of Labor Relations, 519 A.2d 41, 201 Conn. 685.

[19]Bay City Educ. Ass'n v. Bay City Public Schools, 422 N.W.2d 504, 430 Mich. 370; and Overseas Educ. Ass'n, Inc. v. Federal Labor Relations Authority, 872 F.2d 1032.

circumstances; therefore, before hiring any new teachers, districts may be required to reinstate tenured teachers in the order in which they were laid off.[20]

Clearly, there are many other issues open to negotiation, but these examples illustrate the recent focus of teachers' collective bargaining. In general, courts still tend to support traditional prerogatives of management rather than legitimizing some claims that many teachers believe would help them achieve full professional status. Yet, by associating into bargaining units, teachers have become a force that cannot be ignored.

On the other hand, although unionization and collective bargaining have increased teachers' power, they also have brought some disadvantages to the profession. For example, bargaining tends to draw battle lines that heighten public awareness of educators' disagreements. An orientation of "us versus them" sometimes makes it more difficult for school boards and teachers to resolve their differences. Also, when teachers, administrators, and board members are personally involved in negotiations, they sometimes develop hostilities or hurt feelings that continue long after negotiations end. Remember Gary Nuernberger, the teacher quoted in Chapter 1? He spent five years on the negotiating team for teachers in his district, and he remembers the experience with distaste:

[20]Hodgeson v. Board of Educ. of Buena Vista School Dist., 438 N.W.2d 295, 175 Mich.App. 405; and United Teachers of Flint v. Flint School Dist., 404 N.W.2d 637, 158 Mich.Dpp. 138, appeal denied.

Comparative Perspective on Today's Issues . . .

◆ HAS UNIONISM HURT TEACHERS' EFFORTS TO GAIN BENEFITS AND TO BE CONSIDERED "TRUE PROFESSIONALS"?

The Issue   As teachers have adopted labor-union models of organization, including use of the strike and collective bargaining, many people have concluded that teachers are not professionals in the way that doctors and lawyers are.

YES   When teachers use the tactics of organized labor, they weaken their claim of professionalism. True professionals, like doctors and lawyers, do not strike or go to the bargaining table to improve their work conditions and salaries. They are able to control their professional lives without turning to labor-union methods. Furthermore, when teachers assess the financial and personal outcomes of striking, they find that they have gained little, if anything.

NO   Throughout the ages people of similar occupational training and experience have banded together in order to influence and control their market. Originally such groups were called guilds, and later unions. Ultimately some occupational groups, as in law and medicine, were called professions "when people . . . [forgot] that they were unions." Therefore, it is not the union model that is the problem; it is the fact that teachers still must answer to lay boards and do not control the standards for entry. See James H. Sutton, "The Ideological Basis of Teacher Organization, or Why We Do What We Do," ED 275 634, 1986.

I went through a bad time when I was doing negotiations. It was really bitter. We didn't go on strike, but we might as well have, for the feelings between the staff, administration, and school board. Of course I got written up. We [teachers on the negotiating team] had a big race that year about who would get the most letters [of administrative reprimand]. I think I tied with another teacher. Almost every week I was called on the carpet. I would sit there, listen to the nonsense, nod my head—then go teach. I closed my door and I taught, and I just ignored the administration and school board."[21]

For reasons like these, approximately half the country's school boards and about the same number of bargaining units now hire professional negotiators to represent them. This practice tends to lower the stress and tension between teachers and administrators.[22] A few systems are experimenting with alternatives that make negotiations collaborative and more positive.[23] One widely hailed approach is a strategy called "win-win." School board members, teachers, and administrators *must* participate in negotiations, but rather than emphasizing "power relationships, concessions, credibility challenges and personality conflicts," the win-win process stresses "problem solving, considering mutual interests, [and] sharing of information, and it aims at positive relations."[24] Many educators who have negotiated in this way are pleased with the process and its results.

OTHER UNION ACTIVITIES   If collective bargaining has been the most visible focus of the NEA, the AFT, and local affiliates, it by no means has been their only interest. Among the most important activities of teacher organizations is their active engagement in politics. Given that state legislatures, local school boards, and many city councils are intimately involved in funding schools and setting educational policies, teacher organizations have become extensively involved in policial activities that shape opinion and legislation. The NEA, the AFT, and the NEA's state-level organizations have formed **political action committees (PACs)** to actively lobby politicians and influence educational legislation. These groups and a number of locals also routinely endorse political candidates, and they regularly publish politicians' voting records. In Casper, Wyoming, for example, members of the Natrona County Education Association successfully opposed school board candidates whom they considered to be "far right extremists."[25] Finally, state and national organizations annually adopt comprehensive platforms, or statements of belief, which center on educational matters but also support positions about such issues as women's rights, peace, and many other topics.[26]

Another major focus of unions is members' welfare, in cases where arbitration, grievance procedures, or court decisions have not yielded satisfactory results. For example, when a school board in southern Georgia refused to reinstate a teacher after she was acquitted in court of charges relating to marijuana, the Georgia Education Association publicized her story and appealed for contributions to a support fund for her, noting that the teacher had two children to care for.[27] In West Virginia, when a parent insisted on removing *Scary Stories to Tell in*

[21]Interview with Gary Nuernberger, 3 December 1989.

[22]Iris McGinnis, "Board Members Should Give the Bargaining Table a Wide Berth," *American School Board Journal* 176 (August 1989): 22–23; and Edward E. Eiler, "Follow These Golden Rules, and Negotiate a Solid Labor Contract," *American School Board Journal* 176 (August 1989): 25–26.

[23]Robert A. Hansen, "Good-bye Adversarial Negotiations—We've Found a Better Way to Bargain," *American School Board Journal* 176 (August 1989): 23–24.

[24]Joe Thiele, "Collective Bargaining: How Not to Lose at Win-Win," *Illinois School Board Journal* 55 (January–February 1987): 19–20.

[25]"Locals Recognized for School Board Victories," *WEA News* 57 (April–May 1989): 10.

[26]Julie Schwindt, "Speaking Out: Political Commitment Ensures Education on Candidate's Agenda," *WEA News* 56 (May–June 1988): 2; Bob Leinius, "Why WEA *Must* Make Endorsements," *WEA News* 57 (April–May): 3; "District 12 Wins PAC Race with $53.88 per Delegate," *VEA News* (May 1989): 3; and "Did Your Legislators Vote Pro-Education?" *VEA News* (April 1989): 8.

[27]"Association Notes: School Board Refuses to Reinstate Acquitted Teacher," *The Update* (September–October 1989): 4C.

Beyond collective bargaining, an important activity of teacher organizations is political action to shape public opinion and legislation. Teachers lobby, form PACs, endorse candidates, and support positions on a wide variety of social and ethical issues.
—UPI/Bettmann

the Dark from the elementary school library, the West Virginia Education Association gave the story prominent space in its publication.[28]

Examples like these show the wide range of issues that teacher organizations handle on behalf of members. But are today's organizations the final word? No one can know for sure, of course, but the following discussion of professionalism suggests that teachers and their organizations are in a transitional phase.

PROFESSIONALISM AND THE PUBLIC SCHOOL TEACHER

With so much attention on unionization and collective bargaining, where does teaching stand on the professional ladder? Those who study occupational and professional developments generally agree that teachers are not on the top rung with lawyers and doctors, even though, as Chapter 1 pointed out, the professions of law and medicine were both held in little esteem a century ago.

Today, however, medicine and law share a set of characteristics that lets doctors and lawyers enjoy high social status, much prestige, and generous financial remuneration—the last of which is not seen as being in conflict with their public-service missions. Teaching, on the other hand, is regarded as an **emerging**

[28]"1927 Story Collection Instigates Complaint," *WV School Journal* 118 (November 1989): 4.

profession because it does not involve the same number of characteristics to the same degree that law and medicine do; nor do teachers enjoy the same status or financial rewards as lawyers and doctors. It will be helpful, then, to examine the general characteristics of professionalism, and to assess how teaching measures up to those characteristics.

Generally defined, a **profession** is an occupation, vocation, or "calling" that requires study in the liberal arts or sciences as well as intensive, often-lengthy preparation in specialized areas of knowledge. Social scientists and educators have defined the term more precisely, viewing a profession as "an occupation with a crucial social function, requiring a high degree of skill and drawing on a systematic body of knowledge."[29] These definitions imply that a certain set of conditions or characteristics must be present before one can be considered a professional.

The literature on professionalism is extensive, and many lists of characteristics have been offered to describe what a truly "full" professional does.[30] For our purposes, however, the characteristics can be grouped into four categories:

1. Professionals are trained in a recognized and exclusive body of knowledge from which they gain expertise and permission to practice.

2. Professionals apply this expert knowledge and skill as a valued service to clients, for their welfare and benefit.

3. Professionals have a high level of autonomy in making decisions about clients and in controlling and maintaining the standards of their profession.

4. Professionals have a sense of collegial identity, and their cooperation is fostered by a formal organizational structure.

Now let's assess teaching in relation to these four characteristics of professionalism.

A Recognized, Exclusive Body of Knowledge

Many people have argued that teaching is an art with only a distant tie to science and that it has no agreed-upon knowledge base.[31] They do not believe that teaching is bound by a comprehensive set of scientific rules and methodologies, as the medical sciences are; consequently, many laypeople regard themselves as education experts. Connected to this belief is the notion that *any* educated person can walk into a classroom and deliver daily lessons to a group of twenty-five or thirty children.

RESEARCH SAYS

For Tomorrow's Education . . .

Certain specific practices and behaviors of teachers are strongly associated with students' achievement. See "Good Teaching: Do You know It When You See It?" *Harvard Education Letter* 5 (May–June 1989): 1–3.

---

[29]Hugh Socckett, "Towards a Professional Code in Teaching" (paper presented before the Annual Meeting of the American Educational Research Association, Chicago, 31 March–4 April 1985), 2.

[30]For descriptions of the characteristics and limits of professionalism see, for example, Arthur E. Wise, "Six Steps to Teacher Professionalism," *Educational Leadership* 48 (April 1990): 57–60. Also see David Ozar, Francis J. Catania, and Elizabeth O'Connell, "Professions and Professional Obligations," chap. 2 of an unpublished manuscript entitled "Ethical Issues in University Administration"; Albert Shanker, "In Support of Teachers: The Making of a Profession," *NASSP Bulletin* 482 (September 1985): 93–99; John J. Bergen, "The Professional Role of the Teacher: Three Important Dimensions and How They Interact," *Education Canada* 3 (Fall 1987): 26–29; Y. L. Jack Lam, "Determinants of Teacher Professionalism," *The Alberta Journal of Educational Research* 3 (September 1983): 168–179; and Linda Darling-Hammond, "Teacher Professionalism and Accountability," *American Educator* 12 (Winter 1988): 8–12, 36–43.

[31]See David Dill, *What Teachers Need to Know* (San Francisco: Jossey-Bass, 1990); and Allan C. Ornstein and Daniel U. Levine, *Foundations of Education* (Boston: Houghton Mifflin, 1993), 43.

A significant body of research shows such beliefs to be mistaken. In one recent study, for example, three college graduates who had strong training in their disciplines but no education coursework were hired to teach in high school settings. Their experiences during the first year were then compared with the experiences of other first-year teachers who *had* received pedagogical coursework as well as the typical training in their disciplines. Researchers found that the three without education coursework did not know (1) how to motivate students to learn, (2) how to plan a lesson, or (3) how to present material in a way that facilitates learning. The teachers who had professional preparation *did* know how to accomplish these essential aspects of successful teaching. The study concluded that "while subject-matter knowledge, good character, and the inclination to teach are important characteristics of beginning teachers, they do not necessarily lead to a pedagogical understanding of subject matter nor to a theoretical understanding of how students learn a particular subject."[32]

Other education researchers believe that the field of teaching is on the threshold of creating a scientific base which the public will accept as *truly specialized knowledge* similar to knowledge in the medical field. They also believe that the methods and forms of education research compare favorably with those found in the chemical and physical sciences.[33]

RESEARCH SAYS

For Tomorrow's Education . . .

Research in education and social sciences is no better, nor worse, than in the hard sciences. See L. Hedges, "How Hard Is Hard Science, How Soft Is Soft Science: The Empirical Cumulativity of Research," *American Psychologist* 42 (May 1987): 443–455; and David C. Berliner, "The Teaching Profession," *Equity and Excellence* 24 (Winter 1989) 2: 4–19.

Several commission reports have agreed that the preparation of teachers is insufficiently rigorous to provide trainees with a uniformly high level of professional development. They call for extended academic programs to provide additional professional preparation as well as a stronger liberal arts background. One popular model to reform teacher training calls for a five-year program like the one mandated by Oregon (see Chapter 1), while another insists on six years. In both cases prospective teachers would earn a bachelor's and a master's degree. Most of the five-year proposals would devote the fifth year to professional coursework and training, following four years of liberal arts and sciences. Advocates of the six-year plans do not agree about how best to sequence the academic and the professional preparation. Some would offer the professional training during the last two years, while others believe that integrating liberal arts courses with pedagogical preparation throughout the six years would be more effective.[34]

To maintain higher professional standards, these commission reports have also called for more rigorous, more uniform procedures for licensing and certification. This recommendation has led many states to reform their certification

[32]Pamela L. Grossman, "Learning to Teach without Teacher Education," *Teachers College Record* 2 (Winter 1989): 207, 191–207. Also see Dona M. Kagan, "Professional Growth Among Preservice and Beginning Teachers," *Review of Educational Research* 62 (Summer 1992) 2: 129–169; and "Education Reformer Learns Experience Is the Best Teacher," *Chicago Tribune*, 28 June 1992, sec. 6, p. 1.

[33]David C. Berliner, "Knowledge Is Power," *Equity and Excellence* 24, (Winter 1989) 2: 4–19. Also see Harriet B. Morrison, "The Holmes Group Plan vs. a Phenomenological Scenario for Teacher Education: An Epistemological Methodological Comparison" (paper presented at the Annual Meeting of the American Educational Research Association, San Francisco, 22 April 1992).

[34]See, for example, National Commission for Excellence in Teacher Education, *A Call for Change in Teacher Education* (Washington D.C.: American Association of Colleges of Teacher Education, 1985), 17–18.

procedures so that prospective teachers are required to pass competency tests in the arts and sciences. Critics of such tests maintain that the level of knowledge they require is not much higher than what average sixth-graders know—and, hence, that tests do not promote high standards. In contrast, supporters of certification tests argue that their purpose is to ensure minimal standards of literacy and competence in the subjects to be taught by the candidates.[35] The tests are not designed to measure teaching skill, and so they do not predict whether a candidate will be a successful teacher. Consequently, many school districts require prospective teachers to pass the National Teachers Examination, which does focus on professional and methodological matters.[36]

APPLICATION OF KNOWLEDGE FOR CLIENTS' WELFARE

Teachers who remain in the field for five or more years seem to have a strong commitment to students' learning. As pointed out in Chapter 1, most teachers *like* teaching, even if they are not so happy about some of the conditions under which they teach. Furthermore, the public generally views teachers as providing a valuable service to students and to the population at large.[37] Because schooling is compulsory, teachers are vested with a strong moral obligation to safeguard their clients' physical, mental, and emotional health. Coupled with this is the parental act of surrendering their children to the school, which demonstrates a considerable amount of trust. Thus teachers provide a valued service to children, who are compelled by the state to be in the teachers' charge for a defined period of time. In this way teachers become the "mediators of the relationship between parent, child and the state."[38]

RESEARCH SAYS

For Tomorrow's Education . . .

One common problem for beginning teachers is that they do not adequately understand their students; nor do they have the appropriate ethical training to stretch beyond their own value structure. See Landon E. Beyer, "Schooling, Moral Commitment, and the Preparation of Teachers," *Journal of Teacher Education* 42 (May–June 1991) 3: 205–215; Robert J. Nash, "Theme: The Ethical Responsibilities of Teaching," *Journal of Teacher Education* 42 (May–June 1991) 3: 163–172; Dwight Rogers and Jaci Webb, "The Ethic of Caring in Teacher Education," *Journal of Teacher Education* 42 (May–June 1991) 3: 173–181; and Robert V. Bullough, Jr., J. Gary Knowles, and Nedra A. Crow, "Teacher Self-Concept and Student Culture in the First Year of Teaching," *Teachers College Records* 91 (Winter 1989): 209–213.

AUTONOMY OF TEACHERS

What has been most problematic for teachers in their efforts to become fully professional centers on issues of autonomy—on their ability to regulate their workplace and to monitor and control the standards of their profession.

[35]Wise, "Six Steps to Teacher Professionalism," 57–60; and "If We Are Ever to 'Professionalize' Schoolteaching, Universities Must Redesign Education Programs," *The Teacher Educator* 4 (Spring 1984): 29–32; and Arthur E. Wise, Linda Darling-Hammond, and Susanna Purnell, "Impacts of Teacher Testing," in *Licensing Teachers: Design for a Teaching Profession* (Santa Monica, Calif.: Rand Corporation, R-3576-cstp, November 1987).

[36]W. Dean Marple, "Teacher Testing in Illinois," *Illinois School Research and Development* 1 (Fall 1988): 9–14.

[37]See Chapter 1 concerning the public's valuing of teachers.

[38]Roger Soder, "Professionalizing the Profession: Notes on the Future of Teaching" (Occasional Paper No. 4, Seattle, Wash., Institute for the Study of Educational Policy, College of Education, University of Washington, June 1986), ED 298 648. Also see Dwight Rogers and Jaci Webb, "The Ethic of Caring in Teacher Education," *Journal of Teacher Education* 42 (May–June 1991) 3: 173–181; and Irene Murphy, "Characteristics of a Good Teacher," *The Delta Kappa Bulletin* 57 (Fall 1990) 1: 39–45.

AUTONOMY IN THE WORKPLACE   For the most part, teachers do control their classrooms. As Mr. Nuernberger put it: When he closes his classroom door, no one bothers him. He is left alone to teach. He is in charge.

Difficulties arise, however, when it comes to making decisions about curricula, or about school regulations and general procedures. In these areas teachers are not usually consulted as knowledgeable experts. Instead, in typical "top-down" management style, teachers are *told* (by the central, district, or building administration) what the policies, procedures, and practices will be. As one teacher put it:

> Even teachers recognized by the community as "a cut above"—teachers whom parents go out of their way to request for their children—may find their expressed views on curriculum unheeded, their requests for innovative disciplinary action ignored, their thirst for scholarly growth unwatered.[39]

To remedy this defect of management, some districts have initiated school-based management or shared decision-making models that include representatives from the teaching staff in various administrative functions. Chapter 3 will discuss these in greater detail.

AUTONOMY IN THE PROFESSION   When prospective teachers finish their training, they undergo a state certification process in which standards and criteria have been set by people other than members of the teaching profession. Unlike doctors and lawyers, teachers have not been involved in monitoring and regulating their own certification or licensing process.

One of the reform reports produced by the Carnegie Taskforce on the Teaching Profession (entitled *A Nation Prepared*) recommended "an assessment process that certifies teachers to show a high level of competence."[40] In response to this recommendation, and to implement the assessment process, the **National Board for Professional Teaching Standards** was created in May 1987. The board and its work are unique to the profession in two ways: (1) two-thirds of its sixty-four members are practicing schoolteachers who are balanced by geographical region, grade level, and subject area; and (2) the board develops national advanced specialized standards for various fields and levels (such as English, grades 9 through 12). Practicing teachers who already are state-certified (or

[39]Nuernberger interview; and Victoria C. Esarey, "What Does It Mean to Be a Professional?" *Virginia Journal of Education* (7 April 1989): 13.

[40]Gary Sykes, "National Certification for Teachers: A Dialog," *NEA Today* (special issues, January 1989): 6. Also see Carnegie Taskforce on the Teaching Professional, *A Nation Prepared: Teachers for the 21st Century* (New York: Carnegie Forum on Education and the Economy, 1986); and Rob Jones, "National Certification," *Virginia Journal of Education* 83 (December 1989): 6–12.

RESEARCH SAYS

For Tomorrow's Education . . .

Teacher and student portfolios may become an effective supplementary mode for assessing the performance of both. See Jay Sugarman, "Teacher Portfolios Inform Assessment," *Harvard Education Letter* 5 (May–June 1989): 5–6; also see the winning entries of a national competition to develop radical education changes (conducted by the New American Schools Development Corporation, a nonprofit group of business leaders), such as "Bensenville's Vision Earns Education Grant," *Chicago Tribune*, 10 July 1992, sec. 1, p. 1.

licensed) can choose to be assessed to determine whether they meet the standards in one or more specialty. If so, they will be eligible for this special certification, just as doctors can be board-certified in one of twenty-three specialties.[41]

Certification by the National Board for Professional Teaching Standards is optional, and it signifies a high level of competency in one's specialty. State certification is comparable to the initial license that is required by most professions; it signifies basic or entry-level professional competence. Thus specialty certification can be used as a criterion for awarding privileges, more benefits, or better compensation to a teacher. The type of benefit is a local matter, not a national one. For example, some districts use specialty certification as part of a **career-ladder plan** that identifies various levels of expert knowledge and provides evaluative criteria for assessing each level. As outstanding teachers climb the rungs of the career ladder, they attain greater compensation and more professional ways to utilize their talents and expertise, such as mentoring.[42]

Today at least twenty-six states are implementing or considering forms of career ladders, either statewide or as a district option. One example of a career ladder (or differentiated staffing) has five levels: Level 1 is an *apprentice teacher* who has a bachelor's degree and three or more years of experience with average performance; level 2 is an *associate teacher* who has a bachelor's degree with three or more years of above-average performance; level 3 is a *senior teacher* with a bachelor's degree and six or more years of above-average performance; level 4 is a *master teacher* who has a master's degree and nine or more years of above-average performance; and level 5 is an *expert teacher* who has at least a master's degree and twelve or more years of above-average performance. Such a career-ladder plan—with its specific levels and criteria—goes far beyond **merit pay**, which is simply a monetary bonus for a job well done.[43]

COLLEGIALITY AMONG TEACHING PROFESSIONALS

In 1975 the publication of Dan C. Lortie's *Schoolteacher: A Sociological Study* confirmed the assumption that teachers—because they spend most of their work hours as the *only* teacher in the classroom—are isolated from each other and, therefore, do not have the benefit of collegial relationships with peers. Whether or not this is true, and whether or not it differs significantly from medical practitioners (who also spend many work hours alone with clients) has yet to be determined systematically. Even so, research does suggest that schools which

RESEARCH SAYS

For Tomorrow's Education . . .

Indiana's "Teachers Teaching Teachers" is a voluntary state-supported program that helps teachers share ideas and learn new skills through staff development. Participants say that the program has increased their collegial relationships and enhanced their classroom performance. See "Indiana's Training Waves," *NEA Today* 8 (October 1989): 1.

[41]Sykes, "National Certification for Teachers"; and Jones, "National Certification."

[42]Richard D. Packard and Louann Bierlein, "Career Ladder Abstract and Incentive Programs for Teachers: Will It Work in Arizona?" ED 287 797. Also see Jean Fontana, "The Rite of Passage: The Mentor Teacher/Intern Program," *The Delta Kappa Gamma Bulletin* 57 (Fall 1990) 1: 31–38; and Margaret F. Ostlund, "Partnership in Education: A Model for School/University Collaboration" (paper presented at the Annual Meeting of the American Educational Research Association, San Francisco, 23 April 1992).

[43]David Nelson and others, "Implications of the Texas Mandate for Comprehensive Performance Appraisal" (paper presented at the Annual Meeting of the International Society for Educational Planning, Washington, D.C., October 1986), ED 280 161; and Richard L. Flander, "A Systems Approach to Management Effectiveness Training" (paper presented at the Annual Meeting of the American Association of School Administrators, Dallas 1985), ED 270 085.

Like other professionals, teachers—and schools—benefit from collegial relationships with other teachers. Today many districts have staff development programs to foster professional growth and collegiality among educators. —Jay Wiley/Monkmeyer

[44]J. Howard Johnston, Glenn C. Markle, and Joanne M. Arhar, "Co-operation, Collaboration, and the Professional Development of Teachers," *Middle School Journal* 3 (May 1988): 28–30.

[45]Walter H. Moore and James R. Hutton, "Collegiality: Professional Collaboration in Action," *Catalyst for Change* 1 (Fall 1988): 21–23; and "Teaching Professionalism Classes Draw Strong Response," *Chicago Union Teacher* 6 (April 1988): 1; and Douglas F. Waring, "The Effects of a Mentor-Mentee Program on the Learning Environment" (paper presented at the Annual Meeting of the American Educational Research Association, Chicago, 3–7 April 1992), ED 333 357.

encourage collaborative planning, collegial relationships, and opportunities for professional growth through staff development programs tend to show greater achievement among students.[44]

In recent years many school districts have encouraged collegiality through staff development programs and other means. Examples include Mississippi's Continuum project, which provides teams of support teachers as resources for their peers, and Chicago's Educational Research and Dissemination Program, which offers classes in "Beginning of the Year Classroom Management and Effective Group Management." In addition, many education faculty are collaborating with teachers in conducting *on-site*, or *action, research*.[45]

The increasing collegiality of teaching professionals and their application of an exclusive body of knowledge for the benefit of clients give teaching relatively high marks in terms of the four components of professionalism. In matters of autonomy, however—in teachers' ability to control and regulate their workplace—greater strides need to be made. Recent reform efforts are aimed at strengthening this component of professionalism.

CONCLUSIONS

■

The development and growth of teaching have gone through several transformations during this century. In recent decades, particularly, teachers have borrowed elements of industrial unions in an effort to gain control over and monitor their professional lives. At times school boards and teacher unions have taken on an adversarial relationship in which management forced unions to bargain for work conditions while dictating the nature of teachers' "products" and "production processes." This kind of relationship lies behind the charge that teaching is not truly a profession like medicine, law, engineering, and accounting; it is also what lies behind the rhetoric that defines students as "products."

Several reform documents claim that school systems "*need* the advice and information that teachers can offer concerning client needs and the educational process." Thus "rather than something that boards and administrators give to teachers, involvement in educational policymaking is now being redefined as something that they get from teachers."[46]

Such arguments and redefinitions are changing the rhetoric along with the relationship between teachers and school boards. In this view teachers are described as managers of their classrooms, where they are also prime decision makers regarding the type of work that students will do, the manner in which they will do it, and how the work will be evaluated. Concomitantly, students becomes clients, not products. In this view "the product" is the act of teaching itself.

Educators who advocate this perspective believe that it will help change the relationship between school boards and teacher unions. What school boards really need from teachers, they argue, "is not blind obedience, but active cooperation in translating general into specific objectives, plans, and activities. Boards of education and school administrators are thoroughly dependent on teachers to cooperate in this respect."[47]

Indeed, the interdependency of administrators and teachers is the basis for a more cooperative relationship. No one suggests that the two groups will always (or even usually) see "eye to eye"; administrators will remain more concerned about managing and coordinating, while teachers will continue to focus on their work conditions and resources. Collective bargaining can still be used to mediate their different priorities so that one group does not dominate the other. But such an adjustment in their relationsip will have far-reaching effects on the nature of schools.

Compared with professionals like medicine and law, teaching is usually regarded as an emerging profession. However, when it is evaluated according to four basic components of professionalism, teaching gets fairly high marks. It has an exclusive body of knowledge that it applies for clients' welfare, and teachers are building a strong sense of collegiality. The greatest strides need to be made in teachers' autonomy, so that they can better monitor and regulate their own professional lives.

[46]Samuel B. Bacharach, Joseph B. Shedd, and Sharon C. Conley, "School Management and Teacher Unions: The Capacity for Cooperation in an Age of Reform," *Teachers' College Record* 1 (Fall 1989): 103.
[47]Ibid., 102.

KEY TERMS

National Education Association (NEA)	American Federation of Teachers (AFT)
tenure	collective bargaining
political action committee (PAC)	National Board for Professional Teaching Standards
emerging profession	career-ladder plan
profession	merit pay

SUGGESTED READINGS

Marshal O. Donnoley, *Power to the Teachers* (Bloomington, In.: Phi Delta Kappa, 1975). This book traces the development of teacher unions.

Joan K. Smith and L. Glenn Smith, "The Changing of the Guard," *Texas Tech Journal of Education* 8 (Winter 1981); 5–43. This series of two articles traces the change in the power structure of the NEA—a change that resulted in membership privileges for teachers in the NEA.

Robert L. Reid, ed., *Battleground: The Autobiography of Margaret A. Haley* (Urbana, Ill.: University of Illinois Press, 1983). This autobiography tells the story of Haley's political struggles as a Chicago union leader who worked to improve the work conditions of teachers.

Managing Schools

3

One evening at dusk, I stood in the shadows of the greatest mountains in the world—the Himalayas. I sought to see Chomolungma, . . . or Mount Everest. I thought of the challenge of the mountain . . . of climbing not the foothills but the mountain peaks. . . . And then I thought of our role in education. . . . All about us are the mountain peaks of ignorance and apathy. Our challenge is: Will we tackle the mountains of ignorance which surround us, or will we be content to live in the valleys of senility? In many ways . . . the vitality and endurance which are necessary to be a strong leader and school board member, trustee, are not significantly different from that which it takes to climb Chomolungma. . . .

—William Georgrades, "The New America for the Third Millennium" (paper presented at the Annual Conference of Louisiana Association of School Business Officials, New Orleans, 6–8 February 1986), 9–10, ED 293 316

Managing Schools

ADVANCED ORGANIZERS

In this chapter you will learn

What school-based management is

What it means to be an effective principal

How well women and minorities are faring in administrative positions

What functions and duties are performed by principals, superintendents, and board members

How we pay for education

CHAPTER OUTLINE

SCHOOL-BASED MANAGEMENT IN ACTION

A PRINCIPAL AT WORK
  The Principal as Effective Leader
  Principals Profiled

WOMEN AND MINORITIES IN ADMINISTRATION

SUPERINTENDENTS PROFILED
  Duties and Responsibilities of Superintendents
  The CEO as Effective Manager

SCHOOL BOARDS PROFILED
  Working with the Superintendent
  Duties and Responsibilities of the School Board

EVOLUTION OF SCHOOL BUREAUCRACIES
  Growth of School Legislation
  Development of Specialized Functions

PAYING FOR EDUCATION
  Evolution of School Financing
  Sources of Revenue for Education
  Current Issues about School Funding
  Alternative Programs to Improve Education

CONCLUSIONS

At 7:30 A.M. Dr. William Griffin enters his office for a brief meeting with one of his school principals, Jack Roberts, before dashing off to a school board meeting. It is budget time again, and as general superintendent of a midwestern school district with nearly five thousand students, Griffin must contend with the major problem facing most superintendents and school boards: growing financial needs but limited revenues. Griffin's district has a particular problem, because a medium-sized factory has just left the area to relocate in the Sun Belt. This reduces the district's tax base at a time when elementary school enrollments are growing.

Three years ago Griffin initiated a school-based management approach in his district. It has been implemented in the high school, the two junior high schools, and all six of the elementary schools—including Roberts's school. The district's proposed budget for the coming fiscal year must be reduced, and Griffin needs to know which items Roberts intends to cut. School principals are in charge of their own budgets, and Griffin has met with all the other princpals already; this meeting with Roberts will be his last one before preparing the district's budget.

SCHOOL-BASED MANAGEMENT IN ACTION

If you join the teaching force sometime during the 1990s, your school will probably practice some form of **school-based management (SBM)**, meaning that the central district will delegate authority to the school and will share decision making with its representatives. Your SBM may be similar in form to the approach first implemented in 1987–88, in Dade County, Florida, where 53 of the county's 259 schools submitted proposals, and 32 pilot schools were selected and evaluated after one year. The typical decision-making cadre in these cases included five to twelve school staff and community members, supported by ancillary committees that identified and examined issues relating to the new management process. The evaluation phase pointed out the main obstacles and problems that resulted from starting something new, and these were corrected.

Or perhaps your SBM model might be similar to one started in 1989–90, in five of the public schools in Prince William County, Virginia. Each school was given its prorated share of the district's budget, and each had the freedom to allocate funds as it saw fit. One stipulation was that management had to consult an advisory committee made up of teachers, parents, and—ideally—students, if the principal so decided. These management teams were responsible for hiring employees, arranging building maintenance, paying utility bills, and allocating instructional funds. Each school's budget had to be in keeping with state regulations, accreditation standards, school board policies, and administrative regulations. Once developed, the budgets were submitted to the central office for review; if problems were found, the superintendent had power to correct them.

As it turned out, these management teams found that SBM required more time and consultations with experts than they had expected. But the pilot programs were successful, and the county's entire system adopted SBM in the early 1990s.[1]

These examples illustrate the two key elements of school-based management. The first necessary ingredient for SBM is that the central district must delegate authority to the schools. Next, there have to be mechanisms to share decision making with the teaching staff and, possibly, with community representatives. Decision-making authority relates to three critical areas: budgeting, staffing, and the curriculum. The degree of authority may vary, and sometimes budgeting decisions may not include staff salaries, depending on the rules and regulations in union contracts or state policies. Nonetheless, the school is given a lump sum of money to allocate for equipment and supplies, curricular materials, and staff development.[2]

Allocations for staffing are usually based on "staffing units," which are determined by the average cost of a teacher, including benefits. Staffing decisions center on defining positions and filling them. Although the central district actually issues the contract to a new employee, it does so on the recommendation of the principal and the teacher and community representatives. Once the teaching staff has been hired, the few dollars remaining can be used to hire support staff: clerical workers, various specialists, and part-time instructional aides.[3]

Under SBM, curricular decisions are often limited to those supporting the goals and core curriculum which have been formulated by the district and, often, by the state. And since individual students may change schools within the district, mechanisms are needed to coordinate curricula across the district's sites. Yet each school's staff can make textbook decisions, create new curricular materials, and help to develop the curriculum. As the school's management representatives, they may also be asked to serve on a district curriculum committee aimed at coordinating general master plans. Site representatives may also share in decisions relating to new technology, promotions, scheduling, and the assignment of pupils.

Usually, decision making under SBM occurs through a school council composed of teachers and (often) parents, students, and community representatives. The council can be elected or appointed on the basis of grade level, other committee membership, or community work. Whatever the process, most systems

[1]Richard G. Neal, "School-based Management Lets Principals Slice the Budget Pie," *Executive Educator* 11 (January 1989): 16–19.
[2]Jane L. David, "Synthesis of Research on School-based Management," *Educational Leadership* 46 (May 1989): 45–53.
[3]Ibid., 46–47.

Since the nation's founding, the American democratic tradition has been exercised in school governance. The direct local approach provided "invaluable laboratories of democracy in which . . . many Americans learned . . . that their vote made a difference." —Mimi Forsyth/Monkmeyer

find that SBM promotes teachers' satisfaction, professionalism, and collaboration. But SBM needs to be planned carefully before it is implemented so that everyone's new roles, routines, and relationships can be learned; it takes time to put this new kind of management team into place. Currently, Boston, Chicago, Hammond (Indiana), Los Angeles, New York City, Pittsburgh, and San Diego have implemented school-based management options. In addition, over one hundred school districts in Florida, Illinois, Michigan, Minnesota, and New York are practicing some form of SBM.[4]

A PRINCIPAL AT WORK

■

You now should have some idea of what to expect in terms of your school's management approach. But what about the leadership of your school—your principal? Who is this person? What does she or he do all day?

Not surprisingly, the real picture of a principal's daily life can be characterized as one interruption after another. One study tracked the typical activities of principals and found that about 58 percent of their workday was spent in the headquarters area of the school; they were in their offices about 48 percent of the time. Twelve percent of their office time was devoted to written communication, and half to three-quarters of it related to personnel matters. Other

[4]Paula A. White, "An Overview of School-based Management: What Does the Research Say?" *NASSP Bulletin* 73 (September 1989): 1–8.

paperwork and record keeping took up the rest of the time spent on written communication.

RESEARCH SAYS

For Tomorrow's Education . . .

Outstanding principals are those who have a vision for their school, are dedicated to learning, have a good knowledge of their school, are active and highly visible in their school, are good communicators, and are not concerned with students' socioeconomic status or low teacher morale. These factors are related positively to students' achievement. See Ronald H. Heck, "Principals' Instructional Leadership and School Performance: Implications for Policy Development," *Educational Evaluation and Policy Analysis* 14 (Spring 1992) 1: 21–34; and Del Stover, "Principals Who Save Troubled Schools Are Relentless Optimists," *Executive Educator* 11 (September 1989): 22–26.

The remaining time in the office was devoted to answering and returning telephone calls; meeting with teachers, support staff, parents, and visitors; and responding to various emergencies and minor crises. Some of these necessitated movement around the building, which the principals did throughout the day. Specifically, they spent about 11 percent of their time in school corridors, and 9 percent in classrooms. Another 13 percent of the day was spent outside the building at other sites.[5]

THE PRINCIPAL AS EFFECTIVE LEADER

Given the pace and variety of a typical workday, a principal needs to maintain a flexible administrative style. This can be crucial to a school's effectiveness, and most research agrees that "the principal of a school is the key to its success."[6]

A principal needs a flexible management style in order to adapt to daily events or a teacher's innovation without having to change school policies or structures. For example, as a beginning teacher you might want to experiment with some innovative classroom techniques, and you should be able to do so without disruption or interference from your principal or your colleagues—unless, of course, you seek their advice. Such a trial-and-error approach might be bothersome to a principal whose management style aims to control all aspects of the school environment, including the smallest detail.[7]

Let us also hope that your principal has strong ethical values and interpersonal skills, for these are also important qualities of effective principals. In other words, they are good communicators, and they are committed to the school's mission and goals. They can articulate a vision of the school's values and can communicate it to others. Such principals tend to be visible within their schools, and they support their professional staff. They recognize and reward accomplishments, even as they confront and correct unacceptable behaviors. They delegate

[5]Van Cleve Morris, Robert L. Crowson, Cynthia Porter-Gehrie, and Emmanuel Hurwitz, Jr., *Principals in Action* (Columbus, Ohio: Merrill, 1984), 33–50.

[6]John E. Roueche and George A. Baker, *Profiling Excellence in America's Schools* (Arlington, Va.: American Association of School Administrators, 1986), 26.

[7]Ibid., 46–97.

The key to a school's success is its principal, and the best ones tend to be visible within their schools—articulating and communicating a vision of the school's values. Strong but flexible leadership holds a school together. —Bob Daemmrich/Stock, Boston

authority in order to get a job done, and they welcome collaboration in solving problems.

Finally, your principal should be a role model for you and your colleagues. Research shows that effective principals are those who serve as instructional leaders. They are concerned about the quality of teaching and about the level of students' achievement. As a result, they assist teachers in developing the curriculum; they help identify and evaluate learning goals; and they communicate policies and procedures effectively to the entire school community.[8] When you go to an interview for your first teaching position, see what you can learn about the principal's management style. Remember: You can ask questions, too!

PRINCIPALS PROFILED

ELEMENTARY SCHOOL PRINCIPALS   If you join an elementary school faculty, your principal will probably be like the one mentioned at the beginning of the chapter—Jack Roberts, who fits the national profile of elementary principals. For the most part he enjoys his job, except during budget time. Like his national counterparts, Roberts ranks board relations and financial matters near the bottom of the list of things he likes about his work. He and his peers much prefer the activities and responsibilities that relate to community relations and to the administration and supervision of their schools.

Nationally, Jack Roberts shares other demographic characteristics with typical elementary school principals (see Table 3.1). He is a white male in his mid-

[8]Ibid. Also see Morris et al., *Principals in Action*, 13–14.

TABLE 3.1   Demographic Characteristics of Principals (Percentages)

Characteristic	High School Principals	Middle School Principals	Elementary School Principals
Average salary	$61,768	$57,394	$53,856
Sex			
Male	87.9	79.5	60.3
Female	12.1	20.5	39.7
Ethnic background			
Black	6.8	13.0	6.8
White	93.2	81.7	87.1
Hispanic	—	3.1	2.5
Asian	—	1.5	1.9
American Indian	—	0.8	1.0
Other	—	—	0.6
Age			
Under 30	—	—	0.2
30–35	5.1	2.3	3.1
36–41	10.9	10.7	14.4
42–47	35.4	42.0	31.3
48–55	31.4	35.1	32.1
56–64	17.1	9.9	18.5
Over 65	—	—	0.4
System enrollment			
Less than 1,000	36	15	20
1,000– 4,999	40	54	39
5,000– 5,999	7	9	15
10,000–24,999	8	10	14
More than 25,000	9	11	12
Length of educational service			
5 years or fewer	—	—	—
6–10 years	4	—	4
11–15 years	14	9	11
16–20 years	24	28	27
21–25 years	26	29	26
26–30 years	15	18	18
More than 30 years	17	16	15
Years in current job			
Less than 1 year	10.2	7.6	7.4
1–3 years	31.8	29.0	22.4
4–5 years	12.5	10.7	16.5
More than 5 years	45.5	52.7	53.7
Age planning to retire			
55 or younger	24	26	25
56–59	31	40	31
60–64	32	28	32
65–69	11	6	10
70 or older	2	1	2

TABLE 3.1   Continued

Characteristic	High School Principals	Middle School Principals	Elementary School Principals
Percent who consider compensation adequate	43.9	42.3	45.5
Assessment of job security			
None	6.3	3.0	4.5
Little	13.7	12.9	8.2
Some	41.7	36.4	41.9
Great deal	38.3	47.7	45.4
Political affiliation			
Democrat	47.4	46.6	46.1
Republican	32.6	30.5	30.7
Independent	16.0	13.7	16.2
Other	1.1	0.8	1.4
None	2.9	8.4	5.7
Political classification			
Conservative	69.6	65.4	64.0
Liberal	29.8	34.6	36.0
Average hours worked per week			
30–40	0.6	0.8	0.6
41–50	11.9	10.6	29.1
51–60	40.3	57.6	48.4
More than 60	47.2	31.1	21.9
Highest degree earned			
Bachelor's	—	0.8	0.8
Master's	61.4	65.6	66.3
Specialist	19.9	16.8	23.2
Doctorate	18.8	16.8	9.7

Sources: Judith Brody Saks, "Education Vital Signs," *American School Board Journal* 179 (December 1992): 38–39; "You're Overworked, Underpaid, but Reasonably Happy Anyway," *Executive Educator* 11 (November 1989): 20–21; and Luvern L. Cunningham and Joseph T. Hentges, *The American School Superintendency, 1982: A Summary Report*, ED 225 295, 39.

forties, and he earns about $42,000 annually—a level that he does not find adequate for the job. Like 58 percent of his peers, he has held his current position for longer than five years; and like 92 percent of them, he feels secure in it. He works from 51 to 60 hours a week, but usually does not work on weekends.[9] He has been an educator for more than twenty years, along with 59 percent of his colleagues, and he is planning to retire when he reaches age sixty. Roberts is completing work toward a doctorate degree, which is another growing national trend among elementary school principals.

MIDDLE SCHOOL PRINCIPALS   If you join the faculty of a junior high or middle school, chances are that your principal will also fit the national profile

[9]Judith Brody Saks, "Education Vital Signs," *American School Board Journal* 179 (December 1992): 38–39; "You're Overworked, Underpaid, but Reasonably Happy Anyway," *Executive Educator* 11 (November 1989): 20–21. Also see Luvern L. Cunningham and Joseph T. Hentges, *The American School Superintendency, 1982: A Summary Report* (American Association of School Administrators, 1982), ED 225 295, 15–24.

shown in Table 3.1. Middle school principals are more content with their salaries (around $45,000 per year) than are elementary or secondary school principals. Your principal, too, will probably be a white male who has been in education for longer than twenty years. He will have been in his current position for more than five years, and he plans to retire before age sixty. He will probably be in his middle to late forties, and he recently completed a doctoral program at a nearby state university.

HIGH SCHOOL PRINCIPALS   Finally, if you join a high school faculty, your principal is likely to have been in his position for about four years, and he probably feels overworked and underpaid (see Table 3.1). Compared with elementary and middle school principals, your high school administrator thinks that his position has the most stress. Like his national counterparts, he is a white male in his forties, and he has been an educator for twenty years. His pay range is similar to that of junior high principals, but he puts in more weekend hours and feels less secure in his job.

WOMEN AND MINORITIES IN ADMINISTRATION

■

It must be clear by now that your prospective school administrator is likely to be white and male. Although the numbers of African-American and female administrators are increasing slowly, the picture presented in this chapter does conform to reality. As Table 3.1 shows, at the elementary level only 32 percent of the country's principals are female, and even smaller percentages of women head up middle schools and high schools: 17 and 10 percent, respectively. As far as the superintendency is concerned, only 5 percent of the nation's school systems are run by women, and they generally are found heading up smaller systems (see

RESEARCH SAYS

For Tomorrow's Education . . .

The *small* percentage of female superintendents is not likely to increase in the near future, nor is the even smaller percentage of African-American female superintendents. One explanation is that the ranks of teachers continue to remain short of minorities, thereby denying minority students the role models they need to inspire a teaching career. See, for example, "U.S. Classrooms Short of Men and Minorities," *Chicago Tribune,* 7 July 1992, p. 5; and Nancy L. Arnez, "Selected Black Female Superintendents of Public School Systems," *Journal of Negro Education* 51 (Summer 1983): 309–317.

TABLE 3.2   Percent of Women
             Superintendents
             by District Size

District Size	Percent Headed by Women	
25,000 or more pupils	3.5	
3,000–24,999 pupils	20.2	
300– 2,999 pupils	52.6	76.3
Less than 300 pupils	23.7	

Source: Luvern L. Cunningham and Joseph T. Hentges, *The American School Superintendency, 1982: A Summary Report*, ED 225 295, 73.

Table 3.2). Female administrators earn less money than their male counterparts, even though they tend to have completed more years of academic study.[10]

When it comes to administrative positions, members of minority groups fare even less well than women do (see Table 3.1). For example, 7 percent of elementary school principals are African-American, and 2 percent are Hispanic; among middle school principals each group can claim only 1 percent. Hispanics also make up 1 percent of high school principals, while African-Americans constitute 5 percent. At the superintendency level, 2 percent are African-American, and 1 percent are Hispanic.[11]

Regardless of race or ethnicity, female superintendents feel a greater degree of discrimination than male superintendents do (see Table 3.3). Discrimination in hiring and promotion was regarded as either a major or a minor problem by 80.8 percent of white females and by 83.2 percent of minority females; in contrast, 60.3 percent of minority male superintendents and 53.8 percent of white male superintendents saw discrimination as a problem, and most of the males considered it a minor problem.[12]

TABLE 3.3   Discrimination Problems for Women and Minority
             Superintendents (Percentages)

Degree of Discrimination	White		Minority	
	Male Sup'ts	Female Sup'ts	Male Sup'ts	Female Sup'ts
Major problem	12.2	43.3	15.0	32.7
Minor problem	41.6	37.5	45.3	50.5
Total	(53.8)	(80.8)	(60.3)	(83.2)
Little/No problem	46.1	19.2	39.6	16.8

Source: Luvern L. Cunningham and Joseph T. Hentges, *The American School Superintendency, 1982: A Summary Report*, ED 225 295, 27.

[10]Ibid., and Cunningham and Hentges, *American School Superintendency*, 72–73.
[11]Saks, "Education Vital Signs," 38–39; and "You're Overworked," 20–21.
[12]Cunningham and Hentges, *American School Superintendency*, 27.

SUPERINTENDENTS PROFILED

■

As a beginning teacher, you will not often have contact with your school district's **superintendent**, or chief executive officer (CEO). There may be a districtwide orientation meeting at which he will welcome you; and if you teach in a large city system you may see him quoted in newspapers or interviewed on television. But even if you get no closer than this, it is important for you to know something about your superintendent and the school board, because they will set the general tone of your school system.

Once again you will notice that we are using the pronoun *he*. In fact, there is a 95 percent chance that your superintendent will be a man (see Table 3.4).

TABLE 3.4   Demographic Characteristics of Superintendents (Percentages)

Characteristic	Superintendents	Deputy/Assistant Superintendent
Average salary	$83,342	$69,315
Percent who consider compensation adequate	56.1	
Sex		
Male	89.5	
Female	10.5	
Ethnic background		
Black	1.9	
White	97.1	
Hispanic	0.5	
Asian	—	
American Indian	—	
Other	0.5	
Age		
Under 30	—	
30–35	1	
36–41	4.8	
42–47	35.2	
48–55	31.4	
56–64	26.7	
Over 65	1	
System enrollment		
Less than 1,000	40	1
1,000– 4,999	44	44
5,000– 9,999	7	23
10,000–24,999	6	16
More than 25,000	2	17

Sources: Judith Brody Saks, "Education Vital Signs," *American School Board Journal* 179 (December 1992): 38–39; "You're Overworked, Underpaid, but Reasonably Happy Anyway," *Executive Educator* 11 (November 1989): 20–21; and Luvern L. Cunningham and Joseph T. Hentges, *The American School Superintendency, 1982: A Summary Report*, ED 225 295, 39.

Table 3.4   **Continued**

Characteristic	Superintendents	Deputy/Assistant Superintendent
Length of educational service		
5 years or less	—	1
6–10 years	1	2
11–15 years	6	4
16–20 years	18	21
21–25 years	26	26
26–30 years	25	26
More than 30 years	25	20
Years in current job		
Less than 1 year	13.3	
1–3 years	28.4	
4–5 years	14.2	
More than 5 years	44.1	
Age planning to retire		
55 or younger	15	25
56–59	32	30
60–64	38	34
65–69	13	7
70 or older	2	4
Highest degree earned		
Bachelor's	—	
Master's	33.8	
Specialist	25.2	
Doctorate	41.0	
Assessment of job security		
None	10.1	
Little	16.8	
Some	47.6	
Great deal	25.5	
Political affiliation		
Democrat	37.1	
Republican	39.5	
Independent	18.0	
Other	0.5	
None	4.9	
Political classification		
Conservative	72.9	
Liberal	27.1	
Average hours worked per week		
30–40	1.0	
41–50	11.9	
51–60	54.3	
More than 60	32.9	

The superintendent you met at the beginning of this chapter, Dr. William Griffin, is typical of most superintendents in the United States. He is male, white, and between the ages of forty-eight and fifty-five. He is employed by an upper Great Lakes school system with an enrollment of 1,000 to 4,999 students. He is married, has two children, and owns his own home. Although his parents did not attend college, his wife is a college graduate. Dr. Griffin completed his Ed.D. several years ago, thus joining the growing number of superintendents who have felt a professional need to earn the doctorate. He now earns $75,000 per year and is perceived by his community as having above-average to high social status.[13]

Like most of the nation's superintendents, Griffin maintains that teaching is still his first love, and he looks back fondly on the seven years that he taught social studies in a neighboring high school. Although he admits that his present job is stressful, especially during budget time, he likes its other planning responsibilities as well as its supervisory activities and curricular decisions. Thus he doesn't mind the 60-hour workweek that the superintendency requires. And since his wife is an elementary school principal in a smaller system nearby, she understands the demands of his job.[14] Having stayed at home while their children were young, she recently joined the small but growing number of superintendents' wives who also have education careers.

Dr. Griffin has been the district's superintendent for five years, having been elected after serving for five years as a high school principal and then for four years and six years as the superintendent of two smaller districts. He is currently involved in the aspect of his job that he enjoys least: budgeting and finances. Even so, he is glad that the situation is not complicated by declining enrollments—a problem with which he struggled during his two previous superintendencies. He is also glad that he enjoys a good relationship with the school board. So far he has had little difficulty in getting the board to approve his policy recommendations.[15]

DUTIES AND RESPONSIBILITIES OF SUPERINTENDENTS

Someday *your* superintendent, like William Griffin, will be responsible for the duties listed in Table 3.5. As chief executive officer he or she will recommend and execute policies—as do 75 percent of American superintendents, who generally take the lead in recommending new policies to their boards. An example is Griffin's proposal for school-based management, which the board subsequently approved.

In most annual evaluations of him, the board has given Griffin high marks for meeting its expectations—which is one of the main reasons he has been reelected. As chief executive officer he is credited with having recruited and hired a good group of administrators and teachers. Since he has been in office, student achievement for all grade levels has risen above national averages. He has implemented an effective curriculum and has provided in-service training for both teachers and administrative personnel—even when budgetary contraints made it difficult. Griffin has kept abreast of curricular and administrative trends and developments, and he has articulated them to the board as well as to the community at large. It is not at all unusual for him to have several speaking engagements each week at various civic meetings and events.[16]

[13]Saks, "Education Vital Signs," 38–39; and "You're Overworked," 18–21. Also see Cunningham and Hentges, *American School Superintendency*, 15–24.

[14]"You're Overworked," 18–19.

[15]Ibid.; and Saks, "Education Vital Signs," 38–39.

[16]Cunningham and Hentges, *American School Superintendency*, 30–37; and Mark Littleton and Lynn Turner, "A Descriptive Study of the Role of the Superintendent as Viewed by School Board Members in Texas" (1984), ED 251 935, 11–18.

TABLE 3.5   Duties of the Superintendent

1. Acts as executive officer for the board
2. Executes policies
3. Recommends policies
4. Conducts personnel transactions
5. Develops programs
6. Provides leadership
7. Presents, interprets and analyzes budget and financial transactions
8. Makes reports to board
9. Determines school, plant and needs
10. Oversees school plant construction
11. Interprets school program to the board and community
12. Evaluates the work of all school personnel, instructional programs, and other aspects of the board

Source: Mark Littleton and Lynn Turner, "A Descriptive Study of the Role of the Superintendent as Viewed by School Board Members in Texas" (1984), ED 251 935, 15.

THE CEO AS EFFECTIVE MANAGER

When Dr. Griffin was hired as district superintendent, he faced the typical problems of the early 1980s: declining enrollments and a lack of funds. To meet these challenges, he decided to implement a participatory management approach that would include the various constituencies of the school and community. (This was stressed as an effective administrative approach in the literature Griffin read while studying for his doctorate.)

RESEARCH SAYS

For Tomorrow's Education . . .

Effective superintendents are likely to have completed formal graduate education, especially the doctorate; to have been involved in professional associations and activities; and to have worked as principals and high-level central administrators before assuming CEO positions. They also report having good relationships with their school boards. See Joan Gibson Burnham, "Superintendents on the Fast Track," *School Administrator* 46 (October 1989): 18–19; and Thomas E. Glass, *The Illinois Superintendency: A Summary Report of the 1991 Survey of Illinois Superintendents* 6 (Springfield: Illinois Association of School Administrators, April 1992).

Budgetary adjustments were the first problem to be addressed. Instead of making recommendations directly to the school board, Griffin created opportunities that allowed the staff, parents, students, and citizens to discuss ways to cut several million dollars from the budget.[17] Separate discussion meetings were

[17]For a discussion of this process see Nancy C. Roberts, "Transforming Leadership: A Process of Collective Action," *Human Relations* 38 (November 1985): 1023–1046.

held for each constituency, and Griffin studied the many recommendations that resulted. Then he presented his final recommendations to the school board, which approved them.

This experience led to the development of participatory task forces aimed at solving other problems. Eventually, a model of decentralized school-based management evolved, which allowed each school to have greater autonomy in making decisions that directly affected it.

SCHOOL BOARDS PROFILED

There are seven members on William Griffin's **board of education**, which, like boards throughout America, sets school policy. Members decided to run for office because they thought the schools had some problems that they wanted to help solve.[18] Six of Griffin's board members are white, and one is African-American. Two of the white members are women; one has a professional career, and the other is a homemaker and former schoolteacher. All the male board members have college degrees, and three have also earned professional degrees (two in law and one in medicine). All the board members are married homeowners, and their annual incomes range from $35,000 to over $125,000. One has lived in the community for ten years; the other six have been residents for more than twenty years. In most ways they are typical of American school board members (see Table 3.6). They see themselves as public servants rather than as politicians, and they are not paid for performing their main task, which is to set school policy.[19]

Of the current seven members, five were on the board that selected Dr. Griffin and reelected him twice for three-year appointments. The two newer board members have served for four years and two years, respectively. Nationally, school board members serve an average of five years.

WORKING WITH THE SUPERINTENDENT

[18]Cunningham and Hentges, *American School Superintendency*, 30; M. A. Awender, "The Canadian School Board Member: A Comparison with the American Counterpart," *Education* 103 (Spring 1983): 281–287.

[19]Lorn S. Foster, "Political Culture: A Determinant of Public Regardingness Among School Board Members," *Urban Education* 18 (April 1983): 29–39.

[20]Littleton and Turner, "A Descriptive Study," 13.

[21]Ibid., 11–12.

Superintendent Griffin has been active in educating his board members about the latest trends in education, and he has been their major source of information about the state of the district's system. Generally, the relationship between him and the board has been cooperative, although there have been some minor clashes over textbook selection, curricular changes, and budgetary matters. Such differences are typical of interactions between school boards and superintendents.[20] For the most part, however, Griffin's board has been pleased with his performance. They see him as a leader who exhibits the characteristics needed for effective administration: good judgment, scholarship, energy, loyalty, self-confidence, good interpersonal skills, fairness, political acumen, flexibility, stability, and reliability.[21]

TABLE 3.6   Demographic Characteristics of School Board Members

Characteristics	Percentages	Characteristics	Percentages
Ethnic background		$40,000– 59,999	30.5
Black	3.1	$60,000– 79,000	20.6
White	93.9	$80,000– 99,999	12.3
Hispanic	1.5	$100,000–149,999	11.0
American Indian	8	$150,000 and more	6.7
Asian	2	*Sex*	
Other	5	Male	60.1
Years lived in community		Female	39.9
0–5	2	*Age*	
6–15	18	Under 25	2
16–35	35	26–35	3.8
36+	45	36–40	14.2
Education		41–50	47.2
Less than high school	7	51–60	20.9
High school	22	Over 60	13.7
University/college	47	*Where board members live*	
Graduate or professional school	25	Small town	26.4
Home ownership		Suburb	30.7
Yes	84	Rural area	29.8
No	16	Urban area	8.7
Income		Other	4.4
Under $20,000	2.2		
$20,000– 39,999	16.7		

Source: Judith Brody Saks, "Education Vital Signs," *The American School Board Journal* 179 (December 1992): 37; M. A. Awender, "The Canadian School Board Member (A Comparison with the American Counterpart)," *Education* 103 (Spring 1983): 283.

DUTIES AND RESPONSIBILITIES OF THE SCHOOL BOARD

Generally, the school board of your system will have major responsibility for setting the education policies that your superintendent will administer. Board members will be concerned about your community's educational needs, and they will seek to ensure that schools operate successfully. More specifically, school board members (1) adopt salary schedules, (2) approve budgets, (3) propose bond issues, (4) review financial procedures, (5) decide on school construction and closings, (6) evaluate the superintendent and school programs, and (7) fill board vacancies that occur between elections.[22]

Dr. Griffin is lucky to work with a school board that is above national norms in how it executes its duties and fulfills its responsibilities. We hope your board will be as capable, for its roles have been delegated by the state, which has final

[22]Ibid., 9–11.

RESEARCH SAYS

For Tomorrow's Education . . .

A recent nationwide survey asked school board members to identify their top concerns. Highest on their list was "the continuous effort by state legislators and governors to dictate the responsibilities of local school boards, usually without providing additional funds to meet these responsibilities." This concern was followed by facility maintenance and growing enrollments. See Daniel M. Seaton, Kenneth E. Underwood, and Jim C. Fortune, "The Burden School Board Presidents Bear," *American School Board Journal* 179 (January 1992) 1: 32–37.

authority over public education. As a teacher in the system you will know whether or not things are running smoothly, *and*, of course, your contract will have been signed by the board's president. Beyond such matters, however, the president and board members will not be very visible in your daily professional life.

EVOLUTION OF SCHOOL BUREAUCRACIES

The preceding profiles of principals, superintendents, and school boards show that each of these administrative units has specific responsibilities and well-defined relationships with the others. Such compartmentalization is a common characteristic of most administrative structures, and it is certainly one overriding feature of most American schools today. Sociologists call such structure a **bureaucracy**—that is, a system characterized by specialization of functions, adherence to fixed rules, and a hierarchy of authority. America's largest school districts are extraordinarily complex, but even the few simple systems that exist tend to be bureaucratic. For the last several decades the number of our school districts has been declining even as their average size has increased. This is a recent phenomenon in the history of schooling, and some reformers and critics regret it.

For more than two centuries after Europeans colonized North America, schooling arrangements were simple in organization. From the 1620s—when New England settlers first attempted formal schools—to the 1850s, every school was an entity unto itself. Almost all schools had only one teacher; in a few of the largest ones, an "usher," or assistant, helped the master. Occasionally a school might have two assistants. Until the nineteenth century was well under way, however, neither law nor practice formally linked two or more schools together into a larger organizational unit.

The supervision of such a one-teacher community school—which came to be called a **common school**—was direct. Each school usually served ten to twenty families who lived within 5 miles of each other. In Massachusetts and Connecticut the first officials who were charged with overseeing school matters were known as **selectmen**. Each township—a governmental and geographic unit of 30 to 40 square miles—elected two selectmen, and these governing bodies were the forerunners of state legislatures. Selectmen's duties after the 1640s included making sure that any township with more than fifty families had a teacher of basic English reading and writing and of computing; they also decided which families were too poor to pay for their children's schooling.

The Europeans who owned and ran the land settlement companies assumed that every township (measuring about 5 to 7 miles on each side) would have one village in which all the township's residents would live. In classic European manner each farmer owned several small strips of land scattered throughout the township (see Figure 3.1). Each morning farmers left the village to work one or more strips of land, and each evening they returned to the security of the village. Every family lived within a short walk of the village's school and church.

Within a few years of settlement, immigrants to North America began to buy, sell, and trade strips of land to consolidate their holdings into one spot. They also built homes on their farmland; thus, instead of the European model of one village per township, individual houses were scattered throughout the township—generally a few hundred yards from each other. Subdistricts developed in the townships, and they needed a school and a church so that families would not have to travel too far to use these essential services (which the law required them to support). See Figure 3.2.

By 1700 New England colonial governments routinely approved requests from citizens to start schools (and churches) within subdistricts of townships. Since the selectmen found it difficult to supervise these, **trustees** took charge of the schools. Trustees were citizens—meaning property owners—who either were chosen by general consent or were elected. Their task was to hire a teacher and oversee the maintenance of a school building. The number of trustees in a subdistrict varied, but three was a typical number. To lead the group, often one trustee emerged either naturally or was elected.

Most parents took a direct interest in school-related decisions. The teacher routinely ate some meals and slept one or more nights in the homes of pupils. Parents who wished to do so could visit the school to observe the teacher. In addition, most heads of households attended meetings to help the trustees make important decisions, such as hiring or firing a teacher, selecting a school site, constructing or repairing a building, setting a teacher's salary, and establishing the "rate" that each family would pay for schooling.

If a teacher pleased parents and pupils, that news usually traveled quickly. Neighboring communities often competed for a well-regarded teacher, in which case the trustees might have to offer a substantial salary increase or lose the valued teacher. On the other hand, a teacher who displeased a substantial number of parents and pupils usually wasn't rehired and was not likely to be recruited by a nearby community.

This direct local approach to school governance was the opposite of bureaucracy. The only specialist involved was the teacher. The community supervised the school directly and expressed decisions through its unpaid elected

FIGURE 3.1   Seventeenth-Century Township Plan Showing Ideal Residential and Land Ownership Patterns

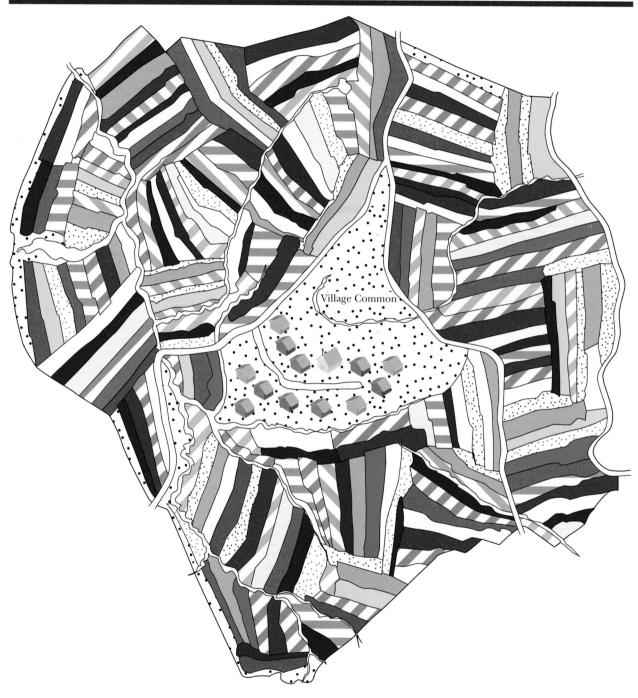

Village Common

representatives. Each year the teacher negotiated salary directly with the trustees, and all the money needed to operate the school came from a combination of tuition and local taxes. Most citizens participated directly in deciding how money would be spent. "It would be as difficult to exaggerate the contributions these

FIGURE 3.2   Eighteenth-Century Township Plan Showing Houses and District (Common) Schools

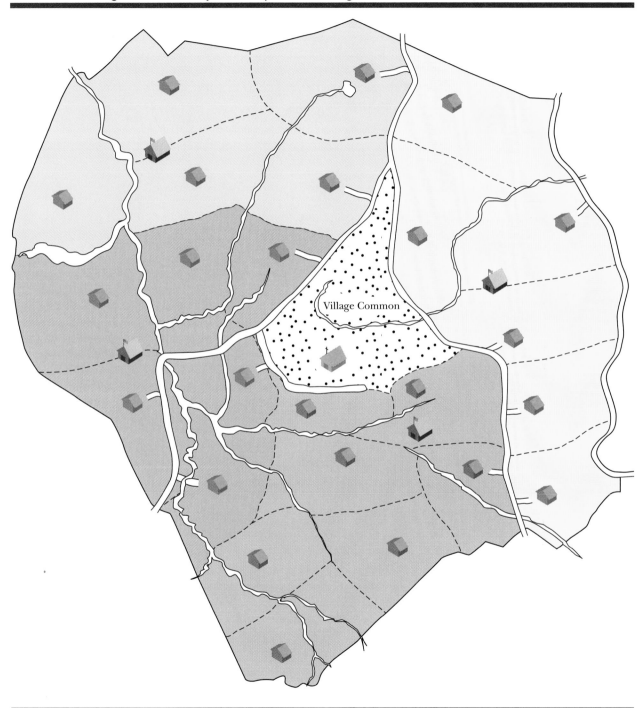

Village Common

small school districts made . . . as to imagine rural America of that period without them," writes one historian. "They were invaluable laboratories of democracy in which . . . many Americans learned . . . that their vote made a difference, that they could change what they did not like, and that democracy actually worked."[23]

[23]Wayne E. Fuller, *The Old Country School: The Story of Rural Education in the Middle West* (Chicago: University of Chicago Press, 1982), 45.

Comparative Perspective on Today's Issues . . .

◆ **SHOULD SCHOOL SYSTEMS IMPLEMENT LOCAL SCHOOL COUNCILS THAT HAVE AUTHORITY OVER POLICY MAKING AND DECISION MAKING?**

The Issue   In an effort to involve neighborhood communities in education, some school systems, including Chicago's, have created local school councils that perform the major administrative functions of the particular schools they serve. Many people think that the school councils undermine the roles and responsibilities of education professionals.

YES   Local school councils allow parents and communities to have direct involvement in their schools and influence over them. If the concept of giving a lay school board control over school policies is viable, then it stands to reason that a local board for each school is even more valuable, because it involves the laypeople who are most committed to improving the operation of their particular school. This is a return to the original concept of a lay board, and it allows minority groups to control predominantly minority schools.

NO   The concept of involving parents and the community in the operation of their local school is a valiant one. But taking away the decision-making and administrative functions from the experts—from teachers and administrators—is unprofessional and counterproductive; it undercuts the efficient management of the school. Lay members of a local council do not have the expertise needed to operate the school, and it would be costly and time-consuming to train them for such roles and responsibilities. Since members are elected for only a specific period of time, the school would face expensive, periodic training sessions.

The change to an education bureaucracy came about during the second half of the nineteenth century. As early as the 1820s and 1830s a small number of people began to advocate "state systems" of schooling. James G. Carter and Horace Mann in Massachusetts are the best known of these, and through their efforts Massachusetts created a state-level office of education in 1838. Horace Mann was the first head of the Massachusetts State Board of Education, and he made it famous during his twelve-year tenure.

The Civil War lent considerable impetus to the movement to centralize school governance. The newly formed Republican party took a strong position on education, arguing that the "War of the Rebellion" had happened because the South did not have state *systems* of education such as Massachusetts had developed. One condition for the seceded states' readmission to the Union was that they present new constitutions that provided for state supervision of local schools.

In 1867, having gained some bipartisan support from a few Democrats in states that had not seceded, the "radical" wing of the Republican party sponsored the creation of the United States Department of Education. Some vocal advocates wanted this to be a state and federal partnership, with the national office having a dominant role. But given the country's long tradition of localism, the legislation that created the U.S. Department of Education restricted the department's duties to gathering and disseminating information and to "promoting the cause of education" throughout the country.[24]

At about the same time courts began to view education as a *state* function rather than a local one. Today courts see school boards—despite their local character—as extensions of state government. Although local boards have substantial discretion in many areas of education, state legislatures *can* regulate local schools extensively. In addition, some federal laws and regulations strongly affect local schools.

GROWTH OF SCHOOL LEGISLATION

When Europeans began to settle the New World, no one thought that education and religion even could (much less *should*) be separated. The concept of church and state coexisting almost independently—now widely accepted in the United States—was unthinkable to the most forward-looking seventeenth-century theorists.

Two factors, particularly, shaped early American attitudes toward education. One of these was religious reform, which swept Europe between the late fifteenth century and the early eighteenth century. During this long period both Protestant and Roman Catholic reformers focused on education as the primary means of achieving their goals, and settlers brought this central trust in education to North America with them.[25] The other factor, which fit neatly with the first, was the settlers' fear of the decivilizing aspects of the wilderness, which Europeans set out to tame. It was not only immigrants who paid attention to providing schools for themselves; from the sixteenth to the eighteenth centuries, missionaries in what are now Canada, the United States, and Mexico also made special efforts to establish schools.

By 1787, when recently independent Americans were writing a constitution for their new government, the idea of separating church and state was strong. In fact, some delegates to the Constitutional Convention in Philadelphia advocated a national school system, but because they were in a minority, the final document made no reference to education. This responsibility was thus left to each state.

By the 1820s many New Englanders began to fear that migration South and West would weaken the new nation's educational (and moral) fiber. Such fears were intensified by the addition of millions of acres of new territory in the 1819 purchase of Florida from Spain, and by the election in 1828 of President Andrew Jackson. As mentioned earlier, people like James G. Carter and Horace Mann began a crusade to establish state-level systems of schooling to ensure that no local area could shirk its educational duties or deviate from statewide norms.

Not everyone agreed, of course. After two hundred years of letting each community make its own education decisions, many people resented the suggestion that they would not educate their children properly unless the state was watching. For several decades—from the 1830s to the 1860s—many people debated about this, and, as we have noted, the Civil War precipitated a resolution in favor of state-level education systems. In 1874 the Michigan Supreme Court

[24]L. Glenn Smith, "Founding the U.S. Office of Education, *Educational Forum* (March 1967); and Donald R. Warren, *To Enforce Education* (Detroit: Wayne State University Press, 1974).
[25]L. Glenn Smith,"For the Glory of God: Religious Competition and Educational Improvement, 1565–1650," *History of Elementary School Teaching and Curriculum,* eds. Giovanni Genovesi et al., 1 (Hanover, Germany: 1990): 1–8.

decided the **Kalamazoo case**, which was brought by a group of local-control advocates who favored state supervision. Since then both state and federal courts have accepted the primacy of state over local school jurisdiction.[26]

The legal basis for state control over education is found in the Tenth Amendment of the U.S. Constitution: "The powers not delegated to the United States by the Constitution nor prohibited by it to the States, are reserved to the States respectively, or to the people." By defining education as a state function, courts set the stage for today's complex organizations of school systems. Under this interpretation each state has extensive power over education within its borders; state constitutions and legal codes are quite influential in determining how education will be structured and administered within every community in the state.

On the other hand, several forces temper a state's authority. One is the federal Constitution itself. States (and their school systems) must honor Article 1, Section 10, which forbids states to pass any "law impairing the obligation of contracts." Regarding education, this means that states cannot arbitrarily change laws about teachers' salary, tenure, or retirement to the detriment of teachers. Collective bargaining might not be enforceable without this provision. The First, Fourth, Fifth, and Fourteenth Amendments also restrain states in important ways.

Over the years the federal government has limited state power and increased its control over education through the congressional passage of acts and statutes. For example, provisions of the Civil Rights Act of 1964 that prohibit discrimination in employment apply to public schools. Other statutes regulate the conduct of state and local authorities that receive federal money—specifically, conduct that relates to "race, color, or national origin," "sex," and "otherwise qualified handicapped individuals." Section 1983 of the civil rights legislation also provides for federal protection of students and teachers. If they believe that a school rule infringes on their federally protected civil rights, they can go to federal court; the court will "pass on the regulation" and adjudicate the complaint.[27]

Still another restraint on state prerogatives is the long tradition of local control over education. Even though courts have defined local school districts as *state* agencies for more than a century, in practice state authorities are often careful not to intrude too far into areas where local feelings are strong. For example, state education officials have often wanted to consolidate many of the smaller school districts of the fifteen thousand districts in the country. But citizens usually resist consolidation, and local elected officials tend to restrain state bureaucrats from angering local constituents.

An additional factor that limits state power over education is the bureaucracy itself. This can happen in several ways. For example, remember that state education agencies themselves make up large systems of self-interest; hundreds or thousands of permanent civil servants who live and work in the state capital make an effective lobbying force. Most of these bureaucrats are unlikely to encourage legislation that radically alters what they do or how they do it. Even so, legislators occasionally do pass laws that state-level education bureaucrats dislike. But new laws must be implemented through detailed regulations that are written,

[26]Stuart v. School Dist. No. 1 of Village of Kalamazoo, 30 Mich. 69 (1874).

[27]E. Edmund Reutter, Jr., *The Law of Public Education*, 3d ed. (Mineola, N.Y.: Foundation Press, 1985), 9.

interpreted, and enforced by the employees of state agencies. Thus state civil servants can subtly—sometimes overtly—modify the law's original intent.

Still another limit on how education legislation works in practice is that it is interpreted by local systems. Besides the state-level bureaucracy there are many local bureaucracies. In larger cities these are quite extensive organizations. For example, New York City's local education establishment at 110 Livingston Street employs 130,872 people. Even if state legislators in Albany put something in motion, Livingston Street can stop it in its tracks if it is unpopular with local bureaucrats.[28]

DEVELOPMENT OF SPECIALIZED FUNCTIONS

When James G. Carter and Horace Mann in Massachusetts, and similar thinkers in many other states, began to agitate for state and township systems of schools administered by specialists, they did not envision today's huge, complex bureaucracies. Most likely they thought of a few elementary schools and perhaps one higher school in each large city. Probably no school would have more than four to six teachers, with one being the lead, or principal, teacher. A superintendent with an assistant or two and a secretary completed their picture of a school system in a city like Boston. Smaller cities would have proportionally smaller "systems."

By the early twentieth century, however, what emerged was a two-tiered approach within a one-directional bureaucracy. The administration of schools and systems gradually became a separate career track from teaching. Elementary teachers usually had completed high school and from one to three years of "normal" school (teacher education). High school teachers often had a bachelor's degree.

At first, elementary principals came from the ranks of teachers and, therefore, might have a normal diploma rather than a college degree. By the 1920s, however, many superintendents encouraged school boards to avoid hiring any principal who did not have at least a bachelor's and preferably a master's degree in education. Since most women in school settings were elementary teachers with normal diplomas rather than college degrees, many were blocked from the principalship. In 1920 more than 80 percent of elementary principals were women, but by the 1970s fewer than 30 percent were—even though over 90 percent of elementary teachers were women.[29]

As school administration became an increasingly specialized career path within the field of education, many universities began to offer graduate courses and degrees to prepare specialists for emerging roles. Working closely with state education bureaucrats, universities began to offer certification programs for counselors, psychologists, principals, superintendents, and business managers. Most often such certificate programs were closely tied to graduate degrees. Harvard developed the degree Doctor of Education (Ed.D.) to meet the needs of the most advanced specialists. Other universities offered either Doctor of Philosophy (Ph.D.) degrees with majors in education or followed Harvard's lead with Ed.Ds. Some offered both degrees. Increasingly, the most prestigious administrative positions were filled by people who had doctorates.

Administrative theory in this century has often followed industrial and busi-

[28]U.S. Department of Education, National Center for Education Statistics, *The Condition of Education 1992* (Washington, D.C., 1992): 130.
[29]Linda McPherson and Joan K. Smith, "Women Administrators in Historical Perspective: Toward an Androgynous Theory of Leadership," *Educational Horizons* 60 (Fall 1981): 22–25.

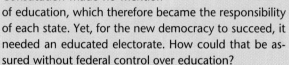

Horace Mann
1796–1859

One problem facing eighteenth-century America was how to create and monitor a system of schools. This was particularly a problem because the U.S. Constitution made no mention of education, which therefore became the responsibility of each state. Yet, for the new democracy to succeed, it needed an educated electorate. How could that be assured without federal control over education?

One of the pioneers in forming a system of schools common to all Americans was Horace Mann, who was born in Franklin, Massachusetts, in 1796. His parents, Thomas and Rebecca, had three boys and two girls; Horace was the second-youngest child. Although his family was the third generation to be farmers, Horace knew early that farming was not for him. He turned instead to learning, which was provided at home and in the nearby one-room district school.

Mann discovered that he wanted to go to college, and at eighteen he began studying to pass Brown University's entrance examinations. After a year of studying alone, he hired a tutor for the classics and for mathematics. He later recalled that he regarded this period as real learning—more rigorous than anything else he had experienced in Franklin. He did pass the entrance exams, and he entered Brown as a sophomore. In 1819 he graduated as valedictorian with a bachelor of arts degree, and then he worked briefly in a law firm before deciding to go to Tapping Reeve's Law School in Litchfield, Connecticut. After completing the course of study, he moved to Dedham, Massachusetts, where he began a successful law practice. Finally, he moved to Boston in 1827, when he was elected as Dedham's representative to the General Court.

Mann's first humanitarian focus was on the treatment of the insane, and he helped bring about legislation to improve their conditions. During this time he married Charlotte Messer, the third daughter of Brown University's President, Asa Messer. Unfortunately, they were married for only two years; in 1832 Charlotte died of consumption at age twenty-three. Her death hit Mann hard, and for three years he became somewhat of a recluse, a morose, unkempt figure about whom his friends worried—until they convinced him to run for the Massachusetts Senate. He was elected in 1835, and in 1837 he took up the cause of education by becoming the first

Yesterday's Professional

secretary of the newly created state board of education. This helped him to recapture his zeal; he traversed the state, scrutinizing the status of its schooling and writing about its poor conditions in the first of twelve annual reports to the state legislature.

Mann's reports had far-reaching effects, and his name became linked with educational improvements across the country. He started and edited the *Common Schools Journal*, in which he appealed to the business community to support common schools. The tenets he advanced included tax-supported schools, uniformity of textbooks, free schooling for all, a bureaucratic administrative structure, uniform school hours, and a greater number of compulsory schooldays.

In 1843 Mann married Mary T. Peabody, and in 1848 he left the Massachusetts state board of education to become a U.S. Congressman, filling the seat vacated by the death of John Quincy Adams. In Congress his crusade was for the abolition of slavery—a cause that jeopardized his political career so much that he lost his congressional seat as a Whig, but he gained it back as a Free Soiler.

Finally, in 1852 Mann accepted the presidency of Antioch College, in Ohio, where he fought against sectarianism and for coeducation. But the college was struggling financially and went bankrupt in 1859, when some of Mann's eastern friends bought it. Exhausted by the pressures of his job, Mann developed typhoid fever and died in August of that year.

Source: *Based on L. Glenn Smith and Joan K. Smith et al.,* Lives in Education: People and Ideas in the Development of Teaching *(Ames, Iowa: Educational Studies Press, 1984), 197–206.*

ness models. And since many schools were large by the 1960s, with high schools enrolling five thousand or more students, it was not unusual to hear administrative language that was reminiscent of factory management. Thus students became "products," and teachers became assembly-line workers. In keeping with this kind of imaging, many administrators saw their job as ensuring "efficiency" and "productivity"; they generally believed that small school systems were less efficient than large ones, and they encouraged consolidation of smaller neighboring districts. One result has been that for several decades the total number of school districts has steadily decreased while their average size has increased.

As district size—and the number of nonteaching specialists—increased, parents and teachers grew isolated from their school board and from the administrative bureaucracy. This tendency was evident as early as 1900, when Ella Flagg Young (later the superintendent of Chicago's schools) wrote her doctoral dissertation on the subject. By the 1960s and 1970s many observers of American schools were commenting unfavorably about the effects of bureaucratic isolation. Both parents and teachers expressed dissatisfaction with how schools were working, and they often pointed to features of the bureaucracy as being either central or contributing causes. During the 1980s many state legislatures passed laws (often referred to as reform legislation) to correct educational arrangements that had come to be cited by the media as less than satisfactory. Although little of such legislation directly addressed the bureaucracy, much of it did aim at improving the educational climate by increasing the involvement of parents in what schools were doing. In response to all this attention and concern, school boards turned to the school-based management models described earlier. Administrators began to give teachers, parents, and students a larger role in decision making.

PAYING FOR EDUCATION

■

Schooling in the United States costs more than $200 billion annually. As we have noted, budgetary and financial matters are among the most vexing problems for boards of education and for administrators. How these problems are resolved is a vital issue for teachers as well, because when teacher unions and their agents enter into collective bargaining, they need to have a clear and realistic idea of what the school system can pay to support their services. Figure 3.3 shows the growth of expenditures per pupil in elementary and secondary public schools from 1959–60 to 1989–90.

EVOLUTION OF SCHOOL FINANCING

The financing of schools evolved in a way that parallels their governance and structure. That is, drawing on a long European tradition, colonial Americans saw education as primarily a family responsibility. There was widespread agreement that parents should see to it that their offspring were literate, moral, and able to

FIGURE 3.3   Expenditures Per Pupil in Elementary and Secondary Schools, 1959–60 to 1989–90 (Constant 1989–90 Dollars)

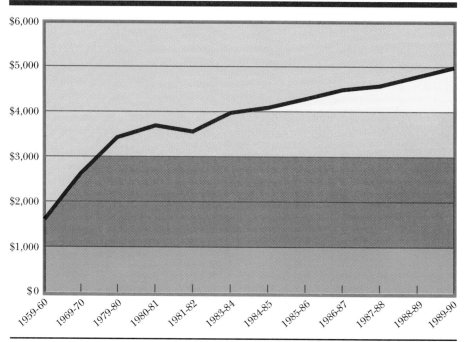

Source: *Digest of Education Statistics 1992*, National Center for Education Statistics, U.S. Department of Education, Office of Educational Research and Improvement, p. 161.

Early Americans saw education as a family responsibility, to be financed by those who actually used the schools. By the mid-nineteenth century it was argued that all citizens should help pay for schools. But what about parochial schools?
—*Bob Daemmrich/The Image Works*

earn a living. In the case of orphans or families struck by severe circumstances, the community as a whole generally tried to ensure at least minimal instruction in these three areas. And, of course, both Roman Catholics and Protestants felt obliged to provide advanced schooling and to ensure some access for able, highly motivated youngsters who could not afford to pay for their education.

In the partnership that emerged from these attitudes, it basically became a social responsibility to make schooling available to those who needed it. The community as a whole provided a building and secured a teacher, and parents whose children actually attended the school were expected to pay most (or all) of the teacher's salary and to supply wood or coal for heat. Sometimes the teacher charged a specific fee for each skill or subject, and parents paid for the ones they wanted and could afford for their children. In other cases the teacher specified a fee for instructing all the children in a community in agreed-upon subjects, and parents divided the total cost as they thought fair.

Americans paid for their common schools in this fashion until the mid-nineteenth century, when other plans were advanced. Part of the argument that Horace Mann and others made against communities' operating their own schools was that *all* citizens benefited from education and thus should pay for schools—not just the parents who used them. Mann wanted state legislatures to provide some funding for education, and the states' power to withhold payment put muscle into their new grip on schools.

Many who favored stronger state and weaker local control also wanted federal funding for education. This campaign reached its peak in the 1880s, but disagreements between Protestants and Roman Catholics about whether parochial schools would receive federal funds led to an impasse.[30] The federal government did supply money for some items, such as vocational education, and in 1917 it passed the Smith-Hughes Act, which provided annual income to secondary schools to support programs in home economics and agriculture.

During the 1930s the federal government passed many acts to relieve conditions brought on by the Great Depression. One example was the Civilian Conservation Corps (CCC) of 1933, which provided vocational training for three million youth. During World War II Congress passed three important acts that provided for the building and maintenance of schools (Lanham Act of 1941), for the education and occupational training of disabled veterans (Occupational Rehabilitation Act of 1943), and for veterans' higher education and training (the "GI Bill," or Servicemen's Readjustment Act of 1944). Concern over the "space race" with the Soviet Union led in 1958 to passage of the National Defense Education Act, which directly linked education to the country's security and defense. Programs funded under this act ranged from science and math, to foreign languages, to counselor training, and to teacher training for disadvantaged students.

In the 1960s general federal aid to education became available through two major acts. The first was the **Civil Rights Act of 1964**, which stated that all federally funded education programs must be administered without discriminating against any group (that is, minority Americans). The other was the **Elementary and Secondary Education Act (ESEA) of 1965**. Seen as part of President Lyndon Johnson's "War on Poverty," ESEA made money available for a variety

[30]For the background leading up to this dispute see F. Michael Perko, S.J., *A Time to Favor Zion: The Ecology of Religion and School Development on the Urban Frontier—Cincinnati* (Chicago: Educational Studies Press, 1988).

of public school programs. The act ultimately had eight titles, or chapters, under which schools could propose programs to reduce or eliminate inequality of educational opportunity.

SOURCES OF REVENUE FOR EDUCATION

For any level of education the main source of revenue is taxation, which almost always leads to controversies over the need, fairness, convenience, and efficiency of the tax. To be effective a tax should be regarded by the citizens as being necessary; its burden should be distributed and collected in an equitable manner; it should be easy to pay and to collect; and it should be flexible enough to respond to changing conditions (during inflation, for example, when costs rise, taxes also should rise; and during recession, when expenses fall, so should taxes).

Much controversy about taxation centers on equity. In other words, should people pay in proportion to the benefits they receive from the government? And should those with the highest income pay the same proportion of taxes as those with the least income? Some people favor the **ability-to-pay principle**, arguing that a citizen's tax burden should relate to how much he or she can afford to support government services. When wealthy citizens pay more than the moderately wealthy, who pay more than poorer citizens, a tax is said to be *progressive*. Others favor the **benefit principle**, saying that citizens should pay only for the government services that they receive.

At the federal level the major sources of education revenues come from personal and corporate income taxes. These taxes are regarded as progressive, because the tax rate increases in proportion to one's income. Schools receive this revenue either as a **categorical grant** (which is designated for a specific purpose) or as a **block grant** (which can be used for broadly defined purposes). Categorical grants were common during the 1960s and 1970s, but since the early 1980s most federal funding has been in the form of block grants.

State revenues for education are generated in the form of vehicle taxes, toll-road fees, sales taxes, corporate and personal income taxes, and (in some states) profits from the sale of lottery tickets. At the local level, property taxes are the main source of revenue.

CURRENT ISSUES ABOUT SCHOOL FUNDING

Advocates of state and federal funding of schools—as opposed to local funding—argue that this is the only way to guarantee good schools for poor communities as well as for rich ones. As stated earlier, at the heart of most debates about schools and taxation is the issue of fairness. In practice, however, state and federal funding have not equalized the revenue for schools, nor have they equalized citizens' tax burdens. In almost every state, some school districts have dramatically less money per pupil available to pay their costs, even though they tax themselves at several times the rate of other, often nearby, districts. Their salary schedules are lower, their curricular offerings are more limited, and their extra services are fewer. Yet their taxes are relatively high.

At the federal, state, and local levels, taxation produces the main revenues for education, and there is much controversy about the fairness of taxes. State lotteries, however, avoid such issues: Everyone knows "You have to pay to play." —AP/Wide World

In the late 1960s critics of state systems that allowed dramatically uneven funding by local districts mounted a massive legal assault. The issues came sharply into view in a 1971 decision by the California Supreme Court. A school official had advised a parent named Serrano—himself a teacher—to sell his house and buy one in a nearby wealthier district if he wanted his sons, who were good students, to be prepared for college. Instead of taking this advice, Serrano brought suit in an effort to get California to equalize funding for local school districts. Known as *Serrano* v. *Priest*, the case led to a court decision that a funding scheme which makes the quality of a child's education dependent on the wealth of the school district unfairly discriminates against the poor.[31]

When a three-judge district court in Texas adopted the same reasoning in 1973, the U.S. Supreme Court struck the decision down, arguing that the U.S. Constitution did not explicitly or implicitly guarantee a right to be educated.[32] Although this decision blunted the movement for equalizing funding in order to provide better education, the issue continues today. For example, in 1992 eleven communities received education grants in a national competition that responded to President George Bush's call to redesign education. These communities needed greater financial support in order to revitalize their educational systems. One winning proposal was based on a business concept: total quality management. Known as **Total Quality Education (TOE)**, this approach assumes (1) that there is more than one way for students to learn, (2) that the learning

[31]Serrano v. Priest, 5 Cal. 3d 584, 96 Cal.Rptr. 601, 487 P.2d 1241 (1971).
[32]San Antonio Independent School Dist. v. Rodriguez, 411 U.S. 1, 93 S.Ct. 1278, 36 L.Ed. 2d 16.

environment must reach beyond the walls of schools, and (3) that teacher-student roles and expectations must be redefined.[33]

ALTERNATIVE PROGRAMS TO IMPROVE EDUCATION

Since the 1980s several programs have attempted to improve and balance the educational performances of schools in a system. One approach is a **choice plan**, in which various schools in a system provide options in the form of magnet schools or special-purpose schools; parents and students then can choose which school best meets their needs. The idea is that each school will spend its revenues and use its resources to improve its unique mix of programs. The results of this approach are uneven. For example, some school systems have implemented a controlled form of choice plan, so that schools with the best reputations could not develop into monopolies; however, this did not ensure a high quality of education throughout the system. In other cases, systems have tried to encourage school monopolies by limiting or closing the less effective schools; obviously, this also resulted in uneven performance.

Another approach is the **voucher plan**, in which parents receive vouchers worth a specified amount of money that they can spend at the school of their choice. The problem with this approach is to ensure that all parents have equal amounts of voucher money to spend, and to prevent wealthier parents from using other sources of income that are unavailable to poorer parents.

A third alternative uses a **tuition tax credit** to equalize parents' ability to pay tuition at a private school. In some plans that have been proposed, parents' income tax would be reduced by the difference between tuition costs and their income tax.

CONCLUSIONS

■

If you become a teacher in a public school, you probably will work with a principal who is male, white, and somewhere in his midforties. It is also likely that—along with members of your community—you will participate in managing the school under some form of school-based management (SBM). Your district's school system will be managed by a lay school board and a superintendent (probably also a white male).

The type, amount, and quality of education available in your school are fundamental issues, and policies that regulate who decides these questions—and who governs and pays for education—are among the most important in any society. Because of constitutional provisions in the United States these policies have been formulated at state and local levels. Traditionally, principals and district superintendents have been responsible for implementing education policies, although the federal government has played an increasingly large role by providing revenues for specific programs. The following chapters will reveal that many social, political, and philosophical matters are intertwined with the policies, roles, and responsibilities of educators at every level.

[33]See, for example, Casey Banas, "Bensenville's Vision Earns Education Grant," *Chicago Tribune*, 10 July 1992, p. 1.

KEY TERMS

school-based management (SBM)	Elementary and Secondary Education Act
superintendent	ability-to-pay principle
board of education	benefit principle
bureaucracy	categorical grant
common school	block grant
selectmen	*Serrano* v. *Priest*
trustees	choice plan
Kalamazoo case	voucher plan
Civil Rights Act of 1964	tuition tax credit

SUGGESTED READINGS

David Tyack and Elizabeth Hansot, *Managers of Virtue* (New York: Basic Books, 1982). This book describes the role of administrators in the nineteenth century and early twentieth century and concludes that—because of the school's focus on moral and ethical matters—administrators of public education were managers of virtue.

Joan K. Smith, *Ella Flagg Young: Portrait of a Leader* (Ames, Iowa: Iowa State Press, 1979). This biography traces Young's life from her early years as a teacher in Chicago, through her study with John Dewey at the University of Chicago, and finally to her 1909 appointment as the first female superintendent of Chicago's public schools.

Ronald F. Campbell, Thomas Fleming, L. Jackson Newell, and John W. Bennion, *A History of Thought and Practice in Education Administration* (New York: Teachers College Press, Columbia University, 1987). This book traces the development of educational administration from the nineteenth century into the twentieth and places current reform practices in a historical context.

F. Michael Perko, S.J., *A Time to Favor Zion* (Chicago: Educational Studies Press, 1988). This book describes the development of common schools in regard to issues of taxation and funding of public and parochial schools.

Van Cleve Morris, Robert L. Crowson, Cynthia Porter-Gehrie, and Emmanuel Hurwitz, Jr., *Principals in Action* (Columbus, Ohio: Merrill, 1984.) This work describes the results of extensive interviews with Chicago's principals, and it also discusses school-based management.

Social Class and Education

Sociological Foundations A

4

While education begins and ends with [the hu]man it always functions through a social system. Thinkers from Aristotle to George H. Mead have proclaimed the obvious; i.e., that [the hu]man is a social animal who achieves . . . humanity through a social system. Formal education becomes the vehicle through which the young are inducted into the social system.

—Clarence J. Karier, The Individual, Society, and Education
(Urbana: University of Illinois Press, *1986*), xxi

Since its introduction to America the intelligence test has been used more or less consciously as an instrument of oppression against the underprivileged—the poor, the foreign born, and racial minorities.

—Leon J. Kamin, "Heredity, Intelligence, Politics, and Psychology," in The Shaping of the American Educational State: 1900 to the Present, Clarence J. Karier, ed. (New York: Free Press, *1975*), 367

Social Class and Education

ADVANCED ORGANIZERS

In this chapter you will learn

How America's social classes are defined and characterized

How women and minorities fit into the social-class structure

How social class relates to educational opportunities and achievement levels

How we account for social and educational inequality

How intelligence measures relate to educational inequality

How various social scientists relate heredity and environment to intelligence and educational achievement

CHAPTER OUTLINE

CHARACTERISTICS OF SOCIAL CLASS
    Social Stratification in the United States
    Social Structure and Community Size

SOCIAL CLASS AND EDUCATIONAL ATTAINMENT
    Use of Correlation in Social Research
    SES and Postsecondary Opportunities
    Reading Achievement and Parents' Educational Attainment
    Family Income and High School Dropout Rate

ACCOUNTING FOR SOCIAL INEQUALITY
    Heredity vs. Environment
    Intelligence
    The Heredity Argument
    The Environment Argument

CONCLUSIONS

*M*ark Sommerfield is a junior at Phillips Academy in Andover, Massachusetts. It is fall, and today is the day that he will take the SAT (Scholastic Aptitude Test). Like most of his classmates Mark hopes to be accepted into Harvard or one of the other Ivy League colleges when he graduates from the academy, and he must do well on the SAT to realize his goal.

Mark thinks that he is pretty lucky to have been accepted at Phillips. He is the first in his family to attend such a prestigious private secondary institution. His father is an attorney with a large firm in Boston, having graduated from the University of Virginia's law school. His mother is a graduate of Wellesley, in Massachusetts. Mark has a younger sister who still lives at home with his family in an affluent section of Boston's greater metropolitan area.

CHARACTERISTICS OF SOCIAL CLASS

Mark Sommerfield's family belongs to one of the upper social classes: the upper-middle class. A **social class** is a group of people who have similar values, habits, and lifestyles as well as "common political and economic goals and interests related to their position in the social structure."[1] Nineteenth-century philosopher Karl Marx (1818–1883) was among the first to conceptualize social class, using the term to refer to distinctions that are determined by the economic functions of a set of occupations or professions. Related to these distinctions are issues involving the power that one occupational group might have in influencing economic decisions.

Marx and his followers distinguished among five basic social groups:

1. The *Capitalists,* who operate according to the profit motive and control large amounts of capital
2. The *Bourgeoisie,* or middle class, who are large property owners and who exert power and control over certain types of investments, production, and labor
3. The *Petitbourgeoisie,* or lower middle class, who also own property and control investments and some production, but not labor
4. The *Proletariat,* or the manual and skilled workers, who have no economic control
5. The *Lumpenproletariat,* who are the poor and unskilled workers

Marx also described a group called the *Intelligentsia,* or educators and professors, who derive power and wealth from knowledge instead of from material goods.

Sociologist and philosopher Max Weber (1864–1930) argued that societies are stratified on the basis of several dimensions, not just economic factors. Again, however, these dimensions are related to social status—to the lifestyle and life

[1]Daniel V. Levine and Robert J. Havighurst, *Society and Education* (Boston: Allyn & Bacon, 1992), 3.

Karl Marx divided society into classes based on economic factors: One's relative status depends on one's power over economic decisions. But other factors also influence social status.   —Culver Pictures

chances one has in addition to the social estimation of prestige and political clout.

Regardless of the type of society, all nations—whether primitive or modern—are stratified based on the social rank of their members. Leaders and others with much prestige make up the highest class, followed by those in semi-leadership or middle leadership positions, and ending with those who have no political, military, or economic power. More recently American sociologists have described U.S. social stratification in terms of five variables: (1) family background, including race or ethnicity and whether the family's wealth is inherited or earned; (2) one's economic level; (3) the status or prestige level associated with one's job; (4) the level of education attained by the parents of the household; and (5) one's living patterns, including religious affiliation, values, and leisure activities.[2] These variables are reflected in the following descriptions of five social classes or five levels of **socioeconomic status (SES)**. Traditionally

[2]See, for example, the work of W. L. Warner, M. Meeker, and K. Eels, *Social Class in America* (New York: Harper Torchbooks, 1960).

RESEARCH SAYS

For Tomorrow's Education . . .

Fewer women are finding employment in the international workplace. Their proportion in the workforce has peaked and will continue to decline worldwide during the rest of this century, according to the United Nation's International Labor Office. (See *Women in the World of Work: Statistical Analysis and Projections to the Year 2000*, U.N. International Labor Office, 1989.) In the United States in 1990 professional women made up 6 percent of all partners in law firms, 16 percent of doctors, 7 percent of engineers, 6 percent of newsmedia executives, and 2 percent of Congress, according to Sandra Day O'Connor in her keynote speech at the "Women in Power" conference hosted by Washington University, in St. Louis on 14 November 1990. Also see "No Matter What They Do, Women Lag in Workplace," *Chicago Tribune*, 22 July 1992, sec. 8, p. 19.

women have been ranked according to their husbands' or fathers' social position, but as more and more women have entered the workforce, sociologists have begun to assess them independently.

SOCIAL STRATIFICATION IN THE UNITED STATES

UPPER CLASS   At the top of the social hierarchy in the United States are the people who have inherited wealth and whose family's prominent social standing can be traced back for several generations. The **upper class** usually makes up the community's *Social Register* and is found on the governing boards of museums, symphonies, and opera houses. They are graduates of Ivy League colleges and prestigious secondary prep schools, and they are strongly represented in such professions as architecture, medicine, and law. Women in this class are rarely professionals themselves, but they engage in the philanthropic activities of social clubs and civic organizations. They are members of Episcopal, Presbyterian, Congregational, or Unitarian churches, and they generally fit the stereotype that has come to be called WASP (white Anglo-Saxon Protestant). Upper-class people usually try to keep a low social profile and generally maintain conservative or inconspicuous lifestyles. They make up about 2 percent of the nation's population.[3]

UPPER MIDDLE CLASS   Although they are second- or third-generation Americans, people in the **upper middle class** do not come from aristocratic families,

The upper middle class seems to have it all—comfortable homes, new cars, and time to enjoy the good life. But it took effort to get where they are, and they know it will take effort to stay there. A good education is an important part of the picture. —Tom McCarthy/The Picture Cube

[3]Levine and Havighurst, *Society and Education*, 5–30.

and they have not inherited their wealth. Instead, their ambition has allowed them to rise to this class from lower beginnings, and they now belong to prestigious professions or are business executives. Many of the women in this class also work in professional or technical fields, and quite a few of them engage in philanthropic activities. The women may be members of the League of Women Voters, while the men often belong to Rotary or Kiwanis clubs; they are likely to be leaders in the chamber of commerce, medical and bar associations, or the National Association for the Advancement of Colored People (NAACP). In their leisure they attend symphonies, ballets, and operas, and they read such magazines as *Atlantic Monthly*, *The New Yorker*, and *Harper's*.

People in the upper middle class live in comfortable homes, drive new cars, and can afford adequate insurance and pension plans. They are active in Presbyterian, Congregational-Christian, Methodist, Midwest Baptist, and New England Unitarian churches, although they also are found in Lutheran and Roman Catholic churches and Jewish synagogues. They tend to be easygoing and non-dogmatic in their relationships with others, and they are relaxed and flexible in their child-rearing practices. Most of their children attend public elementary and secondary schools and then go on to state universities, small liberal arts colleges, or Ivy League colleges. Education is very important to the upper middle class because it is the vehicle that allows them to move socially upward. They expect that education will help their children to maintain their social status. Currently about 16 percent of the population is in the upper middle class.[4]

LOWER MIDDLE CLASS   Often referred to by the two higher classes as the "common people," members of the **lower middle class** hold white-collar sales and clerical jobs, are supervisors in factories, or are leaders in other labor settings (such as railroad engineers and conductors, electrical and small building contractors, and plumbers); most farm owners also belong to the lower middle class. Their income is at or near the national average, and their leisure activities are those which are the most popular. They read the most popular magazines and comic strips, watch the most popular television programs and sports events, and participate in the most popular sports and recreational activities. They make up the membership of men's fraternal organizations like the American Legion, and of women's auxiliary associations. Although they are mostly Protestant or Roman Catholic, Jews are also found in this group. Usually their parents or grandparents were immigrants.

People in the lower middle class are thrifty but economically independent. They live in modest or tract housing in neighborhoods that often border working-class sections. They value education as essential for obtaining good employment, and they have usually graduated from high school. They expect their children to be respectful and attentive in school; about 75 percent of their offspring go on to college. The lower middle class makes up about 32 percent of the nation's population.[5]

UPPER WORKING CLASS   Because this group shares many characteristics with the lower middle class, some sociologists predict that these two groups will become a single class—the **common-person class**. But people in the **upper working**

[4]Ibid.
[5]Ibid.

People in the lower middle class and those in the upper working class make good neighbors. They have much in common and share many values, including that they see education as essential for obtaining good employment
—*David Woo/Stock, Boston*

class are not white-collar workers; they are blue-collar workers, or the skilled and semiskilled workers. Although they live in the less expensive, lower-status parts of towns and cities, their homes are usually well kept and respectable. These people are Catholics and fundamentalist Protestants as well as Methodists and Baptists; a portion of this group is not affiliated with any church.

People in the upper working class are upwardly mobile in terms of mechanical gadgets and conveniences, which they enjoy having as much as their upper-class counterparts do. They are members of veterans' and fraternal associations, and they enjoy hunting and fishing. In their leisure time they read newspapers and like to watch television or fix up their homes. They value schooling as the means to a good education, and although they themselves may not have finished high school, they plan for their children to graduate; some of their offspring will enter college and other postsecondary institutions. About 32 percent of the population belongs to the upper working class.[6]

LOWER WORKING CLASS   People in the **lower working class** are poor and live in tenements and housing projects. They have few skills and consequently have difficulty finding jobs. Sociologist H. P. Miller has described four subclasses within this group. First, there are unskilled but employed workers who have stable home lives. Second, are the strained but employed unskilled workers who manage to hold on to jobs but who have many personal problems. Third, are the copers who have stable family relationshps but many economic difficulties.

[6]Ibid.

RESEARCH SAYS

For Tomorrow's Education . . .

African-American men continue to earn 33 percent less than white men, even when they have the same level of education. In the business world this has been chronicled through interviews with 122 African-American men who tell of "Catch-22" situations when it comes to advancement and the social obligations that coincide with promotions. Middle-class African-Americans also continue to experience all types of discrimination in employment and housing. Data from the U.S. Census Bureau support these conclusions, and a recent book by Dempsey J. Travis entitled *Racism: American Style, A Corporate Gift* (Urban Research Press, 1990) confirms it. Also see Charles M. Madigan, "Blind to Change: Blacks Find Success Doesn't Bring Acceptance," *Chicago Tribune*, 17 May 1992, sec. 4, "Perspective."

And finally there are the unstable, who have both personal and economic difficulties; they are the people who often depend on public assistance.[7]

The lower working class has traditionally included newly arrived immigrants who take on menial labor and other low-paying jobs. Today Hispanics, Asians, and African-Americans are the dominant subgroups of this class, and their children are often considered "problem children" in schools because of truancy, discipline matters, and learning difficulties. About 18 percent of the population belongs to the lower working class.[8]

UNDERCLASS   Recently sociologists have begun to use the term **underclass** to identify people at the bottom of the social-class ladder in larger cities. These are the most depressed among the lower class, and they tend to have little hope of escaping their conditions. Blocking movement out of this class are such factors as that (1) most people in the underclass are from minority groups, and many have been stranded in this social environment for more than one generation; (2) underclass households (when they exist) tend to be headed by females, and social welfare policies have discouraged the traditional family structure; and

RESEARCH SAYS

For Tomorrow's Education . . .

American College Test scores are still closely related to the types of courses that have traditionally been found in college preparatory programs in high schools—that is, four years of English and three years of math, social studies, and natural sciences. (See the ACT publication *Activity* 28 [November 1990], 1.) Also, a recent report by the National Commission on Testing and Public Policy found that multiple-choice tests harm minority students and interfere with educational reform efforts (Boston College, 1990).

[7]H. P. Miller, *Rich Man, Poor Man: The Distribution of Income in America* (New York: Crowell, 1964).

[8]Levine and Havighurst, *Society and Education*, 5–30.

(3) underclass families are highly disorganized and dysfunctional, and they cope with high levels of crime and gang activity because the controlling influences of schools and law enforcement agencies have broken down.

In such cities as Los Angeles, Houston, and New York a high proportion of the underclass is Hispanic, while in other cities the largest portion is African-American. Recent analysis of census data reveals that anywhere from two million to four million people have become stranded in the urban underclass. The working classes tend to move out of this inner-city environment as soon as they can afford to, and so underclass ghetto neighborhoods have grown larger and more isolated than ever before.[9] Those who have studied the underclass have concluded that people have been stranded in it for generations because of family structures and social factors. Structurally, underclass families transmit few occupational skills, and therefore subsequent generations do not learn how to compete for very limited job opportunities. Socially, members of the underclass experience such isolation and hopelessness about shaping their own future that they grow dependent on public assistance for survival. Males thus become afraid to marry and take on economic and family responsibilities when their chances for employment are so limited. There is little to do except return to the street corner for friendship and support, just as they probably did as teenage members of gangs.[10]

Solutions to the problems of the underclass will need to take into account the factors that perpetuate these conditions. Sociologists Daniel Levine and Robert Havighurst have asserted that education and schooling will play a central role:

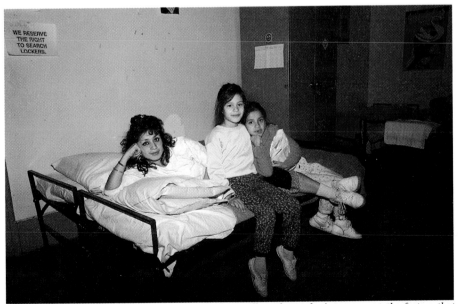

Solutions to the problems of the underclass will need to take into account the factors that perpetuate their conditions. Education is certain to play a central role, not only in job training but also in combating isolation and hopelessness. —Yvonne Hemsey/Gamma Liaison

[9]Ibid., 14–15. The percentage of the population living in inner-city neighborhoods grew from 32 percent in 1960 to 39 percent in 1970 to over 40 percent by 1989.

[10]For descriptions of the hardships faced by the underclass see Elliott Liebow, *Tally's Corner* (Boston: Little, Brown, 1967); D. G. Glasgow, *The Black Underclass: Poverty, Unemployment and Entrapment of Ghetto Youth* (San Francisco: Josey-Bass, 1980); and Ken Auletta, *The Underclass* (New York: Random House, 1982).

Along with programs to provide employment and income, education also is a central component in carrying out a comprehensive program to improve conditions for the underclass in big cities. Desegregation of the public schools, for example, should be concerned with reducing the social isolation of the poor. Whether the poor acquire good jobs in the future will depend to an extent on what low-status youth learn in schools.[11]

In considering the points made here about social class in the United States, keep in mind that, historically, the lower the social class from which students come, the less likely they are to climb the educational ladder. Although Native Americans live mostly in rural settings, on reservations, they often experience conditions similar to those of the underclass.

SOCIAL-CLASS BIFURCATION   During the late 1980s and early 1990s sociologists began suggesting that blue-collar workers are decreasing in numbers as new technologies call for a labor force with higher skill levels. One study concluded that by the year 2000 computer-based automation will eliminate twenty million jobs now required by existing technologies. This would mean that mil-

[11]Levine and Havighurst, *Society and Education*, 24.

Sara Winnemucca

1844–1891

Domestic worker, translator, and educator, Sara Winnemucca was one of the first Native American women to walk between the worlds of Indians and whites. She was born in Nevada, the daughter of a Paiute chief; her grandfather had traveled to California with Freemont; and she learned English while working in the home of an army officer.

When she was around sixteen years old, Sara and her sister matriculated in a convent school in California. But white parents objected to the girls' attendance, and so the sisters withdrew from school and returned to Nevada. Sara again did domestic work, and she tried to continue her education by teaching herself through reading. But she was never satisfied with her educational attainment and prowess.

As an adult Winnemucca became a translator for the Paiutes and whites, working with the military and with the Bureau of Indian Affairs (BIA). She had little use for

the BIA and spoke out against the bureau's fraudulent practices, appointments of unqualified agents, and misuse of labor and land. This made her the target of a BIA investigation, but her military connections and the contacts she had made on speaking engagements shielded her, and she went on to pursue her interest in education.

Sara became acquainted with Mary Taylor Mann

Yesterday's Professional

(the wife of legislator and educator Horace Mann) and with her sister Elizabeth Palmer Peabody, an early supporter of kindergarten education. Mann helped her publish a book entitled *Life Among the Paiutes: Their Wrongs and Claims*, and both women encouraged Sara to pursue her dream of opening a school for Paiute children. The school opened on her brother's farm in 1886, but—even with Peabody's help—it ran into financial problems and closed after 1887. Winnemucca went back to domestic work until her death in 1891.

Source: Based on L. Glenn Smith and Joan K. Smith et al., *Lives in Education: People and Ideas in the Development of Teaching* (Ames, Iowa: Educational Studies Press, 1984), 243–244.

lions of workers would be employed in higher-status jobs with higher skill levels, but millions of other workers would either hold lower-status jobs or be unemployed. If this comes about, the middle segments of American society will shrink, because more people will be in higher stratas and more will be in lower stratas. Thus the U.S. class structure would exhibit **social bifurcation**.[12]

SOCIAL STRUCTURE AND COMMUNITY SIZE

The social-class makeup of a particular community depends on the size of its population. Small rural towns tend to have a three-class structure: upper middle, lower middle, and lower. Such a community may range in size from a few hundred to five thousand people. In towns of this size, working-class farmers and blue-collar industrial workers usually predominate.

Small cities of six thousand to fifty thousand inhabitants generally have a five-tiered social structure, although which class is largest will depend on economic conditions. For example, a city that has a university will have a large upper middle class, while a city with a refining industry will have a larger number of working-class people.

Large cities exhibit the five-tiered social structure with many subclasses including an underclass. Determining who belongs in which class is done by assessing the occupational status of the head of the household, the type of neighborhood and house of the family, their ethnic heritage, and the types of leisure activities pursued by the head of household.

SOCIAL CLASS AND EDUCATIONAL ATTAINMENT

The preceding descriptions of the five social classes included the percentage of people who are found in each class. We also discussed whether or not the children in each class would be likely to finish high school and continue on to college. Table 4.1 shows the percentage of the population in each social class along with the proportion of high school seniors who entered two- or four-year colleges or universities in 1984. We can see that there is a close relationship between a person's SES and the amount of education completed. People in the upper SES quartile are much more likely to attend college than those in lower quartiles. In 1984, for example, 88 percent of students whose parents were in the highest SES quartile went on to two- or four-year colleges or universities, whereas only 59 percent of their counterparts in the middle quartile—and only 39 percent in the lower quartiles—entered college.

One factor to which many educators point as promoting the connection between SES and educational attainment is **tracking**, or the practice of separating students into different classrooms and curricula according to their achievement levels. High achievers receive the strongest academic courses within the college-preparatory track; average students receive more practical courses in the voca-

[12]Ibid., 23–25.

TABLE 4.1　　High School Seniors Who Entered College
in 1984 (Percentages)

Socioeconomic Status (SES)	Social Class (Percent)	2-year College	4-Year College	Total
Upper quartile	upper (2%)	27	61	88
Middle quartile	upper middle (16%)	27	32	59
Lower half	lower middle (32%) upper working (32%) lower working (18%)	20	19	39

Source: Levine and Havighurst, *Society and Education* (Boston: Allyn & Bacon, 1989), 7, 58, citing National Center for Education Statistics, 1984.

tional track; and low achievers are placed in the general track, where they focus on remedial work in essential courses and also take elective courses in such subjects as art and home economics. Lower-SES students are located predominantly in the general tracks of secondary schools.

Many lower-SES students receive postsecondary education in proprietary schools (vocational schools that offer courses in such trades as allied health, business, secretarial, cosmetology, aviation, and electricity). It is estimated that more than six thousand proprietary institutions compete with similar programs in two-year community colleges. However, the dropout rate for students in proprietary schools exceeds 50 percent, and it is even higher in community colleges.[13]

USE OF CORRELATION IN SOCIAL RESEARCH

Two variables that are so closely associated, such as SES and schooling, are said to be highly correlated; in other words, if one variable is present, the other will also be found. Technically, **correlation** is a statistical concept that numerically expresses how closely associated two or more variables are. For example, identical twins almost always have the same eye color. Because correlation is usually expressed as a two-digit number ranging from +1.00 to −1.00, the correlation of eye color in identical twins would be about +.99. This correlation is a positive number because knowing the color of one twin's eyes tells us that the other twin will have the *same* color eyes. The correlation would be a negative number (−.99) if knowing the color of one twin's eyes were to tell us that the other twin has eyes of a *different* color. (The only reason for expressing the correlation as .99 instead of 1.00 is that, if we examined enough twins, we might discover a pair whose eyes were different colors.) If there were no relationship at all between two variables, the correlation would be expressed as .00 or 0.00.

We need to remember one other feature of correlation as a way of describing associations between variables. The two-digit number that expresses correlation does *not* literally say how much the two items have in common (or the extent to which one "predicts" the other, as statisticians put it). For example,

[13]Ibid., 62.

suppose we know that the correlation between two people's scores on a test is .80. This does not mean that the two people answered 80 percent of the test items the same; it means that only about 64 percent of their responses were alike. Why? Because in using a correlation *coefficient* (.80 in this case) to estimate how closely associated two items are—or estimate how frequently we can predict one item knowing its associated counterpart—it is necessary to *square* the coefficient (.80 × .80 = .64). This concept is critical in understanding statistical reasoning, and we will return to this point later.

Because SES and schooling have such a high correlation, SES is the best predictor of a student's educational attainment and success in school. In fact, SES is a better predictor than a student's earned grades or aptitude test scores. The following three sections describe some of the research that confirms the correlation between SES and educational attainment.

SES AND POSTSECONDARY OPPORTUNITIES

An early researcher into the relationships among SES, occupation, and post-secondary educational opportunity was Joseph A. Kahl. He found that sons of fathers with major white-collar jobs, such as those in managerial and professional fields, had much higher college aspirations than did sons of fathers from lower-SES occupations. In fact, sons of high-SES fathers had 2.5 times the chance to enter a postsecondary institution than did sons of lower-SES fathers. For college entrance the ratio of high-SES sons to low was 4:1; for graduating from college it was 6:1; and for entering graduate or professional schools the ratio was 9:1.[14]

READING ACHIEVEMENT AND PARENTS' EDUCATIONAL ATTAINMENT

Reading achievement has also been correlated with parental educational attainment and social class. In a 1985 study the National Assessment of Educational Progress (NAEP) obtained estimates of the reading proficiencies of children aged nine, thirteen, and seventeen and compared these scores to parents' educational attainment (see Table 4.2). Reading scores were categorized in the following manner:

- A score of 150 meant that the student possessed *rudimentary* skills in reading, such as following simple written directions and reading simple phrases that described a picture or object
- A score of 200 meant that the student had the *basic* knowledge needed to understand simple paragraphs, stories, and news articles
- A score of 250 placed the pupil at an *intermediate* level where he or she could read more complex material and could locate and organize information in relatively lengthy material
- A score of 300 indicated that the individual was *adept* at understanding and analyzing relatively complicated material
- A score of 350 indicated that the student could extend and restructure *advanced* material in technical and highly specialized texts.[15]

[14]Joseph A. Kahl, *The American Class Structure* (New York: Holt, 1957).
[15]Levine and Havighurst, *Society and Education*, 45–48.

TABLE 4.2   Reading Level and Parents' Educational Attainment

Reading Score	9-Year-Olds	13-Year-Olds	17-Year-Olds
350 (Advanced)			
310			
300 (Adept)			*
290			
282			#
280			
270			
267			+
265		*	
260			
255			
253		#	
250 (Intermediate)			
247		+	
240			
230			
224			
220	*		
211	#		
210			
200 (Basic)			
197			
193	+		
190			
180			
150 (Rudimentary)			

Notes: * Parents who had postsecondary experiences.
      # Parents who graduated from high school.
      + Parents who did not graduate from high school.
Source: Levine and Havighurst, *Society and Education*, 46, citing the NAEP, 1990.

All nine-year-olds were below the intermediate level (250), and the children of high school dropouts were below the basic level (200). The thirteen-year-old children of dropouts were still below the intermediate level, while the children of high school graduates and postsecondary students were beyond the intermediate level. Finally, the seventeen-year-old offspring of parents with postsecondary experiences averaged slightly under the adept category (300), and seventeen-year-olds whose parents were dropouts or graduates were midway between intermediate and adept levels, with scores of 267 and 282, respectively.

FAMILY INCOME AND HIGH SCHOOL DROPOUT RATE

Students from families with low incomes are more than twice as likely to drop out of high school as are those from families with high incomes (see Table 4.3).

TABLE 4.3   High School Dropout Rate
            and Family Income

Family Income	Dropout Rate (Percentage)
Low quartile	33
Low–middle quartile	15
Middle–high quartile	15
High quartile	10

Source: Levine and Havighurst, *Society and Education*, 50–51, citing the National Research Council, 1989.

Only 10 percent of students from high-income families drop out, compared with 33 percent of students from low-income families; the dropout rate is about 15 percent for all other income groups. When race and ethnicity are considered, 40 percent of Hispanic, 24 percent of African-American, and 28 percent of white students dropped out.[16]

ACCOUNTING FOR SOCIAL INEQUALITY

■

Whenever we address issues of inequality, including educational inequality, our analyses inevitably rest on assumptions about the nature of reality—that is, about how things really are (and, by implication, how they *must* be). In an effort to understand the numerous, often conflicting explanations of why inequality exists, and how or whether it can be reduced or eliminated, we must examine some of the basic assumptions about reality that different people have made to account for inequality.

HEREDITY VS. ENVIRONMENT

Since the nineteenth century much of the discussion about inequality has been rooted in opposing views about the extent to which a person's skills, abilities, talents, or intelligence are inherited through genetics or are determined by environmental factors. This debate is at least two thousand years old. In Athens around 430 B.C. two famous philosophers, Socrates and Protagoras, argued about whether virtue was inherited or learned. Protagoras said that most people were capable of learning enough to govern themselves; Socrates thought that only a few people were virtuous enough and intelligent enough to govern and that they possessed these qualities through birth, not education. In our own day the Swiss educationist Jean Piaget is noted for saying that anyone can learn anything if properly taught (his ideas are discussed in Chapter 6). Of the numerous educational psychologists who disagree with Piaget, one of the best known is Professor Arthur Jensen of the University of California. Jensen first caught the attention of most educators in 1969, by arguing that ''intelligence'' is 80 percent inherited

[16]Ibid., 51.

and that teachers thus should concentrate on students with high intelligence quotients (IQs), leaving the remainder to learn vocational skills.

As it turned out, Jensen based his argument primarily on faulty data in the work of Cyril Burt, a British psychologist with whom he had studied. Burt undertook his work with the conviction that "genius" is inherited, and he spent many years assembling data that would support his belief. As a psychologist for the schools of London he had access to the test scores of all students in that large city, which had just begun administering IQ tests about the time Burt began his work in the 1920s.

Already convinced that "intelligence" is genetically determined, Burt spent years studying test data for identical twins. He correlated IQ and achievement scores for each pair of twins whom he could locate in London, and then he divided them into two categories: (1) twins who for various reasons had been separated at an early age and were raised in different households and (2) twins who had been reared together in the same family environment. Burt expected to find little difference in the average correlations of twins reared apart and those reared together because he thought that the environment was an unimportant influence on intelligence. We have already noted that a statistical correlation does not literally express how closely related two variables are, because first the coefficient must be squared (thus $.80 \times .80 = .64$). This is one key concept in understanding Burt's (and Jensen's) reasoning. Another is the concept of intelligence itself, which is not as clearcut as many people think.

INTELLIGENCE

Originally a Latin word, **intelligence** long signified "the ability to learn or understand or to deal with new or trying situations."[17] Early in this century, however, the word came to be synonymous with performance on a few scholastic aptitude tests, the concent of which reflects what *most* students have learned or achieved by certain ages. Recently some people have called for returning the term to its original meaning, because the more recent definition is too narrow and limited.[18]

This twentieth-century development was not accidental. It actually began during the eighteenth century, with the apparently unrelated speculations of Abraham De Moivre about the probability of obtaining a certain number of "heads" in ten flips of a coin. In doing so he was able to develop a mathematical formula that came close to describing the curve of the tops of the line in Figure 4.1. This **normal curve**, as it came to be called, appealed to a nineteenth-century English "gentleman" named Francis Galton (1822–1911). A first cousin of Charles Darwin, Galton had an interest in many things, including science, and he had enough of an inheritance from his physician father to live a life of leisure. Although he had not graduated from a university, Galton believed that himself was a person of considerable intellectual talent.[19]

Among Galton's interests was statistics, and he, in fact, worked out the concept of correlation discussed earlier. Given his belief that "genius" was inherited, it was natural for Galton to see the "normal curve" as an accurate representation of how intellectual talent was distributed. That is, a tiny percentage

[17]*Webster's New Ninth Collegiate Dictionary.* (Springfield, Mass.: Merriam-Webster, Inc., Publishers, 1984), 629.

[18]William Gardner, *Frames of Mind: The Theory of Multiple Intelligences* (New York: Basic Books, 1985). Also see Gardner's *Unschooled Mind: How Children Think and How Schools Should Teach* (New York: Basic Books, 1991).

[19]Gene V. Glass and Julian C. Stanley, *Statistical Methods in Educational Research* (Englewood Cliffs, N.J.: Prentice-Hall, 1970), 96–106.

FIGURE 4.1   Normal Distribution of Probabilities and De Moivre's Curve

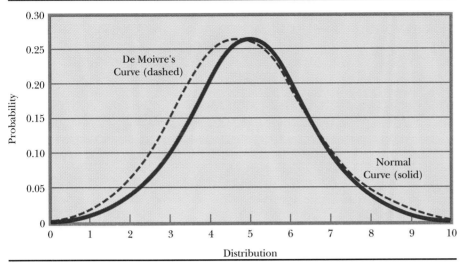

Source: Based on Gene V. Glass and Julian C. Stanley, *Statistical Methods of Educational Psychology* (Englewood Cliffs, N.J.: Prentice-Hall, 1970), pp. 97, 99.

of the population had an enormous amount of ability, and at the other end of the spectrum were "morons," "imbeciles," the "feebleminded," and "backward children"—to use the language of his day; the great mass of people lay somewhere between the two ends of the curve.

Galton thought that intellectual ability was mostly genetic in origin and that the larger a person's head, the greater the intelligence therein. (He had a large head himself.) He also thought that women were intellectually inferior to men, but he believed that aristocratic women were more likely to be intelligent than their sisters of lower social standing. He wanted to encourage marriage between the most talented people, and so he advocated separating "feebleminded" individuals from the rest of society, hoping to prevent them from having children. Galton *assumed* that high SES was a good indicator of genius in mature adults; but he was not sure how intelligence could be measured in people who had not yet—because of youth or other circumstances—been able to show what they could do in life.

French psychologist Alfred Binet (1857–1911) took up the challenge of devising a practical scheme for measuring "intelligence" in response to a request from the government of France. The French wished to identify the most severely incapable people and to separate them from the general population. The minister of public instruction asked Binet to develop a way of identifying children who were likely to fail in regular schools so that they could be put into special asylums. Binet, with the help of his student Theodore Simon, devised a series of tasks that seemed to test childrens' listening, comprehension, recognition, sequencing, and obedience skills. Binet and Simon arranged these tasks from simple to more complicated, and they asked each child to perform the tasks in order of difficulty, beginning with the simplest. Children who could do the fewest tasks successfully seemed to be the most likely candidates for special services. Although

What is "intelligence," and is it based more on heredity or on environmental factors? If the answers seem obvious, think again. Research in these areas has been full of good intentions, questionable results, and dramatic controversies. —Lew Merrim/Monkmeyer

Binet cautioned against using the test for any purpose other than the one for which he designed it, people quickly generalized the process.

Psychologists in the United States took an early and leading role in adapting Binet's procedures—with terrible results, according to science historian Stephen Jay Gould: "If Binet's principles had been followed, and his tests used as he intended, we would have been spared a major misuse of science in this century."[20] First, Henry Goddard of Vineland, New Jersey, translated Binet's items from French into English, and then Lewis Terman, a professor at Stanford University, revised the items for American use. This form of the test became known as the Stanford-Binet Intelligence Scale. (Figure 4.2 shows the normal curve for the fourth edition of the scale). Designed primarily for use with children, the test required one to identify objects that were common to everyone's experience and to perform sequenced tasks that depended on memory and visual-spacial perceptions. The objects were presented as fairly realistic miniatures or were depicted in simple sketches, with each being shown on a separate card so they could be displayed one at a time.

The Stanford-Binet test was administered by an adult to one child at a time. By asking many children of different ages to perform sequenced tasks and to identify objects or sketches, the test makers arrived at a "Standard Average Score" for each age; "norm tables" summarized the scores and ages, beginning at age two. It was *assumed* that everyone had been exposed to basic skills and knowledge, and so differences in performance must result mainly from differences in "general ability." Although the Stanford-Binet eventually came to in-

[20]Stephen Jay Gould, *The Mismeasurement of Man* (New York: Norton, 1981), 155.

FIGURE 4.2   Normal Curve for the 4th Edition of the Stanford-Binet
Intelligence Scale

IQ	67	68	78	79	88	89	110	111	120	121	131	132	IQ

Mentally Retarded	Slow Learner	Low Average	Average	High Average	Superior	Very Superior

←——————————————— Ability Classification ———————————————→

Source: Robert L. Thorndike, Elizabeth P. Hagen, and Jerome M. Sattler, "Stanford-Binet Intelligence Scale," *Technical Manual*, 4th ed. (Chicago: Riverside, 1984), tab. C.1, p. 127.

clude fifteen subtests (such as vocabulary, verbal relations, copying, paper folding and cutting, memory for digits), the test's *Technical Manual* emphasized that all the subtests measured *g*, that is, "mental energy," or "primary mental ability."[21]

Terman's and Goddard's work led to the concept of an **intelligence quotient (IQ)**. The idea was to find the test taker's "mental age," or **mental level**, by seeing which Standard Average Score was closest to the individual's raw score on the test. This then became the person's mental age and was expressed in years and months. Then the person's actual chronological age—also expressed in years and months—could be divided into the mental age to yield a ratio, or quotient. Multiplying this by 100 gets rid of the decimal and results in the IQ.

It should be noted that the Standard Average Score was often not very different from one age to another. For example, a twelve-year-old with a raw score of 23 was average; 5 points less would yield a mental age of nine, while 5 points more would yield a mental age of fifteen years, eight months. Thus the difference between an IQ of 120 and 80 might actually reflect only a 10-point difference in a child's performance on the test.[22] (Figures 4.3 and 4.4 show the performance norms of various groups of students, depending on ethnicity and parents' occupations.)

In 1917 Harvard Professor Robert Yerkes developed two forms of group tests to help the U.S. Army select potential officers. Known as the Army Alpha and Beta tests, these were the first IQ tests to be administered on a large scale. Yerkes and others analyzed the test results and found reinforcement for their beliefs that the most intelligent Americans had family roots in northern Europe, particularly in Great Britain, Scandinavia, and Germany. As Terman wrote about two Native American and Mexican children who had taken his test:

[21]Robert L. Thorndike, Elizabeth P. Hagen, and Jerome M. Sattler, *The Stanford-Binet Intelligence Scale: Fourth Edition, Technical Manual* (Chicago: Riverside, 1986), 1–32.
[22]Ibid., 136.

Comparative Perspective on Today's Issues . . .

◆ **DOES TRACKING SUPPORT EDUCATIONAL INEQUALITY?**

The Issue   During the 1920s and 1930s high school curricula became more differentiated as education became more compulsory. The application of differentiated curricula became known as *tracking*, and the tracks seemed to coincide with society's social-class structure. During the 1960s and 1970s, as equality of educational opportunity became a national goal, the practice of tracking came under attack.

YES   During the 1980s educational policy makers began to focus on academic excellence, and the goal of equal educational opportunity lost momentum. Those seeking academic excellence assume that it is sacrificed when schools stress social equality, but such an assumption is likely to "lock schools into patterns that make it difficult to achieve *either* excellence *or* equality" (290). Tracking is an example of how schools claim to be committed to excellence and equality while they provide curricula that encourage neither ideal. Instead, tracking places the highest academic hurdles in front of poor and minority students, thereby perpetuating educational and economic inequalities. Data on student outcomes in tracked settings support the argument that tracking can "*prevent* rather than *promote* educational goals" (291).

—*Jeannie Oakes, Associate Professor, UCLA, and Social Scientist, Rand Corporation*

NO   Despite the criticism of tracking, it represents a common, long-standing educational practice: that of ability grouping. As soon as a teacher divides a class into those who know something and those who do not, tracking has occurred. As far as inequality of educational opportunity is concerned, no one should suppose that it occurs simply by putting all students into the same type of class. Trying to treat all children exactly the same actually results in the most dangerous form of inequality, for it ignores individual differences.

In fact, research supports tracking by demonstrating that there is little effect on achievement levels of average or below-average students. Indeed, appropriate tracking—that promotes structures which enhance individual differences and needs—can help low-level students to move toward higher achievement levels; they will be less likely to get lost in classes that are learning material which is intellectually out of their reach.

—*Charles Nevi, Director, Curriculum and Instruction, Puyallup School District, Washington*

Source: Based on James Wm. Noll, ed., *Taking Sides: Clashing Views on Controversial Educational Issues*, 5th ed. (Guilford, Conn.: Dushkin, 1989), 288–305.

Their dullness seems to be racial, or at least inherent in the family stocks from which they come. The fact that one meets this type with such extraordinary frequency among Indians, Mexicans, and negroes suggests quite forcibly that . . . there will be discovered enormously significant racial differences . . . which cannot be wiped out by any scheme of mental culture.[23]

Goddard asked, "How can there be such a thing as social equality with this wide range of mental capacity?"[24] Terman worried about preventing "as far as possible the propagation of mental degenerates."[25] Many of the early proponents of intelligence testing were active in the eugenics movement, an organized effort that sought to change social policies in order to slow down or prevent

[23]Lewis M. Terman, *The Measurement of Intelligence* (Boston: Houghton Mifflin, 1916), 91–92.

[24]H. H. Goddard, "Mental Levels and Democracy," in Clarence J. Karier, ed., *Shaping the American Educational State, 1900 to the Present* (New York: Free Press, 1975), 186.

[25]Lewis M. Terman, "Feeble-minded Children in the Public Schools of California," *School and Society* 5 (1917): 161–165.

FIGURE 4.3   Ethnicity and Performance Norms on the Stanford-Binet (Ages 12 Through 18–23)

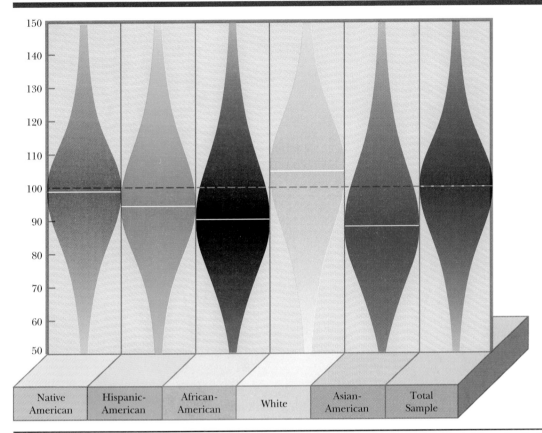

Source: Robert L. Thorndike, Elizabeth P. Hagen, and Jerome M. Sattler, "Stanford-Binet Intelligence Scale," *Technical Manual*, 4th ed. (Chicago: Riverside, 1984), tab. 4.5, p. 34.

"idiots," "imbeciles," criminals, and other "undesirables" from having children.

The new "science of mental levels" quickly found two applications of far-reaching significance. First, it resulted in the immigration law of 1924, which for the first time set quotas on the basis of national origin. In practice this law was anti-Semitic and racist, and it discouraged immigration from Latin and Slavic countries. Second, ability testing in schools became the basis for hiring "guidance counselors" who "guided" high school students (and their parents) into making "appropriate" curricular and career choices. Reinforced by "standardized tests," upper-middle-class students generally chose the college preparatory track; working-class or underclass students usually populated the vocational track, or they dropped out.

Educators embraced the testing movement for two main reasons: (1) because it was "scientific" and mathematically precise and (2) because it solved their problem of organizing unprecedented numbers of students who were staying in school longer—a result of changing economic and social conditions. Thus educators were ready to believe psychometricians, who told them that reliable and effective instruments were available to solve their problems "objectively."

FIGURE 4.4   Parental Occupation and Performance Norms on the Stanford-Binet (Ages Through 18–23)

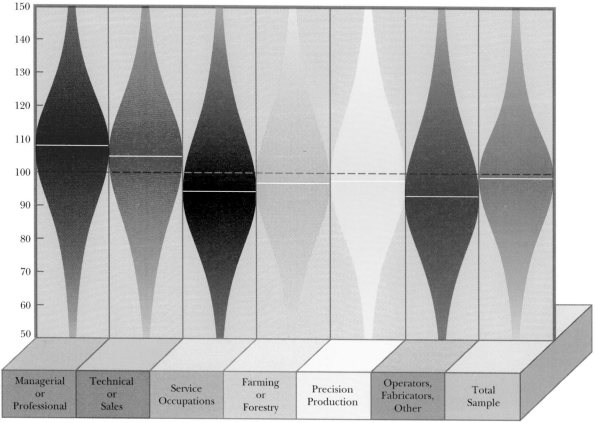

Source: Robert L. Thorndike, Elizabeth P. Hagen, and Jerome M. Sattler, "Stanford-Binet Intelligence Scale," *Technical Manual*, 4th ed. (Chicago: Riverside, 1984), tab. 4.5, p. 35.

The fact that the tests supported the status quo—the idea that those who had the most money and control were the people who *should* have them—may have helped the testing movement gain acceptance.

THE HEREDITY ARGUMENT

For standardizing testing to command general acceptance, scientific evidence was essential. This is why Cyril Burt's work was so important. No other researcher was able to find correlations that offered such solid support for the proposition that "general ability" was inherited. The fact that Burt's findings reached the intellectual community through the pages of a journal that he himself edited did not cause alarm for many years. But in the 1970s Leon Kamin, a psychologist at Princeton University, began to read Burt's reports carefully. He discovered contradictions, inconsistencies, and vague descriptions that gradually aroused suspicions. After carefully assessing Burt's work, Kamin concluded that "the numbers left by Professor Burt are simply not worthy of serious scientific attention." After examining three other reports of twin studies and three of "adoptive'' studies, Kamin reported that there was ''no unambiguous evidence what-ever in these studies for *any* heritability of IQ test scores.''[26]

What Burt had published was a comparison of fifty-three sets of identical twins reared apart and ninety-five sets of twins reared together. Based on group tests, the average correlation of the ninety-five pairs of twins reared together was .944. (Remember: Squaring this number yields an average estimate of the extent to which each pair of twins got similar test results—89 percent, in this case.) Twins reared apart produced a correlation of .771 (59 percent) on the group test. To minimize the substantial difference between 89 percent and 59 percent, Burt gave some twins individual tests (the Stanford-Binet), and he adjusted scores in some cases. He called the result of this process a ''final assessment'' correla-tion. For the twins reared together he ended up with .925 (86 percent), and for those reared apart the average was .874 (81 percent). Thus, using the latter correlation, Burt concluded that ''general intelligence'' was about 80 percent inherited.[27]

Arthur Jensen based his whole argument on Burt's estimate of intelligence being 80 percent inherited. Jensen concluded that schools can do little to change a child's ability if it is overwhelmingly inherited. That children from the under-class or lower working class scored about 30 points lower on IQ tests than did children from the upper middle class struck Jensen and others who accepted his basic assumptions as an unalterable fact of nature. Similarly, that some racial and ethnic minorities were disproportionately located in the bottom half of the social hierarchy was also simply a fact of nature for those who accepted the assumptions about inherited ability. Jensen advocated an academic curriculum for students who did well on IQ tests and a nonacademic course for those who did not.

RESEARCH SAYS

For Tomorrow's Education . . .

Studies of the heritability of intelligence continue to be conducted, and their results continue to be debated. Thomas Bouchard at the University of Minnesota has been involved in this research for many years. His recent findings support the notion that heredity plays a significant role in intelli-gence, as evidenced by data he collected about identical twins reared together or apart. However, other psychologists, such as Urie Bronffen-brenner at Cornell University, criticize Bouchard's report for continuing to generalize about environmental variables without analyzing their impact as was done with heredity variables. See Tina Adler, ''Seeing Double? Contro-versial Twins Study Is Widely Reported, Debated,'' *APA Monitor* 22 (January 1991): 1.

[26]Leon J. Kamin, "Heredity, Intelli-gence, Politics and Psychology," in *The Shaping of the American Educational State: 1900 to the Present*, Clarence J. Karier, ed. (New York: Free Press, 1975), 367–393.

[27]Cyril Burt, "The Genetic Deter-mination of Differences in Intelli-gence: A Study of Monozygotic Twins Reared Together and Apart," *British Journal of Psychology* 57 (1966): 137–153.

Cyril Burt received a knighthood for his research, but soon after his death in 1971 a scandal emerged. A historian of psychology named Leslie Hearnshaw undertook a biography and discovered—partly from Burt's own diaries and correspondence—that Sir Cyril had faked at least some of his data. Arthur Jensen took an indignant public stance about the controversy, but in a book defending his own hereditarian views he admitted that "all [Burt's] massive purported data on inheritance of mental ability must now be treated as worthless."[28]

More recently, the heredity argument has received renewed scientific support from experimental studies of identical twins reared apart. This investigation was conducted by psychologists at the University of Minnesota, who purport to have avoided Burt's methodological flaws.[29]

THE ENVIRONMENT ARGUMENT

ROSENTHAL AND JACOBSON   Even before it was known that Cyril Burt's twin studies were fraudulent, Leon Kamin concluded: "We had better build a better psychology; and we had better help to build, quickly, a better society."[30] Among those searching for a "better psychology" were a Harvard professor named Robert Rosenthal and a teacher named Lenore Jacobson. They described one of their experiments (and many related studies) in a book entitled *Pygmalion in the Classroom*. The title referred to George Bernard Shaw's play *Pygmalion* (better known as the Broadway musical and motion-picture *My Fair Lady*), which makes the argument that a person's social standing is an entirely artificial construct—that is, people's perceptions of us define who we are. This point is made in the story when Eliza Doolittle is transformed from an uneducated "flower girl" living on the streets of London into a "lady" simply by learning standard English pronunciation and usage and by acquiring the manners of "polite society." As Eliza puts it, when a significant person in her life threats her like a flower girl, she is a flower girl; and when she is treated like a lady, she is a lady. In short, Eliza becomes the person that significant others *expect* her to be.

Rosenthal called this phenomenon the **Pygmalion effect**, or the experimenter effect, and he set out to investigate the extent to which students' school performance is affected by the basic attitudes, expectations, and fundamental perceptions that their teachers have of them. To set up their experiment Rosenthal and Jacobson told elementary school teachers in a working-class section of California that they had developed a new test which would predict "early academic blooming." The new test was actually a standard IQ test that they had administered to students in each of the school's eighteen classrooms (six grades each divided into three classrooms designated "low," "middle," and "high"). Then, ignoring the actual test results, the two researchers *randomly selected* 20 percent of the students in each classroom and told their teachers that the test had selected these students as being likely to blossom—to do much better than they had been doing, whatever that was. Eight months later, they retested the students using the same test.

Between the two testing cycles, both the students who were designated as "bloomers" and those about whom nothing was predicted gained IQ points, but the "bloomers" gained an average of 4 points more. Rosenthal and others did additional studies, and Rosenthal identified the following four reasons to explain why students performed better when teachers' (or parents') expectations were high than when their expectations were not so high:

[28]Arthur R. Jensen, *Straight Talk about Mental Tests* (New York: Free Press, 1981), 124–127.

[29]Tina Adler, "Seeing Double? Controversial Twins Study Is Widely Reported, Debated," *APA Monitor* 22 (January 1991) 1: 1; citing the work of Thomas Bouchard on identical twins at the University of Minnesota.

[30]Kamin, "Heredity, Intelligence, Politics and Psychology," 393.

RESEARCH SAYS

For Tomorrow's Education . . .

Exceptional performance by students in the first grade was related to teachers' characteristics—especially their work conditions—and to students' maturity and academic self-image. Family background had a negligible effect, according to Aaron M. Pallas, Doris R. Entwistle, Karl L. Alexander, and Doris Cadigan. Their results are reported in "Children Who Do Exceptionally Well in First Grade," *Sociology of Education* 60 (October 1987): 257–271.

1. *Climate:* Teachers create a warmer socioemotional mood around students whom they regard as "special."

2. *Feedback:* Teachers give more positive assessments when students whom they expect to perform well do so, and they give *more negative analysis* to students who *don't perform well* when they expect them to.

3. *Input:* Teachers present more and harder material to students who are expected to perform well. "A teacher's expectations about a student's performance are not simply transmitted in subtle voice nuances and a casual facial expression. The expectations may be translated into explicit, overt alterations in teaching style and substance."

4. *Output:* Teachers give students whom they regard as able more opportunity to respond than they give to students whom they regard as less talented. This is seen both in the number of additional cues or prompts teachers give and in the amount of time teachers will wait for a response—usually they allow several seconds for able students to respond and often less than one second for students who are regarded as less able.[31]

Rosenthal and Jacobson found one other interesting phenomenon: Teachers had positive attitudes about those students in the 20 percent of "bloomers" *who did improve;* but they had *negative* feelings about students in the 80 percent not designated as bloomers *when those students did better than they had been doing.*

Rosenthal further explored teachers' attitudes by interviewing teachers in four schools, two with students from middle-income families and two with students from poor families. In each economic category one school's students were predominantly black, and the other's were white. Here are Rosenthal's conclusions:

> The teachers were much less favorable to the lower-class children than they were to the middle-class children; 40 percent of their comments about the poorer children were negative compared to 20 percent about the middle-class children. And the teachers were more likely to talk negatively about black children than white children, 43 percent to 17 percent. . . . I.Q. scores of the middle-income children, both black and white, were clearly related to the

[31]Robert Rosenthal, "The Pygmalion Effect Lives," *Psychology Today* (September 1973): 56–63.

positive attitudes of their teachers. This relationship did *not* hold for the low-income children; in fact, it was reversed. That is, lower-income children who had *higher* I.Q.s tended to have teachers who viewed them *negatively* and this was especially true for lower-income children who were black. The children who surpassed their teachers' expectations got resentment and complaints for their pains.

Thus children who are both black and lower-income have a double handicap. And this result cannot be attributed to white teachers' bias; both of the teachers of the black children were themselves black. The prejudice of stunted expectations knows no race barrier.[32]

RESEARCH SAYS

For Tomorrow's Education . . .

In a study completed by Deborah R. Dillon secondary low-track English-reading students who were low in SES and predominantly African-American were helped to increase their participation in lessons and their learning from them. This was accomplished through the caring attitude of the white male teacher, who constructed a social organization in the classroom that utilized the students' cultural background. He did this by (1) establishing a risk-free environment in which students could feel good about themselves; (2) planning activities that fit students' interests and structuring them to meet their needs; and (3) providing an atmosphere that encouraged students to be active, successful learners. See Deborah R. Dillon, "Showing Them That I Want Them to Learn and That I Care about Who They Are: A Microethnography of the Social Organization of a Secondary Low-Track English-Reading Classroom," *American Educational Research Journal* 26 (Summer 1989): 227–259. More recent studies support the importance of a caring attitude on the part of teachers. See Dwight Rogers and Jaci Webb, "The Ethic of Caring in Teacher Education," *Journal of Teacher Education* 42 (May–June 1991) 3: 173–181.

SKEELS   One of the most compelling studies which supports the view that environment is an important influence on ability was completed in 1966 by a psychologist named Harold Skeels. He started his professional life in the 1930s in Iowa, where he noticed a dramatic improvement in two young retarded orphans who had been affectionately "mothered" by an older retarded girl. To investigate this Skeels selected thirteen other young orphans (average IQ = 64, highest IQ = 89) and got them assigned to a ward for retarded older girls. He then selected a control group of children with similar characteristics, including IQ, who continued to live normally in the orphanage. Three years later children in the control group had lost an average of 20 IQ points, while those who were assigned to the older retarded girls had gained an average of 28 IQ points. Two years after that, eleven of the thirteen "mothered" children were adoptable, whereas no child in the control group had been placed in an adoptive home.

[32]Ibid., 63.

Several years later Skeels tracked down twenty-five of the twenty-six children in his study (one child in the control group had died at age fifteen). "The differences found in the adult life experiences of the two groups were enormous," as one author put it.[33] All thirteen children whose adopted "aunts" had given them individual care had become self-supporting adults, whereas five of the twelve remaining control-group children were still institutionalized. The six control-group children who were employed were earning only one-fourth as much as the children in the experimental group, who also had completed more than 2½ times as many years of school. Eleven members of the experimental group had gotten married, and they had twenty-eight children among them. Their children had an average IQ of 104; not one of them was retarded.

In 1966 Skeels published his study, and the Kennedy Foundation gave him an award for research. The young man who presented the award—although he had not known it until that time—was one of the thirteen children whom Skeels had gotten assigned to special care. "Shortly after the televised event, this formerly 'retarded' young man announced that he would probably switch careers and enroll in a doctoral program in child psychology." He had been working toward a master's degree in business administration.[34]

CONCLUSIONS

When asked, most Americans say that they are middle class. Yet society's class structure is based on many variables—such as income, educational attainment, family background, and living patterns—and there are large disparities in these variables. Social class and SES nonetheless continue to correlate positively with school success. Many educators are trying to overcome this relationship, however, since they believe that all children *can* learn and that schools must try to maximize learning. Such beliefs have led to widespread dissatisfaction with standardized testing, with curricular tracks based on tests, and with the assumption that academic talent is limited to a small percentage of the population.[35] Educators who are dissatisfied with tracking are convinced that it leads to inequality of educational opportunity. However, the debate about whether intelligence is influenced more by genetics or by the environment continues to rage. Proponents of the heredity argument believe that some populations are innately less intelligent than others, while advocates of the environmental argument believe that a person's intelligence is related to social and educational factors.

[33]Lewis P. Lipsitt and Hayne W. Reese, *Child Development* (Glenview, Ill.: Scott, Foresman, 1979), 53.
[34]Ibid.
[35]Jean Evangelauf, "Reliance on Multiple-Choice Tests Said to Harm Minorities and Hinder Reform; Panel Seeks a New Regulatory Agency," *Chronicle of Higher Education*, 30 May 1990, pp. 1, A31.

KEY TERMS

social class

socioeconomic status (SES)

upper class

upper working class

lower working class

underclass

social bifurcation

tracking

correlation

upper middle class

lower middle class

common-person class

intelligence

normal curve

Intelligence Quotient (IQ)

mental level

Pygmalion effect

SUGGESTED READINGS

Ken Auletta, *The Underclass* (New York: Random House, 1982). This book identifies and profiles the conditions and circumstances surrounding the plight of students from underclass settings. It is an ethnographic study.

D. G. Glasgow, *The Black Underclass: Poverty, Unemployment and Entrapment of Ghetto Youth* (San Francisco: Josey-Bass, 1980). This book describes the conditions that today's urban youth experience.

Mary R. Jackman and Robert R. Jackman, *Class Awareness in the United States* (Berkeley, Calif.: University of California Press, 1983). This book defines and analyzes the variables that constitute social class in America.

Clarence J. Karier, *The Individual, Society, and Education* (Urbana: University of Illinois Press, 1986).

Karier provides a psychological and historical picture of the development of education in American society.

Daniel V. Levine and Robert J. Havighurst, *Society and Education* (Boston: Allyn & Bacon, 1992). This book comprehensively presents the social and cultural topics and issues that influence education.

Joel Spring, *American Education: An Introduction to Social and Political Aspects* (New York: Longman, 1985). This book offers a current and comprehensive view of the major issues affecting education.

Stephen Jay Gould, *The Mismeasurement of Man* (New York: Norton, 1981). This book presents a careful historical analysis of the mental-testing movement in America, including its impact on social and educational policies.

Education for Equity and Diversity

Sociological Foundations B

5

To endorse cultural pluralism is to endorse the principle that there is no one model American. . . . [It] is to understand and appreciate the differences that exist among the nation's citizens . . . as a positive force. . . . Cultural pluralism is more than a temporary accommodation to placate racial and ethnic minorities. It is a concept that aims toward a heightened sense of being and of wholeness of the entire society based on the unique strengths of each of its parts.

—American Association of Colleges for Teacher Education, "No One Model American:
A Statement of Multicultural Education" (Washington, D.C.: AACTE, 1972), 9

5

Education for Equity and Diversity

ADVANCED ORGANIZERS

In this chapter you will learn

What it means for a society to be multicultural, or culturally pluralistic

What the historical antecedents of cultural pluralism were

How schools have attempted to equalize educational opportunities in a multicultural society

How well minority groups achieve in American schools

What constitutes an effective school for minority students

How well females achieve in American schools

CHAPTER OUTLINE

SCHOOLING IN A MULTICULTURAL SOCIETY
  Evolution of Cultural Pluralism
  Discrimination and Minority Groups
  Equalizing Educational Opportunities
  Federal Funding and Discrimination

NATIVE AMERICANS AS A MINORITY GROUP
  European Policies in North America
  The Politics of Self-Determination

MINORITY STUDENTS IN THE SCHOOLS
  Theories about Learning Problems
  New Patterns of Segregation
  Academic Achievement of Minority Students
  Dropout Rates of Minority Students
  Influences on Academic Performance of Minority Students

GENDER AND EDUCATION
  Access to Education
  Purposes of Education
  Curricular Differences
  Power Relations Between the Sexes

CONCLUSIONS

R osita lives in a lower-working-class neighborhood in San Antonio, not far from the city's downtown business area. She is eleven and is in fifth grade at the nearby elementary school. Like most Hispanic students in her class, Rosita is bilingual. Her teacher is Hispanic also and grew up in the same neighborhood. In fact, 80 percent of the school's students are from minority groups (primarily African-American and Hispanic). Seven years ago the school implemented a bilingual program so that instruction is given in both English and Spanish; before then, teachers spoke only English in the classroom.

Rosita is described as polite, conscientious, and friendly. She is talkative except in large-group discussions, when she is somewhat shy and withdrawn. Unfortunately, most instruction does involve large groups. The teacher has concluded that Rosita has limited abilities, because she has trouble conveying information in English even though her vocabulary is adequate. She communicates much better in Spanish, but her academic vocabulary is less extensive than in English. After evaluation by an educational consultant who observed Rosita in various settings, it was determined that her language skills are not limited; instead, the classroom environment does not encourage her to use them fully and express herself.

SCHOOLING IN A MULTICULTURAL SOCIETY

Rosita was lucky because her educational situation was changed and she now can perform better in the smaller groups and one-to-one settings that the school has provided. Her problems, however, are not unique in a society that includes so many cultural traditions and so many racial and ethnic groups. Probably more than any nation the United States can be described as **multicultural**, or **pluralistic**, in that our society is composed of many racial and ethnic groups that voluntarily live and work together while acknowledging and recognizing their original cultures.

Many ethnic and racial groups contribute to America's pluralism. The dominant, or majority, group is white (about 83 percent of the population), followed by African-Americans (around 12 percent) and Native Americans (more than 3 percent). In addition, each of these groups includes people whose Spanish-speaking ancestors came from Europe and from countries in Central and South America. Known collectively as Hispanics, they compose about 9 percent of the population (no one really knows, because many enter the country illegally). By the year 2000 the Hispanic population is expected to be close to 11 or 12 percent and growing.[1] All other ethnic groups—including Asian-Americans—make up less than 2 percent of the U.S. population.

For demographic purposes Hispanic Americans (mainly Mexican and Puerto Rican), African-Americans, Native Americans, and Asian-Americans are generally classified as **minority groups**, and—except for Asian-Americans—most

[1] Daniel V. Levine and Robert J. Havighurst, *Society and Education* (Boston: Allyn & Bacon, 1992), 366. The growth rate of the Hispanic population is expected to exceed that for both whites and African-Americans.

have become disproportionately stranded in lower social classes. They thus are said to have low socioeconomic status (SES). As we saw in Chapter 4, because SES and educational attainment are so closely related—and because minority groups make up such a large proportion of lower classes—minority students do not generally achieve as much in school nor climb so far up the educational ladder as their majority classmates do. A look at history will help us understand America's multicultural heritage and its implications for education.

EVOLUTION OF CULTURAL PLURALISM

It is often repeated that the United States is a "melting pot," a country of immigrants from many lands. In fact, the parents, grandparents, or great-grandparents of most Americans were born in foreign countries and emigrated to the United States as children. Yet, as Figure 5.1 shows, the patterns of immigration have not always been the same. During the colonial period, for example, other than the shiploads of Africans and Jamaicans who had been sold into slavery, most immigrants came from Great Britain and the Protestant areas of Europe. And because the largest number of people came from Great Britain, English became the new country's dominant language.

By the middle of the nineteenth century the immigration pattern shifted to include many Catholic, non–English-speaking groups, particularly the Irish, Italians, and Germans. Beyond the colonies, opportunities for schooling and a respectable livelihood on the expanding American frontier continued to beckon to foreigners, and the immigration rate surged as the twentieth century approached. From 1870 to 1920 the immigration pattern shifted again, this time to include many East European groups (Poles, Greeks, Hungarians, Russians, and other Slavic peoples). Meanwhile, the country was changing from an agri-

FIGURE 5.1   Legal Immigrants and Where They Came From

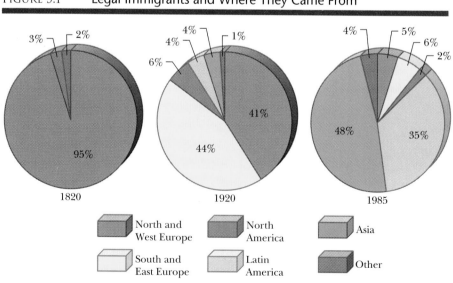

Source: Based on data from the U.S. Census Bureau.

cultural to an industrial society, and these new Americans found their economic opportunities in the factories and foundries of large cities. Thus Chicago, for example, doubled its population in just five years (from 1885 to 1890 it grew from 629,985 to 1,205,669), becoming a city in which 80 percent of its people were foreign-born. Over the next two decades—from 1890 to 1910—its population increased by a million.[2]

RESEARCH SAYS

For Tomorrow's Education . . .

Multicultural education during the 1970s and 1980s was not very different from practices in the 1940s, when the concept of pluralism was recognized. See Michael R. Olneck, "The Recurring Dream: Symbolism and Ideology in Intercultural and Multicultural Education," *American Journal of Education* 98 (February 1990): 147–174.

The most recent dramatic shift in immigration began in the 1960s and has drawn many people from Asian and Latin American countries. By the late 1980s nearly half of legal immigrants were from Asia, and at least one-third were from Latin America. Overwhelmingly these people have been drawn to the largest coastal cities, particularly to New York and Los Angeles, but large numbers also have settled in Miami, Chicago, San Francisco, San Diego, and Houston.

DISCRIMINATION AND MINORITY GROUPS

Although slaves were emancipated as a result of the Civil War, African-Americans have long experienced social, economic, and educational hardships as racism continued and as immigrants displaced them in the marketplace. Ethnic tensions also have been strong enough to erupt into public disorder, such as in Chicago's Haymarket Square riot of 1886. At such times great hope has always been placed in the ability of schools to act as the "melting pot." Here was the place where ethnic groups would be transformed through **cultural assimilation** into an "Americanized" population that basically espoused Anglo-American ideals and values. In schools as in society generally, the white Anglo-Saxon Protestant (WASP) became the dominant cultural identity.

During and after World War I the large number of non-Anglo, non-northern European immigrants led to restrictions on immigration quotas. Thus, by 1924 the proportions of various immigrant groups that were allowed to enter through ports like Ellis Island had to conform to the ethnic proportions that existed in the 1890 American census, when the Anglo, northern European percentages were higher than they became in the 1920 census. The quotas became a particular problem in the 1930s for Jewish immigrants seeking to escape Hitler's Third Reich.[3]

The concept of the "melting pot"—and the value of cultural assimilation and conformity—gradually lost its social and educational grip as Jews, Hispanics,

[2]Joan K. Smith, *Ella Flagg Young: Portrait of a Leader* (Ames, Iowa: Educational Studies Press, Iowa State University Research Foundation, 1979), 40.

[3]Leon J. Kamin, "Heredity, Intelligence, Politics and Psychology," in *The Shaping of the American Educational State: 1900 to the Present*, Clarence J. Karier, ed. (New York: Free Press, 1975), 367–393.

Survival on the American frontier demanded that Europeans learn from the people who already understood the environment; but Europeans saw no need to learn about the educational techniques that Native Americans used in rearing their young. —Bettmann

and African-Americans sought to retain their cultural roots and identities. By the 1970s assimilation was replaced by the idea of cultural pluralism, or **biculturalism**. Unfortunately for African-Americans and Hispanics, however, discrimination had become entrenched over the years, and African-Americans in particular had been stranded in the lower social strata of American cities. By the 1950s many Americans were working to eliminate discrimination and to equalize social opportunities and civil rights.

EQUALIZING EDUCATIONAL OPPORTUNITIES

In education the practice of discriminatory policies dated to 1896, when the U.S. Supreme Court in *Plessy v. Ferguson* established the standard of "separate but equal accommodations" for black people and white people. This became the legal basis for segregation in education, so that African-American children were placed in separate schools that generally were inferior to schools for white children. In the South two entirely separated school systems arose and resulted in **de jure segregation**, or segregation "under the law." Nor was the North free of racial inequality in education. Since patterns of housing were segregated, that allowed affluent white neighborhoods to provide better schools for white children; in this case the result was **de facto segregation** (segregation "in fact").

It took fifty-eight years for the "separate but equal" standard to be overturned by federal court decisions rendered in the famous cases of *Brown v. the Board of Education of Topeka* (1954 and 1955). In these two landmark cases the courts ruled that both de jure and de facto segregation of schoolchildren by race was illegal, and that the country's educational system must be desegregated with "all deliberate speed."

Bringing an end to segregated schools and housing patterns was not easy for the federal government, because these matters came under state and local jurisdictions, not federal. Finally, at the urging of President Lyndon B. Johnson, Congress passed the **Civil Rights Act of 1964**. As discussed in Chapter 2, this act gave the federal government the power to bring desegregation lawsuits into federal court and to deny federal aid to school systems that did not comply with desegregation regulations. For Hispanic students *Cisneros v. Corpus Christi Independent School District* (1970) brought an end to legal (de jure) segregation.

RESEARCH SAYS

For Tomorrow's Education . . .

Academic achievement can be improved in underclass and minority students when certain cultural boundaries are crossed. For a discussion and an example of this crossing of boundaries see Diane S. Pollard, "Against the Odds: A Profile of Academic Achievers from the Urban Underclass," *Journal of Negro Education* 58 (Summer 1989): 297–300; and "Teachers Alter Roles in Language," *New York Times*, 16 April 1992.

Ending the problem of de facto segregation has been much more difficult, given the complexities and subtleties that support it. People's attitudes, of course, are part of the problem (see Figure 5.2 for a specific example). But even when school districts are redrawn to compensate for segregated housing patterns, or when children are bused to schools outside their neighborhood, students are often grouped or tracked by academic achievement records, which continues to segregate them.

FEDERAL FUNDING AND DISCRIMINATION

Despite housing patterns that lead to de facto segregation, the federal government has continued to enact legislation to remediate discriminatory practices. In 1965, as part of President Johnson's "War on Poverty," Congress also passed the **Elementary and Secondary Education Act (ESEA)**, which aimed to alleviate educational inequality by providing financial aid to disadvantaged schools, whether public or parochial (see Chapter 2). About 78 percent of the money was earmarked for educational programs for disadvantaged students, money that came from Title I of the act (now called Chapter I). The other five titles provided resources to implement the programs funded through Title I. In 1972, Title VI was amended to include provisions for the educationally handicapped, and titles

FIGURE 5.2   Racial Attitudes in Chicago, 1993: Willingness to Mix

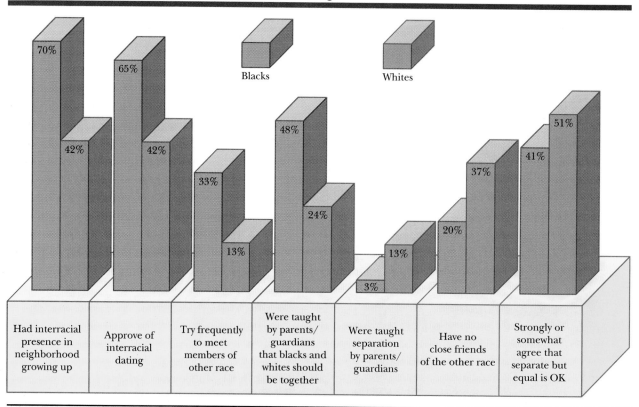

Source: "The Great Divide: Racial Attitudes in Chicago," *Chicago Sun-Times*, January 10, 1993, p. 16.

VII and VIII were added to the original six. (Title VII provided revenue for bilingual education, and Title VIII funded dropout prevention programs.) Thus money from ESEA and other federal projects was spent to improve educational facilities, equipment, teacher aids, and other materials designed to correct, or "compensate" for, deficiencies in the disadvantaged backgrounds and lifestyles of lower-income (mostly minority) children. Known as **compensatory education**, these programs also included preschool education, through projects like Head Start.

Meanwhile, federal desegregation guidelines were set to withhold ESEA and other federal monies from school districts that were not making satisfactory progress. In 1964 Congress commissioned an extensive study to assess conditions in the nation's schools and the magnitude of the problem of educational inequality. Directed by sociologist James Coleman of the University of Chicago, the study was completed and published in 1966. Entitled *Equality of Educational Opportunity*, but better known as the **Coleman report**, the study related that 80 percent of white first- and twelfth-grade students were attending public schools that were 90 to 100 percent white. The study concluded that the achievement gap between majority students and minority students continues to widen through the elementary grades and that "the facilities and the curriculums of the schools

Mary McCleod Bethune
1875–1955

One of the first African-Americans to hold a prominent government office, under President Franklin D. Roosevelt, Mary McLeod Bethune is considered an early champion of civil rights. First and foremost, however, she was an educator. Born in 1875 to former slaves, Mary was the youngest of fifteen children, and the only one who was born free. Her parents struggled so that she could attend the local Presbyterian Mission School for Negroes; she later continued her education at Barber-Scotia College in North Carolina and at Chicago's Moody Bible Institute, from which she graduated in 1895.

After college McLeod taught at Haines Institute in Augusta, Georgia, and then at Kindall Institute in Sumter, South Carolina, where in 1897 she met and married fellow teacher Albertus Bethune. The following year their only child, Alber McCleod Bethune, was born, and soon after she moved with her son to Palaatka, Florida, to teach at a school for African-American children. In 1904, concerned about the plight of black railroad workers, Bethune moved to Daytona Beach to open the Daytona

Normal and Industrial School for Girls. Within two years the school had 250 students—including boys.

For the next twenty years Bethune expanded the Daytona school to offer both day and night programs with academic, vocational, and religious curricula. She also opened a hospital for African-Americans, who were denied service at the local hospital. Prominent people vacationing in Daytona (including James M. Gamble, of

Yesterday's Professional

Procter and Gamble) became her friends and helped to support her school.

Bethune served on the National Child Welfare Commission under presidents Coolidge and Hoover, and she was vice-president of the National Urban League; during the Roosevelt administration she served as adviser and counselor on Negro education. In 1935 she founded the National Council of Negro Women (NCNW), and from 1936 to 1943 she was director of the Division of Minority Affairs under the National Youth Administration (NYA). In 1945 she was a special representative to the San Francisco conference that established the United Nations.

The Daytona School became Bethune-Cookman College, and until her death Bethune was one of the most prominent and most influential women in America. She died of a heart attack in Daytona on May 18, 1955.

account for relatively little variation in pupil achievement" as measured by standard tests.[4] The report implied that school achievement depended more on a student's social class and family background.

NATIVE AMERICANS AS A MINORITY GROUP

Although Europeans began to explore and colonize the New World about five centuries ago, for more than half that time—until the early nineteenth century—people of native American ancestry outnumbered Europeans of all kinds. Strictly in terms of numbers, then, those who traced their roots back to pre-European discovery were not "minorities." In every way except for numbers,

[4]James Coleman et al., *Equality of Educational Opportunity* (Washington, D.C.: U.S. Government Printing Office, 1966), 3, 20–21.

however, Americans of native ancestry were usually dominated whenever they came into regular contact with Europeans. Such **hegemony** (dominance or authority) of European language, culture, economy, military force, and religion is of primary significance in understanding the educational development of Native American groups. Europeans were eager to acquire the land, raw materials, products, and crafts of Native Americans. In return they offered Christianity, alcohol, economic exploitation, and limited access to schooling in European languages—mainly Spanish, English, Portuguese, or French.

From the very beginning, European countries exhibited mixed motives in colonizing newly discovered territories in Africa, in the Pacific, and in North and South America. Governments sought economic and military advantages in the nationalistic competition that involved most ambitious European countries. And most Christians welcomed new converts—not only because conversion was part of Christianity's inherent beliefs but also because the competition was intense among Christian subgroups reacting to the sixteenth-century Reformation.

EUROPEAN POLICIES IN NORTH AMERICA

Europeans generally assumed that any people they might encounter in colonizing would need to be "civilized" and converted to Christianity. The Spanish founded missions in what are now Florida, Texas, New Mexico, Arizona, and California. The French did the same in Canada and the Mississippi Valley, and the English planned to instruct natives in Massachusetts and Virginia. "Compel a Barbarous People to Civilitie" was the way one English author put it.[5] Some natives adopted European dress, religion, language, and attitudes, but many resisted assimilation.

For a time Europeans assumed that Native Americans who did not want to assimilate could continue to live as they had, but outside the areas that Europeans wanted for themselves. Thus began the long history of broken treaties, massacres, and forced moves to reservations—and then more forced moves to new reservations as European settlers demanded the land of earlier reservations.

Native Americans taught the Europeans new techniques of farming, cooking, hunting, architecture, healing, and fighting. Indeed, survival demanded that European immigrants learn from the people who already understood the environment. But Europeans did not see any need to learn about the educational techniques that Native Americans used in rearing their young. Instead, Europeans thought of themselves as having "no higher calling in the world than to be missionaries of our idea to those people who have not yet reached the Anglo-Saxon frame of mind," to quote the U.S. commissioner of education.[6] This idea eventually included the native populations of Samoa, Hawaii, Puerto Rico, and Alaska, when they came under U.S. rule during the nineteenth century.

The nation's commissioner of education spoke in 1872 of saving the children of Alaska "from growing up in the grossest ignorance and barbarism."[7] His successor in 1902 described exactly what this meant:

> If the natives of Alaska could be taught the English language, be brought
> under Christian influences by the missionaries and trained into forms of in-

[5]Thinking of conquered peoples in colonial territories as barbarous and uncivilized was a common attitude among seventeenth- and eighteenth-century Europeans. For a discussion of this attitude and related educational practices see L. Glenn Smith, " 'Compel a Barbarous People to Civilitie': The Roots of Compulsory Education in America," in *Conference Papers for the Eighth Session of The International Standing Conference for the History of Education*, 6 vols., Giovanni Genovesi, ed. (Parma, Italy: Universita di Parma, Bollettino C.I.R.S.E., 1986), 1: 291–301.

[6]William Torrey Harris to Julia Ward Howe, 22 January 1901, Outgoing Correspondence of the Commissioner of Education, Record Group 12, National Archives of the United States, Washington, D.C.

[7]*Report of the Commissioner of Education for the Year 1872* (Washington, D.C.: U.S. Government Printing Office, 1873), 134.

Comparative Perspective on Today's Issues . . .

◆ *SHOULD LITERACY BE BASED ON THE DOMINANT CULTURE?*

The Issue   Traditionally our schools have taught only the knowledge that came from the dominant culture, and they have imparted skills and knowledge through one language only—American English. Recently, with the greater awareness of biculturalism and biliteracy, such policies and practices are being questioned.

YES   During the 1980s such education critics as Allen Bloom (*How Higher Education Has Failed Democracy and Impoverished the Souls of Today's Students*, 1987) and Mortimer Adler ("Paideia Proposal: Rediscovering the Essence of Education," *American School Board Journal*, July 1982) raised a call to redirect education back to the study of works that reflected America's European heritage. All U.S. citizens—whatever their socioeconomic status—need to be able to participate in the national culture; this means that schools must teach and expose students to a common body of materials.

—*E. D. Hirsch, Jr., Professor, Department of English, University of Virginia*

NO   Other critics are concerned that education so strongly emphasizes the Eurocentric perspective. Ira Schor's book *Culture Wars: School and Society in the Conservative Restoration, 1969–1984* (1987) claims that the underlying motivation for basing literacy on the dominant culture is that it allows society's conservative elements to establish authority from the top down, while discounting the liberal perspective of the 1960s. Students do not become enculturated by learning bits and pieces of traditional culture in a structured sequence. Cultural literacy is a product of several contexts besides the school, including the home, the neighborhood, and the workplace.

—*Stephen Tchudi, Director, Center for Literacy and Learning, Michigan State University*

Source Based on James Wm. Noll, ed., *Taking Sides: Clashing Views on Controversial Educational Issues*, 5th ed. (Guilford, Conn.: Dushkin, 1989), 220–237.

dustry suitable for the territory, it seems to follow as a necessary result that the white population of Alaska, composed of immigrants from the States, would be able to employ them in their pursuits, using their labor to assist in mining, transportation, and the producing of food.[8]

On another occasion the same commission explained that the best curriculum would be the works of Shakespeare, Dickens, Walter Scott, and their like, because these authors would "arouse and kindle the sluggish minds of the natives of Alaska with sentiments and motives of action which lead our civilization."[9] Not all teachers brought such condescending attitudes to their work, of course, but few could neutralize the effects of this widely held belief in the superiority of the "Anglo-Saxon frame of mind."

Beginning in 1934 the **Indian Reorganization Act** increased the power and self-governing responsibilities of the Native American tribal councils. The Indian Education Act of 1972, augmented in 1975, brought more self-determination in educational matters. Both separatism and assimilation have proponents among

[8]*Report of the Commissioner of Education for the Year 1896–97*, 2 vols. (Washington, D.C.: U.S. Government Printing Office, 1898), 1: xiv.

[9]William Torrey Harris, "Memorandum on Alaskan Text Books," typescript in a folder marked "Commissioner Harris, 1889–June, 1906, Record Group 12, National Archives of the United States, Washington, D.C.

Native Americans. Some see bilingual instruction (which has been widely practiced since the early 1970s) primarily as a way to learn English; others think bilingual instruction is empowering, because it gives children pride in their native tongue and leads to greater self-acceptance and a better self-concept.[10]

THE POLITICS OF SELF-DETERMINATION

For Native Americans, increased community control over schooling has also brought an increase in segregated education. The founding of more than twenty community colleges run for and by Native Americans, and the better staffing of reservation schools, has led to higher enrollments in schools that are exclusively or predominantly Native American. Some people have argued that segregated schools—even when they are preferred by the minority group—cannot offer high-quality education, but there is good research evidence to the contrary.[11]

Integrated schools with a majority of Anglo teachers and administrators are sometimes less friendly and less supportive than schools that are all Native American, Eskimo, or Aleut.[12] Overreliance on standardized tests in majority schools may seriously underestimate the abilities of Native American students.[13] When the self-concept of students is undermined, ''scholastic demoralization'' often occurs. This phenomenon (which is the opposite of the Pygmalion effect discussed in Chapter 4) ''begins several years before entry into high school [and] is a primary cause of educational marginality and dropping out.''[14]

The educational issues confronting Native Americans are similar in most respects to those facing students of Hispanic backgrounds. Among the factors

[10]Daniel McLaughlin, "The Sociolinguistics of Navajo Literacy, *Anthropology & Education Quarterly* 20 (December 1989): 275–289.

[11]Linda Pertusati, "Beyond Segregation or Integration: A Case Study from Effective Native American Education," *Journal of American Indian Education* 27, 2 (January 1988): 10–19; and Pauline Rindone, "Achievement Motivation and Academic Achievement of Native American Students," *Journal of American Indian Education* 28, 1 (October 1988): 1–7.

[12]Daniel Sanders, "Cultural Conflicts: An Important Factor in the Academic Failures of American Indian Students," *Journal of Multicultural Counseling and Development* 15, 2 (April 1987): 81–90.

[13]William Brescia and Jim C. Fortune, "Standardized Testing of American Indian Students," Office of Educational Research and Improvement (Washington, D.C., 1988), 13 pp., ED 296 813.

[14]Norman F. Watt et al., "Psychological Study of Educational Attainment Among Hispanics" (Colorado State Department of Education, 1987), 68 pp., ED 298 198; and Benjamin Lloyd Atencio, "Perceptions of High School Climate in New Mexico: American Indian Enrollment as a Variable," Ph.D. dissertation (Arizona State University, 1988), 232 pp.

Integrated schools with a majority of Anglo teachers and administrators are sometimes less friendly and less supportive than schools that are entirely populated by the minority group they serve. —Eastcott-M./The Image Works

RESEARCH SAYS

For Tomorrow's Education . . .

Native American students can benefit from more cooperative learning environments that acknowledge their cultures' different belief systems. See Helen M. Thilde and Lawrence D. Shriberg, "Effects of Recurrent Otitis Media on Language, Speech, and Educational Achievement of Menominee Indian Children," *Journal of American Indian Education* 29 (January 1990): 25–43; and Carol Locust, "Wounding the Spirit: Discrimination and Traditional American Indian Belief Systems," *Harvard Educational Review* 58 (August 1988): 315–330.

contributing to lower educational achievement are the need for literacy in two languages, a preference for cooperative learning styles, internalized feelings of personal and academic marginality, families with severely limited incomes, and restricted employment opportunities—especially for males and for those without a bachelor's degree. One challenge for a democratic society is to find ways to creae true equality of educational opportunity for members of minority groups that historically have been underserved.

MINORITY STUDENTS IN THE SCHOOLS

Figure 5.3 compares the 1976 and 1990 minority-group enrollments in American schools. You might want to return to this figure from time to time as you read about minority students' problems and achievements—and the factors that influence both.

THEORIES ABOUT LEARNING PROBLEMS

That minority students were disproportionately stranded in the lowest social classes and that such an impoverished environment was related to low academic achievement led many educators to formulate the **cultural deprivation theory** to account for the learning problems of minority students. It was claimed that the culture of poverty into which minority students were socialized resulted in a lack of academic success.[15] Thus compensatory education programs were seen as a means of remediating the impoverished environment and faulty socialization of minority students.

By the late 1960s and early 1970s—when it looked as though most compensatory education programs had fallen short of the mark—the idea of cultural deprivation came under sharp attack by educators who looked for other explanations. Harvard sociologist Christopher Jencks re-analyzed the data collected in the Coleman study and concluded that, while schooling and SES were closely

[15]James A. Banks, "Ethnicity, Class, Cognitive, and Motivational Styles: Research and Teaching Implications," *Journal of Negro Education* 57 (Fall 1988): 452–460.

FIGURE 5.3   Minority-Group Enrollment in U.S. Schools, 1976 and 1990

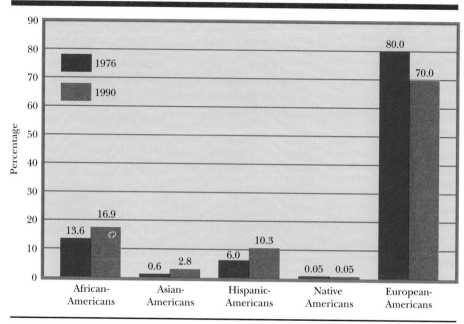

related, these variables did not determine how much a person would be paid in the job market. In *Inequality: A Reassessment of the Effect of Family and Schooling in America* (1972) Jencks argued that economic success depends both on some on-the-job competence and on random factors like luck. For example, if we examined a sample of U.S. lawyers who came from similar backgrounds and who all had IQs of 130 + when they were eighteen years old, we would discover that their incomes varied greatly. According to Jencks, compensatory education will not affect economic disparities, and he proposed that wage levels be guaranteed for certain occupational categories.[16]

Other education experts returned to Jensen's and Burt's emphasis on heredity to explain the failure of compensatory education. Still others supported psychological or sociological explanations related to Rosenthal's Pygmalion effect and Skeels's nurturing study (see Chapter 4 for a summary of these arguments).

Another explanation that arose during the 1970s, as compensatory education programs failed, was the **learning disabilities theory**. It was claimed that compensatory education had failed because it sought to bring minority students up to some "mythical norm" of achievement. In contrast, disabilities theory stated that minority students have *different* cognitive styles, different ways of thinking and learning that need to be diagnosed and treated. Thus inner-city schoolteachers have to be able to identify and prescribe for "particular and discrete 'learning problems.'" This approach gained strong support among educators, and many programs based on such theories qualified for federal money. Today learning disability theory and training are a major focus of most teacher preparation programs.[17]

[16]Christopher Jencks et al., *Inequality: A Reassessment of the Effect of Family and Schooling in America* (New York: Basic Books, 1972), 226–232.

[17]Joan K. Smith and L. Glenn Smith, *The Development of American Education: Selected Reading* (Ames, Iowa: Iowa State University, 1978), 233. Also see Louise R. White, "Effective Teachers for Inner City Schools," *Journal of Negro Education* 42 (1973): 308–314.

The theories about minority students' learning problems have not borne as much fruit as would be hoped. Unfortunately, educational integration and equality of opportunity have remained unrealized goals. While some compensatory education programs, such as Head Start, have had moderate success, their minority graduates continue to achieve less in school than majority students do. Some educators continue to account for this with genetic theories like those put forth by Jensen and Burt (see Chapter 4). But other educators, psychologists, and sociologists point to students' environments—both at home and in the classroom—saying that they inhibit minority students from learning. Learning disability theories continue to find strong support among educational psychologists. (Chapter 6 discusses theories of learning and cognition.)

NEW PATTERNS OF SEGREGATION

Despite legal restrictions on segregation, the proportion of minority students who attend minority-dominated schools has remained high. For example, 64 percent of African-American students and 71 percent of Hispanic students attend schools in which more than half the students are from minority groups; about one-third of all African-American and Hispanic students attend schools that enroll more than 90 percent minority students.[18] Among the many reasons for this de facto form of segregation is what might be called "white flight" into the suburbs. Especially during the 1970s and early 1980s white middle-class families who lived in large cities began to move to the suburbs, where schools and educational opportunities promised to be better. As white people left the cities, minority families moved into the vacated neighborhoods, hugely increasing the minority population of most urban schools. (Minority families also move to the suburbs, of course. Figure 5.4 gives an interesting comparison of suburban and city attitudes among African-Americans and whites.)

Mandatory busing, which once aimed to alleviate segregated patterns of schooling, has proved to be impractical. Given the long distances and commuting times that often are involved in busing students out of their neighborhoods, parents and communities have opposed mandatory busing (voluntary transportation to schools—if parents want it—is still an option in many school districts). For many reasons the steps to desegregate schools that were taken during the 1970s have turned out to be temporary, and new patterns of segregation began to emerge in the 1980s.

This trend can be seen in Chicago's public schools, where African-American and Hispanic students now make up about 83 percent of the enrollment; Asian-Americans account for another 3 percent, and white students total 14 percent. The pattern was different in 1970, when 35 percent of Chicago's students were white and 55 percent were African-American. Hispanic and Asian-American students were both listed at 1 percent, but 1970 was the first year that census data separated Hispanics from whites.

Chicago's efforts to integrate the small population of white students took such forms as voluntary transfers, redrawn attendance areas for schools, compensatory education programs, and **magnet schools** (which provide instructional programs and materials not usually available in neighborhood schools). Similar

[18]Levine and Havighurst, *Society and Education*, 302–303.

FIGURE 5.4   Racial Attitudes in Chicago, 1993: City and Suburbs

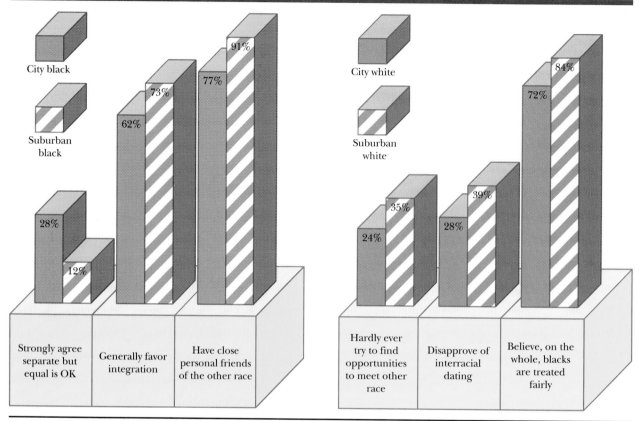

Source: "The Great Divide: Racial Attitudes in Chicago," *Chicago Sun-Times,* January 10, 1993, p. 16.

efforts to balance the student population were made in many other urban school systems.

More recently, as part of a larger reform effort, Chicago created **local school councils** (see Chapter 3). Composed of parents, community members, and teachers, each school's council is charged with setting and implementing educational policies for that school. It is hoped that local councils will result in better programs and better teaching approaches—and, consequently, better educational opportunities for each community's students.[19]

ACADEMIC ACHIEVEMENT OF MINORITY STUDENTS

During the 1970s white middle-class families began leaving urban schools in which desegregation policies were being implemented. They were responding to two main fears: that the quality of instruction would deteriorate and that the level of student achievement would decline. The first concern is difficult to assess, although some studies seem to indicate that in lower-class school districts content is often watered down and relations between teachers and pupils are often poor (see the discussion of Rosenthal's study in Chapter 4).

[19]Chicago Board of Education, *Annual Reports* for 1970 and 1987; and Levine and Havighurst, *Society and Education,* 145, 485.

TABLE 5.1   Average Scores of High School Sophomores
and Seniors, 1980–1982

Group	Language Score*	Math Score*	Science Score*
African-American	14.5	6.5	6.4
Hispanic	15.6	7.7	7.4
Asian-American[†]	25.2	16.6	11.0
White	27.8	15.5	11.2

*Scores are based on the following total points: 57 for language, 38 for math, and 20 for science. The language score includes vocabulary, reading, and writing skills.

[†]Asian-American students on the West Coast.

Source: National Center for Education Statistics, *High School and Beyond* (Washington, D.C.: NCES, 1980), 58.

The second concern, regarding achievement levels, has been studied by many experts, who have generally found that minority students achieve less than majority students (and less than Asian-American students). As can be seen in Table 5.1, out of a total language score of 57, the African-American average for high school sophomores and seniors was 14.5, and the Hispanic average was 15.6. The African-American average was about 11 points lower than the Asian-American average and 13 points lower than the white average. The Hispanic average was about 10 points lower than the Asian-American average and 12 points lower than the white average. The pattern was similar for math scores (total = 38) and science scores (total = 20), with math showing the greatest differences between African-American and Hispanic students as compared with Asian-American and white students. Keeping in mind the relationship between social class and educational achievement (discussed in Chapter 4), it is not surprising that 45 percent of these African-American students were in the lowest SES quartile, as were 43 percent of the Hispanic students. In contrast, only 22 percent of the Asian-American and 18 percent of the white students were in the lowest SES quartile. (Although these data are from the early 1980s, the picture has not changed substantially since then.)

DROPOUT RATES OF MINORITY STUDENTS

Although high school completion rates for African-American and Hispanic students have increased over the last decade, they continue to remain below the graduation rate of white high school students (see Table 5.2).

Although the dropout rates of African-American and Hispanic high school students are declining, they are getting worse in four-year colleges and universities. Fewer students from these two groups are attending colleges, and even fewer are graduating. In 1971, for example, 24.6 percent of African-Americans aged twenty-five to twenty-nine had completed one or more years of college; by 1981 the percentage was 41.5; and by 1991 it had leveled off to 42.5 (after exceeding 44 percent in the early 1980s). The percentage continues to hover at around the 1991 level. Of the 42.5 percent of African-Americans who attended college in 1991, only 13.6 completed four or more years, compared with 17 percent in the late 1970s.[20]

[20]U.S. Department of Education, National Center for Education Statistics, *The Condition of Education, 1992* (Washington, D.C.: U.S. Government Printing Office, 1992), 44—48, 62.

TABLE 5.2   High School Completion Rates,
1980–1985 (Percentages)

Student Group	1980	1982	1984	1985	1988
White	84	84+	84	85	82+
African-Americans	74	74+	80	81	76
Hispanic	56	60	60	67	60

Source: U.S. Department of Education, National Center for Education Statistics, *The Condition of Education,*
1992 (Washington, D.C.: U.S. Government Printing Office, 1992), 58.

The percentage of Hispanic high school graduates who completed one or more years of college in 1971 was 24.9; in 1981 it was 40.1; and in 1991 it had leveled off to 41.3 (after exceeding 44 percent in the mid-1980s). The percentage of Hispanic students who completed four or more years of college in 1991 was 16.4, compared with 18 percent in the mid-1980s.

In contrast, the percentage of white high school graduates with one or more years of college *increased*—from 44.9 percent in 1971, to 51.2 percent in 1981, to 54.9 percent in 1991. The percentage of white students who completed four or more years of college in 1991 was 29.7. These ratios have generally remained the same during the early 1990s.[21]

INFLUENCES ON ACADEMIC PERFORMANCE OF MINORITY STUDENTS

CLASSROOM VARIABLES   Researchers who have continued to study the academic achievement of African-American and Hispanic students have produced a growing body of literature that focuses on classroom atmosphere rather than on family background, socialization, or the personal characteristics of students, such as low self-esteem. (In fact, it appears that low-SES minority families have high aspirations for their childrens' education, and that the children seem to like themselves as much as white middle-class children do.[22] Some newer research reports that minority students perform less well than majority students because school settings are organized around individualized, highly competitive work. Such an atmosphere is not common in minority cultures, which often socialize children by emphasizing cooperation and group effort. Thus the socialization process is different from the dominant, majority pattern, which promotes individual effort and performance. Not surprisingly, then, minority students tend to learn better in situations that stress peer-group cooperation. In recognition of this, the classroom environment should be organized in ways that emphasize group learning and peer evaluation. Teaching strategies that enforce isolated instruction ("Do your own work") are a disadvantage for minority students, who want to seek peer assistance freely without being labeled "cheaters."[23]

Hispanic and Native American students seem to benefit from classroom environments that encourage interaction between their primary cultures and the English-speaking environment. The bilingual and bicultural programs that work best take this into account by incorporating Hispanic and Native American com-

[21]Ibid. Also see "Study: Fewer Blacks, Hispanics in College," *Chicago Tribune,* 14 January 1990. Also see "The Wooing of Black Scholars," *Chicago Tribune,* 3 March 1992, p. 1; and "Drop in Black Ph.D.'s Prompts Debate," *New York Times,* 21 April 1992, p. A1.

[22]See, for example, Mzobanzi M. Mboya, "Black Adolescents: A Descriptive Study of Their Self-Concepts and Academic Achievement," *Adolescence* 21 (Fall 1986): 689–696; and Diana T. Slaughter and Edgar G. Epps, "The Home Environment and Academic Achievement of Black American Children and Youth: An Overview," *Journal of Negro Education* 56 (Winter 1987): 3–18.

[23]Ibid. Also see Lynn A. Vogt, Cathie Jordan, and Roland G. Tharp, "Explaining School Failure, Producing School Success: Two Case Studies," *Anthropology and Education Quarterly* 18 (December 1984): 276–286; Barbara J. Shade and Patricia A. Edwards, "Ecological Correlates of the Educative Style of Afro-American Children," *Journal of Negro Education* 56 (Winter 1987): 88–99; and Peter J. Burke, "Academic Identity and Race Differences in Educational Aspirations," *Social Science Research* 18 (1989): 136–150.

RESEARCH SAYS

For Tomorrow's Education . . .

Bilingual classrooms may not be set up to allow Hispanic students to demonstrate their full range of biliteracy and their conceptual abilities, according to Nancy L. Commins and Ofelia M. Miramontes in "Perceived and Actual Linguistic Competence: A Descriptive Study of Four Low-Achieving Hispanic Bilingual Students," *American Educational Research Journal* 26 (Winter 1989): 443–472. Also see Lucinda Pease-Alvarez and Kenji Hakuta, "Enriching Our Views of Bilingualism and Bilingual Education"; and Luis C. Moll, "Bilingual Classroom Studies and Community Analysis," in *Educational Researcher*, Special Issue on Bilingual Education, 21 (March 1992): 4–6, 20–24.

munity interests into the classroom and by allowing instruction to proceed both in English and in the student's primary language.[24] In general, it appears that the less a school requires minority students to ignore or deny their family's cultural heritage, the more they will achieve. Environments that promote small-group interactions with peers and teachers also seem to work best for bilingual minority students.[25]

HIGH EXPECTATIONS   During the early 1980s Marva Collins received national recognition for her work in Chicago's West Side Prep School. The publicity centered on the high achievement levels of her students, even though they came from lower-class and underclass backgrounds. The methods Collins used were not unusual: She expected teachers to hold students to high standards of achievement while presenting a curriculum that was not watered down.

Another example of a good school for gifted minority students from poor families is De La Salle Academy in New York City. Its junior high school students are chosen from public schools through an admissions process that includes a

RESEARCH SAYS

For Tomorrow's Education . . .

Catholic high schools seem to provide a greater margin for minority achievement than public schools do. This is thought to occur partly because Catholic schools maintain a more demanding curriculum; see the work of Timothy Z. Keith and Ellis B. Page, reported in "Do Catholic High Schools Improve Minority Student Achievement?" *American Educational Research Journal* 22 (Fall 1985): 337–349. As a result of this perception, more minority parents are seeking Catholic and nonpublic schooling for their children. See Robert T. Carter, Faustine C. Jones-Wilson, and Nancy L. Arnez, "Demographic Characteristics of Greater Washington, D.C., Area Black Parents Who Chose Nonpublic Schooling for Their Young," *Journal of Negro Education* 58 (Winter 1989): 39–49.

[24]Ibid.
[25]Nancy L. Commins and Ofelia M. Miramontes, "Perceived and Actual Linguistic Competence: A Descriptive Study of Four Low-Achieving Hispanic Bilingual Students," *American Educational Research Journal* 26 (Winter 1989): 443–472.

The movie Stand and Deliver *dramatized the success of Jaimie Escalante in teaching calculus to Hispanic-American students in a Los Angeles public high school. Escalante's high expectations challenged the students to join and advance the group's efforts. —Jerry Ohlinger's*

test administered by the school, standardized test scores, grades from previous schools, personal interviews, and a statement of financial need. Each fall hundreds of students compete for the school's fifty openings, and graduates go on to enter the best private schools in the region. Once again, the curriculum is academically stringent, teachers focus on discipline and standards, and students are expected to excel. Parents like the school's "wholesome learning environment" and its cultural diversity (students are predominantly African-American and Hispanic, with much smaller percentages of Asian-Americans and whites). Students who previously felt peer-group pressure *not* to achieve in public schools enjoy this school's challenge to excel.[26]

Happily, there also are examples of public schools that have promoted high achievement among minority students. In the late 1980s nearly everyone became familiar with the success story of Jaimie Escalante, a high school calculus teacher in Los Angeles whose victories in spurring the mathematical achievements of minority students were dramatized in the movie *Stand and Deliver*. Another success story from Los Angeles involves the Audubon Junior High School, which since the late 1980s has been recognized for creating an educational environment that fosters higher levels of academic achievement. Composed predominantly of African-Americans and a small percentage of Hispanic students, this

[26]"N.Y. School Targets Poor, Gifted Youth," *Chicago Tribune,* 28 January 1990, sec. 1, p. 25.

RESEARCH SAYS

For Tomorrow's Education . . .

Compared with the mid-1970s, today fewer African-American and Hispanic students are going to college, and even fewer are graduating; among college graduates fewer study to become teachers, and more go into business. These are the findings of a 1990 study conducted by Deborah Carr for the American Council of Education. For a summary see, for example, Mike Royko, "Study: Fewer Blacks, Hispanics, in College," *Chicago Tribune*, 14 January 1990; and "Drop in Black Ph.Ds Prompts Debate," *New York Times*, 21 April 1992, p. A1.

The picture has not improved much for women on campus either. Although the number of female students, faculty, and administrators has increased over the last eighteen years, women are not strongly represented among the higher ranks of faculty and administrators, nor are they numerous in the more prestigious fields of study. Female faculty are also less likely than males to receive tenure. See Bernice R. Sandler, "The Chilly Climate for Women on Campus," *USA Today*, July 1988, pp. 50–53.

On the other hand, the higher-education picture *is* improving somewhat for Native Americans, especially through the founding of tribal colleges. See Carnegie Foundation for The Advancement of Teaching, "Trendlines—Native Americans and Higher Education: New Mood of Optimism," *Change* 22 (January–February 1990): 28–30.

school has prompted about 75 percent of its students to earn grades of C or better. Teachers are committed to their fields and to providing an outstanding educational experience for students. Parents are actively involved in the school, and there is a sense of pride in the accomplishments of its students and teachers. In terms of the criteria given in Chapter 3, Audubon Junior High is an example of an "effective school."

GENDER AND EDUCATION

Although females outnumber males in the general population, their educational experiences have been—and to some extent remain—unequal, separate, and different. Chapters 8 and 9 present the historical evolution of women's education, but here we want to examine issues relating to equity between males and females. Specifically, we will look at access to education, its purpose, curricular differences, and power relations between the sexes.

ACCESS TO EDUCATION

When questions about the education of females first arose, they focused primarily on the fact that males had much greater access to schooling. Christine de Pisan, in fifteenth-century France, and Sor Juana Inez de la Cruz, in seventeenth-century Mexico, wrote eloquently about negative male attitudes toward educated women. Their challenges were renewed in the late eighteenth century, in England, by Mary Wollstonecraft.[27] By the time Americans adopted a constitution, there were a dozen degree-granting colleges and many academies available for males, but no college and few academies admitted females. This is not to say that women went uneducated; but they did have to either join religious orders or find "nonformal" ways to acquire the same knowledge that was readily accessible to their brothers.

Between about 1820 and 1860 a limited number of "higher" education opportunities became available for American women. Among the first were Troy Female Seminary and Elmira College, in New York, and Berea College, in Kentucky. After the Civil War, Iowa and Colorado (among other states) founded new universities that admitted women; and by the end of the nineteenth century a number of women's colleges existed, along with many coeducational institutions. During this same period women were becoming much more active politically, in an effort to gain the right to vote and to expand their economic and occupational choices. This became especially noticeable in 1848, when the **Woman's Rights Convention** met in Seneca Falls, New York, in order to secure for women "an equal participation with men in the various trades, professions, and commerce." The effort culminated in 1920 with ratification of the Nineteenth Amendment, which grants voting rights to women. The 1920s also witnessed the early development of an equal rights amendment (ERA) by a somewhat radical wing of the women's movement—the National Woman's Party. Calling for equal pay for working women, the amendment ran into strong opposition from social reformers of both sexes, and by 1930 it had died from the intense conflict.[28]

Gender inequities continued in the workplace. Women were concentrated in lower-paying jobs than men, and they were paid less even in the same jobs and having the same educational background; women who were in training on

[27]Chapters 8 and 9 more fully discuss the history of education for females.

[28]Ellen Boneparth, ed., *Women Power and Policy* (Elmsford, N.Y.: Pergamon, 1982), 55–60. For a historical perspective on attitudes toward women in educational leadership roles see Linda McPheron and Joan K. Smith, "Women Administrators in Historical Perspective: Toward an Androgynous Theory of Leadership," *Educational Horizons* 60 (Fall 1981): 22–25.

RESEARCH SAYS

For Tomorrow's Education . . .

When it comes to science and math, female students are more likely than males to be placed in lower ability groups. However, this does not seem to affect females' achievement levels in math, according to researchers Maureen T. Hallinan and Aage B. Sorenson, in "Ability Grouping and Sex Differences in Mathematics Achievement," *Sociology of Education* 60 (April 1987): 63–72. On the other hand, a recent report by the American Association of University Women reviewed hundreds of studies and revealed that females of all ages are discriminated against in schools; high school females lag behind males in tests of math, science, and verbal skills. The report concluded that textbooks either ignore or stereotype females and that tests are biased against them. See Marcel C. La Follette, "Daring Steps Are Needed to Increase Women's Role in Science," *Chronicle of Higher Education*, 3 October 1990, p. A56; and Peter Jennings, "ABC Evening News," 12 February 1992.

the job also received less pay than training men did. Finally, the **Equal Pay Act of 1963** was the beginning of several legal developments aimed at ensuring equity between the sexes. Title VII of the 1964 Civil Rights Act prohibited employment decisions based on gender, and presidential Executive Order 11246 was amended in 1967 to do the same in the hiring practices of contractors who receive federal money. Similarly, Title IX of the Education Amendments of 1972 prohibits gender discrimination in educational employment, activities, or programs that receive federal money. Also, during the 1960s and 1970s efforts to pass the ERA were renewed, but the amendment failed to win ratification in three-fourths of the states, as the Constitution requires.

It is too soon to assess all these measures aimed at equity between the sexes. Before they can be implemented fully, society must undergo subtle changes in fundamental beliefs about what is appropriate and desirable. As long as significant numbers of vocal people believe that some occupations—and some forms of education—are more appropriate for one sex than for the other, discrimination based on gender will remain.

PURPOSES OF EDUCATION

Opponents of advanced education for women originally based their arguments on nature, saying that too much education would be harmful for women—either

Until very recently, the longstanding assumption that males and females should be educated to fulfill specific gender roles led to important differences in their curricula. Even today, female students tend to choose traditionally "safe" fields of study. —Bettmann

As long as significant numbers of vocal people believe that some occupations—and some forms of education—are more appropriate for one sex than for the other, discrimination based on gender will remain.   —Bob Daemmrich/Sygma

morally or physically, or both. In 1873 a faculty member of Harvard medical school wrote a book claiming that women would suffer dire physical symptoms (even premature death) if they pursued higher education. No less an authority than the U.S. commissioner of education refuted this claim, offering statistical evidence that women who graduated from college lived longer, on average, than women who did not.

If women's health was no longer an issue, there was still extensive disagreement about *why* women would pursue advanced education. Not everyone agreed that a college education would maximize women's choices in life, including occupational choices. In fact, to some degree in the United States—and in many other societies—conventional wisdom has held that education for women should aim to enhance their nurturing roles as wives and mothers. Such an attitude perhaps helps to explain why—when more U.S. females than males have finished high school in this century—only recently have as many women as men graduated from college. And it is still the case that fewer women than men complete doctoral programs.

CURRICULAR DIFFERENCES

Given the longstanding assumption that males and females should be educated for different roles, it is no surprise that both subtle and overt curricular differences exist. One result is that more males than females specialize in science, mathematics, and engineering.[29] Another is that females tend to internalize feelings which encourage them to choose "safe"—that is, traditionally approved—fields of study.

There is evidence that the conflict between realizing one's potential as a person and accepting cultural role expectations is even more intense for African-American, Hispanic, and Native American girls and women. This is true partly because males in these groups are discouraged from continuing their education much more than white males are. In addition, minority women—who disproportionately face financial and other impediments to earn advanced degrees—also face greater difficulties in finding a male partner whose educational interests and attainments match their own.[30]

POWER RELATIONS BETWEEN THE SEXES

The last decades of this century have witnessed numerous movements in many countries to throw off the shackles of colonial domination. Bonnie Cook Freeman has suggested that women's experiences be related to the concept of **colonialism** (the domination of one group by another in an unequal relationship that benefits the colonizer at the expense of the colonized). According to Freeman's analysis the unequal status of females is neither accidental nor a result of well-intended mistakes. Instead, in Freeman's view males have used their position of power—of being in charge of the dominant culture—to "colonize" females and thus enhance their income and psychological sense of well-being.

Leaving the issue of intent aside, much recent feminist literature concludes that the *effect* of education has been to leave females in a subordinate position to males—forcing them to internalize the negative self-esteem that accompanies longstanding disadvantages in power relations. Those who write about the effects of colonialism note that depression (or inturned aggression) and lowered self-concept are inevitable results of long-term domination. In a diverse society like the United States today, the problem of how to achieve equity is both extremely important and extremely difficult. For American educators the task is to transform schools that historically were developed to serve the needs and interests of middle-class white males into schools where students of both sexes and all cultural backgrounds can flourish.

CONCLUSIONS

■

Cultural pluralism—a reality in today's society and schools—has come about through a long, difficult process in which minority cultures first were ignored and then were expected to assimilate into the majority American culture. Now most Americans want to preserve their cultural heritage and coexist—equally—with the dominant culture. In terms of education, however, African-Americans, Hispanics and Native Americans do not generally achieve as much as white students do. Nor are their families as well represented in upper social classes; they

[29]Jerilee Grandy, "Ten-Year Trends in SAT Scores and Other Characteristics of High School Seniors Taking the SAT and Planning to Study Mathematics, Science, or Engineering: Research Report" (Washington, D.C.: National Science Foundation, 1987).

[30]Judith Teresa Gonzales, "Dilemmas of the High-achieving Chicana: The Double-Bind Factor in Male/Female Relationships," *Sex Roles* 18 (April 1988): 367–379; J. N. Baraka-Love, "Successful Women: A Racial Comparison of Variables Contributing to Socialization and Leadership Development," Ed.D. dissertation (Western Michigan University, 1986); and "Report Says U.S. Schools Fail to Give Science Top Priority," *New York Times*, 27 March 1992.

often become stranded in low-income urban environments where their children attend schools that predominantly include other minority students.

Despite legal restrictions that call for all students to be integrated in schools, new patterns of segregation have emerged. White families have moved from urban areas to less integrated suburbs, and mandatory busing has proved to be impractical. Although the current emphasis is on providing better programs in low-achieving urban schools, minority students continue to lag behind on standardized academic tests, and their dropout rates remain high. Hope for the future lies in a growing body of research that identifies particular classroom variables which can affect students' performance positively.

Although female students outnumber male students, they too have experienced unequal treatment and unequal educational opportunities. In many respects it is as though females have been "colonized" by males—suffering disadvantages not only in economic matters but also in terms of access to education and its results.

American schools are no longer expected to be a "melting pot" in which all students become the same. Rather, schools are expected to *treat* all students the same so that students can progress as far as their talents and interests may take them, without regard to race, ethnicity, or gender.

KEY TERMS

multicultural (pluralistic) society

minority groups

cultural assimilation

biculturalism

de jure segregation

de facto segregation

Civil Rights Act of 1964

Elementary and Secondary Education Act of 1965 (ESEA)

compensatory education

Coleman report

hegemony

Indian Reorganization Act of 1934

cultural deprivation theory

learning disabilities theory

magnet schools

local school councils

Woman's Rights Convention of 1848

Equal Pay Act of 1963

colonialism

SUGGESTED READINGS

James Coleman et al., *Equality of Educational Opportunity* (Washington: U.S. Government Printing Office, 1966). This is the original report that attempted to relate curriculum variables and the condition of school facilities to students' achievement. Results showed virtually no or little relationship.

Christopher Jencks et al., *Inequality: A Reassessment of the Effect of Family and Schooling in America* (New York: Basic Books, 1972). Jencks re-analyzed the Coleman data and concluded that schooling has very little to do with income inequality in the United States.

Benjamin D. Stickney and Jody Fritzpatrick,
Coleman's Inequality Twenty Years Later: The Origins, the Issues and the Implications (1987), ED 297 422. This paper looks at the Coleman report's original conclusions in terms of the rash of compensatory education programs that were funded during the next twenty years. Then it focuses on programs and results in Colorado.

Maureen B. Slonium, *Children, Culture and Ethnicity* (New York: Garland, 1991). This reference is a cross-disciplinary study of the effects of culture and ethnicity on children's development.

Angela L. Carrasaquillo, *Hispanic Children and Youth in the United States,* Reference Books on Family Issues series, 20 (New York: Garland, 1991). This is a guidebook that discusses the characteristics, demographics, and future outlook for Mexican-American, Puerto Rican, Dominican, Cuban, and South American children in the United States.

Patricia G. Ramsey, Edwina B. Vold, and Leslie R. Williams, *Multicultural Education: A Source Book* (New York: Garland, 1989). This book covers a wide range of philosophies, policies, research, and issues related to multicultural education.

Valora Washington and Ura Jean Oyemade, *Project Head Start* (New York: Garland, 1987). This book presents a historical study of Project Head Start, examining both its original purposes and its current programs.

Donna M. Gollnick and Philip C. Chinn, *Multicultural Education in a Pluralistic Society* (St. Louis: Mosby, 1983). This book provides an overview of various U.S. subcultures in terms of ethnicity, religion, language, SES, and demographic trends. It concludes by offering strategies for effective multicultural education.

II

YESTERDAY AND TODAY

By developing an appreciation of our past heritage—including its social, psychological, philosophical, and educational dimensions—we can better understand the forces that shape our culture in general and our schools in particular. Too often educational policies and practices reflect the pressures of the moment or concerns about the near future. Reflecting on the past can add a valuable perspective.

In Part II we examine the main influences on our changing American society and its system of education. Specifically, we explore the psychological, historical, and philosophical foundations of education. Chapter 6 brings a psychological perspective to the theoretical aspects of teaching and learning. It describes the important ideas that psychological theorists have had about how human beings process and organize knowledge, and about how these ideas influence our understanding of teaching and learning.

Chapter 7 shifts the focus from theory to application by considering how various learning theories result in classroom curricula and practices. We examine the instructional issues that emerge when curricular materials are adopted, and we also describe curricular developments and programs aimed at special populations of students.

Chapters 8 an 9 explore the historical foundations of American education. Chapter 8 begins by describing ancient societies, including Greece and Rome, and then examines European developments that have shaped American education. In each case we consider such questions as Who taught? Who got educated? What was taught? And how did this society contribute to American education?

Chapter 9 transports European educational practices across the Atlantic to the American colonies. After examining the historical forces and developments that came to bear on American education, the chapter describes how they were transformed into a unique enterprise on this side of the Atlantic.

Finally, Chapter 10 looks at American education in terms of philosophical patterns of thought. The philosophical foundations of education lead us to consider the differences between science and philosophy, the ways in which philosophical ideas can be organized, how philosophical ideas have permeated and affected American schools, and how you can select and develop your personal philosophy of education.

Learning

Psychological Foundations A

6

As soon as I knew that I had at my disposal a class of little children, it was my wish to make of this school a field for scientific experimental pedagogy and child psychology. . . . My intention was to keep in touch with the researches of others, but to make myself independent of them, proceeding to work without preconceptions of any kind. I retained as the only essential, the affirmation, or, rather, the definition . . . that "all methods of experimental psychology may be reduced to one; namely careful observation of the subject."

—Maria Montessori, The Montessori Method *(New York: Schocken, 1974), 72–73*

No one would be so rash as to claim that it makes no difference what food a child has, that the only question is how does its stomach attack the food. Yet certain educators maintain that the "significant question in education is how children learn and not what they learn."

—Ella Flagg Young, *"Scientific Method in Education,"* Chicago Decennial Publications, *ser. 1, 3 (Chicago: University of Chicago Press, 1903), 147–148*

Learning

ADVANCED ORGANIZERS

In this chapter you will learn

How the process of learning was viewed in the past

The impact of empirical sciences on ideas about the learning process

The contributions of John Dewey, Maria Montessori, and Jean Piaget to learning theory

The contributions of cognitive science to our understanding of the learning process

CHAPTER OUTLINE

EARLY IDEAS ABOUT LEARNING
  Rationality and Inborn Potentials
  Empiricism

TWENTIETH-CENTURY IDEAS ABOUT LEARNING
  Behaviorism
  Other Empirical Theories of Learning
  Empirical Learning Theories in Perspective

LEARNING THEORY TODAY
  Cognitive Science and Learning Theory
  Classroom Applications of Cognitive Research

CONCLUSIONS

S uppose you are a teacher and have been asked to join a group of educators who are observing various classrooms—both traditional and innovative—throughout the country. It is early morning as you walk into a classroom where thirty children, aged four to seven, are dispersed around the room and are engaged in all sorts of activities. You glance around quickly and discover two surprising conditions: There are no desks in the room, and the teacher is not readily discernible. Finally you spot her—sitting on the floor with a couple of four-year-olds who are fitting together the pieces of a puzzle.

As you observe more closely, you see that all the children are busily engaged, alone or in groups, in a variety of activities. Everyone is absorbed in his or her chosen pursuit. Pupils are conferring quietly, or returning materials to their place and selecting others, or drawing and writing on the blackboard; in general, they are going about their business without disrupting others. On the walls are pictures that would interest children as well as pictures of classic works of art. Your attention is caught by a girl who has knocked over a chair; she quietly picks it up and returns it to its place. This makes you notice that nothing *is out of place in the classroom except for materials that are being used at the moment.*

When the teacher notices your group, she comes over to introduce herself. Her name is Lois Rivera, and she is eager to answer your questions. But first she tells you that this is a Montessori school, and so she is called a "directress," not a teacher. When one of your group asks why the children are playing with "toys," Rivera dispels another misconception: Each object that the children are using is called a **didactic material**, because it gives instruction in a specific learning concept, such as spatial relations (the puzzle) or sequential organization (a set of stacking blocks). All the materials have been especially designed to help children "unlock" or learn the concepts inherent in them by means of concentrated self-activity. Rivera also tells you that the children's activities are not called play but work, because the children are engaged in learning. Finally, she says that the classroom is regarded as a "prepared environment" in which children learn through self-activity. She says that Dr. Maria Montessori discovered these ideas and practices by carefully observing children. As you leave the room, you feel energized by seeing so many children engaged happily and busily in their work. You wonder what you can do as a teacher to revitalize the learning process in your own classes.

It is not unusual for teachers to be concerned about the study of learning processes. Since ancient times educators have been interested in pedagogical theories and ideas about how human beings think and learn. **Pedagogy**, or the art of teaching, has been the subject of much writing throughout history, and different ideas have dominated at different times. Only recently have researchers been able to confirm and verify some of the ideas about human thought and learning—and to apply them to teaching techniques and the curriculum. Before we look at current theories, however, let's examine some selected pedagogical ideas from the past to see how they relate to thinking and learning. Although it is difficult to separate theory entirely from practice, this chapter will focus on pedagogical theories, and Chapter 7 will explore teaching methods and curricula.

EARLY IDEAS ABOUT LEARNING

◼ RATIONALITY AND INBORN POTENTIALS

For centuries before the Christian era Greek education was based on the idea that the human mind had to be trained or exercised in order to think well. This need for **mental discipline** or training stemmed from the belief that an infant's mind at birth was endowed with innate ideas. Plato and Aristotle articulated this theory of innate ideas, and they considered learning to be a process of providing logical exercises so that the inborn thought patterns could be remembered and strengthened through practice. For them all branches of mathematics—especially geometry—were the most logical subjects and, therefore, the best subjects for study. But even boxing was regarded as logical and requiring mental discipline, because the boxer had to learn mental schemes or game plans—strategies—in order to play and win.[1]

Besides the *rational* faculty of the mind, the Greeks conceptualized four other faculties. Aristotle envisioned them this way: The *vegetative* faculty was responsible for growth; the *appetitive* faculty was necessary for sustaining life; the *locomotive* was needed to control motion; and the *sensory* faculty was responsible for connecting us to the physical environment. During the nineteenth century this verion of the mind as possessing specialized compartmental structures that must be exercised came to be known as **faculty psychology**. Its roots, however, were in ancient Greek thought, which dominated Western educational beliefs for centuries.

Although Aristotle was Plato's pupil for about twenty years, the two held different ideas about some points. For example, Plato did not believe that our senses put us in touch with any useful knowledge, because they connected us to the physical environment, which for Plato had little to do with an individual's inborn intellectual potential. Aristotle, on the other hand, acknowledged the senses as being a useful faculty of the mind, but he regarded the rational faculty as being more important, because it was unique to human beings. (The other faculties were possessed by members of the animal kingdom as well.)

RESEARCH SAYS

For Tomorrow's Education . . .

Teaching by inquiry has been demonstrated to be a powerful approach that can improve learning and increase students' interest in a variety of subjects, according to Walter L. Bateman. He describes his methods in *Open to Question* (San Francisco: Jossey-Bass, 1990).

---

[1]Morris L. Bigge, *Learning Theories for Teachers* (New York: Harper & Row, 1971), 22–34; and L. Glenn Smith et al., *Lives in Education: People and Ideas in the Development of Teaching* (Ames, Iowa: Educational Studies Press, 1984), 15–24.

Aristotle's theory of learning also held that ideas are remembered best when they are associated with other ideas. He described four types of associations that aided the memory process. One was *contiguity*, or the proximity of two ideas;

thus, if a teacher explains that whales live in the ocean, students will think of the ocean when they hear the word *whale*. The second type of association depended on the *similarity* of two ideas, as in the comparison "An airplane is a giant bird." Another Aristotelian connection is based on the *succession* of ideas, which is often used in learning and remembering numbers in sequence. The fourth type of association that he described is *contrast*, as when a person connects two opposite ideas, like hot and cold, or laughing and crying.

These theories of innate ideas, faculties of the mind, and learning by association led to a pedagogy based on rote memory activities. Indeed, that approach dominated educational thought and practice in America until well into the nineteenth century. The following description exemplifies such a pedagogy in practice:

> Ms. Putnam teaches fourth grade and is starting the day with a reading lesson. She asks all forty of her pupils to get their books out and to turn to the story that they will read. First she asks the students to take turns reading one paragraph each, in order. (At other times all forty pupils read the entire story in unison with Ms. Putnam.) When students stumble over a word, she stops them, pronounces it for them, and asks them to repeat the word the way she pronounced it.
>
> Next Ms. Putnam asks the students a series of questions; they are to respond by reading passages from the story that contain the answer. She repeats this process until every student has had a chance to respond. Then Ms. Putnam writes ten words—along with their definitions—on the blackboard. These are the new vocabulary that students will need to know in reading tomorrow's story. She tells all forty pupils to copy each word and its definition ten times.

EMPIRICISM

The preceding picture of a tedious class based on rote memory in order to exercise students' mental faculties became the target of educational reformers and critics during the late nineteenth and early twentieth centuries. Many called for a more scientific pedagogy—like the one postulated by the seventeenth-century English philosopher John Locke (1632–1704). He questioned the doctrine of innate ideas and a psychology that relied on "rote memory" for mental discipline. Instead, Locke emphasized empirical (sensory) experience and introduced a more scientific theory of thinking and learning. Unfortunately, his influence on American educators was slight for two centuries.

The basic difference between Locke and Plato lay in how they defined what an idea is. For Locke an idea is the result not of an intuitive, inborn mental potential but rather of an individual's sensory experience.[2] He believed that an infant's mind is blank—a **tabula rasa** ("blank tablet")—that accumulates, in an organized way, the impressions of an individual's sensory experiences. A kind of complex filing system, the mind takes a sensory impression (including its related feelings) and files it appropriately as a discrete, or single, idea. Thinking, therefore, is the recollection of an arrangement of discrete ideas at any particular time.[3]

[2]For a discussion of Locke's educational philosophy see, for example, John Locke, *An Essay Concerning Human Understanding*, ed. Alexander Fraser (New York: Dover, 1959); for a description of his practical education to fit a gentleman see, for example, H. H. Quick, *Locke on Education* (New York: Macmillan, 1902).

[3]Ibid.

Empiricist John Locke held that an infant's mind is blank at birth, not—as the Greeks believed—filled with innate ideas. For him, learning results from sensory experience, not from disciplined recall.
—New York Public Library Picture Collection

Locke also thought that the objects with which a person comes into contact by sensing them (touching, seeing, smelling, hearing, and tasting) possess three types of qualities: primary, secondary, and tertiary. *Primary qualities* of an object are those which an individual can measure and quantify in some way, leading to assessments of its size, shape, weight, and so on. A primary quality is universal; that is, everyone experiences it in much the same way. An object's *secondary qualities* are those which give it color, flavor, odor, or sound; secondary qualities are experienced differently by individuals. Finally, although primary and secondary qualities are discernible by examining the object, *tertiary qualities* are not; they are discovered only by using the object and working with it. For example, the combustibility of wood is a property that is discerned only by working with and using wood; one cannot discover that wood is combustible simply by examining or observing it.

In viewing the mind as blank and making the senses the sole means of gaining knowledge, Locke's learning theory is an example of **empiricism** (in contrast to Plato's rational theory of innate ideas). Knowledge is derived from sensory experiences, and perception is the vehicle through which ideas are formed from sensory input. Locke's empiricism also includes the formation of complex ideas, which is accomplished when the mind organizes simple ideas into groups of ideas, or concepts. Given this ability to organize by association, Locke concluded, the mind is not merely a passive receptor of sensory impressions. In other words, although the mind is a blank tablet at birth, it does have a sort of "mental chemistry" that allows it to compare and contrast ideas and to group them in a contiguous or sequential fashion. In these respects, especially,

Locke's theory followed from Aristotle's theoretical groundwork of sensory impressions and **associationism**.

In turn, Locke's empiricism had many followers who tried to implement educational practices that relied on sensory experiences. Jean Jacques Rousseau (1712–1778) was among the first. In his novel *Emile* he postulated the idea that a child learns best in a natural surrounding, because as part of the environment the child can develop naturally and freely. According to Rousseau, nature is good, and human nature—being part of the biological world—is also good. Thus, through a process of natural unfoldment, children learn to interact actively and develop their impulses, feelings, and perceptions naturally. (For more information about Rousseau, see Chapter 8.)

These ideas are empirical because they make sensory experiences the basis of a child's learning. Locke's ideas also came to underlie behavioristic theories of learning, which we will explore later in this chapter. And Rousseau's ideas were put into practice by two of his followers—Johann Heinrich Pestalozzi (1746–1827) and kindergarten founder Friedrich Froebel (1782–1852). Because their contributions affected teaching methods and curricula, we will discuss them in Chapter 7.

One of the next successors to this empirical legacy was German philosopher Johann Friedrich Herbart (1776–1841). He developed a theory based on the notion that the mind is a "battleground" where sensory ideas actively compete to gain recognition and acceptance and to remain in a person's consciousness. When sensory impressions are presented to the mind, they become **mental states**—the aggregate of which is the contents of the mind. Therefore, the mind has no spatial or concrete quality, because it is only a collection of mental states. The mental states themselves (or "ideas") are composed of new and old sensory impressions as well as emotional elements. These can combine, or "associate," because they have the associationistic qualities of contiguity, continuity, and similarity. An idea that does not remain in consciousness becomes submerged and fights to return to the forefront, where it was originally learned. Thus Herbart turned away from a faculty-based psychology and created a psychology of consciousness, along with a series of steps that allowed ideas to be learned.

RESEARCH SAYS

For Tomorrow's Education . . .

Harvard psychologist Howard Gardner has developed a theory of multiple intelligences, arguing that traditional measures of intelligence do not take into account the full range of human intellectual potentials. See, for example, *The Mind's New Science* (New York: Basic Books, 1985).

In Herbart's view the order of steps in learning is successive, and teachers must follow them if their students are to learn material or acquire a new mental state. First is *preparation*, or bringing into consciousness former mental impressions that are going to be relevant to the new information. Second, the new material or concept is *presented*. Third, the new ideas are compared and abstracted, or *associated*, to the former material or mental states. Fourth, a *generalization* that incorporates both old and new ideas is formed. Finally, the expanded concept with its elements of old and new is *applied*. (In Herbart's original scheme, the first two steps were combined into what he called *clearness*; comparison and abstraction were termed *association*; generalization was *system*; and application was *method*. His followers in turn-of-the-century America—including Charles DeGarmo, Frank and Charles McMurry, and Charles Van Liew—expanded and relabeled Herbart's four steps into five.)

Herbart used the term **apperception** to describe the total process by which mental states or presentations associate and get stored, and the totality of mental states he called the **apperceptive mass**. For him perception really was synonymous with apperception; hence, his system of learning is often called the theory of apperception. Note that it is also associationistic in terms of how ideas are learned and concepts are formed. This theory is one of the first complete systems of psychology to be based on the *tabula rasa* notion of the mind.[4]

Herbart was also one of the first theorists to be concerned about student interest—something that the faculty psychologists ignored. But Herbart thought that if new material is presented properly—that is, if it is associated with former mental states—the new will naturally be interesting. Thus, if a new idea can naturally associate with old ideas, students will "feel interest." Herbart and his followers believed in a moral education; consequently, any curriculum had to teach material that was morally appropriate. For the most part Herbartians relied on cultural history and literature as the foundation for building a moralistic education. Hence, their curriculum was enriched with social studies that provided them with tools for a moral education.

Although most educators and psychologists have left Herbart behind, today's teaching methods still have vestiges that can be traced to his psychology of learning. Let's take a quick look at the following lesson and note the apperceptive parts:

Mr. Calhoun is about to introduce his second-graders to a new unit on the solar system and the movement of the planets around the sun. He starts by asking the students if they have ever seen a sunrise (old material, or *preparation*).

After the students respond, Mr. Calhoun goes on to ask them about the sunset: Why is the setting sun in a different place than the rising sun? (more *preparation*) Next, he asks them if they think that the sun has moved, or if there is something else that could have moved. As he raises these questions, he introduces a model of the sun and the earth (new material, or *presentation*). Next, with a demonstration of how the earth orbits the sun, the lesson moves into the *association* part. As the students formulate rules about the sun as the center of the solar system and the orbits of planets around the sun, they *generalize*; finally, they apply the generalizations to a model of the solar system that Mr. Calhoun asks them to construct.

[4]Bigge, *Learning Theories*, 36–46.

TWENTIETH-CENTURY IDEAS ABOUT LEARNING

■

BEHAVIORISM

During the first third of this century, educators moved away from Herbart's version of associationism toward a more physiologically based form that was pioneered by such psychologists as Edward L. Thorndike (1874–1949) and John B. Watson (1878–1958). Both men were influenced by a growing number of psychologists in the late nineteenth century who became interested in the physiological (bodily) functions of behavior—the more observable forms of behavior, rather than the more internal or mental forms.

Experiments by the Russian physiologist Ivan Pavlov (1849–1936) had revealed that when food was put in front of a dog and a bell was rung at the same time, the dog soon started to salivate simply by hearing the bell ring—without the presence of food. In other words the dog had become "conditioned" to respond to the secondary stimulus (the bell), which was associated with the primary stimulus (food). Thorndike followed Pavlov's lead and experimented with chickens and cats as well as dogs. Based on his experiments (especially those concerning cats' behavior before and after they learned to escape from a cage), Thorndike developed laws of learning known as **connectionism**, or **stimulus-response (S-R) bond theory**. These learning principles retained Herbart's associationism of ideas or mental states, but Thorndike called them *mental units* and

Behaviorist B. F. Skinner found ways to control a stimulus in order to increase the likelihood of a desired response. In his view, learning is a change in the probability that a response will occur again—a change that can be reinforced by operant conditioning. —Joseph McNally

defined them as something sensed or perceived. He assumed that every mental unit had a corresponding physiological or physical component that was either a stimulus or a response. Learning occurred when units were connected: a mental with a physical, a mental with a mental, or a physical with a physical.

From his conditioning experiments Thorndike concluded that through trial and error certain responses become connected, or "bonded," with specific stimuli. He also developed three "Laws of Learning":

1. Some connections or bonds are more predisposed or readier to connect than others; when they bond, the individual feels satisfied.

2. By exercising or repeating a bond, an individual remembers it longer.

3. A response is strengthened if it is followed by something pleasurable, and it is weakened if it is followed by something unpleasant.

Thorndike called these the *laws of readiness* (1), *exercise* (2), and *effect* (3).[5]

John Watson pursued a purer form of behavioristic psychology that showed no relationship to Herbart's mental states. He expanded on Thorndike's postulate that any stimulus can be connected to any response, and during the 1920s he developed the capstone premise of behavioristic thinking: Any possible response can be linked to any stimulus.[6]

Following in the tradition of Watson and dominating behavioristic learning theory through the 1950s was Burrhus Frederic (B. F.) Skinner (1904–1990). Known as **operant conditioning**, Skinner's learning theory was based on the type and timing of the activity that reinforces the appropriate behavior, or the operant. (An *operant* is a set of acts that constitutes an organism's response pattern or behavior pattern.) For example, a teacher who wants students to learn to spell the word *tree* must provide a positive reinforcer immediately or soon after they spell it correctly; this will optimize the chances that the learning will be retained.[7]

[5]Ibid., 49–55.

[6]Ibid., 55–57; and Abram Amsel, *Behaviorism, Neobehaviorism and Cognitivism in Learning Theory* (Hillsdale, N.J.: Lawrence Erlbaum Associates, 1989), 2–29.

[7]B. F. Skinner, *Science and Human Behavior* (New York: Macmillan, 1953), 59–106.

[8]Skinner, *Science and Human Behavior*, 73. In connection with negative reinforcement Skinner discusses the definition and role of punishment, which does not have a place in his approach to conditioning. He defines punishment as the removal of a positive reinforcer (taking candy from a child) or the inclusion of a negative reinforcer (spanking). See page 185; also see Bigge, *Learning Theories*, 93.

RESEARCH SAYS

For Tomorrow's Education . . .

It is now possible to design and build complex learning interventions that can strengthen the short- and long-term retention of "at-risk" students, according to Stanley Pogrow. See his article, "Challenging At-risk Students: Findings from the HOTS Program," in *Phi Delta Kappan* 71 (January 1990): 389–397.

In Skinner's view, learning is a change in the probability that a particular response will occur again. Thus operant conditioning is a process that makes a response more probable (or less probable) through the use of positive reinforcers (or negative reinforcers). A **positive reinforcer** is a stimulus (such as food or money) that strengthens the behavior, while a **negative reinforcer** (such as a loud bell or an electric shock) weakens the behavior. Also note that, when a negative reinforcer is removed or absent, the behavior will be strengthened.[8]

Skinner's theory resulted from experiments on lower-order animals like rats and pigeons. He selected such animals because their behavior was simple and thus environmental influences on them were easier to control in the laboratory. In fact, all that he needed for most of his experiments was a box—now called the **Skinner box**—in which an animal was presented with a lever that allowed food (a positive reinforcer) to be released each time it was pressed. This simple environment was devoid of any other stimuli that might complicate the conditioning process. Ultimately, Skinner's goal was to control the environment of human beings and thus predict their behavior. In fact, the main criticism of operant conditioning is that it tries to generalize and predict the complexities of human behavior and learning, based on conditioning experiments with simple animals in sterile environments.

With this brief overview of behavior modification in mind, let's return to Mr. Calhoun's second-graders and their lesson about the solar system to see how operant conditioning might be applied in the classroom:

When Mr. Calhoun asks whether the sun sets in the same place as it rises, Henry says, "No, it sets in the West, which is the opposite side." Mr. Calhoun reinforces this response immediately with, "Good for you, Henry; that is exactly right!" As the class continues the discussion of "What has moved? The sun or something else?" Mr. Calhoun accepts all answers, but he only rewards (positively reinforces) the correct ones that students might know. Finally, he moves to the model of the solar system in which a large ball represents the sun and smaller balls represent the planets. He asks Jenny, who has seemed

In programmed instruction each student, working alone, moves through a sequence of material and is reinforced for each correct answer (or is referred to information that contains the correct answer). Then the student is given another chance to respond correctly. —Jeff Greenberg/ PhotoEdit

to understand the discussion so far, to point out what might do the moving. Jenny points to the planets, and Mr. Calhoun rewards her with, "That's wonderful, Jenny! I can see that you have understood the discussion."

Skinnerian learning techniques are best seen in "programmed instruction," in which each student works individually through a sequence of material and is reinforced for each correct answer. For example, the above lesson would be presented to each student step by step, either by a computer or by a packet of sequential materials. When a student answers a question correctly, the computer or programmed materials reinforce the response with words or a "happy face," and the student is given permission to go on to the next question. If an answer is incorrect, the student is either corrected or is referred to information that contains the correct response. Then the student is given a second chance to respond correctly before moving to the next question. Each student proceeds through the sequence of material at his or her pace, and each is reinforced or corrected after every response.

OTHER EMPIRICAL THEORIES OF LEARNING

One theoretical framework that began to compete with behaviorism was more concerned with an individual's interaction with the environment and the manner in which the individual perceived, or "configured," the interaction. Known by many names (configuration theory, cognitive field theory, and gestalt field theory), this approach went back to Locke via Rousseau and his followers, Pestalozzi and Froebel (discussed earlier).[9] It was also influenced by the contributions of John Dewey, Maria Montessori, and Jean Piaget.

JOHN DEWEY   A philosopher, not a cognitive psychologist, the well-known pragmatist John Dewey (1859–1952) emphasized the mental dimension of Rousseau's educational ideas. He posited that learning is a mental process which involves problem-solving experiences and intelligent action. He described the process as (1) identifying the problem, (2) recognizing and choosing among possible solutions, and (3) incorporating the information gained from experiencing the problem and its solution into one's cognitive framework.

Dewey wrote about the social and psychological aspects of education, holding that children need to be actively engaged in the educational process (not "passive receptacles" like the children in Ms. Putnam's class). In Dewey's view, learning is more than a stimulus-response connection; it is an interactive process in which children intermingle with elements of the immediate environment and learn *through* this interaction. Early in this century Dewey wrote a book with his daughter entitled *Schools of Tomorrow*, in which they described schools that reflected Rousseau's ideas. Still, he is best remembered for developing the philosophy known as pragmatism, which has many influences on education (see Chapter 10.)

MARIA MONTESSORI   Another educational theorist who fits better in the cognitive than in the behavioristic camp is Italian physician Maria Montessori (1870–1952). Her medical practice put her into contact with mentally deficient children

[9]Bigge, *Learning Theories*, 50–51. *Gestalt* is a German word meaning form, figure, shape, organization, or arrangement. The term was used by a group of German psychologists to mean the structure of a person's total perceptions at any given time. Some believed that such perceptual totalities were stored in a field that actually occupied space; others conceived no spatial dimension to the field (just as our thought processes have no spatial dimension). For a discussion of these views see John O'Keefe and Lynn Nadel, *The Hippocampus as a Cognitive Map* (Oxford, England: Oxford University Press, 1978), 5–61.

Maria Montessori
1870–1952

Born in Chiaraville, Italy, to parents of comfortable means, Maria attended the state day school until she was twelve, when her family moved to Rome. Because she liked math, she decided that she wanted to become an engineer—a very unusual choice for a girl at the time. Although her parents wanted her to become a teacher, they did not stop Maria from enrolling in the technical curriculum. By the time she graduated, however, her interest had changed from math to biology, and she decided to become a medical doctor instead of an engineer.

Social opposition to a medical career for women was very strong, but Maria decided to pursue her goal at the University of Rome in 1890. Her father had to accompany her to lectures, and she had to perform laboratory experiments in the evenings, when male students were not around, because it was considered improper for her to dissect bodies in their presence. She overcame other obstacles as well and finally graduated in 1896 with a double honores degree in medicine and surgery—the first female in Italy to accomplish this.

Montessori held a chair of hygiene at a women's college in Rome before being appointed assistant physician in the psychiatric clinic at the University of Rome. In this capacity she visited asylums for the insane that also housed orphaned and retarded children. Observing the conditions in which mentally deficient children lived, Montessori became interested in education. She began

Yesterday's Professional

to study the work of Itard and Seguin concerning Victor, the "Wild Boy" of Aveyron.

In 1904 Montessori accepted the chair of anthropology at the University of Rome, and in 1907 she opened her first Casa dei Bambini in a tenement district in Rome. For the first time she was able to practice her education ideas with normal children. She allowed the preschoolers to work with and manipulate materials in the room, while she observed them. Eventually her work attained international recognition, and she began to train others in her methods. By 1913 she was lecturing all over the world, including the United States, where she was accompanied by such educators as John Dewey and Ella Flagg Young.

Montessori continued her worldwide work on behalf of children for the rest of her life. In 1952 she died in Holland—one of her adopted homes—with her devoted adopted son Mario by her side.

in asylums. Observing the atrocious conditions in which the children lived, Montessori concluded that their problems were educational, not medical. After studying the leading philosophers and social scientists and carefully observing children of various ages in many settings, she opened a house for children—**Casa dei Bambini**—in Rome.

Montessori's views have two basic components: a developmental one and a maturational, or predispositional, one. Regarding human development she postulated that between infancy and eighteen years an individual goes through a mental metamorphosis that can be divided into three stages, or epochs. During the first epoch (birth to age six) the child's mind is like a sponge, absorbing everything it has contact with in the environment. This "absorbent mind" works like a camera and a film developer, snapping pictures (impressions) and storing them in the darkroom of the unconscious mind until the child enters the conscious part of the first epoch, around age three. For several years, aided by self-activities, the child's memory faculty (Montessori espoused a form of faculty psychology) will recall those previously unconscious stored pictures, and will use them to develop new abilities and knowledge.

During the second epoch (ages six to twelve) the child exhibits stable psychic and physical growth in a pattern similar to the first epoch. In other words, little metamorphosis is taking place. But given a correctly prepared environment, the child can learn and store much cultural information. During this stage children become more extroverted; they form gangs for the purpose of socializing.

Finally, the third epoch (ages twelve to eighteen) is subdivided into several years of puberty and several of adolescence. Now the more introverted psychological characteristics emerge: "doubts, hesitations, violent emotions, discouragement, and an unexpected decrease in intellectual capacity, plus a tendency toward creative work and a need for the strengthening of self-confidence."[10] If the environment has been prepared in order to foster the development of these psychological traits, the eighteen-year-old will emerge from the third epoch as a "socially conscious adult . . . member of the human society."[11]

The second component of Montessori's theory was the idea of "sensitive periods" when children are focused on some aspect of the environment like a beacon light "illuminating certain parts of the environment, leaving the rest in comparative obscurity."[12] For example, between ages one and two children need to experience order in their familiar environment. Thus, if Jill's mother decides one day to wear her long hair in a different style—perhaps piled on top of her head—eighteen-month-old Jill might react, perhaps with tears and admonishments to "put hair down." The child is experiencing "disorder" on her mother's person.

Anyone who spends time with children and young adults will appreciate the accuracy in some of Montessori's descriptions. After all, she developed her ideas from observing. But whether her ideas can be generalized to all children has been a point of contention among experts in child development and human cognition. In addition, her acceptance of some aspects of faculty psychology places her somewhat in the nineteenth century. But Montessori captured the importance of sensory experiences and maturation in a child's learning process, and she based her views on observation. Also to her credit, she dispelled many turn-of-the-century notions about mental deficiency. Those who saw her and the students she trained as directresses conduct classes with didactic materials in a prepared environment were usually amazed at the results (as in Ms. Rivera's class, described at the beginning of this chapter). And the marketers of preschool toys certainly came to discover the importance and popularity of materials like hers; today's toy stores are filled with wooden puzzles, stacking blocks, and containers with geometric holes that correspond to geometrically shaped pieces.

JEAN PIAGET   Perhaps the most famous psychologist to follow in Rousseau's cognitive, configurational tradition was Swiss-born Jean Piaget (1896–1980). Although the full impact of his work was not felt in the United States until the 1960s, when behaviorism began to wane, Piaget began to develop his theories as early as 1932, at the Rousseau Institute in Geneva, Switzerland.

[10]E. M. Standing, *Maria Montessori: Her Life and Work* (New York: New American Library, 1962), 114.
[11]Ibid.
[12]Ibid., 19–20.

Developmental psychologist Jean Piaget theorized that each child goes through stages of cognitive growth, picking up skills in a particular order. He argued that the content and structure of a classroom should match the child's level of maturity.
—*Yves De Braine/Black Star*

Like all cognitionists, Piaget was interested in the central organizing processes that shape human intellectual development. He believed that every organism interacts with the environment in an ongoing process that changes and refines the individual's conception and understanding of reality.[13] Two cognitive functions help the organism to adapt to the environment. The first function is **assimilation**, which occurs when an individual takes something from the surroundings and incorporates it into his or her mental structure, or picture of reality. The second function, **accommodation**, is the organism's ability to change or alter the mental picture to fit the assimilated material. Although both functions are always present, they are not always in balance. For example, when children imitate, assimilation outweighs accommodation; and when they play, accommodation outweighs assimilation. But an individual's ability to adapt to the environment is greatest when the two functions *are* in balance, or in equilibrium. Then the individual can best generalize from, differentiate among, and coordinate various mental structures.

Piaget used the term **schema** (Latin), or **scheme**, to refer to the general properties that are needed in order to interact with a particular part of the environment. For instance, a child who is learning to color first learns how to pick up and position the paper, then learns how to grasp the crayon, and finally

[13]For a discussion of Piaget's theories see John L. Phillips, Jr., *Piaget's Theory: A Primer* (New York: Freeman, 1981). Phillips uses the translated term *scheme* instead of Piaget's Latin terms, *schema* and *schemata*.

learns to move the crayon back and forth on the paper to produce color. The three activities of picking up, grasping, and moving the crayon can be applied to *any* crayons and paper; therefore, they form the properties necessary to coloring, or—in Piagetian terms—they are the scheme of coloring.

Known as a developmental psychologist, Piaget described a series of cognitive stages that characterize changes in an infant's intellect as the child eventually matures into adolescence (see Figure 6.1). First is the **sensorimotor stage**, which begins during the first six months and concludes around age two. As the term indicates, the child is developing schemes that pertain to acquiring and coordinating motor skills, such as grasping a favorite object when it is nearby. As the sensorimotor stage progresses, the child learns (through assimilation and accommodation) to find meaning in various signals and symbols, thus creating schemes for these meanings. For example, the smell of apple juice and the sound of it pouring into the child's cup are signals that mean a drink is coming; similarly, seeing Mommy put on her coat symbolizes her departure from home.

Piaget's second developmental stage occurs between ages two and seven and is called the **preoperational stage**. During this period children extend the scope of their activities in order to bring more meaning and order to the environment; they also expand the symbolic schemes that they began to develop toward the end of the sensorimotor stage. In fact, the major difference between the preoperational stage and the sensorimotor stage is that children focus on signals and symbolic manipulations which represent the environment, rather than directly interacting with objects. Preoperational children rely on explanations of symbols as they continue to develop mental structures. During this stage the classification of objects and symbols, guesses about aspects of reality, and the beginnings of logical thought patterns appear. Nonetheless, children at this stage

FIGURE 6.1   Piaget's Stages of Cognitive Development

STAGE OF COGNITIVE DEVELOPMENT	AGE RANGE (Approximate)	MAIN CHARACTERISTICS
SENSORIMOTOR	Infancy to age 2	Coordination of motor skills
PREOPERATIONAL	Age 2 to age 7	Manipulation of symbols representing the environment
CONCRETE OPERATIONS	Age 7 to age 11	Visualization and reversal of concrete operations: more complex classifications (including number concepts)
FORMAL OPERATIONS	Age 11 to age 15	Comprehension of symbolic operations: metaphors, equations, logical propositions, scientific constructs

of development continue to see themselves as the center of their world (called **centering**), and they can only consider their own point of view (**egocentrism**).

The **concrete operations stage**, from about age seven to about age eleven, results in a more advanced system of classification and develops a child's ability to *reverse* operations; that is, besides being able to start with A, add B, and get C, now the child can remove B and return to A. At this stage of development children can begin to comprehend number concepts, and they can visualize many operations in a concrete form but not in an abstract form. In other words they might visualize "love" as a hug from Mom or Dad, but they will not grasp the abstract, more symbolic forms of love.

RESEARCH SAYS

For Tomorrow's Education . . .

The notion that a person is either "right-brained" or "left-brained" has been labeled myth by biopsychologist Jerre Levy in an article entitled "Right Brain, Left Brain: Fact or Fiction," *Psychology Today* (May 1985): 38–44. Levy argues that, while each hemisphere of the brain has specialized abilities, both hemispheres are used regularly.

Piaget's final developmental period is called the **formal operations stage**, which occurs roughly between ages eleven and fifteen. As the term indicates, at this stage of development an adolescent can understand the form of symbolic operations, such as metaphors, equations, logical propositions, and scientific constructs. According to Phillips,

> The adolescent begins where the Concrete Operational child left off. . . . He then *operates on those operations* by casting them into the form of propositions. The propositions then become part of a cognitive structure that owes its existence to past experience but makes possible hypotheses that do not correspond to any particular experience.[14]

As far as teaching is concerned, Piaget's theory of developmental stages argues that the content and structure of a classroom should match the students' level of maturity. Returning once again to Mr. Calhoun's lesson about the solar system, we can see that his use of visualization (when he asked his second-graders to picture a sunrise and sunset) and his introduction of a physical model would generally work well with students in the concrete operations stage. To teach this lesson using other gestalt techniques, Calhoun first would have had to interact with his students in order to assess their developmental level and their perceptual framework. Such an assessment would lead him to provide appropriate instructional materials and situations for his particular students. By interacting with Henry and Jenny, for example, he knew that they would be able to understand the questions that they answered.

[14]Ibid., 163–164.

In planning subsequent lessons about the solar system, Calhoun will need to continue assessing students' individual development, and he will have to provide instructional situations that match their various levels of development. Gestalt teaching techniques in general require an understanding of students' cognitive worlds, which depends on the teacher's ability and willingness to interact with students.

EMPIRICAL LEARNING THEORIES IN PERSPECTIVE

Gestalt theorists differ from behaviorist and stimulus-response theorists in several important ways. First of all—like Dewey, Montessori, and Piaget—they are more concerned about the *way* in which individuals perceive, organize, and bring meaning to the environment. Gestaltists are empirical, but they do not "separate sensation of an object from its meaning."[15] They also have a different view of the relationship between an individual and the environment. Instead of describing a *reaction* to an environmental stimulus, as behaviorists do, gestaltists believe in an *interaction* between the person and the environment; this occurs simultaneously and mutually, and it brings meaning to the individual's purpose at the time of the perception.

The empirical learning theories of this century began to call attention to children as unique individuals who have differences in learning styles. They also pointed to the need for individualized, practical classroom experiences that develop sensory abilities and match students' learning styles. Although operant conditioning and various cognitive theories have been applied to teaching techniques, it is difficult to make each learning situation a one-to-one exchange between teacher and pupil. However, as Chapter 7 will reveal, the practice of grouping students by maturation level or by abilities has been the dominant approach in employing empirical theories in the classroom.

LEARNING THEORY TODAY

■

Figure 6.2 reviews the evolution of learning theories from ancient Greece to modern times. Now we are ready to examine how contemporary science has influenced learning theory.

During the 1960s and 1970s cognitive psychologists were influenced strongly by computer technology and information processing. Many saw the opportunity for new research that focused on the brain as an information-processing unit. Coupled with medical research on the brain, cognitive psychology was subsumed under a broader label with a slightly different research focus. Today **cognitive science** is an emerging field that includes research from neurosurgery, neuropsychology, developmental psychology, cognitive and educational psychology, and information (computer) science.

[15]Bigge, *Learning Theories,* 72.

FIGURE 6.2   Evolution of Learning Theories

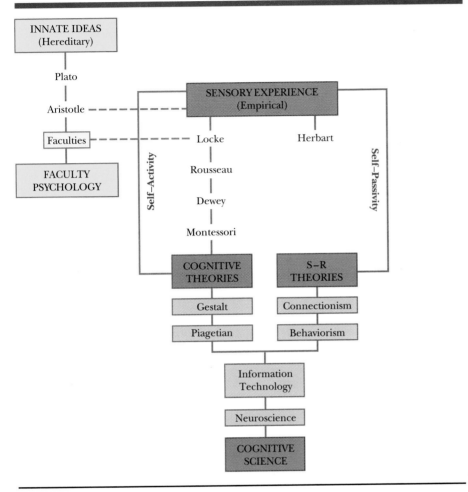

COGNITIVE SCIENCE AND LEARNING THEORY

Interest in developing a "cognitive basis for a pedagogy that fosters thinking and reasoning in school learning" is the basis for current research by cognitive scientists.[16] Following researchers who attempted to understand the higher-order abilities involved in thinking and problem solving, cognitive scientists are studying the "structures and processes of human competence" as well as "the nature of the performance system as a consequence of learning and development."[17] This focus contrasts with past theories that attempted to describe and account for the acquisition and transition processes of learning. In other words, scientists today are studying the cognitive structure as it exists (including its acquired knowledge and skills), whereas scientists in the past aimed to describe and theorize about what is needed for learning to occur. The focus in the past was on *how* the learning process takes place, instead of on *what* learning is. A couple of examples will illustrate the difference.

[16]Robert Glaser, "Education and Thinking: The Role of Knowledge," *American Psychologist* 39 (February 1984): 93.

[17]Robert Glaser, "The Reemergence of Learning Theory Within Instructional Research," *American Psychologist* 45 (January 1990): 29.

RESEARCH SAYS

For Tomorrow's Education . . .
Research and advances in artificial intelligence have led to a technology of
cognitive task analysis. This represents important progress for future models
of learning and instruction. See Robert Glaser, "Education and Thinking:
The Role of Knowledge," *American Psychologist* 38 (February 1984):
93–104; and Robert Glaser, "The Reemergence of Learning Theory Within
Instructional Research," *American Psychologist* 43 (January 1990): 29–39.

First, consider that the manner in which reading is taught, even today, is
based on past learning theories that emphasized the acquisition of knowledge
and skills. The focus has been on teaching such basic communication skills as
word recognition, the correspondence of sounds and letters, and the reverse
process of decoding letters into sounds. Educators have been fairly successful at
designing reading programs based on these basic skills. Even Piaget's work increased our understanding of *how* children acquire certain basic cognitive skills
as they mature. But problems arise when students are asked to progress beyond
basic language acquisitions to develop the critical thinking skills needed for com-
prehending written material. Yes, Johnny can read; but is his reading meaningful
and thoughtful?

Consider a second example. Sam is very good at writing stories with great
plots, exciting turns of events, and dramatic outcomes. But his subject and setting
are always the same: some kind of adventure in the north woods. Sam has been
at home in the woods since he was a small boy, and more recently has become
a camp counselor in the woods. Chuck, his younger brother, knows that a good
story has to have the ingredients Sam includes (exciting plots, turning points,
and outcomes), because he has learned it in school. Although Chuck can readily
identify these elements in Sam's stories, he has never gone camping or exploring
with his brother. He thus lacks the expert knowledge needed to write such stories
himself.

According to cognitive learning theory, Johnny and Chuck have a similar
problem: They lack the organized knowledge structures that are acquired by long
periods of experience and learning. In other words, Johnny will be able to think
critically about what he reads when he develops thought structures that are acquired by studying and applying various bodies of knowledge. Similarly, Chuck
could become a better storyteller by acquiring expert knowledge that can be
fashioned into plot lines. Both boys need to learn more through experience;
lacking experience, they have not acquired the cognitive structures needed for
the skills they seek.

These conclusions are based on recent studies of how human memory is
organized, of what knowledge and information processes are needed to solve
problems, and of the characteristics of human understanding. According to theorist Robert Glaser, cognitive learning research "suggests that the knowledge of
novices is organized around the literal objects explicitly given in a problem state-

ment. Experts' knowledge, on the other hand, is organized around principles and abstractions that subsume these objects.''[18] Successful instruction in schools seems now to depend on research that will produce a knowledge-based curriculum which enhances students' understanding of content and also develops higher-order thinking. Thus, if Tina is an expert at solving an instructional problem in school and Jack is a novice, we can teach Jack to solve the problem by first understanding what knowledge structures Tina has that Jack lacks; then we can help Jack acquire the same knowledge structures.

CLASSROOM APPLICATIONS OF COGNITIVE RESEARCH

For a decade or so some educators have applied recent cognitive research by developing packaged materials that provide teachers with strategies and skills to help students realize higher-order thinking and cognitive growth.[19] Specifically, such materials train teachers to

1. Set up the classroom so that all students can experience the curriculum
2. Help students process new information
3. Help students organize and conceptualize information
4. Design and deliver lessons that students can remember

Regarding item 1, the focus is on providing a variety of sensory experiences so that students are not limited to a single sensory modality, such as listening to the teacher's lecture. For example, in teaching a lesson about the uses of energy, the teacher might start by asking students to tell the class all the things they did

Cognitive research tells teachers to present information in a variety of sensory modes; to organize it in units that help students process it; to conceptualize it in a variety of ways; and to make it relevant (and thus memorable) to students' experiences. —Tony Freeman/PhotoEdit

[18]Glaser, "Education and Thinking," 98–99.

[19]See, for example, the set of materials designed by Joe K. Hasenstab and Geraldine Flaherty, *Teaching Through Learning Channels* (Emerson, N.J.: Performance Learning Systems, 1982).

that day that used energy (the auditory sense). Next, the students could write a list of their energy uses (visual sense) and then could become involved with touch and movement by writing their lists on the chalkboard (kinetic and tactile senses).

In the case of item 2, teachers can learn how to organize lessons into units that help students process information. Going back to Herbart's ideas, teachers need to relate new information to what students already know, so that it can be labeled and incorporated into a generalization and then can be applied. For example:

> In teaching creative writing to tenth-graders, Ms. Rigby focused on the variety of sensations that verbs can evoke. Then she asked students to identify which sensations a number of verbs elicited. Then she asked them to label these verbs in terms of actions (hearing, seeing, feeling) to draw attention to similarities and differences among them. Next, students were asked to read sections of their favorite poems and to identify any verbs that shared one of the above labels. Finally, students were asked to evaluate their previous writing and to change any verbs that could be used more accurately and more effectively.

Comparative Perspective on Today's Issues . . .

◆ **ARE SPECIFIC PROGRAMS TO TEACH THINKING NEEDED?**

The Issue   The recent call that schools should provide excellence has brought attention to the problems involved in accomplishing such a goal. One problem is how to go about developing students' critical and creative thinking.

YES   Recent standardized test results point to gains in basic skills but reveal that some areas are still deficient—for example, students' ability to think critically and to apply basic factual information that they have covered. Thus teachers must incorporate into their lessons various strategies, materials, and activities that emphasize similarities and differences between concepts, that make students aware of their thinking processes, and that explore habits of effective thinking.

—Jay McTighe, critical thinking specialist, Division of Instruction, Maryland State Department of Education

NO   The issue is not that students need to think critically and creatively but that educators are not in agreement about the means for accomplishing it. "There is no such thing as thinking in and of itself" (216). Thinking is not a skill that can be acquired in a vacuum; it must be used and developed in conjunction with all the skills that allow us to use our brains effectively. The purpose of the *Paideia Proposal* is "to turn out thoughtful citizens and learners—persons able to think well and critically in everything they do" (218).

—Mortimer Adler, Director of the Institute of Philosophical Research

Source: Based on James Wm. Noll, ed., *Taking Sides: Clashing Views on Controversial Educational Issues,* 5th ed. (Guilford, Conn.: Dushkin, 1989), 208–219.

Teachers can help students organize and conceptualize information (item 3) in various ways. For example, information can be presented sequentially (like the letters of the alphabet and numbers) or simultaneously (as a brainstorming session in which students call out their ideas randomly).[20] Many concepts can be presented either in physical images or in symbolic images. For example, students can be asked to picture "a pencil" (physical image) or to think of "the word *pencil*" (symbolic image). For any object, what first comes to mind—whether a physical or a symbolic image—is usually the preferred cognitive form. And, of course, some concepts are too complex or too abstract to be pictured physically. But by understanding cognitive organizations and forms, teachers can help students organize and conceptualize information more meaningfully. If high school students are reading a play, the class first might brainstorm to identify its main themes (random organization) and then might be asked to list the themes in the order that the play presents them (sequential organization). To gain a meaningful physical experience of the play, students could be assigned roles to act out in class.

Finally, teachers can help students remember information (item 4). They know that students need to see a reason for learning the material; indeed, many students need to be given a "compelling reason" to learn it. The goal here is much like Herbart's first step in teaching—preparation—which relaxes students and puts them "in the mood" to learn by making them recall personal experiences that can be associated with the new material. Often a particular problem or goal can be tied to learning the new material. Perhaps students are going to collect money for UNICEF at Halloween; that's a good opportunity to present a lesson about the United Nations.

Once students see a reason to learn the new information, the instructor needs to provide memory devices that will help them retain the information. Studies have shown that people find it difficult to remember more than seven items of information in one presentation. Knowing this, the teacher can organize a lesson around seven or less items, or "chunks," of information. And a lesson that repeats the new information three times will help students retain the material in long-term memory.

The example of a Spanish lesson will show these principles in practice. The teacher wants to present the conjugation of the infinitive *estar*, "to be." The students' motivation for learning this information is an upcoming visit by a student from Mexico. The class wants to be able to ask, "How are you?" and to respond, "I am fine." First the instructor presents the six forms of *estar*:

Singular

estoy	I am
estás	you are (informal)
está	he, she, it is / you are (formal)

Plural

estamos	we are
estáis	you are (informal)
están	they are / you are (formal)

[20]See, for example, J. P. Das, ed., *Child Neuropsychology* 1 (Academic Press, 1986): 117–140, 217–239; Sally P. Springer and Georg Deutsch, *Left Brain, Right Brain* (New York: Freeman, 1981), 179–203; and Morton Hunt, *The Universe Within* (New York: Simon & Schuster, 1982).

After presenting the conjugation, the teacher develops a rhythm that fits the six forms and then has the class practice it three times. First the students pronounce the written words on the chalkboard (visual and auditory sense modes); then they say them in rhythm (auditory mode); and finally they write the words on a piece of paper (visual and tactile modes).

The applications of cognitive science in the field of teaching have taken other forms, too, but basically these examples illustrate the approach.[21] Schools of education as well as in-service workshops provided by school districts have exposed both experienced and future teachers to these methods. Although there is always more to discover about human thinking and learning, cognitive science has given educators a solid foundation on which to build better pedagogical theories and techniques.

CONCLUSIONS

Ideas about human thinking and learning have changed throughout history, and so has pedagogy, or the art of teaching. Beginning with the Greeks, including Plato and Aristotle, it was thought that human beings are born with knowledge, or idea potentials. The pedagogical goal was to draw these out and exercise them through mental discipline—especially through the study of logical subjects like mathematics. A related belief was the idea that the mind is divided into specialized faculties, of which the most important is reasoning (the rational faculty). Such ideas lingered in one form or another until well into the nineteenth century, and they are the basis of pedagogical approaches that rely on rote memory.

In contrast to these notions about inborn potentials, in the seventeenth century John Locke formulated a theory that conceived of the mind as a "blank tablet" (*tabula rasa*) that is filled throughout life by sensory experiences. Although this empirical view was unpopular at the time, later philosophers and educators—especially Rousseau and Herbart—followed Locke in postulating theories about the role of the senses in learning. The pedagogical goal became one of providing students with sensory experiences that would help them to associate new information with former information. Herbart proposed that teachers accomplish this through five steps: preparation, presentation, association, generalization, and application.

As the twentieth century approached, educational psychologists began to advance variations on empirical learning theories. Herbart's version of associationism was replaced by behavioristic theories like connectionism, or stimulus-response bond theory, which influences behavior by using positive and negative reinforcers. By the mid-1940s, B. F. Skinner had articulated his ideas about operant conditioning as a means of changing behavior through positive reinforcement, and the approach was applied to learning behavior through such techniques as programmed instruction.

Pedagogical approaches changed again when Skinner's behaviorism was challenged by configuration theory (gestalt field theory), which is concerned

[21]See any articles or materials by Madaline Hunter, such as "Knowing, Teaching, and Supervising," in *Using What We Know about Teaching*, Philip L. Hosford, ed. (Alexandria, Va.: Association for Supervision and Curriculum Development, 1984), 169–92; or "Script-Taping: An Essential Supervisory Tool," in *Educational Leadership* 41 (1983) 3: 43.

with an individual's interaction with the environment and the manner in which the individual perceives that interaction. The emphasis is on the *experience* of learning and on how experience affects a developing mind. Major contributions in these areas were made by philosopher John Dewey, educator Maria Montessori, and cognitive psychologist Jean Piaget; their theories led to efforts to match the content and structure of a classroom to students' maturational levels. It is difficult, however to make each learning situation a one-to-one exchange between teacher and pupil.

Most recently, research in neuropsychology, developmental psychology, cognitive and educational psychology, and information processing has combined in the emerging field of cognitive science. The theoretical focus has shifted from *how* we learn to *what* we learn. Does experience (learning) change the brain's cognitive structures, and how do those structures incorporate new information into the old? Pedagogical goals and approaches have also shifted as teachers learn how to help their students develop cognitive structures that support higher-order thinking.

KEY TERMS

didactic material	negative reinforcer
pedagogy	Skinner box
mental discipline	Casa dei Bambini
faculty psychology	assimilation
tabula rasa	accommodation
empiricism	scheme
associationism	sensorimotor stage
mental states	preoperational stage
apperception	centering
apperceptive mass	egocentrism
connectionism	concrete operations stage
stimulus-response (S-R) bond theory	formal operations stage
operant conditioning	cognitive science
positive reinforcer	

SUGGESTED READINGS

Maria Montessori, *The Montessori Method* (New York: Schocken, 1974). This paperback describes Montessori's developmental and educational theories and their application in the classroom.

John L. Phillips, Jr., *Jean Piaget: A Primer* (New York: Freeman, 1981). Phillips discusses the main tenets of Piagetian theory.

B. F. Skinner, *Beyond Freedom and Dignity* (New York: Bantam Books, 1972). Skinner describes how human behavior can be managed through the influence of external forces. In the classroom this approach overrides unfavorable factors by introducing positive reinforcement.

Carl Rogers, *Freedom to Learn for the 80s* (Columbus, Ohio: Merrill, 1983). Rogers presents humanistic psychology as aiming to achieve an inner state of responsibility, commitment, and will. He also critiques Skinner's behavioristic theory of learning.

S. F. Chipman and R. Glaser, eds., *Thinking and Learning Skills: Relating Instruction to Basic Research,* vol. 1 (Hillsdale, N.J.: Erlbaum, 1985). The authors explore the relationship between instruction and research into thinking, learning, and problem solving.

Robert M. Gagne and Marcy P. Driscoll, *Essentials of Learning for Instruction,* 2d ed. (Boston: Allyn & Bacon, 1988). The authors present a contemporary view of learning that is founded on the most recent cognitive research and theory.

Curricula and Learning

Psychological Foundations B

7

> If there is one battle Mel and Norma Gabler have been winning in the twenty years they have been objecting to America's textbooks, it is their fight to have creationism taught alongside evolution in biology classes: biology texts today often ignore or substantially downplay evolution. Whereas a 1973 Charles Merrill text contained seventeen references to evolution in its index, the 1979 edition has but three. And other texts, such as a 1980 Houghton Mifflin biology book, discuss both evolution and divine creation as possible explanations of the origin of life.

—William Martin, "The Guardians Who Slumbereth Not," Texas Monthly 10 (November 1982): 148

> Depending on your point of view, "Impressions" is either a treasure-trove of children's literature or a passport to perdition. . . . "Impressions" has aroused the righteous indignation of some parents who see in its pages a challenge to traditional family values. . . . One way or another, they want the series out of the school.

—Jeff Merde, "A War of Words," Teacher Magazine 2 (November–December 1990): 38

7

Curricula and Learning

ADVANCED ORGANIZERS

■

In this chapter you will learn

Which subjects were important to study in past societies

What contributions Loyola and Comenius made to education

The child-centered nature of progressive education

How graduate and professional education developed

The role of textbooks in the curriculum

How the needs of exceptional students are met

CHAPTER OUTLINE

■

William Bowen has just won a second term on the school board, and his colleagues have chosen him president. At thirty-six, Bowen is an attorney who has lived in the town of 100,000 for ten years, and he is a partner in the area's most prominent law firm. He is thinking of running for the state legislature, and he hopes that his position as school board president will increase his "name recognition"; recent developments certainly promise to make the board's activities newsworthy.

Significant disagreements, which had been smoldering, became public just before the board's elections. After seeing his daughter's high school biology text, the minister of a large local fundamentalist congregation preached a sermon against "godlessness in the schools." As a result, several members of the congregation formed a citizens' committee to petition the school board to drop the text.

Stimulated by media reports of this controversy, another parent has complained about the American history text, which he believes is unpatriotic because it suggests that American involvement in Vietnam may have been a mistake. He is further displeased by an optional assignment that allows students to write a review of the movie *Born on the Fourth of July*.

Rounding out the agenda for Bowen's first meeting as president are requests to address the board from the chamber of commerce and from LULAC, an organization concerned with Hispanic issues. The chamber of commerce wants to remind the board that several local business and industry leaders have prepared a resolution asking that the schools give more time and attention to "workplace skills." LULAC wants to represent some of the city's Hispanic parents who are distressed about the recent decision to end bilingual instruction in elementary schools. (Nearly 20 percent of the town's population is Hispanic—and the number is growing—but the school system is strapped for money, and some Anglo parents have complained that the bilingual program is both un-American and expensive.)

As Bowen drives into the parking lot of the administration building to chair the meeting, he is barely able to get past a group of demonstrators carrying signs reading, "Keep God in Our Schools" and "Let's Keep America Strong." He smiles and says, "No comment," to Channel 3's reporter and slips through the door, where the superintendent of schools joins him for the walk to the meeting room. "Bill, I know the agenda is crowded, but you will need to save a few minutes to inform the board that we have just been served notice that a parent is suing us. It's about the board's policy that all ninth-graders must take physical education and must wear regulation shorts and shoes. The parent has religious objections to the shorts and says we're abridging First Amendment rights."

Not every new school board president faces so challenging a first meeting, of course, but many wrestle with such issues—and with others just as divisive. The fact is that Americans do not agree about what should be learned in schools or about where the boundaries lie between individual or family rights and professional or social goals. Insightful educators need to be aware of the major controversies, which a look at past beliefs and practices will help illuminate.

EARLY EDUCATION

∎

Curriculum is a Latin word (plural = *curricula*) that originally referred to a defined path or course, such as a race course; in time it came to refer to a defined or particular course of study. Much of today's curriculum has roots in ancient Greece and Rome. The Greeks, for example, taught grammar, logic, and rhetoric to most boys of the citizen class, and many young men also studied music, astronomy, geometry, and arithmetic. Most young women had limited exposure to the same curriculum, which aimed primarily to make them agreeable companions and mothers. Physical conditioning and development were ongoing; sports (running, boxing, wrestling) were emphasized for boys, and dancing (to teach graceful movement) was stressed for girls. We know relatively little about how girls were educated, but it seems to have happened in different settings from those for boys. By age twelve Greek girls were so protected as to be in virtual seclusion.

It was the Egyptians who pioneered the seven "academic" subjects that the Greeks referred to as the **seven liberal arts**: grammar, rhetoric, logic, astronomy, arithmetic, music, and geometry. They used this label because they believed these studies increased human potential by *liberating* people from irrational passions. The Romans adopted, refined, and spread this curriculum throughout their empire, which included most of Europe, much of the Middle East, and some of North Africa. The Christian church added religion and extended the seven liberal arts wherever missionaries traveled. The first three subjects came to be known as the *trivium*, and the last four were called the *quadrivium*.

As noted in Chapter 6, even in ancient times there was a longstanding general belief that learning had a significant innate quality—that a child's "inborn potentials" were exercised and trained through mental discipline. There was also a basic assumption that anyone who had trouble learning either did not have the innate potential (Aristotle thought that women and slaves lacked the capacity for a liberal education and, therefore, should give up the attempt) or was somehow resisting or blocking the process of learning. In the latter case the only remedy most people could think of was physical punishment, usually a thrashing. "The youth has a back and attends [pays attention] when he is beaten," ran an ancient Egyptian proverb. "The ears of the young are placed on the back."

There were, of course, some patient masters and some sensitive parents who disliked whipping, either as a control or as a motivator. As early as the first century A.D. the Spanish-born Roman master named Quintilian wrote that flogging should be avoided completely. A teacher, he said, should be

> strict but not austere, genial but not too familiar; for austerity will make him unpopular, while familiarity breeds contempt. . . . He must control his temper without however shutting his eyes to faults requiring correction; his instruction must be free from affectation, his industry great, his demands on the class continuous, but not extravagant. He must be ready to answer questions and to put them unasked to those who sit silent. In praising the recitations

of his pupils he must be neither grudging nor overgenerous: the former quality will give them a distaste for work, while the latter will produce a complacent self-satisfaction. In correcting faults he must avoid sarcasm and above all abuse: for teachers whose rebukes seem to imply positive dislike discourage industry.[1]

For hundreds of years—from the first century until the sixteenth—curriculum, methodology, and learning theory remained constant in Europe. Even the significant refocusing that the Christian movement brought did not fundamentally alter the main body of academic skills which schools taught, and—admonitions to love one another notwithstanding—religious teachers were as likely to whack hands or lay red stripes across a flagging learner's back as were their secular counterparts. Although individual teachers rediscovered the truths of Quintilian's advice many times, there was no systematic training of teachers and thus no way to generalize a different view of teaching and learning.

"THE RISE OF MODERN SCIENCE"

CHANGES IN SOCIETY

Although the revolution in attitudes and beliefs that took place from about 1400 to 1700 was too complex and too far-reaching to be captured by any single label, the era is sometimes termed "the rise of modern science," and it ushered in educational change. For the most part, schools and universities—representing the most firmly established features of culture—resisted change more than they led the way. Nonetheless, an educational revolution was started, and it is still under way.

It was in the study of astronomy that long-cherished models first began to fail. The Greeks and their successors had conceived of the universe in terms of circles and perfection, and they had elaborated models that were satisfactory for centuries. The explanations began to fail, however, with the Arab importation into Spain of Indian astronomical observations and with the invention of the telescope, which produced a growing body of empirical data that did not fit the assumptions of existing models. At first many people doubted the data; then there were major efforts to explain the new data using old models; finally, with the invention of calculus by Sir Isaac Newton (1642–1727), a new model replaced the old. Other observational discoveries in physics, chemistry, biology, and geology followed, as "scientific societies" arose throughout Europe.

As experimental science began to erode accepted knowledge and conventional wisdom, other aspects of life also came under organized scrutiny. Critics in the Roman Catholic Church, including John Wycliffe (1320?–1384) and John Huss (1369?–1415), called for extensive reform. A little later Martin Luther (1483–1546), a German monk, escalated the debate by advocating rejection of some forms of Church authority to remedy the lack of change. Within a few

[1]Marcus Fabius Quintilianus, *The Instituto Oratoria*, trans. H. E. Butler (London: Heinemann, 1921), bk. 2, ii, 5–7.

When Galileo turned his telescope on the heavens, he challenged models and concepts of the universe that had endured for centuries. Cherished circles of perfection were, literally, bent out of shape by the rise of modern science. —North Wind Picture Archives

decades Roman Catholic reformers were vying with leaders of the new Protestant sects for the hearts and minds of Europeans. This was about two centuries before Locke and Herbart elaborated their sense-based learning theories (discussed in Chapter 6), but it fueled the emerging efforts to ground educational practice in empiricism rather than in tradition. Thus the crucible of religious competition refined the ideas of modern teacher education.

CHANGES IN EDUCATION: LOYOLA AND COMENIUS

Although many people were involved in the revolution in teacher training, it will suffice to consider only the two most famous. One was a Spanish aristocrat, Ignatius of Loyola (1482?–1556), who left professional soldiering in his thirties after nearly dying of a battle wound. While recuperating, he had a conversion experience that led him to return to schoolboy studies as an adult and, ultimately, to form the Society of Jesus, a religious order better known as the Jesuits. The second reformer was a bourgeois Moravian named John Amos Comenius (1592–1670), who was born a little after Ignatius died. Comenius was chief bishop of the Moravian Brethren, a small Protestant sect that no longer exists under that name. He regarded the Jesuits as his archenemy.

Although these two may seem an unlikely pair to reform teacher training, they set a powerful tradition in motion. Loyola did not intend for his society to make education its primary mission; he and his companions were willing to serve in whatever way they were most needed—and this turned out to be in establishing schools. There was considerable demand for effective schools, and the group that developed them was likely to make (or keep) converts among the students as well as their families.

Loyola had three sources on which to base his educational decisions (four sources, if we include prayer). One source was his own experience as an adult learner. Another was the record of those who had written about teaching. And finally there were observations of, and conversations with, teachers of high reputation. (During the early years Loyola required all Jesuit teachers to keep diaries of their teaching experiences and to submit these for periodic review.) Using these sources, representatives from different geographic areas met for more than a year to distill and systematically write out their conclusions about how to organize and approach teaching in a way that would maximize learning. After showing an early draft to a cross-section of experienced teachers, the committee wrote a final version that members of the new society ratified as part of their basic governing document.

The Jesuits' approach to teaching stressed (1) short, well-organized presentations containing a small number of key concepts, followed by breaks for exercise and movement; (2) carefully varied repetition of each key concept; (3) equal treatment of all students, with no segregation or special arrangements for nobility; (4) supervised physical education and games; (5) the use of pupils to teach certain parts of lessons as a reward for doing well; (6) frequent disputations (debates) with appropriate rewards for excellent performance—an approach essentially like what is now called "moot court" in American law schools;

Ignatius of Loyola, founder of the Jesuits, revolutionized teacher training in his efforts to attract converts to Catholic schools. Comenius, a Protestant bishop, was impressed enough to adopt the Jesuits' methods without their theology.
—North Wind Picture Archives

(7) partial self-governance with a variety of offices filled by students; (8) regular holidays interspersed with carefully planned days; (9) the ready availability of books and supplies; (10) student drama as an aid to learning; (11) specific talks with boys who needed correction, rather than general admonitions to everyone; (12) extensive supervision by teachers who were setting good examples (and sparing use of corporal punishment under carefully specified conditions); (13) the grading of pupils by age and readiness; and (14) letting teachers stay with (move up with) younger pupils for two or more years.[2]

Although some Protestant leaders concentrated on doctrinal and political differences with their Roman Catholic competitors, several noted the Jesuits' success in education and began advocating the use of their techniques in Protestant groups. Comenius, for example, argued repeatedly that one did not need to agree with Jesuit theology in order to recognize the educational value of games and plays, of realistically limited amounts of content in each lesson, of frequent periods of rest and diversion, of building on students' interest, of teaching basic and simple concepts before introducing advanced and complex ones. "My whole method aims at changing the school drudgery into play and enjoyment," wrote Comenius. The Jesuits "entice to themselves the most gifted heads of the whole world by their pleasant method, and make them fit, by the exercise of that kind, for their life tasks; while we remain backward in ours."[3] Comenius embraced the theory that learning comes about through the senses (see Chapter 6).

SEARCHING FOR THE ALCHEMIST'S FORMULA

Part of the advance of science which today may seem naive was widespread optimism that experimentation would lead to discovery of the secret of existence and the structure of reality. Those with an eye for profit hoped to be first to discover the secret—and to use the knowledge to turn base metals such as lead into gold, thus becoming fabulously rich.

The dramatic success of Loyola, Comenius, and their numerous followers and colleagues led to similar hopes among those who were interested in educational improvement. That is, either through happy accident or by sustained experiment, they anticipated finding the key to unlock the mysteries of teaching. Some, like Locke and Herbart, used logic or philosophy to examine what learning through the senses (rather than training innate potentials) would imply for how to conduct instruction. Others searched empirically for improvements in technology; in the organization, size, and management of classrooms; in the relationships between teacher and students and among students; and in curricular organization and content. One of the most influential of these experimental movements in America was called the "Lancasterian" or "monitorial" system. It involved all the elements just mentioned.

MONITORIAL REFORM: LANCASTER

Whatever the source of school funding, colonial American teachers (and many in Europe) were paid according to which subjects they taught and how many pupils they had. This encouraged large schools: 75 to 130 pupils daily was typical,

[2]L. Glenn Smith, "For the Greater Glory of God: Religious Competition and Educational Improvement, 1565–1650," in *History of Elementary School Teaching and Curriculum*, International Series for the History of Education, ed. Giovanni Genovesi et al. (Hannover: Universität Hannover Veröffentlichung der International Standing Conference for the History of Education [ISCHE], 1990), 1–7.

[3]Mathew Spinka, *John Amos Comenius—That Incomparable Moravian* (Chicago: University of Chicago Press, 1943), 129–130.

and masters ran even larger operations with the help of paid assistants (or ushers). Masters assigned each pupil a lesson to prepare, and then they or the assistant "heard" each pupil recite. During an individual's recitation the master offered corrections, made a new assignment, and allowed time for preparing a new lesson. The process was then repeated.

Because pupils varied in age from five or younger to over twenty—and because the recitation process was time-consuming—it was not unusual for masters in America to ask older, more accomplished pupils to help younger, less skilled ones. Toward the end of the eighteenth century, people in several coun-

---

RESEARCH SAYS

For Tomorrow's Education . . .

Traditionally the teaching of reading comprehension has focused on teaching a set of subskills that involves sequencing events, predicting outcomes, and drawing conclusions about the story. This approach is being displaced by a new model that views the learner not as passive but as actively engaged in constructing meanings from both old and new knowledge and by using strategies to regulate and preserve comprehension. Teaching also is viewed as an active process, since teachers and students collaborate in mediating the story's meaning by using the instructional climate. See Janice A. Dol, Gerald G. Duffy, Laura R. Roehler, and P. David Pearson, "Moving from the Old to the New: Research on Reading Comprehension Instruction," *Review of Educational Research* 61 (Summer 1991): 239–264.

---

tries began to write and lecture about ways of making "school keeping" more efficient. One of these was Joseph Lancaster, son of a London sieve maker, who as a Quaker was interested in the education of poor children. Lancaster worked out a set of procedures for running a school, and he developed pedagogical aids and experimented with routines known as the **monitorial system**:

> Lancaster's monitorial pedagogy was like a spelling bee all day long. Students in groups of ten or twelve gathered around their monitors in semi-circles to compete in reading or spelling; when one student failed, the next was given a chance to answer correctly and move to the higher position. In studying arithmetic, everyone wrote his [or her] sums on a slate and, at the command "show slates," held it up for the monitor's inspection and correction. It was arbitrary and regimented, but also competitive, active, and possibly, under the supervision of a talented master, fun. Psychologically, the monitorial scheme provided constant activity, immediate reinforcement, and individual pupil progress. . . . Pupils were classified separately in reading, writing, spelling, and arithmetic. . . . Lancasterian advocates often asserted that monitors, being closer in age to their pupils than adult masters, would understand their

Joseph Lancaster's monitorial system solved several problems of classroom management by using older, more accomplished students to hear the recitations of younger, less skilled ones. It was "regimented, but also competitive, active, and possibly . . . fun." —Bettmann

problems better and use a vocabulary more appropriate to the young child. In addition, they claimed, the monitors themselves would learn by teaching.[4]

The groups of students were arranged according to skill, and pupils could be promoted to a higher group any time their skills justified it. For example, one student might be promoted in reading but not in math or spelling, while another might be promoted in spelling and reading but not in math. There was also a system of "merit tickets," each worth a certain amount of money, which were given for good behavior and academic achievement; students could redeem the tickets for such rewards as tops, pictures, balls, and books.

Lancaster started his experiment in 1800. Within ten years it was an organized movement, and he had international fame. He did not handle it well. "He was improvident, arrogant, ungrateful, impulsive, and unreliable," writes one historian. "Having been praised as the benefactor of mankind, he came to believe that society owed him a living. . . . He had other problems: recurring personal illnesses, an incurably deranged wife, and a very exaggerated estimate of his own abilities."[5]

Despite Lancaster's personal failings and difficulties, the movement lasted three decades in the United States and was influential in many other countries. It spawned the first educational journal in America, and it propelled the search for more effective ways to convey the curriculum to students. Some criticized Lancaster's approach as being too mechanistic—which in unskilled hands it could be—but its use of peer teaching and its emphasis on active learning of content are well regarded today.

[4]Carl Kaestle, ed., *Joseph Lancaster and the Monitorial School Movement: A Documentary History*, Classics in Education, no. 47 (New York: Teachers College Press, Columbia University, 1973), 6–7.

[5]Kaestle, *Joseph Lancaster*, 26–27.

OBJECTS, NOT WORDS: PESTALOZZI AND FROEBEL

The philosophy of innate potentials naturally led teachers to an emphasis on symbols and words, on vocabulary and grammatical rules. In practice this often meant extensive rote memorization—and flogging, when children found themselves confused or uninterested. In contrast, proponents of learning through the senses thought that direct experience was much more effective in instruction than words and symbols were. Much of the search for improved empirical teaching methods involved attempts to manipulate learners' sensory experiences. For example, Jean Jacques Rousseau's whole plan for educating little Emile (see Chapter 6) was centered on the parents' or teacher's understanding of how to organize and control the child's "natural" experiences. In fact, Emile was not to have access to *any* reading material until he was twelve.

Of the many experimentors who wrote about how to teach more effectively through the senses, two names stand out: Johann Heinrich Pestalozzi and Friedrich Froebel. Although both men experienced difficulties and unhappiness in their personal lives, their work became symbols and referents in the search for a "science of education."

PESTALOZZI   Johann Heinrich Pestalozzi (1746–1827) was the second of three children born in Zurich to a respectable but poor surgeon who died when Heinrich was five. The boy had an awkward childhood and did poorly in some of Zurich's better schools; as a young adult he lost money farming and turned finally to writing moralistic fiction, which brought him some favorable notice. He also tried with limited success to rear his only son "naturally" (the boy was called "little Jacques," after Rousseau).

When he was past fifty, Pestalozzi stumbled into a relationship with three young men who had been asked by the government to found and run (in an abandoned castle in the town of Burgdorf) a teacher training institute for peasant children who then would become schoolmasters. The three men—Hermann Krüsi, J. G. Tobler, and Johannes C. Buss—experimented with movable letters for teaching reading and spelling; with pebbles and beans to teach counting and arithmetic; with the use of slates and slate pencils, instead of expensive pens and paper; and with the use of drawing as a preliminary step to writing. They considered their techniques a quest for "The Method." After a couple of years a government inspector who had heard good things about their establishment visited it, and his glowing report gave Pestalozzi credit for the activity. The younger

RESEARCH SAYS

For Tomorrow's Education . . .
Encouraging children to become involved in artistic creation can improve their understanding of knowledge that they already possess. See Karen Gallas, "Arts As Epistemology: Enabling Children to Know What They Know," *Harvard Educational Review* 61 (February 1991): 40–50.

men—out of respect for Pestalozzi's age and his need for recognition—allowed the report to stand.

The resulting publicity (first in German, and then in other languages) about "Pestalozzi's method" brought many educators, tourists, and politicians to Burgdorf. Krüsi, Tobler, and Buss recruited other able associates, and for a few years the establishment flourished (even after it was forced to move to Yverdon because of a change in Swiss politics caused by Napoleon). Ultimately, all of Pestalozzi's associates left him over personal differences as his moods swung from elation to depression to anger. The demise of the establishment started before 1810 and happened over several years, but it was little noted by the outside world. Instead, educators from several European countries, fifteen German states, Canada, and the United States wrote and talked about Pestalozzi's method of **object teaching**.

FROEBEL   The youngest of five brothers, Friedrich Froebel (1782–1852) lost his mother when he was only nine months old. His busy minister father remarried a woman who—soon pregnant with her own child–had little time or patience for young Friedrich. Froebel turned inward. Gradually he came to identify consciously with Jesus, and he evolved a personal faith that included elements of mysticism. He tried forestry, the army, surveying, and accounting, and he did some university study (without earning a degree) before turning to his life's work—teaching children. This came about when a favorite brother died, leaving three children, and Friedrich took over their instruction. With friends he formed a succession of schools in different towns and wrote a book, *The Education of Man*, laying out his theories. He had twice visited Pestalozzi's operation in Yverdon.

In 1837 Froebel gave full practical expression to his ideas by founding at Blankenburg (about halfway between Hannover and Leipzig) a "children's garden"; we know this by its German name, **Kindergarten**. Here he developed teaching materials and approaches that he called "gifts" and "occupations." The **gifts** consisted of six sets of geometric shapes. A child could manipulate these shapes, but the shapes themselves did not change; hence, the child learned the universal nature of things. The **occupations** involved materials that could be transformed, as in paper contructing, cardboard cutting, sand molding, clay modeling, and wood building. These activities were to grow out of using the gifts. Other occupations were sewing, weaving, and drawing—all of which require extensive *self-activity*, a vital concept for Froebel. Games, plays, singing, and dancing (more self-activity) completed Froebel's catalog of methods and materials.

Several women helped Froebel develop and popularize these ideas. His first wife, Henrietta Hoffmeister, was a soul mate throughout the development years, but she died in 1839. In 1851 he married Louise Leven, who was much younger than he, and she helped spread the movement after Froebel died, in 1852. So did the Baroness Bertha von Marenholtz-Bulow, who devoted her money, time, and social conscience to propagandizing for Froebel's ideas both before and after his death.

PESTALOZZI AND FROEBEL IN AMERICA   The educational ideas associated with Pestalozzi came to America in several ways. Joseph Neef, for example, had studied at Yverdon and came to the United States in 1806; he wrote about "the method" and started schools in Kentucky, Ohio, Pennsylvania, and Indiana. And the utopian New Harmony settlement in Indiana also imported some Pestalozzian ideas. But neither of these sources was ultimately influential.[6]

Around 1860 Edward A. Sheldon bought a set of "objective teaching materials" in Canada and brought them to Oswego, New York, where he was superintendent of schools. He hired two Europeans—including Hermann Krüsi, Jr., who had experience with "the method"—to instruct him and his teachers in using the materials. Sheldon became an expert on object teaching, and he prepared an entire curriculum around the concept. "Object teaching was distinctive chiefly in its method of instruction," wrote one student. "Whatever objects were used, it was standard practice to have the children name the qualities of the objects. . . . Take apples, for instance. This apple is large, firm, red, wholesome, and so on." From here the discussion could go wherever the teacher's imagination or the pupils' interests took them. The class might have an art lesson and sketch or paint apples. They might eat an apple and talk about taste or nutrition. They might discuss horticulture—or even take a field trip to an apple orchard. Or they might cut apples into sections to illustrate the concept of fractions.

Sheldon insisted on variety and change of pace. He established morning and afternoon recess periods, and he encouraged a warm, sympathetic relationship between teachers and pupils. The curriculum included gymnastics and singing "to give change of position and rest to children, and keep up an animated and pleasant state of feeling."[7] Such applications of "the method" became the basis of training at the Oswego Normal School, which educated a generation of America's most able teachers. After studying at Oswego, one young teacher built an entire curriculum for Chicago's public schools, basing it on the use of common objects. Her name was Ella Flagg Young, and she later became the first female superintendent to head Chicago's schools.

Froebel's ideas came to America a little later than Pestalozzi's. Several women—Margarethe Schurz, who studied with Froebel before immigrating to Wisconsin; Elizabeth Palmer Peabody, from Boston; and Susan E. Blow, from St. Louis—popularized the concept of kindergarten and early childhood education both within the regular school system and outside it. Peabody started a publication entitled *The Kindergarten Messenger*, which purveyed a great deal of information about Froebel. This paper was taken over by the *New England Journal of Education*, which continued to publish a column about the kindergarten (including reminiscences of the Baroness von Bulow).

By the late nineteenth century, the ideas of Herbart, the object teaching of Pestalozzi, and the gifts and occupations of Froebel were well known in American education circles. Such catch-phrases as "near to far," "simple to complex," "things before words," and "self-activity" became part of the vocabulary and standard knowledge of well-prepared educators. Educational "progressives"—that is, people who wanted to reform schools along lines advocated by Herbart, Pestalozzi, and Froebel—proposed variations on, and extensions of, object teaching.

Colonel Francis Wayland Parker, an American farmboy and later Civil War

[6]Gerald Lee Gutek, *Joseph Neef: The Americanization of Pestalozzism* (University: University of Alabama Press, 1978).

[7]Dorothy Rogers, *Oswego: Fountainhead of Teacher Education—A Century in the Sheldon Tradition* (New York: Appleton, 1961), 20–21.

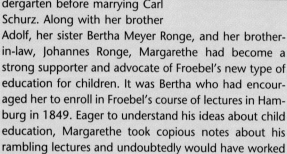

Margarethe Meyer Schurz
1833–1876

One of Froebel's students in Germany was a young woman named Margarethe Meyer, who trained with him to teach kindergarten before marrying Carl Schurz. Along with her brother Adolf, her sister Bertha Meyer Ronge, and her brother-in-law, Johannes Ronge, Margarethe had become a strong supporter and advocate of Froebel's new type of education for children. It was Bertha who had encouraged her to enroll in Froebel's course of lectures in Hamburg in 1849. Eager to understand his ideas about child education, Margarethe took copious notes about his rambling lectures and undoubtedly would have worked for his cause had she not met and married Carl Schurz in 1852.

Because of revolution in Germany, Carl felt it necessary to emigrate to the United States. The Ronges had already moved to England, where they opened a Froebelian "infant garden" at Hampstead in 1851. In fact, Bertha Ronge was responsible for the kindergarten exhibit that caught the eye of American educator Henry Barnard, when he attended the Educational Exhibition in London in 1854. The Ronges had published a manual about Froebel's ideas for English speakers who were interested in teaching in kindergartens.

Margarethe Schurz was also eager to apply her knowledge of childhood education when she arrived in America with her husband. Unfortunately, however, ill health forced her to go to England so that Bertha could care for her. By spring of 1856 she was well enough to return to the United States, and then the Schurzes settled

in Watertown, Wisconsin. There Margarethe set up a school in her home for their daughter Agathe and four of her cousins. In this children's garden she taught the five youngsters Froebelian games and songs, and she used the gifts and occupations in working with them.

The kindergarten was a success, and soon relatives and friends were asking Margarethe to include their children in the group. The expansion in class size forced

Yesterday's Professional

Schurz to move the school to a small building in Watertown in late fall of 1856—the date usually given for the establishment of the first kindergarten in the United States, even though it was taught in German.

In 1859—during a visit to Boston with her husband, who had entered politics with Abraham Lincoln—Margarethe Schurz met Elizabeth Palmer Peabody, the sister-in-law of Horace Mann. Peabody was captivated by the manner in which young Agathe behaved, noting that she was "a miracle—so child-like and unconscious, and yet so wise and able, attracting and ruling the children who seem nothing short of enchanted."* Schurz replied that her daughter's manner was the result of a kindergarten education; she described Froebel's ideas and later sent Peabody the preface of his book *The Education of Man.* In 1860 Peabody made her first attempt to establish a kindergarten herself.

Health problems continued to plague Margarethe Schurz, and she became an invalid after giving birth to a second daughter, who died. In 1867 she returned to Hamburg, Germany, where she died at age forty-two.

*Ruth M. Baylor, Elizabeth Palmer Peabody, Kindergarten Pioneer (Philadelphia: University of Pennsylvania Press, 1965), 35. For a more complete discussion of Schurz's life, see Agnes Snyder, Dauntless Women in Childhood Education (Washington, D.C.: Association for Childhood Education, 1972).

officer turned educator, advocated a **child-centered curriculum** that subordinated subject matter to the interests and motivations of the child. In other words, the child was the curriculum, and school subjects had to be presented in ways that involved the child actively and practically. The combined school and teacher training institute that Parker headed in Chicago was staffed by teachers who understood a wide range of content and who took pupils' interests as their starting point. The generation of educational leaders who followed Parker called for a **project-centered cirriculum**, which to such advocates as John Dewey and William Heard Kilpatrick meant that each child—after a grounding in object teaching and child-centered instruction—would work cooperatively on a major project that involved both manipulative and conceptual skills. For boys this might

RESEARCH SAYS

For Tomorrow's Education . . .

Much of the research conducted during the 1980s concerning the use of media in the classroom has concluded that differences in students' learning levels, if any, result not from the medium used but rather from the methods employed in using it. Robert B. Kozma calls for a broad range of research into the various media and contends that a number of questions about media and their cognitive effects still need to be understood. See Robert B. Kozma, "Learning with Media," *Review of Educational Research* 61 (Summer 1991): 179–211.

mean doing farmwork or building a clubhouse; for girls it was likely to involve something like cooking or clerking in a store (yes, sex-role differentiation was common in schooling early in this century). Advocates of a project-centered curriculum believed that it would improve children's social skills, build on their interests, and show them the connection between academic and practical skills.

Also during this period, an Italian physician named Maria Montessori (1870–1952) developed a system of guided self-activity that drew heavily on Froebel's use of geometric gifts. Today Montessori's ideas (see Chapter 6) have more currency in America's preschools than they did during the 1920s and 1930s, although they were influential then in other parts of the world. After preparing didactic materials that led children to match shapes to shapes or to arrange them in a certain sequential order, Dr. Montessori opened her first Casa dei Bambini ("children's house") in 1907 in a slum area of Rome. Calling herself a directress rather than a teacher (because she guided each child's activities), she allowed a child to select the learning material of his or her choice—perhaps a stacking toy—and to work with it until the child had discovered its unique instructional element. Montessori was amazed to discover that children have strong powers of concentration, love to repeat activities that hold their attention, and need no rewards or punishments to motivate them when engaged in such activities.

ADDING VOCATIONAL SKILLS

Recall that Aristotle's definition of a liberal education included only what one studied to enhance rationality (what one "studied for its own sake" is a contemporary expression of this idea). Thus, whatever one learned in order to make a living was, by definition, *not* liberal and *not* worthy of the time of "free men." This definition fit well with the theory of learning based on innate potentials, discussed in Chapter 6.

The experiential learning theory that was associated with the rise of modern science tended to shift the focus away from "liberal" toward "useful" learning. Because the basis for ideas is experience, and because ideas are the building blocks of knowledge, *all* experience has educational value. Given this reasoning, the curricular challenge lay in identifying the most valuable or most useful experiences for inclusion in schools.

As the criterion for what to teach shifted from liberal to useful, pressure slowly built to expand the curriculum. The traditional liberal arts remained—not only because they were traditional but also because they were useful. Latin was the language of European commerce, scholarship, and diplomacy, and so it was the most powerful tool of communication that people could acquire. At the same time—from about 1300 to 1500—vernacular languages (English, French, German, Italian, and so on) developed both religious and secular literatures, so that extensive study of them was also useful. Study of developments in mathematics and astronomy required more curricular time, and as other scientific fields emerged, there was also pressure to include them.

Long-established schools resisted but gradually absorbed some parts of the new curricula. Schools that were established in response to the Catholic and Protestant Reformation generally incorporated the newer studies. And some of what ultimately became part of the curriculum was taught outside the usual school structure. For example, most classical schools slowly added vernacular grammar, but they left "casting accounts" (bookkeeping) and vernacular writing to independent teachers who often had to travel from town to town and find their own schooling quarters. Applied science, or "mechanical arts" (which we now call engineering), was confined to scientific societies and then to special institutes until the nineteenth century in America and until well into the twentieth century in most of Europe.

The curricula of America's regular schools and universities were more expansive than in European countries for two related reasons. First, most of England's North American colonies claimed the right to set educational policy without consulting the mother country. After 1650 Harvard granted degrees without any English supervision, and lower schools and colleges in most other colonies were just as independent. Second, the three-century process of claiming and settling the United States placed a premium on practical skills. Captain John Smith's group early discovered that a classical European education did not help much in confronting the wilderness. Reading Latin was less useful than understanding the New World's flora and fauna and knowing how to farm, catch game, build a log house, and shoot straight. (Chapter 9 returns to this topic.)

Soon after the American Revolution, newly founded Union College in New York gave practical studies equal status with the classics—something that earlier colonical colleges (despite their tendency to be more utilitarian than European counterparts) had not quite been willing to do. The sentiment for increasing "useful knowledge" built, until in 1862 the U.S. Congress passed the **Morrill Act**, which set aside 30,000 acres of public land for each member of Congress from each state. Any income from these land grants was to be used for collegiate study that—besides liberal arts subjects—would include engineering, agriculture, and military (officer) training. Land grants led to the establishment of major research universities (such as Cornell, Illinois, Iowa State, Michigan State, Nebraska, Ohio State, and Purdue); they also encouraged the evolution of specialized "institutes" into full universities (examples include Rensselaer, M.I.T., Case Western Reserve, and Cal Tech); and they ultimately forced traditional universities like Harvard and Yale to give scientific and engineering studies equal status with the liberal arts.

The Morrill Act both expanded the college curriculum and made it more practical. It also subsidized tuition costs so that more young people from working-class and lower-middle-class families could afford to attend college. In 1890 Congress added appropriations to the original land grants, and for the first time a number of African-American colleges were eligible for money from the "second Morrill Act." Although their shares were not equal to white universities' appropriations, this federal money greatly extended collegiate educational opportunities for African-Americans.[8] Around the turn of the century, other federal legislation, such as the **Smith-Hughes Act** of 1917, added money for training high school teachers of agriculture and home economics.

GRADUATE AND PROFESSIONAL EDUCATION

Thomas Jefferson envisioned a full-scale Continental-style university when he helped found the University of Virginia during the 1820s. He differentiated between the liberal arts as a basis for other knowledge and advanced studies in specialized disciplines. However, most American institutions of higher education were small residential colleges that emphasized a combination of liberal arts and religion. Today's concept of advanced, or graduate, degrees was absent.

The Bachelor of Arts (B.A.) degree was the standard certificate granted at the end of a collegiate course, although many American colleges followed the Oxford model of granting the Artium Magister (A.M.) or the Master of Arts (M.A.) three years after the B.A. to those "fellows" who paid the requisite fees and participated in the college's teaching and governance. While it could be assumed that masters of arts knew more than they had when they finished the bachelor's degree, there was usually no examination for the M.A. Most colleges conferred honorary Doctor of Laws (LL.D.), Doctor of Divinity (D.D.), or Doctor of Medicine (M.D.) degrees on those whom they wished to recognize as especially distinguished—presumably, but not necessarily, in one of the three fields represented by the doctoral degree.

Even in England and on the Continent, attorneys and physicians often learned their fields by apprenticeship rather than by university training. For example, in the 1530s Thomas Platter began practicing medicine when he inherited a "book of remedies and medicines" from a physician who had died of a plague.[9] Attorneys and physicians who held degrees may have enjoyed higher status than those who did not (and perhaps they commanded higher fees), but only ordained ministers or priests could be assumed to have trained in universities.

[8]Clarice Boswell, "The Effects of Educational Policies Between 1980–1988 on the Continued Survival of Selected Historic Black Colleges and Universities," Ed.D. dissertation (Northern Illinois University, 1990).
[9]Paul Monroe, ed. and trans., *Thomas Platter and the Educational Renaissance of the Sixteenth Century* (New York: Appleton, 1904).

American higher education followed the same practices. Dartmouth and King's (Columbia) colleges offered medical instruction late in the eighteenth century, but most physicians learned on the job. Bloodletting was a primary medical remedy throughout the nineteenth century, and as late as the 1870s the universities that offered a medical course did so in a single semester of lectures. The University of Iowa was especially rigorous in that it required medical students to sit through the same lectures two semesters in a row before receiving the M.D. degree. To be admitted for medical study, one needed to have a "common school" education. The study of law was similar, although its knowledge base was more sophisticated. People like Horace Mann and Henry Barnard "read law" *after* graduating from college. There were no licensure examinations in law or medicine until the twentieth century.

Experimentation with new diploma labels began during the mid-nineteenth century as scientific studies pressed for a place in the curriculum. Abbot Lawrence gave Harvard $100,000 for a "scientific school" in 1848; having never attended college himself, Lawrence specified that students should be at least eighteen, have a "good common English education," and post a $200 bond. To differentiate these older students from traditional liberal arts scholars—who resented the intrusion—Harvard designated the degree Bachelor of Science (B.S.) to be granted after one year of study and a public examination. In 1851 Yale began granting the degree Bachelor of Philosophy (B.Ph.) to "scientific students" after two years of study and a public examination. To enter this early form of "adult education," students had to be at least twenty-one years old.[10] By 1870 land-grant colleges, including the one in Ames, Iowa, legitimated the B.S. degree by granting it after a rigorous four-year course of study.

The experimentation with degree titles eventually included the Doctor of Philosophy (Ph.D.), which Yale was first to confer in America in 1862. This was a common degree label in German universities, where it represented the *first* (and only) degree for those who studied in "philosophical faculties"—which included most of the social sciences, humanities, and history. Anyone who completed the *Gymnasium* (high school) and its classical course of study was entitled to matriculate in *any* German university, although most students traveled around to hear the best-known professors lecture. Doctoral candidates might study as little as a year or two before taking an oral, public examination in which they stated, explained, and defended several propositions (theses) to professors (and sometimes to public questioners). On the other hand, some waited for many years before attempting the examination, which was the only requirement for the doctorate. It was exclusively the student's right to decide when and in which university to take the degree exam, while professors claimed the right to say or write whatever they believed true. Taken together, these two privileges constituted what nineteenth-century Germans called **academic freedom**.

A year's travel in Europe had long been regarded as the proper finish to a college education by Americans whose families could afford this luxury. Henry Barnard spent such a year after graduating from Yale in 1830; in his travels he learned German and met people with whom he maintained correspondence, although he did not bother to take an examination for a degree. By the 1860s, however, Americans were discovering that—with the investment of a year or two—they could return home with a Ph.D. from a German university, and by the 1870s this was becoming a "high-status" approach to preparing for college teaching. Besides boosting their status, Americans who studied in Germany benefited from the fact that German academicians were leading the way in such disciplines as history, linguistics, psychology, anthropology, economics, literary and biblical criticism, and chemistry.

In 1873 a Maryland financier named Johns Hopkins died, leaving a $7,000,000 fortune to be divided between a hospital and a university. The university, bearing its benefactor's name, opened in Baltimore with Daniel Coit Gilman as president. Gilman had spent time in Europe after graduating from Yale. He helped form the Sheffield Scientific School at Yale, where the first Ph.D. was granted, and he gathered a faculty that was committed to inquiry (many of them had been educated in Germany). He offered paid fellowships to attract students, more than half of whom already had degrees from American colleges. Recitation, the standard instructional medium at most colleges, was hardly known at Johns Hopkins. Students could sign up for any courses they wanted, and attendance at lectures was—as in most European universities—strictly up to the student. Laboratories, seminars, and independent research were the hallmarks of Johns Hopkins, and the Ph.D. soon became the degree of choice. German-trained scholars, like Herbert Baxter Adams in history, turned out a generation of scholar-teachers who carried the Hopkins idea to other colleges and universities. For example, Frederick Jackson Turner learned historical research from Adams before joining the faculty at the University of Wisconsin; there he revolutionized the study of American history before accepting a position at Harvard.[11]

By 1900 the idea of separating undergraduate and graduate education was firmly established in America. In many fields the master's degree—requiring study, an oral examination, and often a thesis—became an intermediate step on the way to the doctorate. But the baccalaureate was usually the highest degree for teachers, artists, musicians, actors, journalists, engineers, nurses, and architects. A master's degree in these fields was unusual; a doctorate was rare or unknown. Figure 7.1 shows the growth of graduate education from 1970 to 1990.

ACCREDITATION AND LICENSURE

The late-nineteenth and early-twentieth centuries were a time of regularizing many aspects of higher education in America. **Regional accreditation associations** were formed to establish minimal standards for high school and college curricula by applying concepts devised by such groups as the Committee of Ten and the Commission on the Reorganization of Secondary Education (discussed later). The fields of law and medicine also adopted more stringent requirements, including longer courses of study at accredited institutions, higher admission standards, external examinations developed by state-level boards, and standardized curricula reflecting rapidly developing knowledge bases.

During this time there was also a gradual expansion of the disciplines and professional specialties that required doctoral study. Education was among these; indeed, the study of education was a legitimate doctoral specialty in most nine-

[11]Raymond J. Cunningham, "The German Historical World of Herbert Baxter Adams: 1874–1876," *Journal of American History* 68 (September 1981): 261–275.

FIGURE 7.1   Graduate Enrollment, 1970–1990

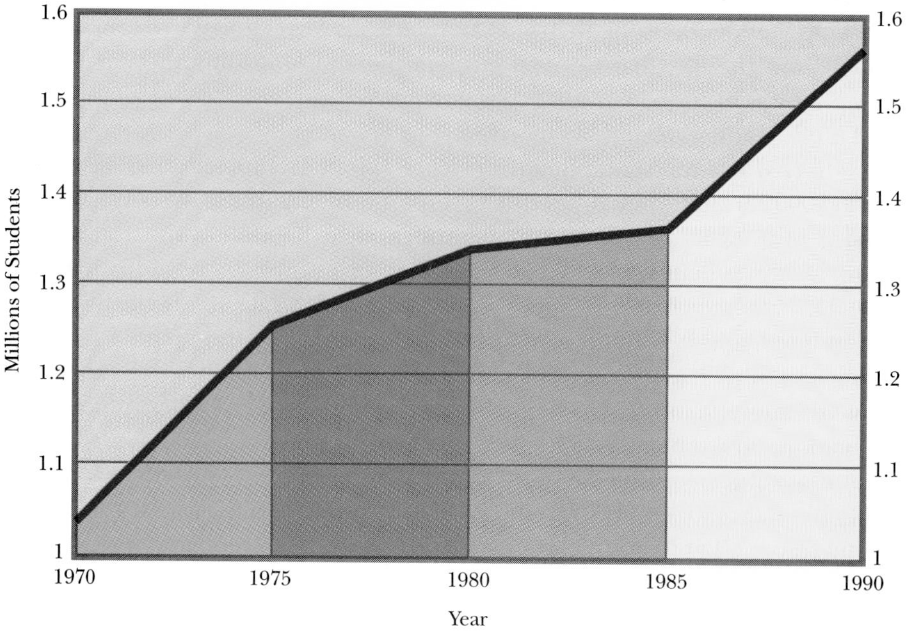

Source: *Digest of Education Statistics 1992*, National Center for Education Statistics, U.S. Department of Education, Office of Educational Research and Improvement, p. 186.

teenth-century German universities. Some American land-grant colleges and universities began to include education as a part of their curricula. The University of Chicago made education a doctoral study from the first, and Columbia followed suit. But most traditional liberal arts colleges resisted. Yale granted doctorates in education for many years but finally abolished the specialty. During the 1920s Harvard compromised by granting the Doctor of Education (Ed.D.). Today both the Ed.D. and the Ph.D. degrees are given, with little practical distinction between them.

DIPLOMA MILLS

In the flurry of institution building, some states eased the requirement for college charters to the simplicity of filing an application, accompanied by a fee; not all impressive-sounding universities were legitimate. When some colleges did poorly in the competition for students, they let profit-minded operators acquire their charters, and they offered diplomas in return for money. This practice was prevalent in the fields of medicine and dentistry, where there were strong disagreements about a very limited body of knowledge. This was a ready market for practitioners who had acquired their training through apprenticeship, and thus the **diploma mill** was born.[12]

   No one can say how many such operations arose, but from a few documented cases it is clear that the phenomenon was widespread. For example, between 1858 and 1880 a man in Philadelphia named John Buchanan estimated that he sold ten thousand degrees—mostly M.D.s.[13] And from 1904 to 1928

[12]Martin Kaufman, "American Medical Education," in *The Education of American Physicians: Historical Essays*, ed. Ronald L. Numbers (Berkeley: University of California Press, 1980), 7–28.

[13]*Report of the Commissioner of Education for the Year 1880* (Washington, D.C.: U.S. Government Printing Office, 1882), cxli–cxlv.

Helmuth P. Holler sold thousands more, using charters for "Oriental University," supposedly in the District of Columbia and Virginia.[14] Both men spent time in prison, but not for selling phony degrees. Buchanan drew a sentence for trying to fool the court by faking suicide (he had hired an expert swimmer to impersonate him and fall overboard from a ferry). Holler did time for mail fraud, after investigators from the FBI, Treasury Department, State Department, and other offices had developed extensive files about his activities.

Buchanan, Holler, and many lesser-known operators did a brisk diploma business in Europe, Asia, and South America. Officials in countries where education was centrally regulated found it difficult to understand why the U.S. Bureau of Education lacked the power to cancel the charters of institutions that were caught selling degrees. But it is a measure of how much Americans value entrepreneurship and corporate sanctity that the selling of diplomas is still a thorny issue. In recent years a small number of operators have been able to continue selling degrees—mainly doctorates in psychology, theology, and education—because American laws and traditions favor individual expression over social concerns in this area.[15]

DEMOCRATIZING SCHOOL ATTENDANCE

THE CURRICULAR RESPONSE

The Reformation's emphasis on training everyone to read religious material in their own languages led to two separate and unequal school systems throughout Europe. Traditional classical schools got new energy and became somewhat more accessible; but because they were supported primarily by tuition fees, their students generally came from aristocratic or middle-class families. Depending on the country they were in, these schools went by different names: In England they were called *grammar schools*; in Germany and Scandinavia they were *gymnasia*; and in France the label was *lycee*. They came to be called **secondary schools**, and university preparation occurred in them.

RESEARCH SAYS

For Tomorrow's Education . . .

Schools that have reorganized their professional relationships to increase teachers' participation in program design and school management have the potential for improving instruction and student learning. However, it is important as well to maintain an organizational structure that the public perceives as providing traditional line authority from board to superintendent to principal to teacher. See William A. Firestone and Beth D. Bader, "Professionalism or Bureaucracy? Redesigning Teaching," *Educational Evaluation and Policy Analysis* 13 (Spring 1991): 67–86.

[14]James O. Wynn, Jr., "Oriental University, Inc.," original typescript of report dated 4 April 1921, in file marked "Commissioner's Office, Case of Oriental University," box 17, record group 12; Records of the Secretary of the Interior, Central Classified Files, 1907–1936, "Bureau of Education: Oriental University," record group 48; and Nugent Dodds to Leo A. Rover, 7 November 1932, Department of Justice Mail and Files Division, file no. 212077, record group 60, National Archives, Washington, D.C.

[15]Robert H. Reid, *American Degree Mills: A Study of Their Operations and of Existing and Potential Ways to Control Them* (Washington, D.C.: American Council on Education, 1959).

Most peasants and working-class people attended vernacular schools, which in England were called **elementary schools** (in France the label was *petit school*; and in Germany and Scandinavia it was *folk school*, meaning "people's school"). These cost less than secondary schools, were lower in status, and did not teach the classical curriculum needed for university study. By the nineteenth century, when many European countries began establishing state-funded systems, it was the elementary school that received funding. Thus, by the end of the century, most Europeans went *either* to an elementary school *or* to a secondary school—not first to one and then to the other.

The English-speaking colonies in North America began in the European tradition, but patterns of settlement did not lend themselves to separate classical and vernacular schools. Parents who wanted classical studies for their children either hired a tutor or sought a schoolmaster who could teach Latin to some pupils (usually for extra pay) while instructing all pupils in English. As American states began to formalize their schooling arrangements into tax-funded systems, they gradually included secondary schools as high schools, not as a separate parallel track but as a second level coming *after* elementary school.

During the 1890s the **Committe of Ten** of the National Education Association, chaired by the president of Harvard, laid out the basic elements of the high school curriculum. With the majority of its ten members coming from colleges and universities, the committee recommended that a four-year curriculum be standardized throughout the country. Providing for relatively few elective subjects, the course of study was to concentrate on English language and literature, modern or classical languages, mathematics, and physical and natural sciences.[16] What the committee recommended was similar to the curriculum described in Table 7.1. The committee overtly rejected the idea of including extracurricular activities, such as student government, sports, clubs, musical groups, and other "nonacademic" activities.

The demand for public high schools continued to grow, and it was met. In 1860 there were only one hundred high schools, but by the turn of the century some six thousand high schools enrolled half a million students. In fact, the ever-increasing mechanization of business and industry represented a threat to unskilled workers, for the kinds of farming and manufacturing jobs that teenage dropouts could easily obtain in 1890 were disappearing a generation later. Given the limited availability of jobs, it was clear that teenagers who were not in school were likely to have—and to cause—social problems. But if most young people were to stay in high school, the curriculum was an issue, for it was aimed primarily at college preparation (and the grading system was designed to sort out students who were not suited for college). Figure 7.2 shows the growth of high school enrollments since 1870.

Recognizing the need to keep teens off the streets and to train workers for jobs in a rapidly changing economy, the NEA sponsored a second high-level committee, the **Commission on the Reorganization of Secondary Education (CRSE)**, which issued a document entitled **Cardinal Principles of Secondary Education**. It listed seven main objectives: (1) health, (2) command of fundamental processes, (3) worthy home membership, (4) vocation, (5) citizenship, (6) worthy use of leisure, and (7) ethical character. The CRSE noted that these seven

[16]*Report of the Committee on Secondary School Studies* (Washington, D.C.: U.S. Government Printing Office, 1893).

TABLE 7.1   Typical High School Curriculum of the 1890s

Math	*History*
Arithmetic	General
Algebra	U.S. Geography
Geometry	U.S. Constitution
English	*Philosophic—Scientific*
Reading	Logic
Grammar	Natural Philosophy (Biology & Physics)
Rhetoric	Moral Philosophy
Declamation (Speech)	Natural Theology
Composition	Christianity
Language	*Practical—Scientific*
Classical Latin*	Bookkeeping
Modern French†	Navigation
German	Surveying
	Mensuration—Measuring
	Astronomical Calculations
	Drawing

*Latin was required for entrance to most colleges; however, more students studied Latin than went on to college.

†French was usually more popular than German.

FIGURE 7.2   Percentage of 17-Year Olds in High School, 1870–1992

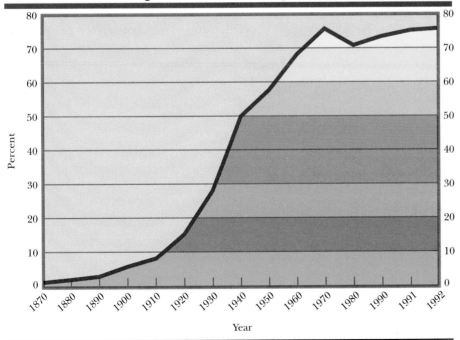

Source: *Digest of Education Statistics 1992*, National Center for Education Statistics, U.S. Department of Education, Office of Educational Research and Improvement, p. 107.

aims did not exhaust the legitimate goals of American education, but it identified these as the primary objectives, and it said that they were applicable from elementary school through college.[17]

Cardinal Principles found such wide general agreement that it quickly became (and remains) the basic justification of American education. Thus the Enlightenment's goals of a secular, rational, vocationally differentiated, socially stable, and scientifically based education system emerged. The heart of the system is a multiplicity of courses organized into six years of elementary school and six years of high school (three years of junior high and three years of senior). Some courses were to be common to all students (health, fundamental processes, citizenship, home membership, and ethics); some depended on a student's curricular track (college prep, agricultural, business, clerical, industrial, fine arts, household arts); and still others were elective courses.[18]

According to the CRSE, children from widely different backgrounds would be unified by the subjects they had in common, by ''social mingling,'' and by participating in shared activities ''such as athletic games, social activities, and the government of the school.'' This reversed the recommendation of the Committee of Ten by saying that the school ''is the one agency that may be controlled definitely and consciously by our democracy for the purpose of unifying its people.'' At the same time, specialization could coexist easily, under the watchful care of guidance counselors. ''Education in a democracy . . . should develop in each individual the knowledge, interests, ideals, habits, and powers whereby he [or she] will find his [or her] place and use that place to shape both himself [or herself] and society toward even nobler ends.'' An individual's growth, choices, and development were to be combined with

> cooperation, social cohesion, and social solidarity. . . . While developing . . . distinctive and unique individual excellencies, the . . . school must be equally zealous to develop those common ideas, common ideals, and common modes of thought, feeling, and action whereby America, through a rich unified and common life, may render her truest service to a world seeking for democracy.[19]

With these social and educational pressures the number of public high schools continued to increase throughout the twentieth century, until the growth stabilized during the 1970s. Table 7.2 shows the demographic mix of high school graduates from 1973 to 1990.

THE SEARCH FOR COMMONALITY

The tension between what the CRSE called ''unique individual excellencies'' and the school's social mandate to develop ''common ideas, common ideals, and common modes of thought'' is prevalent in every society, and it affects curricula worldwide. This tension is a major influence on curricular policy in the United States, and it can be seen readily in the longstanding controversies surrounding the language used for instruction.

Because English is the dominant language in the United States today, it is

[17]U.S. Bureau of Education, *Cardinal Principles of Secondary Education: The Report of the Commission on the Reorganization of Secondary Education, Appointed by the National Education Association,* bulletin no. 35 (Washington, D.C.: U.S. Government Printing Office, 1918); see Sol Cohen, ed., *Education in the United States: A Documentary History* (New York: Random House, 1974), 4: 2278–2289.

[18]Joan K. Smith and L. Glenn Smith, ''The Influence of the Enlightenment on Progressive Education in America,'' in *The Notion of Enlightenment: Conference Papers for the 1st Meeting of the International Standing Working Group on Education and the Enlightenment (within the ISCHE),* ed. Fritz-Peter Hager and Dieter Jedan (Zurich: Working Group, 1986), 139–150.

[19]U.S. Bureau of Education, *Cardinal Principles,* in Cohen, *Education in the United States,* 2278–2289.

Comparative Perspective on Today's Issues . . .

◆ ***SHOULD THERE BE A STANDARD CURRICULUM DETERMINED BY SOME AUTHORITY OR GROUP OF EXPERTS?***

The Issue   Questions about who should determine the curriculum and what it should be are as old as teaching. For Plato, there was only one best curriculum—one that placed geometry at the center of study, because geometry has a logical structure. During the first half of this century, American schools gravitated toward a child-centered curriculum that engaged students' interests through a variety of teaching materials and techniques. In reaction to this approach other educators began to call for a return to a more unified basic curriculum. Some states, including California and Texas, now have state boards to determine and control the content of the curriculum.

YES   The concern is not so much one of who should set the curriculum but that it be set and contain the "basic" education—that it teach those subjects that will provide the knowledge and skills necessary to lay the intellectual foundation to which every human is entitled. Thus, it should include English, foreign language, history, classics, science and math. Through these subjects each student should be able to come away knowing how to read, write, speak, calculate, listen and think.

—*Clifton Fadiman, writer, editor, performer, and associate of* Encyclopaedia Britannica *and the Council for Basic Education*

NO   Students should have the right to decide and control what they want to learn. Without this a person's basic civil liberties are breached. An individual's freedom to learn is an integral part of his/her freedom of thought. This right is currently endangered by school authorities who wish to legally and politically control the curriculum.

—*John Holt, writer, educator, and public school critic*

Source: Based on James Wm. Noll, ed., *Taking Sides: Clashing Views on Controversial Educational Issues,* 5th ed. (Guilford, Conn.: Dushkin, 1989), 18–33.

TABLE 7.2   Percentages of 19- and 20-Year-Olds Graduating from High School

Year	White	African-American	Hispanic	Total
1973	85.9	68.2	54.7	82.2
1978	85.2	67.1	56.0	80.9
1983	85.2	73.2	57.9	81.2
1988	87.1	73.5	53.6	82.1
1990	87.3	77.6	59.7	82.8

Source: U.S. Department of Education, National Center for Education Statistics, *The Conditions of Education, 1992* (Washington, D.C., 1992), 58.

easy to assume that the debate over the language of instruction must be a recent phenomenon. In fact, however, some of the colonies that ultimately became states did not use English predominantly. Swedish, for example, was the dominant language in early Delaware, and visitors to seventeenth-century New York routinely heard more than a dozen languages on the streets (besides Dutch, which was the official language).

It was in Pennsylvania, in the middle of the eighteenth century, that the language of school instruction became visibly controversial. Benjamin Franklin worried that the colony's many German immigrants would not assimilate successfully if they continued to speak German in everyday life, and he supported free primary schools taught only in English. Christopher Sauer, a leader in the German community who published a German newspaper, argued that parents should be allowed to choose the language in which their children would be schooled. He believed that children should preserve their family's culture, including language.

During the nineteenth century this controversy became widespread as immigration increased from China and from southern and eastern Europe. In many communities the pressure intensified to offer instruction in languages other than English. In addition, many non-English-speaking immigrants were Roman Catholic, and they turned to their church for help when their preferences were denied by local schools. Today's extensive parochial school system is an outgrowth of this conflict over language.[20] Although some communities tried to block the use of parochial schools for this purpose by outlawing attendance at schools that were not publicly funded, the U.S. Supreme Court held that compulsory attendance laws can be satisfied through schools that are not tax supported.[21]

The most recent manifestation of the language controversy concerns bilingual education. Although various languages have raised the issue, most often—and most heatedly—the discussion has centered on Spanish, because for so many students that is their first language. Before the mid-1960s many school districts either banned or strongly discouraged the use of Spanish at school, but federal policy has shifted away from this effort to "Americanize" children at the expense of their cultural heritage as Hispanic parents have gained political clout.[22]

In 1974 the U.S. Supreme Court said that non-English-speaking students of Chinese ancestry in San Francisco were entitled to bilingual instruction and that a school's lack of money was an insufficient reason *not* to provide it. The Court based its opinion on Title VI of the Civil Rights Act of 1964, holding that—by having accepted federal funds—the school district was contractually obligated to provide schooling that did not discriminate on the basis of race, color, or national origin.[23] Also in 1974 the Tenth Circuit Court of Appeals held that Spanish-surnamed students were entitled to a bilingual program because their cultural and home environments were so different from the environment of schools in Portales, New Mexico.[24]

These two decisions hinted that students might be entitled to bilingual instruction if they were severely disadvantaged in school because their primary language was not English. But the courts quickly backed away from such a conclusion. In 1975 the Tenth Circuit Court of Appeals reversed a lower court's order that required Denver to establish a bilingual/bicultural program.[25] The

[20]F. Michael Perko, *A Time to Favor Zion: The Ecology of Religion and Educational Development on the Urban Frontier, Cincinnati, 1830–1870* (Chicago: Educational Studies Press, 1987).

[21]Pierce v. Society of Sisters of the Holy Names of Jesus and Mary, 268 U.S. 510, 45 S.Ct. 571, 69 L.Ed. 1070 (1925).

[22]ED 270 239.

[23]Lau v. Nichols, 414 U.S. 563, 94 S.Ct. 786, 39 L.Ed.2d 1 (1974).

[24]Serna v. Portales Municipal Schools, 499 F.2d 1147 (10 Cir. 1974).

[25]Keyes v. School Dist. No. 1, Denver, Colorado, 521 F.2d 465 (10 Cir. 1975).

Ninth Circuit Court of Appeals held that Title VI of the Civil Rights Act does not confer the right to a bilingual education.[26] And courts in New York and North California have said that parents may not keep their children out of school if instruction in the parents' heritage and culture is not offered.[27]

The courts have retreated from asking school districts to minimize the disadvantages that are caused by differences between majority and minority cultures—at least to the extent sought by many minority groups. But this does not mean that school districts need not pay attention to the issue. The Equal Educational Opportunities Act of 1974 calls for a school district to take "appropriate action to overcome language barriers that impede equal participation by its students in its instructional programs."[28] The Fifth Circuit Court of Appeals has ruled that attempts to meet this law should be evaluated on several grounds: (1) how likely the attempt is to implement theory effectively; (2) how well the attempt works in a trial setting; and (3) whether the attempt is a "good faith effort" that takes into account local resources and circumstances.[29]

This important issue of educational equity continues to be controversial and to challenge educators and society. Opponents of Spanish-English bilingual education cite research which claims that—*among Hispanic students who graduate from high school*—those who did have bilingual instruction did not perform differently than those who did not have it. Opponents argue that school systems may as well save the money being spent on bilingual instruction.[30] But advocates of bilingual education point to research which indicates that 40 to 50 percent of children whose backgrounds are classified as being of limited English proficiency (LEP) drop out *before high school graduation*; furthermore, students who get good bilingual instruction early in their schooling are less likely to drop out than those who initially are taught in English only.[31]

There are several reasons why bilingual instruction helps many LEP students. One is that bilingual teachers are more likely than monolingual teachers to understand and appreciate such students' backgrounds and culture. Another is that LEP students are more likely to comprehend concepts and instruction presented in their primary language than in a language they are still learning. A final important reason is that bilingual instruction tends to improve the early academic performance of LEP students, which increases their confidence. As one university administrator who is involved in minority education puts it: "Educational equity goes beyond [issues of] access and includes supportive efforts to increase substantially the chances of academic success for disadvantaged minority students."[32]

TEXTBOOKS AND THE CURRICULUM

As noted in Chapter 3, curricular matters are legally the prerogative of the various states, with some federal qualifications. In theory, given fifty states, the District of Columbia, Guam, Puerto Rico, and American Samoa, one could expect

[26]Guadalupe Organization, Inc. v. Tempe Elementary School Dist., 587 F.2d 1022 (9 Cir. 1978).

[27]Matter of Baum, 61 A.D.2d 123, 401 N.Y.S.2d 514 (1978); and Matter of McMillan, 30 N.C. App. 235, 226 S.E.2d 693 (1976).

[28]20 U.S.C.A. § 1703 (f).

[29]United States v. State of Texas, 680 F.2d 356 (5 Cir. 1982).

[30]See, for example, Linda Chavez, "Español or English?" a review of *Forked Tongue: The Politics of Bilingual Education* by Rosalie Pedaline Porter, *Wall Street Journal*, 3 May 1990, p. A14.

[31]Nancy L. Commins and Ofelia B. Miramontes, "Perceived and Actual Linguistic Competence: A Descriptive Study of Four Low-achieving Hispanic Bilingual Students," *American Educational Research Journal* 26 (Winter 1989): 443–472; Henry T. Trueba, "Culturally Based Explanations of Minority Students' Academic Achievement," *Anthropology and Education Quarterly* 19 (September 1988): 270–287; and Francois Nielsen and Steven J. Lerner, "Language Skills and School Achievement of Bilingual Hispanics," *Social Science Research* 15 (September 1986): 209–239.

[32]Bob H. Suzuki, "Cultural Diversity: Increasing Achievement Through Equity," keynote address before the Los Angeles County Multicultural Conference, 7 October 1987, ED 303 527.

to find substantial local variations in curricula. But several strong forces push school districts toward uniformity. Among the factors that encourage the development of similar curricula are national accreditation of teacher education programs, regional accreditation of colleges and secondary schools, and a mobile population (because so many pupils cross state or regional boundaries when their families move). Yet none of these forces is as powerful as the textbook industry, which for more than a century has been the primary means by which curricula have been delivered.

Most of the textbooks and related materials used in American schools are produced by a small number of national publishers that compete to supply the multibillion-dollar school market. Although most states give local school districts wide latitude in selecting curricular materials, their choices are reduced dramatically by a relatively few Texans (aided by a disproportionate influence from Florida and California). In practice, the other states, districts, and territories have relatively little impact on what school children will read.

This happens because Texas allows its local districts to adopt only the textbooks on an ''approved'' list, which includes no more than five choices for each subject. Textbooks on the list are selected by the state board of education, following public hearings before a fifteen-person committee (at least eight of whom are teachers) that is appointed by the board. The list is updated annually after

In 1993 Joseph Fernandez lost the chancellorship of New York City's schools after many battles with the board. His "Rainbow Curriculum" was just too inclusive for some, who objected strenuously to books like Daddy's Roommate *and* Heather Has Two Mommies. —AP/ Wide World

public hearings; any citizen may present a written "bill of particulars" to the committee or may appear in person to speak about a particular text (there is a ten-minute time limit for each book under consideration). Because only objections and complaints about a book may be presented, publishers naturally try to avoid offending potential critics. Textbook authors and publishers listen to the hearings and may present written responses to the bills of particulars.

One factor that makes Texas so influential in the selection of textbooks is its size—and thus the power of its market. Publishers want to get as many books as possible onto the approved list. "Making the Texas list is practically a guarantee of profit for a publisher," says one analyst. "Failure to make it may doom a book, or a whole series of books, to extinction. Thus most publishers are understandably sensitive to pressures to make their books acceptable for use in this state's . . . districts."[33]

Besides the size of its market, however, Texas exerts a strong influence on textbooks for another reason. Beginning in 1962 a Longview, Texas, couple named Mel and Norma Gabler became concerned about curricular materials in their children's schools, and they began writing bills of particulars about some books each year. When Mel retired from Exxon in 1973, the Gablers turned their four-bedroom home into a review center for curricular materials and became

---

RESEARCH SAYS

For Tomorrow's Education . . .

Attempts to gain control over the curriculum through censorship are becoming widespread. See, for example, Casey Banas, "Wheaton Parents Part of Nationwide Opposition to Book Series," *Chicago Tribune*, 11 November 1990; and Joseph Burton, "Books: A Forearming for Those Who Must Deal with Censors," *Phi Delta Kappan 67* (February 1986); 470–471.

---

full-time advocates of "curricular reform" in American education. Unable to claim any expertise in education, they nonetheless advocated that reading be taught through phonics rather than the "look-say" approach, and they opposed teaching the "new math" because (they said) it held that there were "no absolutes" (thus "every value [the student]'s been taught is destroyed. And the next thing you know, the student turns to crime and drugs").

It is difficult to assess the impact of the Gablers on the textbook review committee or on the Texas Education Agency. No doubt some publishers altered textbooks to avoid conflict with the Gablers and their allied political forces. For example, one publishing house eliminated the word *evolution* from a high school biology text. Among the issues hotly contested by the Gablers and many others is the scientific model on which evolutionary theory rests. Christian fundamentalists prefer a creationist explanation in biology, and they have pressured schools either to replace evolution with creationism or at least to present both "theories." This was the central issue in 1925 in the famous "Scopes monkey trial" in

[33]William Martin, "The Guardians Who Slumbereth Not," *Texas Monthly* 10 (November 1982): 145–148, 150–151, 260–271.

Tennessee, and it was addressed again by courts during the 1970s and 1980s. Some lower courts have supported the critics of "secular humanism" (a code term for the perceived enemies of "creation science"), but appellate courts have tended to uphold the right of schools to base biology instruction on the dominant scientific paradigm.[34]

Textbook publishers do not find it economically feasible to produce different books for different states, and so standardized curricular materials may be disproportionately influenced by a small group of Texans who are neither experts in educational content nor elected to represent any major constituency of the American population. California and Florida have similar but somewhat less restrictive systems of selecting textbooks, and publishers also try hard to satisfy any objections from people in those states.

PREVIOUSLY EXCLUDED GROUPS: EXCEPTIONAL STUDENTS

We have noted the growth in the number and percentage of pupils who stay enrolled in high school longer. Over the past several decades most American school systems have moved gradually toward policies that include *all* potential students of school age. Until recently, however, they did not include many students who had exceptional physical, cognitive, or emotional characteristics. Today considerable attention is directed toward curricula, methods, and social planning that include gifted and talented students as well as those whose special or handicapping attributes influence their progress through school.

In typical school settings it can be difficult to provide for the special needs of a small number of students whose interests and talents enable them to master parts of the curriculum much more rapidly than others. It can be equally difficult to provide for students who need additional time or unusual environments, methods, and supervision. Since President Kennedy's administration in the early 1960s the federal government has passed more than a hundred acts and amendments concerning exceptional individuals. And in 1971 the United Nations adopted seven articles under the title "Declaration of General and Special Rights of the Mentally Retarded." Of particular significance for education is Public Law 94-142, which calls for "inclusive education" or "least restrictive environments" through **regular education initiatives** that give *all* students the right to free, appropriate education.

This approach to educating exceptional students is based on the assumption that categories of handicapping attributes exist and can be identified as separate or different from other attributes.[35] Although it may not be difficult to evaluate physical, visual, or hearing impairments, it is more difficult to assess attributes related to individuals' actions and behaviors. Nevertheless, experts have decided that it is possible to differentiate among such primary behaviors as mental retardation, emotional disturbance, behavior disorder, and learning dis-

[34]Mozert v. Hawkins County Bd. of Educ., 86-6144 (E.D. Tenn. 1986); Mozert v. Hawkins County Bd. of Educ., 87-5024 (6 Cir. 1987); Smith v. Bd. of School Commissioners of Mobile County, 87-7216 (11 Cir. 1987); Aguillard v. Treen, 634 F.2d 426 (E.D.La. 1985); and Edwards v. Aguillard, 197 S.Ct. 2573 (1987).

[35]Bill R. Gearheart, *Teaching Mildly and Moderately Handicapped* (Englewood Cliffs, N.J., 1986): 314–315.

Public Law 94-142 calls for "inclusive education" or "least restrictive environments" that give all *students the right to free, appropriate education. The challenge is to serve exceptional students in ways that are educationally sound.* —Charles Gupton/Stock, Boston

ability. Thus, if a student named Jerry is identified as being primarily **learning disabled**, it means that he has

> a disorder in one or more of the basic psychological processes involved in understanding or in using language . . . which may manifest itself in an imperfect ability to listen, think, speak, read, write, spell or to do mathematical calculations.[36]

Currently, for Jerry to be classified as **mentally retarded**, he would have to be significantly below average in general intelligence (an IQ below 65–69) and also be deficient in adapting appropriately to a particular environment. An assessment of **emotionally disturbed** would mean that Jerry exhibits maladaptive behaviors and has aberrant feelings about himself; and the term **behaviorally disordered** would mean that Jerry has socialization difficulties.[37] The field of special education has an important mission in training teachers to educate such children, who formerly were segregated and shunned because their classmates did not understand their difficulties.[38]

Less federal attention has been devoted to **gifted education**, although Public Law 97-35 (1981) directed schools to accommodate the needs of

> children who give evidence of high performance capability . . . and to require services or activities not ordinarily provided by the school in order to fully develop such capabilities.[39]

The field of gifted education is attempting to move beyond the limitations

[36]Ibid., 4–9.
[37]Ibid.
[38]R. C. Scheerenberger, *A History of Mental Retardation* (Baltimore and London: Brookes, 1983)
[39]Judy W. Eby and Joan F. Smutny, *A Thoughtful Overview of Gifted Education* (White Plains, N.Y.: Longman, 1990).

imposed by IQ tests and other achievement measures to identify exceptional students.[40] A few states have chosen to create special schools, such as the Illinois Math Sciences Academy, to fit the needs of students with unusual talents, but critics argue that segregation is not the best approach.[41] Among the challenges facing today's schools is how to serve exceptional students in ways that are democratic as well as educationally sound.

CONCLUSIONS

■

Educational institutions inevitably reflect a society's tensions and aspirations. This is apparent in many aspects of American education, but nowhere is it more dramatic than in disagreements over what to teach and how to teach it. From the beginnings of formal schooling, for example, until the rise of modern science, students followed a liberal arts course of study, and masters usually believed in some form of corporal punishment. But as experimental science made its way into the curriculum, many aspects of accepted knowledge came into question. Then religious reforms made schooling available to poor and lower-class children, and that revolutionized teacher training as well as instruction in both primary and secondary schools. Particularly influential leaders in education were John Amos Comenius and St. Ignatius Loyola.

As more children received a basic or primary education, further changes occurred in instruction. Two key figures in this transformation were Johann Heinrich Pestalozzi and Friedrich Froebel, who taught by using objects and by involving children in self-activities. In addition, Froebel worked with very young children to prepare them for formal schooling. He called such early-childhood education *Kindergarten*, or "children's garden."

At the secondary level, vocational training slowly made its way into the American curriculum, along with extracurricular activities that promoted democracy and solidarity among students from diverse social and ethnic backgrounds. With the spread of universal education came the need to guarantee standards of education at all levels. This led to greater concern for accrediting schools and for licensing teachers and administrators. It also resulted in controversies over the content and standardization of textbooks and other curricular materials.

As the drive for universal education continued, public policies focused attention on special populations of students. Public Law 94-142 called for "least restrictive environments" that give all children the right to a free and appropriate education. Today, as in the past, curricular matters continue to be at the center of many educational debates; the controversies are especially dramatic and dynamic in a democracy.

[40]Ibid.
[41]David M. Fetterman, *Excellence and Equality: A Qualitatively Different Perspective on Gifted and Talented Education* (Albany: State University of New York Press, 1988).

KEY TERMS

curriculum

seven liberal arts

monitorial system

object teaching

Kindergarten

gifts

occupations

child-centered curriculum

project-centered curriculum

Morrill Act of 1862

Smith-Hughes Act of 1917

academic freedom

regional accreditation association

diploma mill

secondary school

elementary school

Committee of Ten

Commission on the Reorganization of Secondary Education (CRSE)

Cardinal Principles of Secondary Education

regular education initiative

learning disabled

mentally retarded

emotionally disturbed

behaviorally disordered

gifted education

SUGGESTED READINGS

Mortimer Adler, "The Paideia Proposal: Rediscovering the Essence of Education," *American School Board Journal* 169 (July 1982): 17–20. Adler sets forth a plan for a unified basic curriculum for all children, regardless of whether or not they are college bound. The curriculum includes goals and methods for acquiring knowledge, skills of learning, and understanding of ideas and values.

Paul Geisert and Mynga K. Futrell, *Teachers, Computers, and Curriculum: Microcomputers in the Classroom* (Boston: Allyn & Bacon, 1991). This book describes how teachers can integrate computers into the classroom, both to deliver the curriculum more effectively and to aid in decision making.

R. C. Scheerenberger, *A History of Mental Retardation* (Baltimore and London: Brookes, 1983). This book chronicles the history of policies and practices relating to mentally retarded students and their education.

Craig Kridel, ed., *Curriculum History: Conference Presentations from the Society for the Study of Curriculum History* (Washington, D.C.: University Press of America, 1989). This study explores the curriculum from

its historical roots, to curricular plans in specific settings, to biographical sketches of leaders in curricular developments.

Judy W. Eby and Joan F. Smutny, *A Thoughtful Overview of Gifted Education* (White Plains, N.Y.: Longman, 1990). This book reflects on the place of gifted education in the curriculum and describes some recent developments in the field.

John Taylor Gatto, *Dumbing Us Down: The Hidden Curriculum of Compulsory Schooling* (Philadelphia, Pa.: New Society Publishers, 1992). A former teacher of the year in New York, Gatto calls typical American schools "psychopathic"; he proposes home schooling, decertified teachers, and free-market schools.

George Wood, *Schools That Work: America's Most Innovative Public Education Programs* (New York: Dutton, 1992): Wood describes four public schools in which students create the conditions of their own learning and teachers serve as "coaches" rather than authorities.

Henry Louis Gates, Jr., *Loose Canons: Notes on the Culture Wars* (New York: Oxford, 1992). This noted African-American scholar advocates teaching African-American literature as well as traditional Eurocentric classics.

E. D. Hirsch, *Cultural Literacy: What Every American Needs to Know* (Boston, Mass.: Houghton Mifflin, 1987). Hirsch has become well known for arguing that many U.S. graduates are "culturally illiterate."

Michael W. Apple, *Teachers & Texts: A Political Economy of Class & Gender Relations in Education* (New York: Routledge & Keegan Paul, 1986). Apple argues that the curriculum is not neutral—that politics and economics, gender, race, and social class are always reflected in schools.

Carl F. Kaestle et al., *Literacy in the United States* (New Haven, Conn.: Yale University Press, 1992). This book investigates literacy and demographic characteristics, the causes and implications of declining test scores during the early 1970s, the reasons why women's magazines have been more successful than men's, and whether print technology has fostered cultural diversity or consolidation.

Mary M. Huston, "Building New Relationships and Valuing Diversity Through the Information Seeking Process: From Picture Books to Hyper Space," *Multicultural Review* 1 (January 1992): 8–19. "We must . . . learn to inquire, value, and make decisions in new ways," says Huston; she calls for multiple perspectives in developing "legitimate" knowledge.

European Backgrounds

Historical Foundations A

Those who cannot remember the past are condemned to repeat it. Those who are too young must be taught it.

—George Santayana, Life of Reason, *vol. 1 (New York: Scribner's, 1905): 12*

Ignorance or the ignoring of history is the mother of much educational innovation.

—Harry Broudy, *"What Do Professors of Education Profess?" 4th Annual DeGarmo Lecture, Society of Professors of Education, 28 February 1979, 4*

8

European Backgrounds

ADVANCED ORGANIZERS

In this chapter you will learn

The role of education in early societies

What contributions Christianity made to education

How the Renaissance and the Reformation changed education

How science evolved as it became modern

Which ideas of the Enlightenment affected social institutions

CHAPTER OUTLINE

nthony is seven years old. Because his school is a good distance from home, one of the household's servants accompanies him. (His family is well-to-do, and so are the families of his schoolmates.) When Anthony awakens, he washes his face and hands, cleans his teeth, and combs his hair; after he dresses, he leaves his room and kisses his parents good morning. Then he finds his ruler, pen, and exercise book, and he leaves for school with the servant. He doesn't usually have breakfast at home; instead, the servant lets him buy a pastry to eat along the way.

When Anthony arrives at school, he greets his classmates and his teacher, and he takes his usual seat and begins to work on his assignments. He works hard all morning, learning to write and spell properly. He wants to please his teacher so that he won't be spanked for doing his lessons poorly.

When it is time for lunch, the teacher dismisses the class, and Anthony goes home to eat. He has white bread and cheese, along with some fruit and nuts. After lunch Anthony returns to school for the afternoon session, and the teacher tells him to continue with the morning lessons. Finally finished, Anthony shows his work to the teacher, who corrects it. (He hopes that there won't be too many mistakes, because he doesn't want to be whipped.) The teacher says, "Let me see your work! How have you done? It's not bad. All right, I'll let you off this time. . . . "

Their school day finished, Anthony and his classmates leave for home. It is the custom for boys of his age and social station to take a bath before supper. As they part, Anthony bids his friends: "Have a good bath! Have a good supper!"[1]

If asked when and where Anthony lived, you probably would rule out twentieth-century America. After all, few American boys go to school accompanied by a servant (and *very* few seven-year-olds are likely to bathe before supper!). On the other hand, it might surprise you to learn that this typical school day is based on the diary of a Roman boy who lived around A.D. 200—about seventeen hundred years ago!

It is easy to forget that the past is connected to the present, that history is really a prelude to today. Although some things, like technology, often advance rapidly, such things as human relationships and values change much more slowly. Thus we can understand Anthony's school experiences nearly two thousand years later. And by studying cultural and educational history, we can better understand our own educational practices and social experiences today. Understanding the past—like understanding our friends and even ourselves—allows us to see how things came to be as they are. The past helps us to understand the present.

If you didn't know about your past, you would be like an amnesiac. Similarly, if a group does not know and understand its past, it suffers from collective amnesia. History is the means by which we explain our collective selves—the context that helps us understand our present actions, whether they are similar to or different from our heritage. To put it yet another way, history allows us to enter into a dialog with our past so that our consciousness about past and present thought is heightened.[2]

[1]Based on the diary of a Roman boy written around A.D. 200; see H. I. Marrou, *A History of Education in Antiquity*, trans. George Lamb (New York: Sheed & Ward, 1956), 229.
[2]Christopher J. Lucas, *Our Western Educational Heritage* (New York: Macmillan, 1972), 4.

This chapter is devoted to the history of education. By creating pictures of various early and Western societies, we hope to bring today's educational scene into sharper focus. We will emphasize Western societies (Greece, Rome, and Europe) because they are the cultural and educational antecedents of American society and education. But first we will examine early societies, including Sumeria and Egypt, to get an idea of what education was like in tribal and early agrarian societies. Throughout the chapter we will focus on the following questions:

- Who taught what, and who got educated?
- Who were the important figures in education?
- What were the major educational contributions of that society or period?

EDUCATION IN EARLY COMMUNITIES

Education is the means by which a culture transmits its knowledge, beliefs, and customs to the young and thereby perpetuates itself. Kinship was the basis of the most early societies; small groups of related families—called *clans*—banded together for survival. Then groups of clans assembled into a tribe with a leader or chief. Education consisted of teaching the young to survive by hunting for food and (eventually) by planting crops; to secure shelter; to make tools and other utensils; and to learn the tribe's values and regulative rules. Parents, storytellers, priests, and other adults taught children the practical skills needed, and they told them stories that explained the mores (customs) of the tribe. Usually religious practices taught what morality was. In such primitive communities the totem pole was often the link to the past; its symbols and emblems signified the tribe's ancestral clans.[3]

Gradually some hunting and herding tribes learned farming methods and became agrarian societies that placed great value on the land. As communities grew to include more than one tribe, the domination of one tribe over the others replaced kinship as the organizing social force, and laws replaced mores. Social life became much more complex. The need to maintain order, to keep track of crop production and natural resources, to parcel out food, and to trade with other communities made it necessary to develop symbolic methods of record keeping and communication. And as written symbols were devised, more systematic forms of instruction were needed to teach the society's dominant members and future leaders. The earliest schools were actually "tablet houses"—the places where business and cultural records were kept.

The earliest societies that left records were a group of city-states that developed in the Tigris-Euphrates river valley, in Mesopotamia (now in southern Iraq). Known as Sumeria, these city-states—along with some along the upper Nile River in Egypt—became the bases for later social and educational developments in Europe, China, and India.

[3]Ibid., 5–46; and John Bowle, *A History of Europe* (London: Secker & Warburg/Heinemann, 1979), 3–19. For an account of female roles during the beginnings of civilization see Elise Boulding, *The Underside of History* (Boulder, Colo.: Westview, 1976).

EDUCATION IN SUMERIA AND EGYPT

■

SUMERIA

Communities developed in the Tigris-Euphrates river valley around 4500 B.C., when Sumerian hunting tribes conquered the agrarian communities in Mesopotamia. They reached their zenith some fifteen centuries later, around 3000 B.C., before being absorbed by descendants of the natives they had conquered. During their peak period each of several Sumerian city-states was under the rule of a patron god who delegated care of the land and daily operations of the society to a human designate—the priest/king. Sumerian society was polytheistic, and so other gods and goddesses directed all aspects of life: One governed agricultural activities; another oversaw war; and still others directed marriage, travel, trade, and so on.

Sumerian agricultural cities had well-developed irrigation systems, a standard of value based on gold and silver (but no coinage), sailing boats, wheeled vehicles (chariots), a calendar year, and many temples where business and other activities were conducted. These societies comprised a propertied class, a business class, physicians and priests, a poorer class of skilled craftsmen, and slaves. A woman's social station was determined by the status of her father or husband, and she was regarded as his property; she could be sold to pay his debts. A wife who was unable to produce children could be divorced. On the other hand, females could attend school, and a woman could manage her husband's business and household affairs when he was away.

Children had no rights. They could be left to die in the heat of the sun if they were born deformed or of the wrong sex (usually female). In later times, if they incurred their father's disfavor, they could be disowned or banished.

WHO TAUGHT WHAT, AND WHO GOT EDUCATED?   Formal education in Sumeria was conducted in temple schools called **eduba** by priests called **ummia.** Although Sumerians did not have an alphabet, they developed symbols that came to be known as **cuneiform,** which were made by pressing a wedge-shaped stylus into a soft clay tablet. At first cuneiform was used only for business records, but by 2700 B.C. it was also being used for literature. There is evidence that Sumerian language had a grammatical structure and employed over four hundred symbols. Besides language skills the eduba curriculum included basic mathematics (addition, subtraction, multiplication, division, and square and cube roots) and geometry for agricultural purposes. Libraries housed records and literature in many Sumerian cities.

Such was the education for boys from the favored propertied class who planned to join the priestly class and govern the state. To flesh out the picture there is an early account of a young Sumerian who was in trouble with his ummia, apparently because he had spoken out of turn and copied his lessons poorly. Fearing that he would be caned, he asked his father to invite the ummia for dinner and to give him the honored seat at the table. His father consented and gave the ummia not only the seat of honor but also some gifts. The strategy worked; the ummia began praising the boy, telling him that if he applied himself he could become a leader in his time.[4]

EGYPT

During the same period that Sumeria developed, civilization along the upper Nile River was reaching its cultural height. People in the villages that grew up along the river enjoyed cooperative living under a steward king, or pharaoh, who was their god's deputy administrator. Eventually the civilization spread to the lower Nile, and by 3100 B.C. the upper and lower Nile communities united as one kingdom under one pharaoh's rule, forming the first Egyptian dynasty.

From about 2600 B.C. to about 2100 B.C.—during the fourth through sixth dynasties—an elaborate theocratic (religious) government and social system emerged. Egypt's social structure consisted of seven levels, which—unlike Sumeria's social structure—allowed for some mobility. At the top of society was the pharaoh's royal family, followed by priests and then nobility—both of whom served royalty. Next came a "middle class" composed of merchants, **scribes** (learned officials and teachers), artisans, and farmers. The two classes at the bottom of the social hierarchy were serfs and slaves. In addition, there was a professional class of soldiers whose position was independent of the hierarchy. Originally only upper classes enjoyed jewelry and cosmetics, but eventually these luxuries filtered down to lower classes. Female roles were like those in Sumeria, and married women enjoyed a good deal of autonomy.

[4]Lucas, *Western Educational Heritage*, 24; citing Samuel Noah Kramer, *History Begins at Sumer* (Garden City, N.Y.: Anchor, 1959), 2–16.

Egypt, like Mesopotamia, had an extensive system of libraries, including this one in Alexandria. The Sumerians and Egyptians also developed formal schooling and symbolic writing; the Egyptians invented paper as well.
—*North Wind Picture Archives*

Besides its influence on government and the social system, religion also left its mark on art and architecture, especially as evidenced in the tombs, monuments, and pyramids that were built during this time. As already noted, Egyptian priests were the government officials, and it was they who maintained the socioeconomic and political structure. Indeed, this period ended (around 2100 B.C.) because priestly power gradually gave way to the increased power of the nobility.[5]

WHO TAUGHT WHAT, AND WHO GOT EDUCATED? Egypt's priests taught in schools that were connected to temples or (sometimes, in outlying areas) to government offices. Children from the upper classes were taught to read and to write using pictographic symbols known as **hieroglyphics,** which were developed by the priests. In addition, a cursive, more symbolic *hieratic script* was used in business, and a simpler form of it (*demotic script*) was used in informal correspondence. From about age five or six students progressed through Egyptian literature, music, astronomy, arithmetic, and geometry; they also often were instructed in the more practical subjects of surveying and engineering. Such a curriculum occupied six to ten years. After that, promising pupils could study philosophy and theological subjects that prepared them for the learned professions of priest and scribe. (It was not uncommon for women also to hold these positions.) Other men could pursue architecture or medicine. Discipline was very harsh in Egyptian schools. Not only were students flogged, but they sometimes were even imprisoned for breaking rules.

Sometimes youth from the lower classes could attend temple or government schools in order to learn the rudiments of a trade; then they were apprenticed. In the lower schools children wrote on clay tablets, and in the higher schools they were allowed to use papyrus paper. Like Mesopotamia, Egypt also had an extensive library system.[6]

MAJOR CONTRIBUTIONS TO EDUCATION To both Sumeria and Egypt we are indebted for the beginnings of formalized schooling and for the establishment of libraries. Particularly in Egypt, schools developed lower and higher levels of curricular offerings, along with the beginnings of liberal arts and an apprenticeship system. Both cultures also elaborated a system of symbolic writing, which was produced on clay tablets. Finally, to Egypt we also owe the invention of paper.

EDUCATION IN ANCIENT GREECE

Out of Egyptian hieroglyphics and Sumerian cuneiform developed an alphabet in which syllables were separated into individual sounds and were called letters. Phoenician sailors from what today is called Lebanon spread this alphabet throughout the Mediterranean region. Sometime between 1000 and 800 B.C. Greeks refined the alphabet further by isolating and giving vowels individual notations. They also reversed the direction of writing from right–left to left–

[5]Ibid., 30–36; also see Boulding, *Underside of History,* 184–196.
[6]Ibid.

right. Their alphabet had twenty-four characters and was named after the first two—*alpha* and *beta*—or *alphabet* (after dropping the final *a*).

Greek civilization developed on seven fertile plains between about 1200 and 490 B.C.—the year that Athens defeated Persia at the battle of Marathon. From the fifth century to the third century B.C. Greece and particularly Athens enjoyed a flourishing level of culture and education. During these two hundred years Greece colonized much of the Mediterranean area, including towns in Italy and along the French coast. Originally Greek tribes had united in the various plains for religious and military purposes, but it was political reasons that ultimately produced such city-states as Athens, Sparta, Marathon, and Olympia. The center of activity in each state was built upon a hill and was known as the *polis*.

Greek religion was polytheistic, and the many gods and goddesses were believed to live above the clouds at Mount Olympus, the home of the most powerful god, Zeus. Every four years the Greek peoples gathered at Mount Olympus to celebrate Zeus by competing in a variety of games known as the Olympics.

SPARTA

From the sixth to the fourth centuries B.C. the city-state of Sparta was known for military strength. Its government was an oligarchy, meaning the city-state was ruled by a small elite group of elders from a Greek-speaking tribe that had conquered the area's natives. To keep the enslaved natives from revolting, Sparta declared war on them annually. Hence, few cultural developments were realized, and foreign people and their ideas were unwelcome. When Sparta went to war with Athens (the Peloponnesian War), 431–404 B.C., it eventually won the battle but lost its closed and static society to the Athenian culture, which was vibrant, dynamic, and intellectually curious.

One favorable practice that Sparta can be credited with was its refusal to swaddle young children. **Swaddling** is the practice of tightly wrapping infants and

Freeborn Greek males entered a palestra at about age six and were often accompanied to school by their paidogogos; in the early teens they entered a gymnasium. The Greek curriculum was grounded in rhetoric and aimed to develop virtue. —*North Wind Picture Archives*

small children in cloth bands in order to restrict their movement; supposedly, a child's limbs will not develop properly unless they are bound. Some cultures have kept children in swaddling until they walked, and bound children have even been tied to poles and furniture to teach them to stand. Versions of swaddling continued in the Western world until the seventeenth century.

ATHENS

Western societies trace much of their cultural and educational heritage to this Greek city-state. Athens came to prominence after about 500 B.C., as Sparta began to decline, and it is best remembered for its democratic form of government. The franchise, or right to vote, was given to male Athenians at age twenty-one, if both their parents were freeborn and could read. In the middle of the fifth century B.C. the number of franchised citizens was 43,000, out of a population of 315,000. The rest were slaves (115,000); foreigners or resident aliens called *metics* (28,500); and freedmen, women, and children.[7]

A typical day for an Athenian citizen started with a breakfast of wine-soaked bread and was followed by a trip with friends to the barber, who dressed and perfumed one's hair. Next these men of leisure went shopping in the marketplace (the *agora*), where they also had lunch. Then they indulged in a nap before heading for a public gymnasium for exercise and more socializing. Before dinner they bathed. (Since water was scarce, most "baths" involved covering the body with oil and having a slave scrape it and the dirt off with a blunt knifelike instru-

---

RESEARCH SAYS

For Tomorrow's Education . . .

Oral history—the practice of interviewing people to gain firsthand accounts of their experiences—is particularly valuable in expanding information about the history of education. In *Envelopes in Sound: The Art of Oral History* Ronald J. Grele demonstrates how oral-history interviews can be used to combine a subject's language, imagery, and description of social practices into a new understanding of the past (Westport, Conn.: Greenwood, 1991).

---

ment; water stored in large containers was used for rinsing.) Dinner was another social and intellectual occasion. Men reclined while they ate, but women sat erect. If a husband invited a friend for dinner, his wife and children ate in their rooms. Sometimes dinner was the setting for political or intellectual discourse, and at other times it was accompanied by dancers and flute players. An Athenian's day ended after dinner, at sunset. Because the Mediterrean climate was mild, houses were simple: unbaked brick walls and roofed rooms with mud-packed floors opened onto one or more courtyards.

WHO TAUGHT WHAT, AND WHO GOT EDUCATED?   Before the fifth century B.C. Greek education was reserved for freeborn males and consisted of train-

[7]Will Durant, *The Life of Greece* (New York: Simon & Schuster, 1939), 254–255.

ing in the military and studying Homer's *Iliad* and *Oddessy*. These two epic poems gave boys heroic role models like Achilles, who exhibited courage along with a distinctive excellence or virtue that made him superior and honorable. Eloquent speaking, or rhetoric, was also part of the educational ideal. Not only was Achilles' virtue honorable, but Ulysses' oratory was also regarded as an important form of virtue. These distinctive forms of virtue or honor were called **aretè**, and every boy strove to attain it. That was the focus of a Homeric education.

During the fifth century B.C., when Athens had become a growing cultural center through trade and commerce, the curriculum was expanded, although *aretè* continued to be the ideal. Education was still only for freeborn males and began at about age six in a school called the **palestra**. A boy was accompanied to the palestra by his slave (a **paidogogos**, or "boy's slave"). He was typically schooled in three ways. He was taught gymnastics—running, swimming, wrestling, and the use of bow and sling—by a **paidotribe** (masseuse); he was taught to play the lyre as an accompaniment to poetry and other songs by a **cytharist**; and he was taught writing—which included reading and arithmetic—by a **grammartist**. A clay tablet and a stylus were the early writing materials, which later were replaced by papyrus and a crude inkpen.

By the time an Athenian youth was twelve to fourteen years old, he usually left the palestra to attend a municipal school called a **gymnasium**, of which there were several. These were larger and better equipped than the palestra, and their stadiumlike structures were built around a playing field or running track. As time passed, men who were called **philosophers**—who wanted to teach geometry, astronomy, logic, or advanced rhetoric—began to visit the gymnasia seeking clients, because males of all ages could be found at the gyms. Finally, from age eighteen to about twenty-one, Athenian males trained for the military.

Generally, the men who taught were freeborn Athenians and foreigners. Although teaching itself did not confer much status, education for boys was considered very important. In fact, the **Sophists** (as the philosophers were called) developed a questionable reputation because they sold their knowledge and because many people thought that they engaged in deceptive, self-serving reasoning.

Athenian girls were educated at home; their curriculum would be described today as domestic science or home economics, along with singing and dancing. Aristocratic women were expected to remain secluded within the home. They often had their own quarters near those of their young sons and daughters.

Many games and toys were used by Athenian children. They played with dolls, had see-saws, rolled hoops, flew kites, and spun tops. Their games included hide-and-seek, blindman's buff, and marbles. It appears that Athenian parents loved their children and treated them well. Even so, boys were flogged in school, and fathers could exercise their right to expose an unhealthy or abnormal child (putting the infant out in the sun or rain to die within the first week or two of the child's life).

KEY FIGURES IN EDUCATION   The list of well-known Greek philosophers from this era seems endless, but we certainly must recognize Socrates for his emphasis on logic and geometry and for his concern with providing an education that enhanced human virtue. We are indebted for most of what we know about Socrates to his famous pupil Plato, who recorded many written dialogs for us to study. Plato also left us a scheme of education that was designed to select the most academically talented persons to be **philosopher-kings**—intellectually gifted, politically powerful leaders for an ideal society.

Plato's pupil, Aristotle, taught us the significance and value of the Golden Mean—of avoiding extremes in leading a balanced, healthy, and good life. He also demonstrated the value of a contemplative life of study and the importance of the physical world, and he established biological nomenclature. In addition, of course, there were many great Greek rhetoricians—Protagoras, Isocrates, Gorgias—and the philosopher who gave doctors their ethical oath, Hippocrates. (See Chapters 6 and 7 for the learning theories of Plato and Aristotle and how they influenced curricular development.) According to Martin Bernal, however, some of what we attribute to the Greeks may actually have come from Africans (see his two-volume *Black Athens*, published by Rutgers University Press).

MAJOR CONTRIBUTIONS TO EDUCATION   As noted in Chapter 7, we are indebted for the development of the seven liberal arts (grammar, rhetoric, logic, music, arithmetic, geometry, and astronomy) to Athens, and for the refinement of the alphabet and physical education to all the Greek city-states. The practice of flogging children in school continued from Sumeria and Egypt, as did a father's right to expose a newborn infant to the elements. To such dark legacies we can add the bright ones of games and toys; it was the Greeks who saw that children's fun and entertainment hold the potential for learning.

Ancient Greeks, and particularly Athenians, can be honored most for their intellectual curiosity. They questioned everything and posited many speculative answers that became part of Western conventional wisdom until the seventeenth century, when modern science arose. Greek ideas about human nature and ethics were a major legacy to Western civilization.

EDUCATION IN ROME

Greek culture dominated the Mediterranean region until the end of the third century B.C., when Rome conquered Greece and its colonies. Rome may have won the war, but Greek culture was absorbed into Roman society, which had been agrarian until the seventh century B.C., when the Etruscans from the north invaded the Latin and other Italic tribes.

The Etruscans brought with them art, architecture, an alphabet (which the Romans refined into Latin), and an urban lifestyle—the center of which was the Roman *forum*. The Etruscans ruled the Italic tribes until 509 B.C., when the Latins overthrew them and set up a representative form of government called a *republic*. Its governing body was a senate, composed of male heads (*patres*) of the landed Latin aristocracy. Senate officers included a *censor*, who was in charge of the treasury as well as society's morals, and two executives called *consuls*, who were to check each other's political power. Eventually, a merchant class was added to the Senate.

Below the landed and merchant classes were free plebeians, or common people, followed by slaves. During the early years of Roman civilization slaves were treated like members of the family and often were freed upon the death of the patre. Later on, as Rome conquered more and more of the Mediterranean region and Europe, slaves and plebeians were exploited. In exchange for their prowess as foot soldiers in various battles, they were promised greater political rights and some of the newly conquered lands. Unfortunately for them, however, conquered lands usually went to the landed and merchant classes, which created ever-wider political and economic gaps between the upper and lower classes.

It was such treatment of the plebeians and slaves that led to Rome's century-long civil war—from 133 to 30 B.C. The war ended republican government and began the years of the Roman Empire. This came about when one of the two consuls of the Senate became powerful enough to set himself up as emperor (in fact, a dictator). Julius Caesar tried to establish a three-way consulship, or triumvirate, but the other two triumvirs were assassinated, and eventually he was, too (in 44 B.C.). Thus the first true emperor was his nephew and adopted son, Octavius—known throughout history as Augustus Caesar.

The Romans gave us many of our customs. Although their religion was polytheistic (Jupiter replaced Zeus as the most powerful god), Christianity took much of its nomenclature from Rome. Thus patres came to be called priests, because they conducted family ceremonies and performed various public rituals, such as those connected with battle and prophesies. Even the months of the year were named after Roman gods and goddesses; many people still think women should be married in June, the month named after Juno, the goddess of marriage.

A patre was definitely the head of his household, but a Roman woman—especially during the period of empire—was more free than a Greek woman, because she could socialize publicly and could control her own wealth after her patre died. Cato, a famous censor, observed that Roman men ruled all men but were themselves ruled by women. Yet, generally, relations between the sexes followed tribal traditions. When a father gave his daughter's "hand in marriage," it literally meant that he was handing over his authority to the daughter's husband. Daughters also were named after the clan: Julia from the clan of Julius, Claudia from Claudius, Cornelia from Cornelius, and so on.

Roman technology was far superior to Greek. For more than a thousand years Romans built roads and constructed aqueducts to transport water throughout their lands. Roman bathhouses were well-equipped gathering places during the late afternoon, before supper; women's baths were separated from men's, but generally both sexes shared the same elaborate, multiroomed public bathhouse. The Roman home, or villa, was well constructed, and by the third century or so after Christ wealthier homeowners had running water and even a form of glass window. Such technological feats were performed by skilled plebeian craftsmen who formed guilds, some of which eventually provided schools for their sons and financial aid to the families of deceased guild members.

WHO TAUGHT WHAT, AND WHO GOT EDUCATED?   During the years before the Romans conquered the Greeks, an upper-class boy was educated at home by his mother until age seven. Then he went off in the company of his slave—called a **pedagogue**—to a school, or **ludus**. The ludus was conducted in the back of one of the shops in the forum and was taught by a free man called a **ludus magister** or a **litterator**. Reading, writing, and arithmetic were emphasized, although arithmetic amounted to little more than counting. (It is difficult to do much else with Roman numerals, which are based on the fingers of the hand. Thus *I* stands for one finger and represents the number *1; V* stands for five fingers stretched in an open position and represents the number *5*. In many respects Roman numerals can be regarded as sign language.)

Boys also learned to box, swim, spear, and ride horseback. Between ages fourteen and sixteen they spent a year or two accompanying their fathers to the Forum and Senate so that they could learn to socialize and govern. At about age sixteen they began ten years of military training and service, which they needed in order to hold public office.

Roman girls were educated at home. As in Athens, the emphasis was on homemaking. Girls were taught to be efficient slave managers and to have good manners. Later, during the third century B.C., many girls were allowed to attend the ludus.

After Greece was conquered, Roman educational structures were changed to incorporate many of the Greek arrangements. The **Latin grammar school** followed the ludus and taught the seven liberal arts, although the Romans did little with arithmetic, geometry, music, or astronomy. Greek gymnasia were also introduced to Roman society. In addition to Latin grammar school, many aristocratic boys attended these to study Greek language and literature, under the instruction of a Greek pedagogue. By the end of the third century B.C. aristocratic boys often attended a gymnasium in Athens or some other Greek city to perfect their study of philosophy and rhetoric. By this time the goal of Roman education was to combine military prowess with rhetorical skill, in preparation for a political career.

Rome adopted the Greek liberal arts tradition along with such practices as flogging, which went all the way back to Sumeria. Quintilian argued against the rod, but his humane methods were ignored until the Renaissance.
—North Wind Picture Archives

KEY FIGURES IN EDUCATION   Among the best-known Roman orators was Marcus Tullius Cicero (106–43 B.C.), a contemporary of Julius Caesar. Cicero had studied with a Greek pedagogue in Athens. He was concerned about the strong emphasis on rhetoric in the curriculum and thought, instead, that a good orator needed to be educated first and foremost in history; then he would add law, philosophy, politics, ethics, military and naval science, astronomy, geometry, medicine, and even psychology. Unfortunately, Romans paid no heed to his advice and continued to emphasize rhetoric and military preparation. (Much later, during the Renaissance, a well-rounded education did become the ideal.) Cicero was killed by Augustus Caesar, who thought that the orator was among the conspirators who assassinated his uncle Julius Caesar.

Almost a century later Quintilian (A.D. 35–95) also advocated a well-rounded education, except he thought that the study of literature should hold the place of prominence. Quintilian was a rhetorician from Spain. As noted in Chapter 7, he was concerned about the treatment of children in school and wrote against using the rod to motivate them; instead, he favored kindness and the use of play to advance learning.

Other important Roman figures include Virgil (70–19 B.C.), author of *The Aeneid* and *King Midas*; Horace (65–8 B.C.), the lyric poet; Seneca (4? B.C.–A.D. 65), the tragic poet; and Juvenal (A.D. 60?–140?), the satirist. All contributed to the rich legacy of Roman literature.

MAJOR CONTRIBUTIONS TO EDUCATION   From the third century B.C. to the second century A.D. Rome conquered Spain, Hannibal's North Africa, Alexander's Greece, Cleopatra's Egypt, the rest of the Mediterranean region, France, Britain, and part of southern Germany—thereby uniting under one rule a vast amount of what today is Europe. Rome's technological developments became the basis for skilled trade and craft guilds. In addition, many Western social and legal customs can be traced to Rome; our system of jurisprudence, in particular, is rooted in Rome's fertile soil.

During the first and second centuries after Christ the Roman government established schools in all cities of the Empire. Teachers and rhetoricians were paid by imperial governments, which also established many libraries. Romans continued the liberal arts tradition, along with other Greek educational practices—including flogging. They also advanced their very limited counting system of base-10 Roman numerals, which influenced most of the Western world well into the sixteenth century.

During the third century the Roman economy began to falter, ending the occupational and social mobility that had developed. Emperors, such as Diocletian (from 284 to 305) and Constantine "The Great" (from 306 to 337), governed not from Rome but from what is now Turkey (from the city of Byzantium, which then became Constantinople and is now Istanbul); this location offered strategic advantages against invasions by barbarians. Also during this period more and more Romans converted to Christianity, including Constantine himself, so that under his rule the Empire became Christianized. By the fifth century the citizens of Rome embraced Christianity, and Roman society was no longer pagan;

Quintilian

35–95

Remembered as the first public (tax-supported) teacher of the Roman Empire, Marcus Fabius Quintilianus was originally from Calagurris, in northern Spain, and was the son of a *rhetor*, or teacher of rhetoric. His father was called to Rome when Marcus was a boy, and there Quintilian was educated by some of the Empire's best teachers.

Rome was a young empire during Quintilian's life. Octavius (Augustus) Caesar had restored harmony to the war-torn state, but he was followed by his weak stepson, Tiberius, in A.D. 14. When Tiberius died in A.D. 37, the four-year reign of the despot Caligula began; he was followed by the weak Claudius (A.D. 41–54). Quintilian probably arrived in Rome toward the end of Caligula's rule and became a rhetor under Claudius before returning to Spain. The Roman governor of Spain was a man named Galba, and he protected the young teacher.

When the infamous Nero died, in A.D. 68, Galba was called to Rome to be the next emperor. Very likely he brought Quintilian to Rome to teach, but Galba was an unpopular emperor, and the military beheaded him shortly after he ascended the throne. Vespasian (69–79) succeeded Galba, and he appointed Quintilian to the first imperially financed chair of rhetoric. Vespasian also reduced the tax burden for teachers, and he endowed other chairs throughout the Empire; but the chair of rhetoric in Rome was the most prestigious position in education.

After two years of chaos, Domitian (81–96) came to the throne, and Quintilian left his position to tutor the emperor's two grandsons. He also began writing his famous *Institutes of Oratory (Instituto Oratoria)*—an educational plan for Domitian's grandsons as well as his own sons. Unfortunately, Quintilian soon lost his family through death, and he lamented for the rest of his life.

Even by today's standards Quintilian's writings are reasonable and sound. He advocated a well-rounded education based on great literature. Thus students would need to learn both Latin and Greek in order to read the literature. Quintilian understood psychological development. He recognized that children are impulsive and need to have their desires gratified until about age seven. And since children are impressionable, he considered it important that parents seek slaves and pedagogues who were virtuous and well-mannered and who spoke properly.

Yesterday's Professional

In Quintilian's scheme, from age seven to fourteen boys should learn to read and write the languages they speak—Greek and Latin. During these years sensory experiences are important; therefore, games and play should be used in learning. Flogging, to Quintilian, was "a disgraceful form of punishment . . . and should be abolished. It leads to fear which restrains some and unmans others." He recommended that ivory letters be used in learning alphabets. But he also recognized that talent was essential to learning, and that without it the type of curriculum would be unimportant. He thought that schools provided a better environment for learning than individual tutoring sessions did, because schools promoted competition. Yet he thought that classes should be small enough that the teacher could learn each child's talents and weaknesses.

From age fourteen to seventeen students' rational powers were to be developed through the liberal arts, or humanities: grammar, rhetoric, geometry, astronomy, music, and gymnastics. After age seventeen the orator's studies were to be broad—poetry, drama, prose, history, law, philosophy, and declamation—thereby producing a well-rounded, virtuous, and skilled speaker.

In advocating humane educational practices, recognizing individual learning styles, and incorporating play and recreation into learning, Quintilian advanced educational theories and practices that went unacknowledged in the Western world for sixteen hundred years—until his influence reappeared during the Renaissance.

Source: *Based on Aubrey Gwynn,* Roman Education from Cicero to Quintilian *(New York: Russell & Russell, 1964).*

customs either were transformed into the Judeo-Christian tradition or were repressed.

By the end of the fourth century the eastern half of the Empire separated from the western, Roman half. In 476 German barbarians invaded and sacked Rome, and even though the emperor was now in Turkey, 476 was the year the Empire ended, according to English historian Edward Gibbon (1737–1794) in his book *Decline and Fall of the Roman Empire*. A hundred years later the eastern portion of the former empire fell to the Persians.

EDUCATION IN CHRISTIAN EUROPE: THE MIDDLE AGES

From the fifth through twelfth centuries Christianity expanded beyond a religious movement to become a governmental force by taking over the political and bureaucratic structures that had developed under the Roman Empire. Through tithing, the Church assessed taxes, provided medical treatment, housed the poor, and developed a social structure consisting of the traditional aristocracy, high Church officials, lesser Church officials and skilled craftsmen, and finally serfs and slaves.

Waves of Christian reform produced a variety of monastic orders whose main object was to live away from the corruption of city life in rural, undeveloped areas of the European continent. These monastic orders built large self-sufficient fortresses in the wilderness and did much to civilize the northern European frontier. They also provided stopover places for those traveling from one region to another. Life was hard. Plagues, famine, and war diminished the population, while regional kingdoms vied for political and economic power.

During the early ninth century much of the western region was united when Charlemagne (742–814) was crowned emperor of the Holy Roman Empire in 800, but after his death in 814 the region returned to local rule. In many localities a merchant class developed, and they took their social place along side the aristocracy and major Church officials.

WHO TAUGHT WHAT, AND WHO GOT EDUCATED?   Catholic education continued in the Greek and Roman tradition. Old Roman schools either were closed or were Christianized as part of the cathedral structure, and the liberal arts dominated the curriculum. Schools that were affiliated with monastic orders usually provided an internal school for those desiring to become monks and an external school for children of the region's nobility and merchant classes. In larger cities with cathedrals, boys could also learn Latin by being chosen for the choir, in which case they attended a song school. Bishops gave responsibility for running the cathedral school to a Church official called the **scholasticus**; eventually, in some larger cathedrals, the scholasticus hired masters and supervised their teaching.

Both poor and wealthy families aspired to have their sons attend cathedral or monastic schools in hopes that they would climb to upper positions in the Church and monastic hierarchy. During this era the religious community—the clerics—received the most intellectual, most academic education. The sons and often the daughters of the nobility also received liberal arts instruction in several ways: by attending a cathedral school, by attending an external monastic or convent school, or by hiring a tutor. Such an education, however, was usually less academic than the clerics' education.

In addition, the sons of the nobility had to be educated into knighthood. From about ages seven to fourteen a noble boy was usually sent to the home of another aristocrat, where he served as a page. During this time he learned obedience, proper manners, the knightly code, and the skills of jousting and war. Aristocratic girls learned how to entertain guests, to serve a knight at table, and to unbuckle his armor, prepare his bath, and lay out his clothes.

From ages fourteen to twenty-one the young page became a squire and continued developing his military skills. He became an aid to his master knight by carving and serving at his table, helping him mount and dismount his horse, and removing his armor. He also learned heraldry—the history and proper display of family coats of arms. Finally, at age twenty-one, the squire was knighted.

The sons of skilled craftsmen were educated through apprenticeship. From ages seven to fourteen they served a master craftsman who began to teach them the particular skills of his craft. From fourteen to twenty-one the apprentice became skilled enough to become a journeyman; he could be paid for his craft, but he could not take on apprentices of his own or open a shop. At age twenty-one the journeyman became a master craftsman and could join the master guild or union. Now he could open shop and take on apprentices. The profession of teaching has developed in much the same way.

Some smaller communities provided instruction in the rudiments of literacy through parish schools. The reputation of such schools was poor, however, and some were accused of being unable even to provide basic Latin instruction for religious purposes (usually the local priest was the teacher, and he might be barely literate in Latin himself). Under Charlemagne and afterward, laws were passed admonishing Church officials to provide the basics of religious Latin instruction to the young throughout the Holy Roman Empire.

Girls were often included in parish schools, but they also received the best instruction at a monastery or convent school. For the most part, monasteries, convents, and cathedral schools offered the highest form of education, which included instruction in the trivium (grammar, rhetoric, and logic) and enough astronomy and arithmetic to calculate when Easter would occur. Aristocratic young women also served apprenticeships in wealthy households.

THE DEVELOPMENT OF HIGHER EDUCATION   By the eleventh century Paris was an intellectual center of Europe. Young men from all over the Continent came to study in cathedral schools, such as at Notre Dame, or in monastic schools, such as in St. Denis. The teachers were supposed to be members of the masters guild, or **universitas**, and then they were to be licensed by the scholasticus at Notre Dame before opening a school. However, by the twelfth century many teachers were being licensed without first becoming a member of the universitas.

A BRIEF CHRONOLOGY OF THE TIMES

4,500–3,000 B.C.: Sumerian city-states in Mesopotamia

3,100–2,100 B.C.: Egyptian civilization

500–300 B.C.: Classical Greek civilization

4th–1st centuries B.C.: Hellenistic Age

146 B.C.: Greeks conquered by Rome

133–30 B.C.: Civil war leading to Roman Empire

476: End of Roman Empire in West

800: Charlemagne Emperor of Holy Roman Empire

1066: Norman conquest of England

1095: First Crusade

12th century: Rise of towns, Arabic and Greek science

12th–13th centuries: Rise of universities, scholasticism

1215: King John and Magna Carta in Britain

1303–1417: Papacy at Avignon

1348–1349: Black Death

1412–1431: Joan of Arc

1453: End of Roman Empire in East

15th century: Renaissance at its peak

1452–1519: Leonardo da Vinci

1455: Guttenberg Bible

1473–1543: Copernicus

1479–1516: Ferdinand and Isabella of Spain

1492: Discovery of America

1517: Beginnings of Reformation

1519–1522: Magellan sails around the world

1534: Luther's German Bible

1540: Founding of Jesuits

1561–1626: Francis Bacon

1564–1642: Galileo

1564–1616: Shakespeare

1582: Gregorian calendar

1588: Spanish Armada

1611: King James' Bible

17th century: English, French, Dutch in America

1619: First African slaves in Virginia

1632–1704: John Locke

1642–1727: Isaac Newton

1660s: Rise of scientific societies

1661–1715: King Louis XIV of France

1712–1778: Jean Jacques Rousseau

1740–1789: Enlightenment at its peak

1769: Watt's steam engine

1776: American Revolution

1789: French Revolution

1804–1814: Napoleon I

1806: End of Holy Roman Empire

1815: Defeat of Napoleon at Waterloo

Notre Dame's cathedral school made Paris an intellectual center that beckoned to scholars throughout Europe and extended the liberal arts into higher education. Members of the universitas, a guild, were to be licensed by the scholasticus at Notre Dame. —Culver Pictures

Another problem arose from the sheer number of students in Paris. The townspeople and merchants resented the way they seemed to dominate the city, and fights sometimes broke out. Because the students were dressed in clerical gowns, such altercations became known as **town-gown disputes**. After one particularly harsh brawl in which a student was killed, the members of the universitas "walked out" and quit teaching. By this time the masters in the university guild had organized into four faculties, each headed up by a dean—the (preparatory) **lesser faculty** of arts and the (advanced) **higher faculties** of theology, law, and medicine. When the universitas returned, the masters demanded that university rules and regulations be enforced by the Church. From now on, students were to master the arts *before* being voted into the guild, and they were to be licensed *before* pursuing study in one of the higher faculties.

Finally, to protect the clerics from the townspeople, a system of residential colleges was endowed—the first being the Sorbonne, in 1256. Students who were admitted to study at the Sorbonne were taught by members of the various fac-

---

RESEARCH SAYS

For Tomorrow's Education . . .

Traditional accounts of educational history usually take a male perspective and focus on majority groups. In recent years, however, educational historians have drawn more heavily on diverse sources that document the contributions and experiences of females and members of minority groups. Although much work remains to be done in these areas, your library should be able to identify historical materials that go beyond traditional accounts. Also see L. Glenn Smith and Joan K. Smith et al., *Lives in Education: People and Ideas in the Development of Teaching*, 2d ed. (St. Martin's, 1994).

---

ulties. The college built lecture and study halls, dormitories, dining rooms, a library, and a chapel—all enclosed within a stone wall. In time, the Sorbonne became well known for the study of theology.

Other residential colleges were founded on the same pattern, and ultimately the entire universitas was hired by these colleges, each of which offered a curriculum like the Sorbonne's. Thus, unlike the campus of an American university, the medieval European university really constituted a union, or a guild. The residential college provided the physical facilities, and the masters—or professors, as they came to be called—were then hired by the college and often lived on its grounds.

Because European universities offered such a *general* array of studies—not just the arts or one other faculty—this system of a university and its colleges is termed a **studium generale**. Many such systems developed, and by the fourteenth century they could be found throughout Europe: in Bologna and Padua (Italy); in Oxford and Cambridge (England); in Salamanca (Spain); in Prague (Bohemia); and in Orléans, Angers, and Montpellier (France). A center of study that offered only one higher faculty besides the arts was known as a **studium particular**. Eventually, studia generalia—where advanced study in many areas could be pursued—were called universities, while study of the lesser faculty of the arts was begun in a secondary, preparatory school.

The early Church, through St. Augustine (354–430), had found theological meaning in the philosophy of Plato. Augustine had stressed the importance of ideas as reflecting God's nonmaterial transcendental world; for Plato, physical objects had an ideal form envisioned by the mind (see Chapter 10). By the time the university was developing, during the eleventh and twelfth centuries, scholars had discovered Aristotle's writings about objects in the physical world, and they argued that the physical human being had an essence which was connected to God. This theological viewpoint was called **scholasticism**, and it infused the curriculum for studying theology in studia generalia during the late Middle Ages and early Renaissance.

Key Figures in Education   Clearly, Charlemagne was a staunch supporter of education. He so loved learning himself that he strove to make education available to every freeborn person, regardless of social class. He thus is remembered for promoting **universal education**. Also, in 782, he brought to his palace, at Aachen, an English theologian and scholar named Alcuin (735–804), who became his personal adviser concerning education. Advanced schools were opened for learning the liberal arts in pursuit of religious wisdom, and Alcuin recopied the Bible to rid it of errors. He also introduced punctuation into the study of grammar, to clarify textual meanings. Charlemagne became his avid pupil, for he hoped to make Aachen a new Athens. In the palace Alcuin ran two schools: an academy for the pursuit of knowledge and a school to educate boys for ecclesiastical service. With Alcuin's guidance Charlemagne became unusually

Emperor Charlemagne so loved learning that he promoted education for every freeborn person, regardless of class. As Alcuin's avid pupil he strove to make his palace at Aachen a center for education, both academic and ecclesiastical. —North Wind Picture Archives

well educated, except for one thing: Although he could write, he never mastered the art of calligraphy—the fine penmanship so important during the Middle Ages.[8]

Pierre Abélard (1079–1142), a French philosopher and theologian, studied scholasticism in Paris and came to believe that—by weighing each religious argument—a person should decide which point of view was more correct. He explained this idea in the book *Sic et Non* ("Yes or No"), which Christian officials burned because the ideas of religious choice and thinking for oneself were too radical for the medieval Church. Thus Abélard was charged with heresy, which only added to his many troubles. He had already been castrated for having an affair with Héloise, a church official's niece who was an abbess and scholar in her own right. In addition, the masters guild shunned him because he was teaching without having been admitted to the universitas. Nevertheless, in an era when public disputation was considered intellectual as well as entertaining, Abélard supposedly had no equal.

Italian theologian St. Thomas Aquinas (1225–1274) studied at a studium particular in the monastery of Monte Cassino. His main contribution to intellectual debate during the Middle Ages was his argument that a nonmaterial transcendental God had the ability to actualize in the physical world. Hence, physical objects were connected to God through this actualizing process. Aquinas made these arguments in the *Summa Theologica*, which the Church discovered after he died. At that time the arguments were considered heretical, but during the Reformation the Roman Catholic Church adopted them, and Aquinas was sainted.

Scholasticism—the effort to reconcile theological and philosophical ideas—dominated intellectual pursuits during the Middle Ages, until the Renaissance focused attention on the past glories of ancient Greece and Rome. To appreciate how important and dominant scholasticism was during this long time, we offer the following story about Galileo Galilei (1564–1642). Upon viewing the sun through his telescope, he discovered sunspots, and he wrote to a scholastic professor at the university in Paris to relate this discovery. The professor replied that he had read Aristotle very carefully and that the ancient Greek had said that the sun was incorruptible; therefore, he argued, the "sunspots" had to be either in Galileo's eyes or on the lens of his telescope. Case closed. Modern science did not enter easily into the world of scholastic authorities.

CHRISTIAN CONTRIBUTIONS TO EDUCATION   It is difficult to remember that medieval northern Europe was a rough frontier with vast uncultivated and uninhabited lands. It was the massive monasteries of the Christian church that did most of the cultivating, of both land and society. The monasteries developed farming techniques, taught crafts, and provided schools for an advanced liberal arts education. In addition, after a couple had raised a family, the husband and wife often parted; the husband went to a monastery, and the wife entered a convent, to live out their days in a safe environment. Thus medieval monasteries even provided a form of social security for the elderly.

The major educational contribution from Christian Europe was the development of higher education, in the form of studia generalia. In England, where Oxford and Cambridge arose in rural areas instead of cities (where most students

[8]Mother Frances Raphael Drane, *Christian Schools and Scholars*, (London: Burns, Oates, & Washburne, 1924), 117–142.

would live), part of the arts curriculum came to be offered at Latin secondary (grammar) schools located in London and other populous areas. Students would attend one of these **feeder schools** first, and then they would transfer to one of the twelve or thirteen residential colleges at Oxford or Cambridge. Most of these colleges offered similar curricula in both the lesser and the higher faculties of study. An English college, therefore, was a protected residential environment, just as it was in Paris. Today many European universities still consist of several residential colleges in which the members of the university guild teach.

ARABIC AND JEWISH CONTRIBUTIONS TO EDUCATION During the Middle Ages Spain—which had been taken from Rome by various barbaric tribes— had prospered intellectually. By the eighth century Arabs had settled in many Spanish cities alongside their Jewish cousins. Córdoba was one such cultural center from the ninth to the eleventh centuries; others were Granada, Toledo, Barcelona, and Seville. The mosques and temples that date from this time are landmarks of Eastern architecture and aesthetics.

During this period the Moslems translated, into Arabic, the classic Greek texts in medicine, astronomy, and mathematics. In particular, they developed algebra in a text called *Calculation of Integration and Equation*, by Mohammed ibn Musa, which became the standard text in European universities from the twelfth to the sixteenth centuries. Even earlier the Moslems had borrowed numerals from the Persians and Indians, and astronomical tables and arithmetic notation from the Hindus. Using a base-10 system, they developed the concept of zero; that is, if no number appears in the tens place, a circle (*sifr*) is used to indicate that the place is empty. Europeans called this word *cipher*, and the Italians translated it as *zephrum*, or *zero* for short.

In chemistry the Arabs experimented with alchemy, or the art of transforming metals into gold, and in medicine they excelled in ophthalmology and pharmacology. Muhammad al-Razi (844–926) and Abu Ali al-Husein ibn Sina (980–1037), or Avicenna (as he came to be known), wrote medical texts that dominated European university libraries until the eighteenth century. Two physicians who were said to be the most learned of men were Averroës (1126–1198) and Rabbi Moses Maimonides (1135–1204). Averroës was famous for his commentaries on Aristotle; in fact, it is said that even Aquinas learned Aristotle from him. Maimonides wrote ten medical books and monographs. Finally, Islamic Spain is credited with the art of papermaking. It developed in Baghdad during the tenth century and entered Europe via Spain during the twelfth and thirteen centuries, as Christian crusaders captured Spanish cities.

Arabs, Jews, and Christians lived side by side in Spain until 1492. Then, during the reign of King Ferdinand and Queen Isabella, Christian Europeans expelled all non-Christians from Spain.

EDUCATION DURING THE RENAISSANCE, THE REFORMATION, AND THE ENLIGHTENMENT

■

THE RENAISSANCE

The Renaissance—an intellectual and cultural "rebirth," or revival—started in Italy during the fourteenth century and spread through Europe by the end of the sixteenth century. In Italy it was spurred on by trading activity, which many cities—especially Venice—engaged in with Spain. Although Rome had declined as a cultural center, other cities had grown to take its place. Florence was one of them; by the fifteenth century it was the financial capital of the Continent, housing eighty banking centers.

Florence was run by middle-class (bourgeois) guilds: bankers, merchants, manufacturers, and professionals. There were also fourteen minor guilds: clothiers, hosiers, butchers, bakers, vintners, cobblers, saddlers, armorers, blacksmiths, carpenters, innkeepers, masons and stonecutters, oil sellers, and ropemakers. In fact, all men—including former aristocrats and noblemen—had to be members of a guild in order to vote. In addition, there were seventy-two voteless unions and another thousand or so day laborers who were forbidden to organize. Florence was home to the powerful Medici family of bankers, and their influence made the city a noted Renaissance center.[9]

The Renaissance sparked creativity in both the arts and sciences, and it was characterized by a humanistic revival of interest in the art and literature of classical Greece and Rome. **Humanism** (the "new learning") emphasized the study of human beings—the feelings, senses, and physical characteristics described in classical literature. Along with modern science humanism slowly replaced scholasticism as both the repository of valuable knowledge and the basis of educational curricula.

THE REFORMATION

During the sixteenth and seventeenth centuries humanism made its way north to Germany, France, the Low Countries of western Europe, and England, where it ran headlong into the Protestant Reformation. The "great protest" offered hope to the countless illiterates who were still in the clutches of feudal serfdom, who were still tied to the land or barely free. One of the new Protestant tenets was the goal to translate the Bible into vernacular, or common, languages so that uneducated poor people could read and study it for themselves, without the intervention of a priest. For that to be possible, the masses had to be given the opportunity to read and write, meaning that schools had to be made available to them. Thus universal elementary, or primary, education (as distinguished from upper-class secondary education in the classics) was an outgrowth of the Protestant Reformation. Unfortunately, however, it could not occur until most of the religious wars had ended and the break with the Roman Catholic Church was complete. In fact, schooling declined in most parts of the Continent and in

[9]Christopher Hibbert, *The House of Medici: Its Rise and Fall* (New York: Morrow/Quill, 1980), 21–29.

England during the last half of the sixteenth century and the beginning of the seventeenth. Then, as peace was achieved, educational institutions were restored, and the spread of schools got under way.[10]

The Reformation changed the trends in who controlled education. No longer was schooling in the hands of religious and private institutions; instead, civil or public control became the pattern, particularly in northern European countries (Germany, Switzerland, and Scandinavia). One consequence of early civil control in northern Europe was that national systems of education developed in these countries sooner than in Spain, Italy, France, and England. The northern European countries opened secondary schools that stressed humanities and the classics. The schools were called gymnasia, and they were patterned after a school started in Strasbourg by John Sturm (1507–1589) early in the seventeenth century.

In France, Catholicism maintained its stronghold over social, political, and educational matters even as it did battle with the protesters. It also attempted to reform and rejuvenate itself through the Counter Reformation. During this period the Catholic church focused its efforts on making secondary education classical or humanistic and paid relatively little attention to elementary education.

In England the Reformation produced the Anglican church, putting the king at the helm of both religious and civil affairs. Anglican education became a private, philanthropic effort, and secondary (grammar) schools for the upper classes were increased and improved. Although the term **public school** was gradually used to denote such a secondary institution, the schools were neither free nor available to lower-class students. Instead, they were open to middle- and upper-class students who could afford to pay for them, and they were usually endowed by funds from the growing bourgeoisie, or middle class.[11] England also developed a type of private elementary school—the **dame school**—which was conducted by a housewife in her home; she taught the children of the neighborhood and was paid a fee. Some grammar schools also offered elementary or preparatory education, through a department called a **petty school.**

Education for middle- and upper-class girls during this period was available through Catholic nunneries and Protestant elementary schools. In France, Archbishop Fénelon (1651–1715) proposed an educational scheme to prepare Catholic girls for their responsibilities in the home, society, and church. The Ursuline nuns were also dedicated to providing education for girls.

THE ENLIGHTENMENT

Although most people had strong religious convictions during these centuries, skeptics did wonder how so many different religious groups could claim to hold the truth. Some began to question the reliance on theology as the basis for all knowledge, and they searched for truth elsewhere. Astronomy was one such investigation, and it was notably advanced by Nicolaus Copernicus (1473–1543), who developed the theory that the sun is the center of the solar system; by Johannes Kepler (1571–1630), who discovered the elliptical nature of the orbit of Mars; and by Galileo Galilei (1564–1642), who improved the telescope and discovered four of Jupiter's moons.

[10]Ralph L. Pounds, *The Development of Education in Western Cultures* (New York: Appleton, 1968), 137–158.

[11]Ibid., 140. These Latin grammar schools are now England's great public schools, and they often receive government grants; they are no longer completely funded privately, but they are still very prestigious.

Physics and mathematics were other avenues in the search for truth. Trigonometry was advanced beyond its Sumerian and Egyptian beginnings; French mathematician René Descartes (1596–1650) established the foundations for analytical geometry; and Sir Isaac Newton (1642–1727) along with Baron Gottfried Wilhelm von Leibnitz (1646–1716) developed differential calculus.

Through such advances empirical science—knowledge gained through experience and observation—gradually challenged faith as the source of truth. One early proponent of science was the English philosopher and essayist Sir Francis Bacon (1561–1626), who described the scientific method in his *Novum Organum,* or **new method**. Bacon argued that scientists should proceed inductively by first observing facts in nature, then building from such empirical observations an extensive collection of facts, then finding commonalities among them, and finally generalizing from these to form comprehensive formulas and principles. Taking a similarly scientific approach, John Locke (1632–1704) developed sense realism as a basis for learning (see Chapter 6).

During the eighteenth century, belief in science was coupled with the conviction that human reason could improve social and political institutions and thus create a better society for all. The Enlightenment, or Age of Reason, was a time of opposition to authoritarian forms of government, rigid economic and social structures, and unscientific religious dogma (such as arose during the Reformation). German philosopher Immanuel Kant (1724–1804) described this period as a time when people began to use their reason—their rational powers—to direct their lives. Indeed, the Enlightenment might be summed up by Kant's famous command: *Sapere aude!* ("Dare to know!")[12]

Enlightenment thinkers wanted education to assume the responsibility of preparing people for citizenship roles. Hence, many thought that lay teachers would be more committed to civil education than religious teachers would be. Many also supported the idea of a classical humanistic curriculum with the addition of the natural sciences. But since education was still so dependent on religious institutions, the inclusion of science was controversial.

KEY FIGURES IN EDUCATION   After the Middle Ages the intellectual activity of the Renaissance, the Reformation, and the Enlightenment was so various and involved so many people that we must refer you to Chapters 6 and 7 for discussions of the major figures and ideas. Yet there are also many others to mention, such as the humanist Florentine banker Cosimo de' Medici (1389–1464), who collected Roman manuscripts and had them recopied in his academy; he coined the term *humanities*. In the north two Dutchmen merit attention: Rudolph Agricola (1443–1485), who studied the classics in Italy and brought Greek and Hebrew to Germany when he joined the faculty at the University of Heidelberg; and Desiderius Erasmus (1466?–1536), who helped John Colet (1467?–1519) reorganize St. Paul's cathedral school in England into a humanistic Latin grammar school and who advocated play as an approach to learning, along with the use of lay teachers. Besides Colet, we need to note another of England's Puritan humanists—John Milton (1608–1674), who outlined his views of education in a long letter to a friend. Using the term **academy** to label his kind of school, Milton

[12]L. Glenn Smith and Joan K. Smith et al., *Lives in Education: People and Ideas in the Development of Teaching* (Ames, Iowa: Educational Studies Press, 1984), 143–144.

Comparative Perspective on Today's Issues . . .

◆ SHOULD VERY YOUNG CHILDREN RECEIVE ACADEMIC INSTRUCTION?

The Issue The debate about when academic subjects should be taught to children arose with Plato in ancient Greece and got much attention in the eighteenth century when Rousseau argued that children should not receive formal instruction until they are on the verge of adolescence. Today the need for day care has resulted in environments that do present academic instruction to preschoolers. Reading, math, and even foreign languages are being provided—to the dismay of those educators who believe that children should develop naturally in an unstructured environment.

YES Not working on academic skills is not congruent with what we know about child development today. For example, we know that children respond to their environments by learning about them. Thus, if we structure it and shape it to provide higher-order academic skills, it can increase our children's capacities for learning. The result will be that our children will have superior minds and be able to learn school subjects at a faster pace.

—*Siegfried Engelmann, Professor of Education, University of Oregon; and Therese Engelmann, attorney and Ph.D. in psychology*

NO Young children do not learn in formalized settings with abstract and symbolic rules as do older children and adults. Instead they learn by direct interactions and encounters with their concrete nonsymbolic surroundings. What is more, formal instruction can induce stress at an even earlier age. These conclusions are supported by old and more recent research in child development.

—*David Elkind, Professor of Child Study and Resident Scholar, Lincoln Research Center for Citizenship and Public Affairs, Tufts University*

Source: Based on James Wm. Noll, ed., *Taking Sides: Clashing Views on Controversial Educational Issues,* 5th ed. (Guilford, Conn.: Dushkin, 1989), 188–207.

advocated a curriculum of the classics, mathematics, religion, and technical subjects like surveying and bookkeeping.

With his friend and colleague Philipp Melanchthon (1497–1560), Martin Luther (1483–1546) promoted coeducational, compulsory elementary schooling during the morning hours and two hours of apprenticeship in a trade during the afternoon. His ideas about secondary education, however, were traditional and elitist—he proposed having gymnasia in every town for the upper classes. Unlike his Puritan counterpart John Calvin (1509–1564), Luther believed in the separation of church and state, and he viewed education as a function of the state.

Of the many educational thinkers during the Enlightenment, Jean Jacques Rousseau (1712–1778) stands out as offering a philosophy that influenced educators and schooling for centuries. In his novel *Emile*, published in 1762, he laid out the foundations. First, he believed that children are born good and become corrupted only by society. Rousseau reasoned, therefore, that children should be educated in as natural a setting as possible. Thus Emile was to grow

Enlightenment thinker Jean Jacques Rousseau, in his book Emile *(1762), planted the seed of an educational philosophy that eventually sprouted and took root in America.*
—North Wind Picture Archives

up naturally—without being inhibited—in a country setting under the watchful eye of his tutor. After his early physical development was completed, at about age five, he would enter the second phase of his education, in which he would be permitted to ''discover'' nature through his senses, and to develop his physical strength. This stage would last until age twelve. Then, for three years, Emile was to develop a ''taste'' for learning by studying geography and the natural sciences. Now he also would be introduced to his first book, Daniel Defoe's *Robinson Crusoe*, which is set in a natural environment. Finally, at fifteen Emile would learn about society by studying history, philosophy, and politics. (Rousseau's thinking was that by fifteen a youth would be strong enough morally to withstand the corruption and prejudice of society.) Now, with the help of his tutor, Emile was to begin searching for a wife—whom he would find in the country. Her name was Sophie, and *her* ideal education would consist of learning how to please and care for men (because, in Rousseau's view, women were inferior intellectually and morally).[13]

Two women whose lives refuted Rousseau's views of femininity were Christine de Pisan (1364–1470?) and Mary Wollstonecraft (1759–1797). Christine, who was Italian, married a Frenchman but was widowed when she was twenty-five. Well-educated by her father, she began writing poetry—most notably, in response to a century-old French poem, *Roman de la Rose*, which characterized women as selfish, disloyal, untrustworthy, vicious, and easy victims of flattery. Her effective argument even suggested that women might be superior to men, and it supported both equal education and equal rights for women.[14]

This debate about women's political and educational rights continued for

[13]Ibid., 150–161; and Jean Jacques Rousseau, *Emile*, trans. Alan Bloom (New York: Basic Books, 1979).
[14]Smith et al., *Lives in Education*, 88–93.

more than three centuries before it was joined by Mary Wollstonecraft, an English feminist and pedagogical theorist. She thought that women's political rights should be equal to men's and that they should be educated through a curriculum that was as scholarly as men's. Her *Thoughts on the Education of Daughters* and *Vindication of the Rights of Women* are landmarks of feminism. Unfortunately, Wollstonecraft died at age thirty-seven, giving birth to her only child, Mary (the author of *Frankenstein* and wife of the poet Percy Bysshe Shelley).[15]

RESEARCH SAYS

For Tomorrow's Education . . .

The California State Commission objected to a book's new interpretive framework for history that attempted to focus on the contributions of various ethnic groups in order to present a more comprehensive perspective; the text also was written in a narrative style. Interestingly, one criticism of the text was that it did not "go far enough" toward achieving its goals. See "Education Hotline," *Education Week* 9 (1 August 1990): 4. Although this book may have fallen short of its purposes, the trends of a broad, inclusive perspective and a narrative style are becoming more popular. See any of the latest history titles from publishers that go beyond introductory survey texts, such as Greenwood Publishing Group and St. Martin's Press.

MAJOR CONTRIBUTIONS TO EDUCATION   The Renaissance renewed interest in all the liberal arts (which, during the Middle Ages, had been restricted to the trivium and theology). Now all seven subjects were emphasized, as humanism and the rise of modern science refreshed and expanded the curriculum. Secondary schools—like the German gymnasium and the English Latin grammar school—became centers of humanistic study. Universities, however, moved more slowly from scholasticism to humanism.

The Reformation helped bring literacy to the masses and promoted primary, or elementary, schools. Universal coeducational elementary schooling was the vision of most reformers, but there was disagreement about whether it should be separated from religion. Martin Luther advocated separating church and state, with education being a state function, while John Calvin wanted a religious state that would control education. Meanwhile, Catholic reformers focused attention on secondary education, as in the work of St. Ignatius Loyola (see Chapter 7).

During the Enlightenment, scientific enterprise shifted education away from religious emphases and toward empiricism and rationality. Theology was challenged as the source and repository of knowledge. Educating the masses for civil life, by means of lay teachers, became important, and institutions began to be established to train teachers in methods of instruction. Eventually these came to be called **normal schools**, because they prepared teachers to give children a "normal" education in the fundamentals of reading, writing, arithmetic, and character development.[16]

[15]Ibid., 161–170.
[16]Lucas, *Western Educational Heritage,* 261–262; and William Boyd and Edmund King, *The History of Western Education* (Totowa, N.J.: Barnes & Noble, 1975), 203–205, 231–233.

CONCLUSIONS

■

The publication of Rousseau's *Emile* in 1762—describing the psychological, social, and moral development of a child in a natural educational setting—was a
seed that eventually sprouted and developed roots in America more than a century later. But the long history of Western education has been marked by slow
movement toward universal compulsory schooling in literacy and practical skills.
Ancient societies educated only the privileged or the wealthy, and the curriculum
was the liberal arts with an emphasis on rhetoric, which was important for citizenship and politics. By the Middle Ages the Church was the major force in
politics and education. Although the liberal arts still dominated the curriculum,
theology replaced rhetoric as the foundation of knowledge. The Church tenta-
tively began providing literacy to the masses through cathedral and parish
schools.

   Over five centuries the Church gradually lost control of most political and
many educational institutions as monarchs and merchant classes gained power
throughout Europe. During the Renaissance ancient Greek and Roman cultures
were rediscovered, and education focused on the classics for the purpose of
understanding human nature and culture; the term *humanities* came to denote
such study. Meanwhile, discoveries in astronomy and mathematics advanced the
empirical sciences, which ultimately replaced theology as the basis of knowledge.

   The Protestant Reformation led to the establishment of elementary schools,
while Catholicism focused on secondary education. By the end of the eighteenth
century the influences of the Enlightenment had demonstrated the desirability
of a rational citizenry, and governing systems moved away from monarchy toward
democracy. As religious schools and teachers lost their control over education,
training institutions known as normal schools prepared laypeople to teach the
masses. Thus, although the history of education spans some five thousand years,
the training of teachers as a professional activity for laypeople goes back only a
few hundred years.

KEY TERMS

■

eduba	ludus magister, litterator
ummia	Latin grammar school
cuneiform	scholasticus
scribes	universitas
hieroglyphics	town-gown dispute
swaddling	lesser faculty
aretè	higher faculties
palestra	studium generale
paidogogos	studium particular

paidotribe   scholasticism

cytharist   feeder school

grammartist   humanism

gymnasium   public school

philosopher   dame school

Sophists   petty school

philosopher-king   new method

pedagogue   academy

ludus   normal school

SUGGESTED READINGS

Jean Jacques Rousseau, *Emile*, trans. Alan Bloom (New York: Basic Books, 1979). This novel describes the education of a boy and his growth and development through the young adult years to marriage. It became the "Bible" of progressive education.

L. Glenn Smith and Joan K. Smith et al., *Lives in Education: People and Ideas in the Development of Teaching*, 2d ed. (New York: St. Martin's, 1994). This book uses a biographical format to trace the development of Western education from ancient times to the present.

Christopher J. Lucas, "The Scribal Tablet-House in Ancient Mesopotamia," *History of Education Quarterly* 19 (Fall 1979): 305–332. This article gives a good account of education in Sumeria.

Harlan Lane, *The Wild Boy of Aveyron* (New York: Bantam, 1977). This account chronicles the life of Victor, a boy who was found after living in the wild for the first twelve or thirteen years of his life. Many at the time thought that Victor was Rousseau's "noble savage," Emile.

C. M. Bowra, *The Greek Experience* (New York: Mentor, 1957). This gives a cultural account of ancient Greece, including accomplishments in art, science, philosophy, government, and religion.

Jerome Carcopino, *Daily Life in Ancient Rome* (New Haven: Yale University Press, 1940). This is a readable account of life in Rome during the Empire.

Carlo M. Cipolla, *Before the Industrial Revolution: European Society and Economy, 1000–1700* (New York: Norton, 1980). This is a socioeconomic account of Europe from the end of the Middle Ages to the Renaissance and Reformation.

E. H. Gwynne-Thomas, *A Concise History of Education to 1900* (Washington, D.C.: University Press of America, 1981). This is an introductory survey of the main events in Western educational history.

American Developments

Historical Foundations B

9

The great achievements of North America in economics, politics, technology, and agriculture have resulted from the rich diversity of peoples and cultures that have come together in this continent, a mixture that has created new social systems and a uniquely American culture. Beneath the surface of each of these American accomplishments lie indigenous roots. The settlers grafted their civilization onto the native American roots, and together they produced a hybrid civilization of unprecedented vigor.

—Jack McIver Weatherford, Native Roots: How the Indians Enriched America
(New York: Fawcett/Columbine, 1991), 4

9

American Developments

ADVANCED ORGANIZERS

In this chapter you will learn

How European traditions affected colonial education

How the American frontier influenced society and schooling

How religion and politics shaped the new Republic's schools

How high schools and universities developed in America

How American education changed during the early twentieth century

CHAPTER OUTLINE

EDUCATION IN THE NEW WORLD
  European Motives for Schools
  Beginnings of Colonial Schools
  Effects of Wilderness on Schools

A UNIQUE SCHOOL FOR THE COLONIES
  Names for Colonial Schools
  Colonial School Attendance
  Colonial Teachers
  Beginnings of Higher Education

EDUCATION IN THE EIGHTEENTH AND NINETEENTH CENTURIES
  Religious Splintering
  Society and Schools in the New Republic
  Sectional Pride and Competition
  Politicizing Education

BEYOND THE COMMON SCHOOL
  Development of the American High School
  Spread of Higher Education

THE EARLY TWENTIETH CENTURY: PROGRESSIVE EDUCATION

CONCLUSIONS

Y ou have agreed to meet a friend at the student center for a lecture about the history of education. A phone call made you late in arriving, and the lecture is already under way. You slip into a seat trying not to cause disruption. You hear the speaker say:

Children attend not out of compulsion but because of interest. Most pupils range in age from six to sixteen, although some are younger or older. Occasionally adults in their early twenties may attend to remedy some deficiency in their schooling. Such an age spread in one room is an asset rather than a problem, because older students help the younger children with everything from overcoats and boots to academic work and playground disputes.

You suspect that you may have entered the wrong room, but you decide to hear more:

Instruction is highly individualized, allowing each student to proceed at her or his best speed. If Mary wants to race through arithmetic and begin working on algebra, she may. If John finds math difficult or is more interested in art, he may match his pace to his interests and talents.

The school is flexible about curricular materials. Pupils may bring any book from home that their parents want them to use in developing reading skills. With help, some students construct their own basic readers by writing down vocabulary words and sentences of interest; they decorate their readers with sketches of animals, colorful borders of yarn, and so on. Thus reading, writing, spelling, composition, and aesthetics are integrated.

You still aren't sure that you are in the right lecture hall. There was a poster outside the room, but—being late—you rushed past without reading it. Now you want to slip out to check the announcement, but someone has just taken the aisle seat next to you, making it difficult to exit. You settle back to hear more:

The classroom is usually humming with activity, but order prevails. Some pupils read, some work on crafts, and others solve math problems; another group may be outdoors for a nature project. The teacher moves around the room, hearing rec-itations, checking work, correcting errors, and answering questions. The teacher and pupils share decision making, but the teacher has final authority. Some days are devoted to contests, games, or plays, which are often written cooperatively by the class; the most popular of these may be performed for parents and visitors. On pleasant days the class may spend hours tending to the school's garden. This gives the pupils pride in their school as it teaches them about the dignity of manual labor and the value of democratically shared work; it also affords the teacher numerous opportunities to combine theory and practice.

Record keeping is not a major issue. The teacher gives both written and oral examinations, but—aside from spurring competition—these are mainly diagnostic. There is no need to grade the students. The teacher assesses each pupil and assigns an instructional program that fits the child's readiness level. Grades, credits, and permanent records are unnecessary; parents and children get ongoing progress reports. In any case, the ultimate test is practical: How well does the pupil read, spell, write, compute, think, and perform in the areas of instruction?

The speaker pauses to sip water, and the person who took the aisle seat whispers to you: "I thought this was supposed to be a talk about the history of American education." You nod and reply: "We must have the wrong room. This is obviously about schools in some country other than the United States." As the two of you start for the door, you hear the speaker resume:

If this description sounds like an experiment in some distant land, think again. I have just described the kind of school that most Americans attended for over two centuries. It had various names—petty, dame, district, common, subdistrict, old field, or country school. Next I will describe the evolution of this characteristically American institution, which has all but disappeared from memory and the historical record.[1]

Surprised, you pause at the door. Then you see your friend, and you hurry to take a seat next to her.

As surprising as it seems, significant aspects of America's educational past have disappeared from the historical record. This is because history—far from being an objective record of everything that has happened—is always a partial account of selected events as colored by present concerns. Twentieth-century American educators, being preoccupied with increasing the status of their fledgling profession, have given more attention to inherited European traditions than to uniquely American developments. Although European thinking and practices have certainly been part of the story, forces in the New World also shaped how American education evolved; in turn, they influenced how Europeans thought about education.[2]

EDUCATION IN THE NEW WORLD

■

EUROPEAN MOTIVES FOR SCHOOLS

Several European national groups claimed colonial territories in North America and started schools. During the sixteenth and seventeenth centuries Spanish soldiers and religious figures started missions from present-day Florida to Texas to California. The French established missions in the St. Lawrence River valley and along the Great Lakes and the Mississippi River. The English began their attempts to colonize in 1585, and they succeeded in founding a settlement in Virginia in 1607. About two decades later the Dutch established colonies in New York, and the Swedes did so in Delaware; meanwhile, England started a second colony in the Massachusetts Bay region. All these colonizing efforts involved schools.[3]

The educational theories and arrangements that Europeans brought to the New World were those associated with the Reformation (described in Chapters 7 and 8). In that spirit, the colonizing groups considered education important for two main reasons:

1. European families were not willing to settle a distant wilderness without assurances that their children would be prepared to re-enter society in their home countries—and families were essential to the English, Dutch, and Swedish colonizing attempts.

2. Indigenous North American populations were "heathen" (in European terms) and had souls to save; more important, perhaps, was that they were more likely to cooperate in their own exploitation if they were schooled in European concepts.

Together, these motives resulted in classical schools for the children of important colonizers and vernacular-based mission schools for Native Americans who could be convinced to attend them.

Early in the colonizing process a third motive to provide schools emerged. Unlike in South America and Central America, where the Spanish found many native workers, there were relatively few natives in North America, and they withstood European efforts to force them into slave labor. Thus the colonizers had

[1]Adapted from L. Glenn Smith, "The Gillespie/Huftalen Diaries: A Window on American Education," *Vitae Scholasticae* 2 (Spring 1983): 243–265.

[2]William Brandon, *New Worlds for Old: Reports from the New World and Their Effect on the Development of Social Thought in Europe, 1500–1800* (Athens, Ohio: Ohio University Press, 1986).

[3]Floyd R. Dain, *Education in the Wilderness* (Lansing, Mich.: Michigan Historical Society, 1968), 9–32.

to import working-class Europeans as laborers. And given the ever-present "de-civilizing" effects of the wilderness, colony leaders were eager to provide elementary schools to "compel a barbarous people to civilitie."[4]

BEGINNINGS OF COLONIAL SCHOOLS

In 1624 Jamestown Colony founded a flax house (a place for making linen) and guaranteed the support of two poor children from each county to attend it long enough to master the skills of making linen. Earlier the colony had tried unsuccessfully to establish a grammar school and a university. Soon after, it passed a law requiring parents and guardians to ensure that all children had instruction in basic morality and a vocation.

In 1642 Massachusetts Bay Colony issued a law requiring parents to provide basic religious, literacy, and vocational instruction. In 1647 it also adopted a Connecticut law (1644) which decreed that every township, "after the Lord hath increased them to the number of 50 householders," was to "appoint one within their town to teach all such children as shall resort to him to write and read."[5] The teacher was to be paid either by pupils' parents or by all inhabitants of the township. Most towns expected parents to pay tuition, but the town treasury often supplied some support as well. Usually townships paid the tuition for any children whose parents certified that they could not afford it. In addition, the general court (a colony's legislature) often specified that income from some portion of public land go toward supporting what they thought would be the township's only church. An equal amount of land was usually set aside for a school—typically, a grammar, or classical, school. This 1647 law in Massachusetts became known as the **Old Deluder-Satan Law**, because the settlers were convinced that, with education, people would not be "deluded" by Satan.

EFFECTS OF WILDERNESS ON SCHOOLS

Settlement patterns and the rigorous conditions of frontier life altered how schooling evolved in America (see Chapter 3). Although many features of European education could be recognized, school governance became thoroughly community centered, and the curriculum gradually became more utilitarian.[6] This happened in Virginia and the middle colonies as well as in New England.

As is true today, of course, colonial Americans also disagreed about schooling. Middle-class and would-be aristocratic immigrants tended to replicate, as best they could, the kinds of schools they had known in Europe. Working-class immigrants, however, wanted to maximize opportunities for their children; indeed, that was a strong motive for taking on the risks of frontier life in the first place. Although many working-class parents could not afford the time and cost involved in letting their children acquire classical knowledge and attend a university, they could often afford (and were willing to pay for) such marketable skills as writing, bookkeeping, surveying, and modern languages. Both George Washington and Benjamin Franklin, for example, came from families that decided they could not afford a classical course of education.[7]

[4]L. Glenn Smith, "Compel a Barbarous People to Civilitie: The Roots of Compulsory Education in America," in *Conference Papers for the 8th Session of the International Standing Conference for the History of Education*, ed. Giovanni Genovesi, 6 vols. (Parma: Universita di Parma, Bollettino C.I.R.S.E., 1986), 1.

[5]Henry Barnard, "Biography of Ezekiel Cheever with Notes of the Early Free, or Grammar Schools of New England," *American Journal of Education* 1 (March 1856): 303.

[6]Harlan Updegraff, *The Origin of the Moving School in Massachusetts* (New York: Teachers College Press, Columbia University, 1908).

[7]Robert Francis Seybolt, *The Public Schools of Colonial Boston, 1635–1775;* and *The Private Schools of Colonial Boston* (Cambridge, Mass.: Harvard University Press, 1935). Also see Carl F. Kaestle, *The Evolution of an Urban School System: New York City, 1750–1850* (Cambridge, Mass.: Harvard University Press, 1973), 28–59; and Leonard W. Labaree et al., eds., *The Autobiography of Benjamin Franklin* (New Haven, Conn.: Yale University Press, 1964), 52.

What was unique about the one-room school on the American frontier was the way education quickly evolved into a local enterprise. The entire community pitched in to build the school from local materials, and a party culminated their efforts.
—North Wind Picture Archives

RESEARCH SAYS

For Tomorrow's Education . . .

Revisionist history is expanding the picture of the American West to include a more balanced account of "heroism and villainy, virtue and vice, nobility and shoddiness" so that "they appear in roughly the same proportions as they appear in any other subject of human history." Revisionist historian Patricia Nelson Limerick paints such a picture in her book *Legacy of Conquest: The Unbroken Past of the American West* (New York: Norton, 1987). She also thinks that the term *frontier* is "nationalistic, and often racist—'the area where white people got scarce or got scared.' " See "Revisionist Historian Lassos the Mythic West," *Christian Science Monitor*, 18 December 1990, 13.

A UNIQUE SCHOOL FOR THE COLONIES

During the seventeenth and eighteenth centuries schools with a single teacher for pupils of all ages were not unusual. In fact, they were typical. It is a recent practice to group pupils by every year of age and to give a different curriculum to each group. Although such a **graded school** began to develop during the last half of the nineteenth century, it did not become standard until well into this century. As late as 1928, for example, 63 percent of the country's 244,128 elementary schools were still one-room, one-teacher, multi-aged schools.[8] Canada and Australia had a similar pattern of school development.[9]

What was unique about the one-room school on the American frontier was the way it quickly evolved from a government-controlled enterprise to a community-dominated one. We traced part of this development in Chapter 3, where we noted that settlement patterns were scattered rather than concentrated. It proved unworkable to have one church and one school per township (in New England) or per county (in Virginia). Even more important, the basis for participating in government shifted rapidly. Originally the English colonies had specified that to vote or stand for office one had to be male and own substantial property, be at least twenty-two years old, and be a member in good standing of the Anglican church. (Swedish and Dutch colonies had similar rules). By 1650 so many unorthodox and poor immigrants had arrived that most of the adult male population was disenfranchised.

As churches and schools sprang up to meet the needs of isolated settlements, they were often under local control. Historian Wayne E. Fuller has written that such local schools under management of those whose children attended them constituted

> invaluable laboratories of democracy in which rural Americans learned the importance of their vote, how to make laws. Here many Americans learned parliamentary procedures—how to make motions, how to reconsider action already taken, and how to support their motions with arguments. They wrestled with such intricacies as bond issues, taxes, and contingency funds. . . . Democracy was no abstraction to them. . . . They learned . . . that they could change what they did not like, and that democracy actually worked.[10]

Historian Bernard Bailyn has made a similar point in commenting specifically on colonial education:

> Education as it emerged from the colonial period has distinctly shaped the American personality. . . . What was recognized even before the Revolution as typical American individualism, optimism, and enterprise resulted also from the process of education. . . . The transformation of education that took place in the colonial period was irreversible. We live with its consequences still.[11]

NAMES FOR COLONIAL SCHOOLS

Various labels were used interchangeably to refer to American schools during the colonial and early national periods, from the early 1600s to about 1850. The labels arose in Europe, but their meanings evolved further in America. In some cases they changed so much that they now mean something dramatically different. From about the 1850s to the 1870s, for example, a rapid transformation

[8]U.S. Department of the Interior, *Statistics of State School Systems in the United States, 1927–1928*, bulletin 1930, no. 5 (Washington, D.C.: U.S. Government Printing Office, 1930), 30.

[9]Jean Cochrane, *The One-Room School in Canada* (Fitzhenry & Whiteside, 1981).

[10]Wayne E. Fuller, *The Old Country School: The Story of Rural Education in the Middle West* (Chicago: University of Chicago Press, 1982), 45.

[11]Bernard Bailyn, *Education in the Forming of American Society: Needs and Opportunities for Study* (Chapel Hill: University of North Carolina Press, 1960), 48.

occurred in the use of *public* and *common* as applied to schooling; and a few decades earlier the term *free* lost its original meaning. A brief description of the meanings of these three terms and some other related ones will point out important developments in American education.[12]

PUBLIC SCHOOLS   Originally the Latin word *public* referred to "the people," and when the term was associated with education, it described schools that in some sense were available to anyone who could meet their entry requirements and could afford tuition. *Public* connoted group instruction, as opposed to private, or individual, tutorial arrangements. In England the term **public school** came to refer to a classical school (such as Eton, Harrow, and Winchester), because it theoretically was open to any boy in the realm. Parents whose children attended "public schools" paid tuition for their instruction, just as people who ate or drank in a "public house" (the colonial name for a restaurant) paid for what they consumed. There was no connotation of tax support for public schools, and, indeed, even today in England a public school is one of a relatively small number of selective, usually expensive, schools.

FREE SCHOOLS   This term *did* have something to do with money, but it did not imply that the pupils paid no tuition. The term first was associated with a school founded in 1379 at Winchester Cathedral in England. In that year the bishop authorized an **endowment**—that is, provided a continuing income to support the school—so that the school could instruct a small number of boys who were talented but poor. The enabling statutes permitted the master to accept an additional one hundred boys who paid a fee to attend. In practice, this meant that a **free school** actually charged tuition, but it made a few "scholarships" available for those who were fortunate enough to qualify. And since public schools like Eton, Harrow, and Winchester often had a few endowed, or scholarship, places available, they also were called free schools—or, sometimes, free public schools. (These schools were also called grammar schools, because they taught a classical curriculum).[13]

COMMON (PETTY) SCHOOLS   As mentioned earlier, the French term *petites ecoles* referred to elementary schools or departments associated with a grammar school, and *petty* was the most usual early-colonial word for a vernacular elementary school. This was the kind of school mandated for towns with fifty families. Because ordinary, or common, folk—as opposed to aristocrats and the upper classes—attended these schools, they eventually became known as **common schools** (by the 1700s). Their curriculum was reading and writing (in English), some arithmetic, and the basics of Christian morality. As we have seen, parents usually paid tuition for each child (a head tax, or "rate"), and townships often supplemented the master's income. In cases where the community or some religious group provided most or all of the funding (to avoid charging tuition), the common school was called a **charity school**.

LOCAL, COMMUNITY SCHOOLS   European immigrants to North America brought these various terms for schools with them, and during the early years of colonization the terms retained their European meanings. As time passed, how-

[12]Kaestle, *Evolution of an Urban School System*, 16–18, 41–55, discusses public and common pay schools; and his *Pillars of the Republic: Common Schools and American Society, 1780–1860* (New York: Hill & Wang, 1983), discusses common schools in greater detail. Also see F. Michael Perko, *A Time to Favor Zion: The Ecology of Religion and Education on the Urban Frontier—Cincinnati, 1830–1870* (Chicago: Educational Studies Press, 1988), 4–6, 62–64, and 145, for a discussion of Roman Catholic common schools.

[13]Barnard, "Biography of Ezekiel Cheever," 297–314.

ever—and as large numbers of working- and lower-class immigrants adapted to the new wilderness environment—the terms took on new shades of meaning. By the 1600s the adjectives *free, public,* and *grammar* were being used almost as synonyms in reference to schools. And in most of the early English colonies grammar schools and petty schools tended to be combined, because there were rarely enough pupils to support a master who taught a completely separate Latin grammar curriculum. With little notice the adjective *common* joined the other adjectives to describe American schools.

By the 1700s any of these terms, or any combination of them, referred to local, community schools. And because Massachusetts and Connecticut schools grew out of subdistricts within a township, they also were sometimes called **district schools**. (In Virginia and in the South, community schools often were built on unfarmed land or on land worn out by farming, and so they were sometimes called "old field schools.") For a long time no one seems to have thought much about all these different names, but when they used these labels, most people pictured the same kind of establishment: a single-teacher, multi-age school in a church, home, or building constructed specifically for schooling.

School buildings were usually put up in a few days, with everyone in the community pitching in to provide the labor and with a community party culminating their efforts. Building materials were whatever was typical for the community—mostly logs, but also brick or boards or even sod. The building's lighting, heating, ventilation, and furnishings also matched the technology in general use. Some buildings and furniture seem spartan today, but they were within the mainstream of accepted standards in their time, and they would not have struck most pupils as being much different from what they were accustomed to at home.

COLONIAL SCHOOL ATTENDANCE

What percentage of the school-aged population attended school during the colonial period, and for how long did they attend? Such questions are not easy to answer, because no agency collected information about attendance—or even about the number of schools—until well into the nineteenth century. The best we can do, then, is base an estimate on samples of local histories, reminiscences, letters, and other sources. Historians of literacy examine wills (for signatures), consider the circulation figures of newspapers and other periodicals, or base guesses on the size of libraries and the sale of books. But none of these indicators accurately tells us how many people could read. Checking for signatures on documents is not even a good way to estimate people's writing ability, because "making your mark" was so widely accepted in place of a signature that even someone who could write might affix an *X* instead of signing—especially when a witness was present.

The issue is complicated further by the fact that people did not necessarily need schooling to attain literacy. Parents or older siblings often taught children to read and sometimes to write or "cipher" (do arithmetic). Ministers and others offered tutorials, sometimes as a service, but often to augment their incomes. Women at home combined child care with instruction; many mothers taught neighbor's children along with their own, to earn extra money. The more elaborate of such operations was called a **dame school**—as was any school that a woman taught outside her home.[14]

Regarding literacy, it seems safe to say that most colonial adults could read well enough to acquire the information needed in daily life. Probably a majority also could write, but if their livelihood did not require frequent writing, they may have been unable to do so with ease. Some, of course, could write little more than making an *X* for a signature.[15]

During the 1600s and early 1700s, girls were somewhat less likely than boys to attend school; but as settlements moved westward, away from the Atlantic seaboard, the situation changed. At first boys went to school during winter months, when they could be spared from farm duties, and girls attended during summer, when their brothers were in the fields. By 1800 this pattern was breaking down, and coeducation was becoming the norm. There is some indication that, on the frontier—where men were busy hunting, trapping, herding, fishing, or farming—women may have assumed primary responsibility for instructing children in the ABCs at home; they may also have supervised literacy-related activities, such as letter writing and record keeping. In any case, education was a priority for most families, and most boys and girls spent some time—even if only a few weeks—in school.

[14]See, for example, Mary Hall James, *The Educational History of Old Lyme, Connecticut, 1635–1935* (New Haven, Conn.: Yale University Press for the New Haven Colony Historical Society, 1939); and Barnard, "Biography of Ezekiel Cheever," 301–302.

[15]Kaestle, *Evolution of an Urban School System,* 5; also see Lawrence Cremin, *American Education: The Colonial Experience, 1607–1783* (New York: Harper & Row, 1970), 540–549.

There were no attendance records in colonial schools, and we can only guess what proportion of children attended and for how long. But by 1800 most boys and girls spent some time in school—even if only a few weeks—when chores permitted it.
—North Wind Picture Archives

COLONIAL TEACHERS

During the early colonial period, teachers usually had to satisfy the appropriate government official (or, in some cases, an official in their home country) that they held correct religious beliefs. Existing records contain the names of some people who taught, but few of them became famous *as teachers.* An exception was Ezekiel Cheever, who came to the colonies as a young man and devoted his long career to teaching. Another was Elijah Corlet, who taught for forty-three years in Cambridge, Massachusetts, beginning in 1643.[16]

No doubt there were many colonial Americans whose primary occupation was teaching, but few accounts exist of their lives and activities. What is clear from records is that many colonial Americans spent *some* time teaching. Young men often paid all or part of their college expenses by teaching winter terms of school. This practice continued and expanded throughout the nineteenth century, and people were paid well enough to save money for their college tuition and living expenses.[17]

BEGINNINGS OF HIGHER EDUCATION

The first universities in the Americas were established in Lima, Peru, and in Mexico City—both during the midsixteenth century. The printing press had arrived in Mexico City a few years earlier.[18] During the 1660s a seminary opened in Quebec, Canada, and it developed into Laval University. Spain established six other universities in the Americas before England made its first attempt, in Virginia. In 1616 the bishop of London was directed to raise money for "Henrico

With a grant of books and money from John Harvard in 1638, Massachusetts issued a college charter and began building the first American university to grant a bachelor's degree, in 1642. For almost fifty years its graduating class was smaller than nine.
—Bettmann

[16]S.v. "Corlet, Elijah," and "Cheever, Ezekiel," in *Biographical Dictionary of American Educators,* ed. John F. Ohles (Westport, Conn.: Greenwood, 1978); and L. Glenn Smith and Henry Hornbeck, "The Price of a Teacher: A Preliminary Examination of Status and Salary in American Education," in *The Social Role and Evolution of the Teaching Profession in Historical Context,* ed. Simo Seppo, *Conference Papers for the 10th Session of the International Standing Conference for the History of Education* 3 (Joensuu, Finland: University of Joensuu, Bulletin of the Faculty of Education, 1988), 27–32. Seybolt's *Private Schools of Colonial Boston* and *Public Schools of Colonial Boston* both name a large number of teachers and include, if known, their annual salaries.

[17]Smith, "Gillespie/Huftalen Diaries," 243–265.

[18]*Guia de la Universidad: Universidad Nacional Autonoma de Mexico* (Mexico: Secretaria Administrativa UNAM, 1991), 4–6.

College,'' and the London Company set aside 10,000 acres of land to support the effort; however, it did not come into being until 1693, as the College of William and Mary.

Meanwhile, members of the Massachusetts General Court (legislature) accepted a grant of books and money from recent immigrant John Harvard, who died in 1638. Patterning their efforts after Emmanuel College, of Cambridge, England (which a number of the settlers had attended), the colonists started a building in 1638–39 in Newtown, Massachusetts, renaming the town Cambridge. The first nine "young men of good hope" graduated from Harvard College with B.A. degrees in 1642.[19] The Boston-area colonists were able to launch a college sooner than was possible in Williamsburg because the Massachusetts General Court could issue charters; Virginia's legislative could not. In 1693 Dr. William Blair finally got a charter from the newly crowned English rulers, William and Mary.

The number of men who were educated annually at Harvard and at William and Mary remained small (fewer than nine per year at Harvard from 1642 to 1689).[20] College graduates were a tiny fraction of the population even after the Collegiate Institute opened in 1701, in Connecticut (it moved to New Haven and was renamed Yale College in 1718). Until well into the eighteenth century, college teaching was usually the responsibility of the president and one or two assistants. Tuition for higher education was steep enough to rule out most poorer students, although parents often used "country pay"—that is, sacks of flower, cords of wood, barrels of beer, or sides of bacon or beef.

EDUCATION IN THE EIGHTEENTH AND NINETEENTH CENTURIES

RELIGIOUS SPLINTERING

As members of various religious sects emigrated to America, and as longtime residents disagreed over doctrine, people discovered that no one could be forced to acquiesce to beliefs which they did not support nor stay in a community where they felt oppressed. Governance on the frontier was not often tied to any established church, and people quickly learned the value of ignoring differences in personal beliefs. Indeed, the apparent indifference to sectarian religion among frontier residents was worrisome to eastern Americans—or, at least, to New Englanders who had recently moved to the western frontier. The indifference seemed to indicate that established religious values might be in jeopardy.

As a result there were several waves of religious revivalism. The first major one occurred from 1720 to the 1740s and is usually called the **Great Awakening**. During this period several persuasive evangelists advocated that religion express more feeling, more emotional enthusiasm, and their concentrated bouts of preaching led many people to convert. Although the enthusiasm of the moment passed quickly for some new converts, others established new sects—or new

[19]Henry Barnard, "A History of Harvard College, 1636–1684," American Journal of Education 9 (1860): 129–138.

[20]Cremin, American Education: The Colonial Experience, 1607–1783, 221.

RESEARCH SAYS

For Tomorrow's Education . . .

The traditional view of religion in America has typically excluded the educational contributions of, and structures provided by, American Catholicism. F. Michael Perko rectifies this exclusion in his book *A Time to Favor Zion: The Ecology of Religion and Education on the Urban Frontier—Cincinnati, 1830–1870* (Chicago: Educational Studies Press, 1988).

branches of existing sects. Missioning revivalists preached regularly throughout America, sponsored by such sects as the Anglican Society for the Propagation of the Gospel in Foreign Parts (SPGFP) and the Methodists, a dissenting group that eventually broke away from the Anglicans and that sent "circuit riders" to preach throughout the frontier.

Revival meetings became frequent in many parts of the country, especially during summer. In remote areas, these served an important social function as well as the obvious religious one. People came from miles around. They camped out; heard sermons every day; made new friends (young people used revival meetings as an opportunity to meet possible mates); and argued about different theological, political, philosophical, and economic ideas.[21]

From about 1800 to 1830 revivals were so numerous that some historians have referred to the period as the "second great awakening." From it—originating on the frontier in western New York—came such new denominations as the Church of Jesus Christ of Latter Day Saints (Mormons), the Disciples of Christ, and several "spiritualist" groups.[22] Each of these groups later splintered into two or more groups, and older denominations (Methodists, Baptists, Presbyterians) also fragmented into subgroups.

Although this religious activity may seem remote from education today, it had at least two profound effects on how education developed. First, the splintering of Protestant sects provided a forum and a means of self-determination for people who otherwise might have been disenfranchised from schooling. As Chapter 4 explained, people tend to form social groups according to shared status, income and property, and values and beliefs. And within organizations hierarchies of power and influence tend to develop. In American religious sects, then, whenever even a small number of people began to feel excluded or estranged from leadership, there was the opportunity to convince likeminded folk to break away and form a new group. Those who spearheaded such a revolt became instant leaders, and they were influential in establishing the new sect's rules.

The second impact of religious splintering on education was that new groups usually moved quickly to open schools—especially academies, or colleges. A Greek word that was resurrected during the Renaissance, *academy* was the term used by religious dissenters in Scotland and England when they started their own collegiate institutes for sons who were barred from Oxford and Cambridge. When such dissenters, including clergy, emigrated to America, they became

[21]Lawrence A. Cremin, *American Education: The National Experience, 1783–1876* (New York: Harper & Row, 1980), 52.

[22]Frederick Merk, *History of the Westward Movement* (New York: Knopf, 1978), 119.

A NIGHT IN THE GREAT RELIGIOUS REVIVAL IN KENTUCKY IN 1800.

The "Great Awakening" of religious revivalism on the American frontier may have been spurred by theological concerns, but the splintering sects moved quickly to establish competing academies—and greatly broadened America's educational opportunities.
—Culver Pictures

teachers and imported the concept of academies with them. In America an **academy** came to offer two elements: (1) what we now call secondary education and (2) higher, or collegiate, preparation. The curriculum typically included the classical grammar education as well as practical subjects like accounting, surveying, navigation, modern languages, algebra, science, philosophy, and religion.

Although the major preoccupation of a sect in founding an academy was to offer a "purer" theological perspective than its competitors, the overall effect of academies was to broaden America's educational opportunities. An established sect's admissions criteria and tuition policies favored children from the sect, and so recent converts might feel that their children were not so readily accepted and did not belong. This often led them to leave the established sect and start another—along with an academy that welcomed their children. In addition, the tuition charged by an established sect might be beyond the parents' reach, and so a new academy had economic attractions. For both reasons academies and educational opportunities flourished in America.

Compared with the Roman Catholic and Protestant churches during the Reformation, which exerted hierarchical control, in America the new Protestant sects such as Methodists and southern Baptists favored local (congregational) governance. This eventually found ultimate expression in the Disciples of Christ and its splinter groups, the Churches of Christ, which had no organization or officials beyond the local, congregational level. For religion this was the organizational equivalent of the common, or district, school, which recognized no authority beyond that of the local trustees. Religion historian Nathan O. Hatch has summed up the effect on education in America:

> This democratic revolution in theology wrenched the queen of sciences from the learned speculations of Harvard, Yale, and Princeton men and encouraged the blacksmith, cooper, and tiller of the soil not only to experience salvation but also to explain the process. Its genius was to allow common people to feel, for a fleeting moment at least, that they were beholden to no one and masters of their own fate.[23]

SOCIETY AND SCHOOLS IN THE NEW REPUBLIC

The war that American colonists fought for independence from Britain from 1776 to 1783 appeared to have little immediate impact on education. There were disruptions, of course, because of fighting—young men left college to enlist, and sometimes troops were quartered on campus. But neither the Treaty of Paris, which officially ended the war in 1783, nor the following constitutional convention in Philadelphia dramatically affected education in the short term.[24]

Independence, however, brought increased attention to schooling as a means of social development and control, because the peace treaty added new land as far West as the Mississippi River. Through the land ordinance of 1785 and 1787, the Continental Congress surveyed these vast western territories into townships 6 miles square containing thirty-six sections of 640 acres each (see Figure 9.1). The territories were to become states—equal with the original thirteen—as soon as their populations reached fifty thousand.

New citizens who had arrived before the revolutionary war and who had run the risks of breaking with England felt that their investment should be protected from the steady stream of people now pouring in from Europe.[25] Although many of the earlier arrivers had such feelings, those in Massachusetts, Connecticut, and Virginia were especially concerned, because of the prominence their colonies had long enjoyed both culturally and politically. They wanted the territories to be part of the new country, both for future expansion and as a buffer against Spanish and French interests. "We have need of the Floridas and must have them," wrote sixth-generation Bostonian John Proctor in 1818.[26] But Proctor and other New Englanders feared social, moral, and cultural deterioration as settlements pushed beyond the mountain ridges that ran from western New York to northern Georgia. The next day, after writing "And what we must have, we will have," Proctor noted the "more than savage barbarity of [Andrew] Jackson" in Florida, calling it "lawless insolence."[27] (Jackson had hanged two British citizens in Florida for stirring up Seminole insurrections.) New Englanders did not want to be outvoted by western interests.

To guard against the possibility that western settlements might not pay sufficient attention to education, the Continental Congress decreed in its 1787 land ordinance that in the Northwest Territory the sixteenth section (of 640 acres) in each township was to be dedicated to education. Whenever these sections of land were leased, rented, or sold, the proceeds were to be set aside for education. As the territories became states, this plan became the basis for per-

[23]Nathan O. Hatch, "The Christian Movement and the Demand for a Theology of the People," *Journal of American History* 67 (December 1980): 561–562.

[24]Kaestle, *Pillars of the Republic,* 1–61.

[25]The interpretive controversies about the influence of the frontier on America's development are discussed by Paula M. Nelson, "The Significance of the Frontier in American Historiography: A Review Essay," *Annals of Iowa* 50 (Summer 1990): 531–540.

[26]John Waters Proctor Diary, 31 December 1818, Houghton Library, Harvard University.

[27]Ibid., 1 January 1819.

FIGURE 9.1   Northwest Territory Township Survey

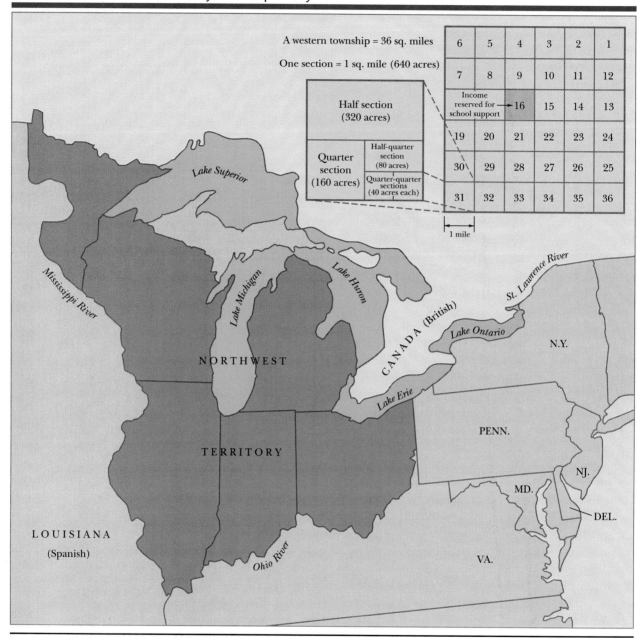

A western township = 36 sq. miles

One section = 1 sq. mile (640 acres)

6	5	4	3	2	1
7	8	9	10	11	12
Income reserved for → school support	16	15	14	13	
19	20	21	22	23	24
30	29	28	27	26	25
31	32	33	34	35	36

Half section (320 acres)

Quarter section (160 acres)

Half-quarter section (80 acres)

Quarter-quarter sections (40 acres each)

1 mile

manent school funds. To protect against too much western influence, eastern interests included the provision that no more than six new states could be created from the Northwest Territory. This ensured that the new states could not outvote the original thirteen in the Senate.[28]

Three forces combined to focus attention on education in the new Republic. One was the fear among well-established Americans that the wilderness would corrupt advancing waves of settlers. A second was the growing faith, rooted in

[28]Merk, *History of the Westward Movement*, 102–111.

Comparative Perspective on Today's Issues . . .

◆ **IS THE SEPARATION OF CHURCH AND STATE BEING THREATENED?**

The Issue   Historically religion has had a close association with schooling, as colonial settlers offered education based on their chosen religious beliefs. While the Constitution mandated the separation of church and state, nineteenth-century Catholic and Jewish immigrants protested the Protestant context in which the public schools provided instruction. By the mid-twentieth century, U.S. Supreme Court cases attempted to remove this influence as they called for the end of religious activities, such as those associated with religious holidays. However, censorship and attempts by some politicians to introduce prayer into the public school curriculum have caused concern among some educators who see such things as a threat to the separation of church and state.

YES   These recent attempts to recast the relationship between the church and state corrode the original intent of the First Amendment—i.e., to forbid "the establishment of religion" by providing any type of federal support. "Acceptance of a narrow, accommodationist view of the history of the establishment clause must not be allowed to be turned into public policies that serve to increase public support for religious schools in any form: vouchers, tax credits, or aid for extremes of 'parental choice.' " Educators must study these issues in terms of the historical scholarship that is available to them (p. 70).

—*R. Freeman Butts, Professor Emeritus, Teachers College, Columbia, and Senior Fellow, Kettering Foundation*

NO   Historical documents do not support an absolutionist view of separation of church and state. The framers of the First Amendment also allowed federal support of religion. For example, Thomas Jefferson signed into law a tax exemption for the churches of Alexandria County, Virginia, and James Madison issued four Thanksgiving proclamations while he was President. The complete record of historical evidence, including accounts of public words and deeds of the founding fathers reveals a narrower, less absolute interpretation of the First Amendment—one that only meant to prohibit the establishment of a national religion or a legally preferred religious position.

—*Robert L. Cord, Professor, Political Science, Northeastern University, Boston*

Source: Based on James Wm. Noll, ed., *Taking Sides: Clashing Views on Controversial Educational Issues*, 5th ed. (Guilford, Conn.: Dushkin, 1989), 64–81.

the European Enlightenment, that human society and conditions could be improved by extending education (see Chapter 8). Thus Thomas Jefferson, Benjamin Franklin, George Washington, and numerous other leaders of opinion authored "educational plans" either for whole states or for the nation.[29] The third force was the Reformation conviction that every individual was personally responsible for acquiring salvation and religious virtue. Indeed, each person was responsible for his or her education. And those whose family or economic backgrounds made schooling inaccessible expanded this line of thought to mean that a person had the *right* to seek as much education as desired.

Until the Civil War the traditions of individual choice and responsibility dominated in America. Except in the most isolated and sparsely populated areas, many kinds of instruction were available. Besides thousands of district schools

[29]Erwin V. Johanningmeir, "Enlightenment and Education in America in the Eighteenth Century," in *Educational Thinkers of the Enlightenment and Their Influences in Different Countries*, ed. D. Jedan and F. P. Hager (Murray, Ky.: Murray State University Press, 1987), 94–112.

and grammar schools, there were teachers of music, writing, accounting, survey-ing, modern languages, navigation, and other specialized skills. After the 1740s these subjects—along with Latin, Greek, Hebrew, algebra, science, philosophy, and religion—were taught in academies.[30] By 1800 the term *grammar school* usu-ally referred to the upper, more advanced part of a district school's curriculum. When grouping students by age became common, during the late nineteenth century, the first two or three years of elementary school were called "primary," while the remainder got the title "grammar grades."[31]

SECTIONAL PRIDE AND COMPETITION

The first half of the nineteenth century was a period of dramatic expansion in America. As the century began, most settlements were still concentrated in the East, and France and Spain claimed much of the territory that would soon be-come part of the country. But as physical expansion occurred, so did educational development. By 1860 hundreds of colleges and thousands of academies had been founded, most of them by religious sects. Today only 20 percent of the colleges and an even smaller proportion of the academies remain. Yet, while they lasted—anywhere from a few months to several decades or longer—they pro-vided a vast array of educational services.

Establishing a college became easy after the American Revolution, because the charter (or legal incorporation) that conferred degree-granting authority came from the states. Although some people—especially in Massachusetts and Virginia—advocated restraint in granting educational charters, most people agreed that one's religious beliefs should not be infringed. This meant as well that individuals should be free to exercise their educational beliefs and rights. Thus the states and the District of Columbia issued educational charters readily, and they were rarely canceled for any reason. As a result of the **Dartmouth Col-lege case** in 1819, in which the U.S. Supreme Court ruled that states could not easily tamper with existing charters, the charters became almost sacred.

The flurry of educational activity did not put everyone at ease. Almost every college and academy was "public" in the longstanding sense of the word, and most communities had common schools. But many New Englanders worried because New York City was surpassing Boston in both population and commer-cial importance. At the same time, commentators in England and on the Con-tinent denigrated American culture as being primitive, and this bothered people who craved European acknowledgment of American legitimacy.[32] It was the free-wheeling, uncouth "westerners" from emerging areas like Kentucky and Ten-nessee who caused Europeans to think of Americans as barbaric—or so, at least, many New Englanders thought. As a frontier teacher wrote back to Connecticut, "You once said to us you thought we might find at the West, as you did at the South, an astonishing stupidity and indolence, and I think I have seen something of it."[33] The election of Andrew Jackson in 1828 was especially galling to many northeasterners.

Many easterners tamed their fear of the frontier with feelings of religious intensity. From 1846 to 1856 nearly six-hundred women left New England under the auspices of the National Board of Popular Education to teach school and to

[30]See Charles Morton, "Considera-tions of the University Oath as Applyed by Some, Against private reading of Philosophy," bMS Am 1259, 12 August 1677, Houghton Library, Harvard University, 34 pp.; Charles Morton to Joseph Dudley, 12 March 1683/4, Autography File, Houghton Library, Harvard Univer-sity, Cambridge, Mass.

[31]Elmer Ellsworth Brown, *The Making of Our Middle Schools: An Account of the Development of Secondary Education in the United States* (New York: Long-mans, Green, 1903), 161.

[32]Noah Webster to Joel Barlow, 19 October 1807, bMS Am 1448; James G. Carter to Henry W. Longfellow, 2 March 1825, bMS Am 1340.2, Houghton Library, Harvard Univer-sity; and Horace Mann to *Providence Patriot*, 25 August 1821, Horace Mann Papers, Massachusetts Historical Society, Boston.

[33]E. Hill to Nancy Swift, 20 De-cember 1862, National Public Edu-cation Board Papers, Connecticut State Historical Society, Hartford.

For Tomorrow's Education . . .

In general, the American West and its educational and religious configurations have become the topic of much renewed thought and discussion. See Brad Knickerbocker, "A Century After the West Was Won," *Christian Science Monitor*, 18 December 1990, 12.

win converts to mainline Protestantism. They were evangelists of culture and of a proper New England attitude.[34] Such activity was overwhelmingly Protestant and has come to seem synonymous with it, but Roman Catholic missioning embodied many of the same values.[35]

POLITICIZING EDUCATION

From the American Revolution to the Civil War, two broad patterns of thought emerged about education. Both favored schooling and saw it as a means of improvement, but they disagreed about how to accomplish it. One group viewed education as a personal, family, or local responsibility, admitting some social obligation for educating the poor. The other group stressed the need for educational planning and control and emphasized social systems (township, state, national government) over individual choices (family, local government).[36]

Until about 1830 the lines separating these two groups were fuzzy, and few people fell cleanly into one or the other. As the Civil War approached, however, the lines grew sharper. Those who favored social control—or **state action**, as it came to be known legally—identified more and more consciously with each other and began to refer to themselves by such labels as "friends of education." The implication was that anyone who was not a *friend* of education must be a foe and, therefore, favored ignorance and vice over enlightenment and virtue. In this way education was becoming framed in a political context.

Friends of education lived in every state and territory but seemed to be concentrated in New England, where three men stood out as early leaders. James G. Carter and Horace Mann were from Massachusetts; Henry Barnard hailed from Connecticut but also worked in Rhode Island and other states. Carter began his work during the 1820s; Mann and Barnard, during the 1830s. All three—and many others who shared their views—advocated state legislation to bring order to individualized approaches to schooling, which they saw as chaotic, undisciplined, and wrong-headed. By the time fighting broke out between Union and Confederate troops in 1861, people's opinions about educational organization and control were politicized. The following sections explain how it was done.

ORGANIZATION AND CONTROL OF EDUCATION   Carter and Mann authored legislation to create a state-level education officer in Massachusetts. When the state board of education became a reality in 1836, Horace Mann left the Massachusetts legislature to become the new unit's full-time executive secretary. Henry Barnard authored similar legislation in Rhode Island and Connecticut,

[34]Polly Welts Kaufman, *Women Teachers on the Frontier* (New Haven, Conn.: Yale University Press, 1984).
[35]Perko, *Time to Favor Zion*, 12, 96–104, and 197–198.
[36]Carl E. Kaestle, "The Development of Common School Systems in the States of the Old Northwest," in ". . . *Schools and the Means of Education Shall Forever Be Encouraged": A History of Education in the Old Northwest, 1787–1880*, ed. Paul H. Mattingly and Edward W. Stevens, Jr. (Athens, Ohio: Ohio University Libraries, 1987), 31–43.

and he also served as both states' first full-time education official. "You are my guide, my hope, my friend, my fellow laborer and fellow-sufferer in 'the cause,' " Barnard wrote to Mann.[37]

From their new positions as official spokespersons for education, Mann and Barnard led other friends of education in arguing for the following inter-related items:

1. All common, or elementary, schools were to be tuition-free, with support to come from local and state taxes.

2. All schools in each township were to be under direct control of a superintendent.

3. All curricular offerings and teaching materials were to be standardized and put under the control of the superintendent instead of parents and individual teachers.

4. All pupils were to be grouped by age into graded schools (this meant that the monitorial approach had to go).

5. All teachers were to be licensed by the superintendent or by the state—after training in normal schools or institutes; unlicensed teachers could not be hired by the trustees.

6. All parents would be compelled to send their children to school for a minimal number of days and a specified number of years, under threat of fines and possible jail terms.

To build public support for this organization and approach, Mann and Barnard wrote many newspaper articles, gave numerous speeches, and lobbied legislators. They claimed that areas which adopted the township organization had superior schools to those which left educational decisions to the individual, family, and community. Other friends of education took up this theme and searched for evidence to support their belief that more state action was needed to beat back the forces of ignorance.

REDEFINING THE TERMS   In a subtle but largely unconscious development during the 1840s and 1850s the friends of education began to redefine several long-standing terms. The term *common school* had long been understood to mean any school that offered elementary instruction, regardless of its funding or religious sponsorship. It was a label with strongly positive connotations, and Mann, Barnard, and others gradually came to use it to refer *only* to schools that were part of the township scheme. The friends of education also began referring to a common school that charged tuition as a **private school**. If a common school was supported primarily by taxes but was not part of a township organization, the friends of education referred to it as a *country*, or *district*, school. In cities they gave the label *charity school* to those charging little or no tuition and not part of a township organization. (Often they included such adjectives as *poor, inadequate,* and *miserable* when mentioning country, district, or charity schools. "The term 'countrified' was an epithet of reproach," said one Connecticut resident of the period.)[38]

[37]Barnard to Mann, 13 February 1843, Mann Papers, Massachusetts Historical Society, Boston.

[38]Denison Olmstead, "On the Democratic Tendencies of Science," *Journal of American Education* 1 (January 1856): 164–171.

RADICAL REPUBLICAN ASSIMILATION   From 1830 to 1860 no predominant political party was associated with the friends of education. Some were Whigs, and some were Democrats. By 1860, however, many of the friends were Republicans. Perhaps a majority were Congregationalists or Presbyterians, and a significant number were Masons (the inaccessibility of Masonic records makes it impossible to guess how many).

Until the Civil War was nearly over, the friends of education tended to play down their political affiliations. After the war Congress struggled with how to reconstruct the Union, including on what terms to re-admit the states that had seceded. Two perplexing questions swirled about: Why had the "Great Rebellion" happened, and how could a recurrence of it be prevented? Several members of Congress who were friends of education offered a simple explanation: The North had free, common, public schools; the South did not. Skeptics countered by pointing out that most of the Confederacy's leaders were well educated. Advocates of the common-school explanation conceded this, but argued that the leaders were evil; the mass of southerners were good but ignorant and did not know that slavery was wrong or that it was illegal to secede from the Union.

This explanation was clearly false if "common school" were defined traditionally. But it was more credible if one used the definition of the friends of education, because most southern states did *not* have statewide systems. (North Carolina was an exception and was ignored by advocates of "the cause" of common schools, newly defined.) Despite the flaws in this explanation, it appealed to enough members of Congress that they made it a prerequisite for re-entry into the Union that a state's constitution provide for common schools.

James Carter died in 1849, followed by Horace Mann ten years later. Henry Barnard lived to 1900. He celebrated "the cause" and many friends of education in the *American Journal of Education*, which he founded and edited from 1855 to 1880. Barnard and other partisans referred to their movement as "the common school revival." Largely because of Barnard's publicity in the *American Journal*, Mann came to be known as the "father of the common school"—a title which misled later commentators into believing that there were relatively few common schools before Mann.[39]

CONSOLIDATING GAINS   In an effort to consolidate their position the friends of education pushed for a department of education as an agency of the federal government. Republican Representative James A. Garfield of Ohio, later to be President, led a congressional effort that resulted in the creation of the U.S. Department of Education in March 1867. Supporters hoped the new department would diffuse "correct ideas respecting the value of education as a quickener of intellectual activities, [and act] as a moral renovator, as a multiplier of industry, and a consequent producer of wealth; and finally, as the strength and shield of civil liberty."[40] Henry Barnard became the first head of the new office.

Opposition to state systems of education was widespread. The idea of a federal system—one that implied either general tax money or national control—appealed only to the most stringent advocates of the new common-school sys-

[39]Ellwood P. Cubberley, *Public Education in the United States* (Boston: Riverside, 1947) made this mistake, which has been repeated in many texts; see Lawrence A. Cremin, *The Wonderful World of Ellwood Patterson Cubberley: An Essay in the Historiography of Education* (New York: Teachers College Press, Columbia University, 1965).

[40]U.S. House of Representatives, 39th Congress, 1st Sess., 1865–1866, *Miscellaneous Documents No. 5*, 1–5.

tems. A move to increase funding in 1869 gave opponents of state systems an opening, and Barnard's political ineptitude weakened Garfield's ability to defend the proposed department of education. Congress changed the unit to a bureau within the Department of the Interior, where it had less authority and status than its advocates wanted for it.[41]

RESEARCH SAYS

For Tomorrow's Education . . .

African-American history continues to receive inadequate coverage in American historical accounts, and much more attention needs to be given to this story. See "American History, Black Americans," *Christian Science Monitor*, 12 October 1990, 20.

Civil War conditions produced important educational developments in two other areas. One was the Morrill Act (see Chapter 7), which passed in 1862 because Democratic opposition to it was reduced by seceding states. The other development was the formation of the Bureau of Refugees, Freedmen and Abandoned Lands in 1865, which grew out of the need to assist four million freed slaves. Known as the **Freedmen's Bureau**, it was supposed to provide land, economic support, and schools. During its brief existence it provided more schools than land or economic aid.

[41]L. Glenn Smith, "Founding the U.S. Office of Education," *Educational Forum* 21 (March 1967): 307–322; and Donald R. Warren, *To Enforce Education: A History of the Founding Years of the United States Office of Education* (Detroit: Wayne State University Press, 1974).

School (Adam's Run), 1925, *by Gari Melchers, depicts an African-American schoolhouse in South Carolina. As volunteers of Freedmen's Aid societies left the South, local communities opened their own schools.* —Courtesy of Belmont, The Gari Melchers Estate and Memorial Gallery

W. E. B.
Du Bois
1868–1963

Will Du Bois (pronounced "Du Boyce") was descended from African, French Huguenot, and Dutch ancestors. His mother, Mary Burghardt, came from a free African-American family that had settled in Great Barrington, Massachusetts, during the late eighteenth century. His father's family was from New York, via the Bahamas, Haiti, and New Haven, Connecticut. His father, Albert, was a barber in Great Barrington, where he met and married Mary against her parents' wishes.

Will was born on February 23, 1868, and shortly later his father left Great Barrington (for unknown reasons, his family did not go with him). A stroke left Mary lame, and so she and Will moved into her parents' home. Will went to school in Great Barrington and finished first in his high school class of twelve. Although there were fifty African-American families in the town, Du Bois was the only black student in his graduating class.

When his mother died in 1885, Du Bois traveled to Tennessee to attend college at Fisk. Racial tensions then were strong in this southern state, and Du Bois later recalled that—before going to college—he had never really experienced racial prejudice. He graduated in 1888 with an outstanding academic record, and his professors encouraged him to continue his studies; he then entered Harvard as a junior and earned another bachelor's degree in philosophy in 1890. At Harvard he kept to himself, socializing little with other students, but his professors included George Santayana and William James, who inspired him to continue his education. At their suggestion he earned a master's degree in history in 1891; the title of his thesis was "The Suppression of African Slave-Trade to the United States of America, 1638–1870."

Next Du Bois set out for Germany to seek a doctorate from the University of Berlin. He was there for two years but did not earn the degree. Instead, he traveled throughout Europe and was amazed to find that he was accepted socially. His academic interests shifted during this period from history to politics, economics, and so-

ciology. When he returned to America, he accepted a position as chair of the classics department at Wilburforce College in Xenia, Ohio. He also completed his Ph.D.—at Harvard in 1895—and a year later he married a Wilburforce coed, Nina Gomer, from Cedar Rapids, Iowa. The couple moved to Philadelphia, where Du Bois became an assistant research instructor for the University of Pennsylvania. His research subject was the African-American community in Philadelphia's seventh ward.

Yesterday's Professional

After completing *The Philadelphia Negro: A Social Study*, Du Bois accepted a position in the sociology department at Atlanta University. He stayed there for thirteen years, studying the conditions affecting African-Americans and trying to influence social policies through lectures and publications. During this time he developed his ideas about the "talented tenth"—the proportion of a population or race that, by becoming cultured intellectuals, can lead the masses. Among his best-known works is *The Souls of Black Folk*, which was written when his sick infant son died because a hospital refused to admit a black child.

Du Bois began to break away from the conservative social stance of such African-American leaders as Booker T. Washington. In 1905 he founded the Niagara Movement, which took liberal social positions, and in 1910 the group merged with the National Association for the Advancement of Colored People. That same year he moved to New York to direct the NAACP's publications and research. After Washington's death in 1915, Du Bois became the spokesperson for African-American politics, and his interest in Africa led him to organize a Pan-African conference in 1919, 1920, and 1921.

Du Bois visited Russia in 1926 and was impressed by how its form of communism aided oppressed people. Increasingly he became convinced that racial equality would never be realized in America, and he began to support segregation and the development of an independent black culture. This position, of course, was unacceptable to the NAACP, which was dedicated to fighting segregation. So Du Bois resigned his editorial position with the NAACP and returned to Atlanta as chair of the sociology department, serving during the presidency of his friend John Hope. But when the university appointed a new president in 1944, its board of trustees voted to

(Box continued)

retire Professor Du Bois without a pension. The NAACP invited him back as director of special research, but before long the old tensions arose again, and he was fired. This time, however, he did receive a pension.

In 1951, a year after his wife Nina died, Du Bois married Shirley Graham, the daughter of an old friend. He also had formed the Peace Information Center, to advance international relations, but since he had not complied with the Foreign Agents Registration Act, he was indicted by the U.S. Department of Justice. Although the case was ultimately thrown out of court, Du Bois contin-

ued to have problems securing a passport. Nonetheless, in 1958 he was allowed to travel to the Soviet Union to accept the Lenin Peace Prize, and in 1961 he left the United States for good; he had become a communist, and he was convinced that authorities would place more limitations on him. He took up residency in Ghana, where he worked on an African encyclopedia until his death on August 28, 1963.

Source: Based on Jack B. Moore, *W. E. B. Du Bois* (Boston: Twayne, 1981); and W. E. B. Du Bois, *The Autobiography of W. E. B. Du Bois* (International Publishers, 1968).

African-Americans in the South generally welcomed the northern teachers who came under the auspices either of the government or of fifty-one voluntary Freedmen's Aid societies. By 1870 there were 2,560 teachers operating 2,039 schools for the government.[42] In addition, a strong movement within the African-American community established many schools—including the first ones for blacks—and sustained them against considerable odds after most northern teachers had returned home. During this Reconstruction period African-American colleges and universities also were founded. Some researchers suggest that the efforts of the Freedmen's Aid societies and Freedmen's Bureau contained elements of condescension and white control that were not in the long-term best interests of African-American education.[43]

In 1870 a chief architect of the Freedmen's Bureau, John Eaton, Jr., became the second U.S. commissioner of education. A Presbyterian and a Mason, Eaton cooperated with Presbyterian missionary Sheldon Jackson in Alaska to secure government aid for schools in that vast territory, purchased from Russia in 1867. Primarily because of Eaton's advocacy, in 1884 the U.S. Bureau of Education (as it was then called) did take over Alaska's schools. For several decades the commissioner of education in Washington set policy for the education of Alaskan natives thousands of miles away.[44]

In 1873 the Michigan Supreme Court made a decision which signaled that the new definition of common school was well established. Known as the **Kalamazoo case**, it brought suit to stop the use of tax funds to pay for a high school and for the salary of a superintendent of schools. Charles Stuart and two other petitioners—all of whom were substantial property owners—thought it unconstitutional (and socially divisive) to spend poor people's tax money to support a school that would be attended only by children of the well-to-do. Stuart himself had attended common schools and strongly approved of such an education; but he understood the term to mean a community-controlled, multi-age school, as it had meant for years. (Stuart had "read law" to become an attorney, and he was a Democrat who had served in both houses of Congress.)[45]

[42]Ronald E. Butchart, *Northern Schools, Southern Schools, and Reconstruction: Freedmen's Education, 1862–1875* (Westport, Conn.: Greenwood, 1979), 4.

[43]Ibid.; and Vincent Harding, *There is a River: The Black Struggle for Freedom in America* (New York: Harcourt, 1981).

[44]Glenn Smith, "Education for the Natives of Alaska," *Journal of the West* 6 (July 1967): 440–450.

[45]Harry L. Selden, "Kalamazoo and High School Too," in Leroy V. Goodman, ed., *A Nation of Learners* (Washington, D.C.: U.S. Government Printing Office, 1976), 120–122.

Chief Justice Cooley defined common schools as did the friends of education. He then cited the Michigan constitution, which authorized common schools, and said that this implied the authority to support by tax any part of the common-school system.[46] A few challenges were mounted in other states, but none overturned this decision. Horace Mann's vision would be realized after all.

BEYOND THE COMMON SCHOOL

DEVELOPMENT OF THE AMERICAN HIGH SCHOOL

The term *high school* came from Europe via German colonists in Pennsylvania; their word *hochschule* (an advanced technical school) was translated into English and came into use during the 1760s. An American named John Griscom, who traveled through Europe during the early 1820s, published an account of his observations of schools in 1824, and he described the Edinburgh High School in detail. In 1825, in New York, Griscom founded an institution called the "high school for boys." At about the same time, the governing committee of the English Classical School in Boston changed the school's name to the English High School—apparently to satisfy the complaints of Latin and Greek teachers who argued that the word *classical* should not be in the name of a school which did not teach those two languages.

A few other institutions called high schools were established before 1850. High schools for girls opened in New York and in Boston during the mid-1820s. (Boston's closed after only two years, probably because the city's male leaders decided that they could not meet the growing demand for girls' schools.) Philadelphia, Baltimore, and Charleston all opened boys' high schools during the late 1830s. By the 1850s some of the friends of education began advocating the inclusion of high schools as part of the common-school system. One researcher estimated that forty high schools existed by 1860.[47] After the Kalamazoo case was decided, high schools multiplied rapidly, while academies disappeared. Some academies were taken over by local school systems and became high schools. Many academies went out of existence, and some became degree-granting colleges.

SPREAD OF HIGHER EDUCATION

The number of American colleges increased substantially after the 1740s. All of them, except for the College of Philadelphia (1754), were associated with a particular religious sect. Even Philadelphia, which became the University of Pennsylvania, represented Benjamin Franklin's liberal deism.

After the American Revolution the number of colleges again increased, as did the number of academies (which essentially offered collegiate coursework). Several southern states—including Georgia, North Carolina, and South Carolina—established what they called universities, but most were not tax supported,

[46]Stuart v. School Dist. No. 1 of Village of Kalamazoo, 30 Mich. 69–85 (1874).

[47]Brown, *Making of Our Middle Schools*, 301–316.

Perhaps about forty high schools existed in 1860, but after the Kalamazoo case they proliferated and replaced academies. By the 1950s high schools had become the centerpiece of the American dream, promising hope and opportunity to all. —Bettmann

and all were liberal arts colleges in terms of their curriculum. Many of their students were from the "supervisory class," and until the nineteenth century almost all were assigned a class rank based on family standing, not on academic performance.

As the population expanded in the West and in the South, colleges arose in large numbers. In fact, most of today's large state universities and many well-regarded independent institutions began as small colleges during the nineteenth century: DePauw University, Duke University, Grinnell College, New York University, Fordham University, the University of Cincinnati, St. Louis University, the University of Pittsburgh, Notre Dame, the University of Chicago, Vanderbilt University, and Wilberforce University. From today's perspective there were also some unlikely sounding colleges that no longer exist, such as Concrete College in DeWitt County, Texas—so named because of the materials from which it was built; it flourished from 1867 to 1880.[48]

In 1862 the Morrill Act expanded the college curriculum and made it more practical. It also subsidized tuition costs so that more working- and lower-class students could afford to attend college. In 1890 Congress added monetary appropriations to the original land grants. This "second Morrill Act" made money available to African-American colleges for the first time. Although their shares were never equitable, this federal money greatly expanded higher-education opportunities for African-Americans.[49]

[48]"Scraps of History about the DeWitt County Area," File A46154 (Miss Nellie Murphree typescript), Dallas Historical Society.

[49]Clarice C. Boswell, "The Effects of Federal Educational Policies Between 1980 and 1990 on the Continued Survival of Selected Historic Black Colleges and Universities" (Northern Illinois University, Ed.D. diss., 1990).

THE EARLY TWENTIETH CENTURY: PROGRESSIVE EDUCATION

■

By 1890 the main features of America's public school system were in place. Harvard President Charles Eliot would shortly chair the Committee of Ten, which would standardize the high school curriculum (see Chapter 7). But not all was well in America's schools. In the spirit of "muckraking" journalism, Joseph Mayer Rice traveled throughout the country examining schools in the largest cities as well as some smaller ones.

Rice's report—first published as a series of articles in *The Forum*—called most schools "unscientific" and said that "the good schools that do exist have been developed, not as a result of the system, but in spite of it."[50] Rice found the schools dehumanizing, characterized by rote memory work, passivity, silence, and no soul. An exception was the Cook County Normal School, under the direction of Francis Wayland Parker. Rice praised Parker as the leading proponent of "the new education," and he called for educators throughout the country to adopt Parker's progressive approaches.

Three years after Rice's exposé was published, a young professor of philosophy named John Dewey moved from the University of Michigan to the new University of Chicago, and Dewey's children attended Colonel Parker's school. Four years later the University of Chicago acquired Parker's Institute, including its faculty and endowment. Parker died in 1902, and Dewey merged his school with the university's department of education. But the merger was not entirely happy, and Dewey soon left for Columbia University in New York.[51]

Among the significant results of Dewey's stay in Chicago were that he developed a strong interest in the problems of education and he met school administrator Ella Flagg Young. She taught him the pedagogical consequences of pragmatic philosophy, and he taught her how to conceptualize educational problems in philosophical terms. Young studied for her doctorate with Dewey and later became the first female superintendent of Chicago's public schools. In that role she implemented progressive educational ideas on a large scale. In 1910 she became the first woman to preside over the National Education Association.

In 1915 John Dewey wrote a book with his daughter Evelyn entitled *Schools of Tomorrow*. It described a progressive school in Fairhope, Alabama, where Dewey drew heavily on the work of Rousseau, Herbart, and Froebel. A year later Dewey published *Democracy and Education*, a book destined to be read by most American educators for two generations. The power of the book is that it melds the progressive intellectual traditions of Europe with the democratic impulses of America and explains how schools draw on and reinforce those traditions. Dewey thus gave educators a philosophical basis for building and expressing their educational ideas.

[50]Joseph Mayer Rice, *The Public School System of the United States* (New York: Century, 1893).

[51]Joan K. Smith, *Ella Flagg Young: Portrait of a Leader* (Ames, Iowa: Iowa State University Research Foundation and Educational Studies Press, 1979), 85–100.

CONCLUSIONS

■

Early colonial education was rooted in British, French, Spanish, Swedish, and Dutch soil. As European settlers pushed West and South, bringing their civilization to the eastern part of the American continent, colonial schools developed into a unique single-teacher, one-room, multi-age institution under control of the community it served.

As the new Republic expanded westward and the pace of immigration increased, control of the country's schools became a concern—particularly for New Englanders whose colonial ancestors had enjoyed political and social prominence. Throughout the nineteenth century a system of American public education gradually emerged, consisting of elementary schools, high schools, and—for those who showed academic promise and could afford them—state colleges and universities. Paralleling this system was a variety of private and religious institutions.

In common with European and Latin American school systems of the same time period, twentieth-century U.S. schools rested firmly on "modern"—that is, Enlightenment—assumptions. These included faith in human rationality and the belief that progress would come through large-scale government programs that rested on social consensus. The preparation of educators, as well as school reform efforts, reflected such beliefs. From the 1960s to 1990s, as numerous attempts to reform schools stopped short of producing hoped-for results, some critics saw Enlightenment assumptions as the problem. They called for "postmodern" solutions predicated on irrational individualism rather than on rational organizations. People like Michel Foucault, Ivan Illich, and Thomas Khun brought serious challenges to advocates of modernity and rational reform.

KEY TERMS

■

Old Deluder-Satan Law

graded school

public school

endowment

free school

common school

charity school

district school

dame school

Great Awakening

academy

Dartmouth College case

state action

friends of education

private school

Freedmen's Bureau

Kalamazoo case

SUGGESTED READINGS

Bernard Bailyn, *Education in the Forming of American Society: Needs and Opportunities for Study* (Chapel Hill: University of North Carolina Press, 1960). This landmark account revised the traditional interpretation of colonial and American education.

Jack Weatherford, *Indian Givers: How the Indians of the Americas Transformed the World* (New York: Fawcett/Columbine, 1988); and *Native Roots: How the Indians Enriched America* (New Fawcett/Columbine, 1991). An anthropologist, Weatherford examines the historical record for a new perspective on the contributions of Native American cultures to modern life.

H. Warren Button and Eugene F. Provenzo, Jr., *A History of Education in the United States* (Englewood Cliffs, N.J.: Prentice-Hall, 1989). This is a comprehensive account of the development of American education from colonial times to the present.

L. Glenn Smith and Joan K. Smith, *Lives in Education* (New York: St. Martin's Press, 1994). The last part of this book deals with the American educational picture and includes biographical sketches of neglected female and minority educators and their contributions.

Vincent Harding, *There Is a River: The Black Struggle for Freedom in America* (New York: Harcourt, 1981). This passionate history of the African-American struggle in the United States makes a powerful argument for understanding the experiences of black Americans and the Afrocentric perspective.

James W. Sanders, *The Education of an Urban Minority: Catholics in Chicago—1833–1965*, (New York: Oxford, 1977). This book supports the thesis that America's public schools were not very successful in separating church and state. Instead, they adhered to a white Anglo-Saxon Protestant ethic that excluded other religious groups. Thus a confederation of Catholic schools sprang up in urban settings, including Chicago.

Averil Evans McClelland, *The Education of Women in America: A Guide to Theory, Teaching, and Research* (New York: Garland, 1991). This book presents a thorough view of the education of girls and women in the United States from colonial times to the present.

Philosophy and Education

Philosophical Foundations

10

*Philosophy is concerned primarily with the general and not with the particular,
with* meaning *and not with* fact.

—*William F. O'Neill,* Educational Ideologies *(Santa Monica, Calif.: Goodyear, 1981), 16*

10

Philosophy
and
Education

ADVANCED ORGANIZERS

In this chapter you will learn

What the categories of philosophy are, and some terminology related to them

How the four traditional philosophical systems view reality, knowledge, and values

How analytic philosophy can be used in solving philosophical problems in education

What the major philosophical movements in American education are

How to build your own educational philosophy

CHAPTER OUTLINE

J ane Fletcher is starting her third year as a fifth-grade teacher in a large city, and this year she is concerned. Her school district has been mandated by a recent law to implement a local council to set policy for the school. Although there is one teacher on the local council, the other six members are laypeople. They will be deciding what should be taught to whom and by whom, what the school's employees should be paid, and what the general approach to discipline should be.

Fletcher questions the wisdom of implementing this new policy-making body, and she wonders how it might affect her status as a professional. Local universities have already been contacted to train the new lay council members so that they can make informed decisions about questions that affect the school's philosophy of education. Until now Fletcher has supported what she saw as a strong system of educational values in her school, and she hopes that the school's goals and values will stay strong. But she is concerned about the year ahead. . . .

In general we can say that philosophy and science both attempt to answer questions and to find solutions to educational problems. But the questions they address and the problems they solve are different. In many ways philosophy picks up where science stops. Noted educational philosopher Harry Broudy has argued that "it is our intellectual duty to exhaust the possibilities of science in the solution of problems before turning elsewhere"; but he goes on to say, "If the facts and scientific theories cannot settle the controversy and if the disputants still wish to continue a rational discussion, they shall have to pass to another level of argument, namely, the philosophical."[1]

DEFINITION OF TERMS

In any discussion of educational philosophy it is necessary to define terms carefully and to specify the context in which they are used. Toward that end, by **science** we mean knowledge that is concerned with the physical world and all its phenomena. The physical, or external, world is a realm of space and objects—both animate and inanimate—each of which has a location and exists in time. The biological and social *sciences*, then, focus on living, or animate, things, such as the factors affecting the growth of plants and animals, or finding cures for diseases, or understanding the causes of juvenile delinquency. A scientific experiment seeks to isolate physical factors or variables and then to observe how they function in special, often-prepared laboratory settings.

[1]Harry S. Broudy, *Building a Philosophy of Education* (Englewood Cliffs, N.J.: Prentice-Hall, 1961), 17–18.

Such a scientific investigation is the basis for **empiricism**—the idea that all knowledge is derived from observation and experience through the process of verification or confirmation. In **empirical verification** the variable or set of variables under scrutiny is observed directly. For example, when Ivan Pavlov conditioned a hungry dog to salivate upon hearing a bell ring (see Chapter 6), he actually observed the dog salivating *after* the bell rang. But it is not always possible to observe a phenomenon directly—especially in the social sciences. In that case, **empirical confirmation** is used; the experimenter is an expert who places a high degree of probability on what occurred in the experiment. In other words, the expert *confirms* that a particular result occurred under the specified conditions. If, for example, starved rats become aggressive but the aggression subsides when they are fed, it is concluded that their behavior change very probably resulted from a reduction in physiological tension when the food was digested. The experimenters cannot directly observe the reduction in tension; they can only confirm it by observing the behavior change. Social science research has gained a great deal of sophistication through the development of statistical techniques that allow researchers to confirm a significant degree of probability in experiments.

In both of these examples we can see that science is concerned with isolating physical factors or variables, manipulating them in controlled settings, and then verifying or confirming changes that occur. Therefore, scientific research questions usually aim to learn which factors are involved in particular changes or how those factors vary in relation to each other. If an experiment is designed and controlled correctly, its results can be generalized to other situations of its kind. For example, when specific dosages of nicotine produce cancerous tumors in laboratory rats, we can conclude that the same amount of nicotine will also produce cancerous tumors in all rats outside the lab and in other mammals of the same size. In fact, we have generalized a step or two further by saying that smoking cigarettes and breathing ''second-hand'' smoke is hazardous to human health. Generalizing beyond the group or species that was used in an experiment has created controversy, among scientists as well as laypeople. Nevertheless, such a research model, or paradigm, has been the dominant way that science has increased our understanding of physical, biological, and (to a lesser degree) social phenomena. Thus a **paradigm** is a carefully delineated model or template that guides research and allows us to add to our knowledge.[2] The science paradigm just described is based on one of the philosophical systems that we will examine in this chapter: modern realism.

Philosophy, in contrast to all this, is not empirical; it is speculative, and it is concerned with meaning and understanding, with discovery and description. It often takes up the cause when science cannot produce explanations or answers. The word *philosophy* literally means ''pursuit of wisdom,'' and traditionally, it has sought wisdom in several related fields that introduce yet more terminology. The main fields of philosophy are (1) metaphysics, including cosmology and ontology; (2) epistemology; and (3) axiology, including ethics and aesthetics.

METAPHYSICS   **Metaphysics** is concerned with the nature of reality. As such,

[2] For a discussion of research paradigms and their history, see Thomas S. Kuhn, *The Structure of Scientific Revolutions* (Chicago: University of Chicago Press, 1970).

it includes **cosmology**, which deals with the universe as an orderly system, and **ontology**, which focuses on the nature of being. Metaphysics seeks to answer such questions as: What is the self? Is existence only a physical reality, or does existence transcend the physical world? How "real" are trees, the sky, and so on? Early in the eighteenth century, one of the central metaphysical questions was posed neatly by the philosopher and Anglican priest George Berkeley (1685–1753), who asked: If a tree falls in the forest and no living being is a witness, is there sound, or does it take auditory receptors for sound to be produced?

EPISTEMOLOGY   **Epistemology** is concerned with the nature of human knowledge and its limits. This category of philosophy is concerned with theories of knowledge and seeks to answer such questions as: What role do our senses play in giving us knowledge? Are there higher forms of knowledge than what we experience? What are the methods of validating ideas? How do we learn? As we saw in Chapter 6, recent advances in cognitive science have revealed much about how human beings process and organize information into knowledge. So science is attempting to answer many epistemological questions. But philosophers are still speculating about the nature of knowledge and how we know it.

A subfield of epistemology is **logic**, or the rules and principles of reasoning. The primary forms of logic are **inductive reasoning**, or making a generalization on the basis of a specific proposition; and **deductive reasoning**, or concluding something specific from a general proposition. Inductive reasoning is usually the kind of logic used in scientific research, as can be seen in the examples given earlier. One of the most common forms of deductive reasoning is the **syllogism**, which procedes as follows: If *A* is equal to *B* and *B* is equal to *C*, then *A* is equal

One of the central questions: If a tree falls in the forest and no living being is around to hear it, is there sound? The answer depends on your philosophy, which often takes up the cause when science cannot produce explanations or answers. —Cary Wolinsky/Stock, Boston

to *C.* Here's a more concrete example: If John is related to Jim and Jim is related to Karen, then John is related to Karen. During the Middle Ages some Christian philosophers tried to prove that God is particularly human, and their argument went this way: If God is the Trinity and the Trinity is three particular persons (the Father, the Son, and the Holy Ghost), then God is three particular persons. Those who were especially outspoken about this belief eventually were charged with heresy, and their argument was deemed false. An argument can be valid in its form and still be false in content.

AXIOLOGY   A third category of philosophy is axiology, which includes ethics and aesthetics. **Axiology** is the study of values, both in regulating human conduct (ethics) and in determining beauty (aesthetics).

Ethics seeks to answer questions about what is right and wrong, or good and bad, both personally and socially. For example, what is the nature of morality? Is it absolute, or does the situation define what is correct behavior? Is it ever right to take another's life, as those in the "Right to Die" movement believe? Or are moral principles universal and timeless, regardless of the situation?

Aesthetics addresses questions about the nature of beauty in art, drama, literature, and music. Is beauty a matter of personal taste, or are there principles that determine what is beautiful? Does beauty change from generation to generation, or is it timeless? Is classical music really "classic"? Is today's music really beautiful, or is it merely noise (as many older people seem to think)? Or are such questions a matter of individual judgment?

TRADITIONAL PHILOSOPHICAL SYSTEMS   Beginning in ancient times, four complete systems of philosophy have evolved. Each has a distinctive way of speculating about metaphysics, epistemology, and axiology. Because each approach thoroughly investigates these three categories—reality, knowledge, and value—each is called a **philosophical system**. In the order in which they emerged, the four philosophical systems are idealism, realism, pragmatism, and existentialism. Next we will examine how each system approaches metaphysics, epistemology, and axiology. (Figure 10.1 summarizes the tenets of these systems, and you will want to refer to it frequently as you make your way through the chapter.)

METAPHYSICS: WHAT IS "REAL"?

■

IDEALISM AND REALITY

The oldest system in Western culture is idealism, which dates back to Socrates and Plato in ancient Greece. Generally, **idealism** holds that *ideas* are the source of reality. Although idealists do not deny that the material world exists, they distrust it because it constantly changes and is characterized by instability. Ideas, on the other hand, are more permanent and enduring.

Plato's Allegory of the Cave demonstrates the difference between the material world and the ideal. In his story prisoners are chained together facing the wall of a cave so that all they can see are the shadows on the wall—shadows that in reality are formed by the world outside the cave. The prisoners have come to believe that the shadows themselves are reality. Imagine one of them getting free and walking out of the cave into the sunlight. That prisoner will then realize that the sun is the source of the light, which reflects objects outside the cave; but the other prisoners do not believe this. Rather, they continue to believe in the shadows, much as (according to idealists) we believe in the material world; we are chained to it by our inability to search for eternal truths and by our lack of concern for what is real.

Plato trusted in the study of mathematics because it shows us that truth can be permanent. Such propositions as that the shortest distance between two points is a straight line and that $3 + 3 = 6$ have always been true, even before people discovered them. Hence, for Plato, the philosopher's quest was a search for universal truth, not only in mathematical fields but in politics, science, religion, and education. The conceptual world of ideas transcends the perceptual world of sensory data and is thus more real.

During the late period of the Roman Empire and the early Middle Ages, idealism became the basis for Christianity. In Platonic idealism the highest form in the world of ideas is the Good. For Christianity it was an easy step to equate this transcendental Good with a transcendental, spiritual God. St. Augustine (354–430) accepted Plato's division of matter and idea, but he preferred to characterize the two realms as the world of human beings (matter) and the world of God (ideal). In his book *The City of God*, darkness, ignorance, sin, and pain come from human qualities, while the world of God holds beauty, light, truth, and happiness. People attain the world of God, he said, only after death; but they can approach it through a life of meditation and contemplation.

During the seventeenth and eighteenth centuries, modern idealism emerged through the works of René Descartes (1596–1650), George Berkeley (1685–1753), Immanuel Kant (1724–1804), and Georg Wilhelm Friedrich Hegel (1770–1831). Descartes added a methodological doubt to idealism; he tried to discover ideas that were undoubtable by doubting everything. Today his approach is known as the **Cartesian method**, and through it Descartes found that he could doubt everything except the fact that he was thinking while he was doubting. As he put it, in Latin: *Cogito ergo sum* (''I think, therefore I am''). This became the first true idea in Cartesian philosophy, and it is in keeping with Platonic idealism because it makes the mind the main force in relation to human beings and the environment.

Berkeley believed that reality was dependent on some mind's perceiving it. In the classic argument about a tree falling—and whether or not there is sound if no living being is around to hear it—he concluded that there is sound, because God is there to perceive it. His strongest critic was David Hume (1711–1766), who said that we have no way to ascertain the reality of material or spiritual substances. Hume represented the empirical viewpoint of objective science, while Berkeley was an adherent of subjective, rational idealism.

Attempting to consolidate rationalism and empiricism, Kant developed a different line of reasoning. Concerned with how a subjective mind can know objective reality, he concluded that the mind cannot know the actual object or

FIGURE 10.1   Summary of Philosophical Systems

SYSTEMS	METAPHYSICS (Theory of ultimate reality): — COSMOLOGY (Universe) — ONTOLOGY (Nature of being)	EPISTOMOLOGY (Nature of knowledge and theories of learning and teaching)	
IDEALISM	Ultimate reality transcends physical world, is spiritual or mental Ideas are more timeless than objects Humans have inborn talents and can make choices	Sensory knowledge is not to be trusted Knowledge is inborn; it emerges through logical, rational study	
REALISM	Physical world exists and is based on natural law	Sensory knowledge is valid	
A. CLASSICAL	Humans have transcendental nature, can make chioces	Reality has a higher, transcendental form	
B. NEO–THOMIST	Humans have transcendental, Divinely created nature, can make choices	Sensory knowledge is valid, but higher forms are Divinely created	
NATURAL REALISM (Scientific)	Reality is independent of the mind perceiving it Humans are determined, do not make substantive choices	All knowledge is sensory and is subjected to complex mental processes	
PRAGMATISM	Reality is experiential, an interaction between humans and their environment Humans make choices, are responsible for choices	Knowledge results from reflective, experiential, problem solving	
EXISTENTIALISM	Physical world exists but is meaningless to humans Reality is individual choice in "becoming" human	Knowledge is matter of individual interest, curiosity	
ANALYTIC PHILOSOPHY	Philosophy is not a system; it is an activity, a critique of language that solves linguistic confusion and dilemmas through empirical verification, confirmation, and linguistic analysis		

"thing-in-itself" (noumenon). The mind can only know its experience or perception of the object (phenomenon). Kant also concluded that science is limited by antinomies (contradictions or paradoxes) and that religion is limited by paralogisms (fallacious or illogical reasoning). His philosophy is dualistic in that it permanently separates mind from matter. In his view, we can never become totally rational because we are implicated by our physical nature, which is reflected in human emotion and passion.

Hegel saw the individual as a spiritual entity—a fragment of the Absolute Idea, or eternal spirit. We each are but part of a highly organized system in which opposing rational and natural forces produce syntheses that are in tune with the

AXIOLOGY (Nature of values): — ETHICS (Moral values) — AESTHETICS (Sensory values)	EDUCATIONAL OUTCOMES	PHILOSOPHERS
Values are absolute, do not change in time There are universal standards for beauty	A liberal study to develop inborn talents, rationality	Plato Hegel Royce Emerson
Values are permanent, objective, exist independently of the mind Arts reflects spiritual, universal nature There is univeral law available to reason Humans need God's help to practice universal law Art reflects spiritual, Divine nature	Comprehensive study of empirical, useful knowledge taught by experts in disciplined environment The above includes religious study	Aristotle Locke Bacon Aquinas Maritain Montessori
Ethical behavior is based on science Art should reflect nature		
Values, morality have social context Art reflects consensus	Study based on tested experience, students' needs, interests; learning by doing (includes reflective, conceptual thinking)	Peirce James Dewey Young
Values reflect individual choices, do not impinge on others' choices Art reflects individual choice	Liberal humanities that provide personal insight into life	Kierkegaard Sartre Buber
		Russell Wittgenstein Schefflers

opposing forces that produced them. A look at history revealed such a system to Hegel. He thought, for example, that every historical period has a thesis which is opposed by an antithesis and that the two opposing forces move toward a synthesis; the synthesis then becomes the next period's thesis. To Hegel, human culture was evolving toward freedom and toward conscious awareness of free spirit in all human beings. This would be the final stage—the final synthesis—in the opposition between idea and matter. Hegel called this evolution a *dialectical process.* Harvard philosopher Josiah Royce (1855–1916) became a spokesperson for Hegelian idealism in America, as did poet Ralph Waldo Emerson (1803–1882) and U.S. Commissioner of Education William Torrey Harris (1835–1909).

In general, then, idealists believe that for every sensible (perceivable) object there is an essence—a universal organizing principle or idea—which is the real or permanent truth. Thus, besides the physical object of a chair, for example, there is the concept of a chair that will endure long after the physical chair is broken or destroyed. For Christian idealists essence is revealed in a personal, spiritual, anthropomorphic God; for others essence is seen as an impersonal universal mind—all-embracing, all-rational—which expresses itself in everything that exists. Yet there is a division, a dichotomy, between the world of sensation and the idea(l) world. We human beings have a spiritual, rational essence that is housed in a physical body. According to idealists, we have free will and can choose to develop our inborn talents and potentials, or we can choose to ignore the development of our potentials.

REALISM AND REALITY

CLASSICAL AND RELIGIOUS REALISM   Like idealism, realism also is rooted in ancient Greece, but it reflects the thinking of Plato's pupil Aristotle (384–322 B.C.). Essentially, he disagreed with his master by emphasizing the importance of the physical world. Aristotle also believed in ideal forms, but he thought that one could better understand them by studying physical matter. For example, every chair has certain physical properties, such as size, weight, shape, color, and material substance. The properties are different for different chairs, but they are part of the idea or essence of a chair—its ideal form is universally the same for

Idealists Socrates and Plato held that ideas are the source of all reality and are more enduring than the material world. Aristotle, Plato's student, was a realist; he emphasized study of the physical world as a means to understanding ideal forms.
—Art Resource, NY

all chairs, past, present, and to come. Instead of placing an object's essence or idea outside it, or transcendental to it, as Plato did, Aristotle said that an object's ideal form or essence was within its matter and was the motivating force that helped it fulfill its purpose.

Regarding human beings, Aristotle concluded that our essence or ideal form was our rationality. In his view there was no dichotomy between mind and matter, because our body can provide our reason or mind with data from sensory perceptions of the environment. He also believed that it is important for people to develop their rational powers through a contemplative life, which will bring happiness. Rational persons will realize that extremes are to be avoided and replaced by a life of moderation—a path between two extremes, which he called the Golden Mean. However, because human beings have free will and can be led astray, not everyone will choose a life of study and moderation. Some will eat too much or smoke, and they may suffer from obesity and poor health by deviating from the Golden Mean. Some people's happiness will be influenced by fame, power, or wealth—all of which can be lost suddenly. Only knowledge and wisdom gained through study are intrinsic to the human form and cannot be taken away.

To help him understand the structure of the ideal world that the mind comprehended, Aristotle also developed logic, especially reasoning based on the syllogism. He argued that all objects and matter point the way toward understanding an ultimate source of power—a god, or an ultimate reality. He called this source the First Cause, and he thought of it as a logical explanation for the design, order, and purpose of the universe. (Indeed, modern science has discovered many principles that underlie the physical aspects of the universe.)

Proponents of **classical realism** subscribe to Aristotle's beliefs, and they also accept Plato's views about human free will and a transcendental or spiritual realm. But they do not necessarily believe that the spiritual dimension is Divinely created. **Religious realism** is philosophically compatible with classical realism, except that it does include a Divine dimension. It was developed in the theology of St. Thomas Aquinas (1225–1274), who used Aristotle's ideas as the underpinning of his Christian philosophy (Thomism, or Neo-Thomism). Aquinas argued that both matter and spirit were created by God and are part of a rational and orderly universe. Taking Aristotle's concept of *entelechy* (the potential to actualize), Aquinas held that God materialized in the soul of the human body. Hence, a human being fuses spirit and matter and, therefore, is immortal.

SCIENTIFIC REALISM   Scientific realism began developing with the works of Francis Bacon (1561–1626) and ultimately benefited from advances in astronomy and mathematics. Bacon's chief contribution was a method of inductive reasoning that generalized from particular *observable* situations. This approach differed from Aristotle's deductive thinking, which began with an assumption or a hypothesis. Hence, Bacon's ideas came into opposition with Thomism.

Following Bacon's reasoning, John Locke (1632–1704) sought to explain how knowledge was developed and stored in the mind, which he said was a *tabula rasa* ("blank tablet") at birth. Locke was an empiricist and had no use for idealism. He thought that objects have primary, secondary, and tertiary qualities.

RESEARCH SAYS

For Tomorrow's Education . . .
Some educational researchers are turning to science to redefine the philosophy of realism so that conflicts among various approaches to educational research might be resolved. See, for example, Ernest R. House, "Realism in Research," *Educational Researcher* 20 (August–September 1991): 2–9, 25.

Primary qualities are characteristics that are measurable and quantitative (such as characteristics associated with an object's size and shape). Secondary qualities are associated with an object's color, flavor, texture, smell, and sound—the characteristics we discover through our senses. And tertiary qualities are those we learn about by working with an object (such as the combustibility of wood or the hardness of a diamond). Locke thought that everyone experiences primary qualities in the same way but that we experience secondary qualities differently. In other words, everyone can agree that a particular amount of spinach weighs 1 pound, but not everyone will agree that its taste is pleasant.

In general, **scientific realism** holds that the physical world is real and permanent and that changes take place in accordance with natural laws. An idea is true if it conforms to those aspects of the world that it claims to describe. But scientific realists do not believe in a spiritual realm, because that cannot be observed. As human beings we are biological organisms with highly developed nervous systems; we are determined by the impact of physical and social factors on our genetic makeup. Thus we have no free will or choice. To scientific realists, choice is an illusion.

PRAGMATISM AND REALITY

This American philosophy—like idealism and realism—is also rooted in Greek thought. In fact, the word *pragmatism* comes from a Greek word meaning "work." Therefore, as a philosophical system, pragmatism is concerned with finding processes and solutions that attain agreeable and appropriate results.

Pragmatism developed into a full-blown philosophical system at the University of Chicago during the early 1900s, when John Dewey and his colleagues published a series entitled *Contributions to Education.*[3] Pragmatists accept the material world as an important part of reality, and they also embrace Darwin's evolutionary theories, especially as they relate to the development of species. But pragmatism is less concerned with "ultimate" reality and more concerned with how human beings interact with their environments; consequently, it focuses on experience as the source of reality. Human beings grow by associating with others in social settings.

Besides Dewey, two other Americans contributed greatly to the development of pragmatism. Charles Sanders Peirce (1839–1914) gave the system its theory of logic, which regards all ideas or concepts in terms of their conse-

[3]John Dewey, ed., *Contributions to Education* (Chicago: University of Chicago Press, 1904).

Pragmatist John Dewey accepted the importance of the material world but was less concerned with ultimate reality and more concerned with the effects of ideas and objects on human beings. For pragmatists, human experience is the source of reality. —Bettmann

quences or effects on human conditions. For Peirce, the facts of the material world are ascertained by scientists; but ideas and objects take on meaning only in relation to their effects on human beings in social situations. Ideas are not knowledge until they are tested by human experience.

Harvard psychologist and philosopher William James (1842–1910) continued Peirce's line of thinking. James assessed ideas in terms of their "workability": There are no absolutes, no essences; the world is open-ended and in the process of changing. Since we cannot be certain that anything will endure, change is central to reality, and individuals have the right to create their own realities.

Finally, John Dewey (1859–1952) added his theory of *instrumentalism* to the views of Peirce and James, by viewing ideas as instruments that can be used to solve problems. Dewey did not separate nature from human experience; rather, he included the sensory experience of nature as part of reality, along with other experiences such as health, emotions, and social conditions.[4]

In general, then, **pragmatism** is a philosophical system that stresses the individual's experiences or interactions with the environment as the main source of reality. Human nature is fluid, flexible, social, and biological. We play an important role in creating our own realities, which makes us *responsible* for this reality process as it does for the social environment in which we interact.

To continue with the example of a chair as a measure of reality, we can conclude that pragmatists certainly would accept that the chair has an important

[4]See, for example, John Dewey, *Experience and Nature* (LaSalle, Ill.: Open Court, 1929); and *How We Think* (Boston: Heath, 1933).

physical presence. But its physical nature alone would not be compelling to pragmatists. They would define the chair's reality in terms of its meanings and uses for human beings.

EXISTENTIALISM AND REALITY

The newest of the four philosophical systems, existentialism emerged late in the nineteenth century and continued to develop throughout World War II (and beyond). With so little hindsight it is somewhat difficult to find the ideas that are common among those who contributed to this philosophy. Generally speaking, **existentialism** holds that human beings live in a meaningless and purposeless world. Although the material nature of the universe is considered real, its existence is absurd to humanity. Instead, what is important to us as individuals are the choices that we make throughout our lives—the focus is on the process of living and on becoming human. Thus, for existentialists, the essence of reality is choice, and we are each fully responsible for the choices we make. Existentialists refer to this continuous choosing throughout life as the process of "becoming." In fact, the only choice that a person does not have to make is whether or not to be born. Existing is our unfortunate predicament ("unfortunate" because it brings the burden of responsibility for all other choices).

The first thinker to develop the existential point of view was Danish philosopher Sören Kierkegaard (1813–1855), who reacted negatively to Hegelian idealism because of all its systemization and submission of the individual to the state. Kierkegaard was a devout Christian who felt that most Christians did not lead truly Christian lives. He noticed, for example, that city officials would "wheel and deal" for six days of the week and then attend church on Sunday. To him this was hypocritical, not Christlike. He concluded that an individual was *defined* by his or her actions: If you act like a Christian, you are; if you act like a "wheeler-dealer," you are.

Kierkegaard went on to describe the individual as lonely, as existing in an impersonal, cold, and scientific world. He said that we know this cold reality through feelings of dread and anxiety, which make us aware of "being." Through fear, we learn what death must be like and thus what its opposite is: existence. At this point we begin to realize that we define ourselves through our actions and that we are completely responsible for them. We know that we are in the process of "becoming," and we accept the burden of choosing.

Vienna-born Martin Buber (1878–1965) moved to Palestine in 1938 and was a professor of social philosophy at Hebrew University in Jerusalem. He believed that a person "becomes" only through a lifelong dialog or communion of the self with the other, which he characterized as an "I-Thou" interaction. In contrast, a "subject-object" or "I-It" relationship he saw as being brought about by our technological, mechanistic world, which teaches us to view everything external to ourselves as part of objective, scientific reality. The problem with this orientation, he said, is that we come to treat other human beings as objects to be manipulated and exploited for our own selfish purposes. However, by developing a lifelong I-Thou dialog, we "become" aware of the true interaction: one

Existentialist Jean-Paul Sartre held that reality is always a human creation. We choose reality, and—through our actions—we choose what we want to become. Such freedom brings the burden of responsibility; each of us is accountable for our actions, for who we are. —Culver Pictures

human being communing with another. Thus we communicate with the other(s) out of our need to be fulfilled as human beings.

Jean-Paul Sartre (1905–1980) added another dimension to the existential perspective. Through his anti-Nazi activities with the French underground during World War II, he came to realize that human rationality (so prized by eighteenth-century Enlightenment thinkers) had not put an end to human destruction and selfishness. While facing death in a Nazi prison camp, Sartre wrote one of his major works: *L'Être et le Néant* ("Being and Nothingness"). In this book he delves into the meaning of consciousness. He concludes that the world has created a human consciousness which tries to play the roles that were assigned to it, either by an absurd and scientifically objective universe or by a God-created universe. According to Sartre, all such "realities" are human creations. Once we realize this, we are free to become whatever we want to become—free to do whatever we choose to do—instead of being what we think we are supposed to be.

In many ways existentialism has taken a new look at Aristotle's idea of essences and has discovered a different dimension. For existentialists, a person's inherent nature is not the sum of his or her rational powers; rather, a person's essence is the sum of his or her actions, which are based on emotions and feelings as well as on rationality. In short, we are what our actions make us, not what our thoughts make us.

To return again to the example of a chair, existentialists agree that the chair exists and has functions and properties. But they think it is meaningless and silly to spend any time being concerned about such things. The important issue is to have a meaningful I-Thou dialogue, whether sitting on a chair, the floor, the ground or standing.

EPISTEMOLOGY: WHAT IS "KNOWLEDGE"?

■

IDEALISM AND KNOWLEDGE

Idealists' beliefs about knowledge follow from their metaphysical, or ontological, perspective. Basically, since ideas are the source of reality, sensory knowledge is to be distrusted because it does not give a true picture of reality and may even be misleading. True knowledge is based on reason and is born within each individual as ideas to be developed. However, not everyone is born with the same idea potential.

Plato recognized that mental talent is distributed across a population, and so he devised an idealistic framework that made education a central focus of the utopian state he depicted in the *Republic*. He described his educational scheme through the Allegory of the Metals. Because people are not born with equal talents, it is necessary, according to Plato, to tell them that the gods had framed them differently. Some people are like iron in that they are predominantly guided by passions and not rationality. Others are like copper in that physical strength is their main talent. Finally, there are those who are rational: The most rational men are like gold and should be trained to rule; other, less rational men are like silver and can best serve society as lesser officials, officers, and administrators.

In Plato's *Republic* all children are wards of the state, rather than belonging to their parents or guardians. At an early age, boys enter public nurseries to learn health, physical education, religion, and patriotism. At age six they are sent to a palestra (elementary school), where they continue their elementary studies. At age eighteen all young men are tested to separate out the iron, who will fill the lowest occupational and military positions. From eighteen to twenty all men serve in the military, and then the remaining three groups (copper, silver, and gold) begin an advanced course of study that Plato referred to as philosophical. At age thirty these men are tested to sift out the copper, who will become soldiers and occupy social levels above the iron. From thirty to thirty-five the remaining men pursue a very abstract course of study, after which they are given a final test to separate out the silver, who will occupy the second-highest rung of the social ladder. The gold then enter into a communal existence and spend the next fifteen years studying and mingling with society in an altruistic fashion. At age fifty these men will become the rulers—the philosopher-kings who combine rationality with power.[5]

Like Plato, most idealists greatly value education, seeing it as the means to preserve a culture's traditions and pass its heritage to future generations. They view people as rational beings who can attain truth through thought. Therefore, an "ideal" education not only should develop thinking and rationality but also should help individuals discover lasting ideas and truths.

For religious idealists, the search for truth (knowledge) is a spiritual search for God. For Hegelian idealists, knowledge is true and valid to the extent that it forms a system—and the more comprehensive the system, the more truth it holds. For followers of Kant, the mind has to have something to work on, and the senses provide that. Therefore, they give more credence to sensory data than

[5]*The Republic*, Benjamin Jowett, trans., in *Great Books*, 7 (Chicago: Encyclopaedia Britannica, 1953): 388–401.

most idealists do. (Kant called sensory information "precepts" and the ideas that arise from sensory data he labeled "concepts.")[6]

Character development is another important aim of education, because idealists believe that a person should be balanced or, as we might say today, well rounded. Thus a truly educated person is intellectually astute, of good character, healthy, and physically attractive. For Socrates and Plato, such adjectives described a virtuous person, which they required all teachers to be. In general, idealists regard the teacher as a model, an example for students to emulate.[7]

For Hegelians, education and human growth occur throughout a series of dialectical stages that can be studied historically. For most idealists, however, education centers on study of the classics. Philosopher and University of Chicago Professor Mortimer Adler, for example, advocates specialized study of the classics based on selections found in the Great Books. His complete educational approach is found in *The Paedeia Proposal: An Educational Manifesto*. He uses the Greek word *Paedeia* in its traditional sense, which refers to the totality of a child's upbringing.[8]

For idealists, then, the educational process encourages and helps students to mature in accordance with their inborn potentials. Knowledge is "wrung out," not "poured in." Idealists see schooling as preparation for life. Through education students learn to become valuable citizens who will take their places in the social order—after they have been prepared to be the best that they can be, given their nature and talent.[9]

REALISM AND KNOWLEDGE

All proponents of realism agree that knowledge comes to us first through our senses, which bring us into contact with the physical world. Empirical data are thus an essential source of knowledge, and—because students learn about the world through their senses—experience is a crucial element in learning. It is also important that the process be controlled and orderly.

Both classical and religious realists believe that there is a higher spiritual order which human beings can attain or know by transcending the material world. Romanticists Ralph Waldo Emerson (1803–1882) and Henry David Thoreau (1817–1862), for example, believed that nature can be transcended and that higher realms can be reached through the power of thought and meditation. Neo-Thomists believe that transcendental experiences lead to knowledge of God and, consequently, should be the aim of all education. Thus they view the church as the primary education agent, since spiritual knowledge comes from revelation, the Bible, and prophecy.

Scientific realists emphasize empirical knowledge, because knowing the material world increases a person's ability to survive and also advances the frontiers of science and technology. They also believe that rigorous, disciplined study is necessary for learning and that certain essential types of knowledge must be taught (rather than permitting students and parents to determine the curriculum). Essential subjects include the "three Rs," advanced mathematics, science, and the liberal arts. Organizations such as the Council for Basic Education have been formed to promote this type of realistic education. In addition, scientific realists believe that individuals have the ability to undertake complex thought

[6]Van Cleve Morris and Young Pai, *Philosophy and the American School* (Boston: Houghton Mifflin, 1976), 128.

[7]Colvin Ross, "An Educational Philosophical Inventory: An Instrument for Measuring Change and Determining Philosophical Perspective," *Journal of Thought* 4 (1970): 20–26; and *Test Manual and Specimen Set: Ross Educational Philosophical Inventory* (Storrs, Conn.: 1969).

[8]Mortimer J. Adler, *The Paedeia Proposal: An Educational Manifesto* (New York: Macmillan, 1982), 1–29.

[9]William E. Hug, "Are You Philosophically Consistent?" *Science Education* 54 (1970): 185–186.

Ella Flagg Young
1845–1918

John Dewey said that Mrs. Young was a practicing pragmatist long before the doctrine was ever in print. She had helped him formulate his form of that philosophy, known as instrumentalism, and he said that she constantly gave him ideas that translated his theories into practical outcomes.

Born Ella Flagg in Buffalo, New York, on January 15, 1845, she was the youngest of three children. Her mother regarded her as delicate and sickly, and she was kept out of school to benefit from fresh air and sunshine. Her father worked at a forge, and Ella spent hours visiting him there and asking questions about his work. She was a curious child who taught herself to read by age nine, and then she read everything she could; she also taught herself to write. Finally, by age eleven, Ella's mother let her enter school, and she liked it immediately. She soon became a class monitor (helper) in math.

In 1858, when Ella was thirteen, the family moved to Chicago, where foundry management opportunities were better for Mr. Flagg. Ella was ready for high school, having completed the grammar grades in Buffalo, but she was told that she needed to complete one more year. She soon became bored with the repetition and dropped out of school. In 1860 she had the opportunity to enter the normal department of the high school, and in two years she was ready to graduate. (She set up her own practice teaching arrangement; such training was not

Yesterday's Professional

part of the regular program at the time.)

In the fall of 1862 Ella began teaching in the Chicago schools, and over the next thirty-seven years she experienced every aspect of them: elementary and secondary teacher, head of practice teaching, principal of a large grammar school, and, finally, assistant and district superintendent. In 1862 she also married William Young, an older family friend who died shortly after the marriage.

In 1899 Young resigned from the superintendency to study full time at the University of Chicago, under John Dewey, and in 1900 she earned a Ph.D. Her dissertation was published as a book; entitled *Isolation in the School*, it described how the tenets of pragmatism can be ap-

processes which relate them to the environment. Following Locke's notion that an infant's mind is a "blank tablet," they see knowledge as being "poured in," not "wrung out." The methods to accomplish this are logical and psychological, such as the behavioral techniques described in Chapter 6.

To realists, the teacher is the expert who decides which essentials are to be learned and the manner in which they should be taught. Critics of a realistic education charge that—by promoting objective, empirical knowledge of a fixed, rational, and physical universe—it sacrifices knowledge relating to an individual's emotions and irrational impulses. Those who oppose scientific realism further charge that behavioral techniques are too mechanistic and treat students and education as an exercise in robotics.

PRAGMATISM AND KNOWLEDGE

Pragmatists see education as an interactive process between an individual and the environment; its purpose is to promote individual growth and social change. Although pragmatists acknowledge that the physical world exists, they do not view it as a "thing" waiting to be known. Rather, the physical world is to be

(Box continued)

plied to curricula and school management. Young joined the faculty at the University of Chicago and contributed to a series that Dewey edited about philosophy and education. In general, her greatest contribution to education was the ability to apply philosophical and theoretical concepts in the classroom.

In 1904 both Dewey and Young left the University of Chicago. Dewey went to Teachers College, at Columbia University in New York, and Young became principal of the Chicago Normal School—the position held by Francis Wayland Parker a few years earlier. In 1909 she was appointed superintendent of Chicago's schools, becoming the first woman to head a major public school system, and her appointment was front-page news in the *New York Times*. During the first several years, when she had the support of the school board, her administration was progressive and pragmatic. But toward the end of her six-year term, political struggles emerged as her administration dealt with the growing Chicago Teachers Federation (CTF), a powerful women's union whose members—under Margaret Haley—were seeking greater control over their professional lives.

At first Young was successful in reconciling differences between the CTF and Chicago's board of education; in fact, they jointly supported her successful bid for

the presidency of the National Education Association (1909–1910), which was another first for a woman. But by the end of 1913 tensions had arisen, and the board failed to reappoint Dr. Young. Many said that this resulted from a plot by a few board members who disliked Young's recognition of the CTF. In any case, the citizens of Chicago were very concerned about this move and held mass protest meetings all over the city; the board was pressured by the public and the mayor to reinstate Young. She remained superintendent for two more years, until 1915, when she retired at age seventy.

During retirement Young visited school systems throughout the country, and she planned to write a book about schools. But the outbreak of World War I changed her plans; she joined the Liberty Loan Committee and traveled the country selling war bonds. In 1918 she fell victim to Spanish flu, which had reached epidemic proportions. Nevertheless, she refused to take care of herself until she had safely deposited her loan revenues with the secretary of state in Washington. By then she had pneumonia, and she died in the nation's capital on October 28, 1918.

Source: Based on Joan K. Smith, Ella Flagg Young: Portrait of a Leader (*Ames, Iowa: Educational Studies Press/Iowa State University Research Foundation, 1979*).

understood through an individual's interactive experiences with it. Thus pragmatic education is a "process of" acquiring knowledge, not an "end to" learning. The process always involves individual growth, which, in turn, leads to more growth. The aim of the learning process is to become an effective solver of intellectual, social, and practical problems.

The pragmatic learning process begins when an individual experiences a new problem. As the person reflects on it, former problematic experiences are recalled, and the individual considers former solutions and their consequences. Finally the person chooses a solution from the viable alternatives. If the new problem is solved, the experience has taught the individual what to do in the next similar situation. But if the new problem is not solved, the individual learns that the solution was ineffective, and so that solution will not be tried again in similar situations. In other words, a student learns both from making correct (effective) choices and from making mistakes (ineffective choices). Again, education is a process, not a product, and the test of its success lies in its practical consequences.

For pragmatic educators the curriculum should train students in this problem-solving learning process. Among the labels to describe such a curriculum are the Project Method, the Project Approach, Problems-Centered Learning, and the Activity Method. Basically, students are presented with a problem. In solving it, they bring their past experiences to bear on it, along with resources that might help—books, videos, periodicals, field trips, interviews with experts, and so on. The classroom is designed to permit a great deal of flexibility. In fact, John Dewey and William Heald Kilpatrick (1871–1965) saw the classroom as a laboratory in which educational resources are the basis of experiments designed to confront new information and experiences. The interests and curiosity of students are essential ingredients in such problem-solving and learning, and the teacher acts as a director or facilitator in the process.

Critics of pragmatic approaches point out the difficulties of individualizing instruction to this great extent when there are twenty-five or thirty students in the class. Also, since students' interests drive the problem-solving process, some (or many) may miss essential instruction. For example, one student in Dewey's Laboratory School at the University of Chicago (1894–1904) said that he had never learned to spell, because he did not like spelling. Others admitted that to enter college they had to hire tutors to teach them math and science, which they had neglected at the lab school.[10]

EXISTENTIALISM AND KNOWLEDGE

"Who am I?" "Where am I going?" "How do I learn to make choices and be responsible for my actions?" These are central questions for existentialists, but it is difficult at best to design a curriculum and classroom around them. Taking a less speculative approach, existential educators have advocated a humanities-based curriculum that provides students with knowledge from others who have experienced and pondered life. Learning what the great thinkers and writers of the past have said about the human predicament and how to solve the human dilemma is a more manageable way to approach education.

Martin Buber developed the I-Thou relationship as an approach to education. He described it as a continuing dialog in which each student embarks on an adventure in the classroom and thus encounters the teacher. In turn, the teacher surveys the classroom of students in search of one genuine, inquiring face; that student and the teacher then enter into a communion, or meaningful dialog. Other students eventually join in when they grasp the meaning of the

[10]Richard J. Storr, *Harper's University: The Beginnings* (Chicago: University of Chicago Press, 1966), 297–301.

RESEARCH SAYS

For Tomorrow's Education . . .

In the realm of epistemology, the "immersion approach" shows promise of developing higher-level thinking in students. In this approach students are regarded as members of a "discourse community" that is actively engaged in the pursuit of common understandings. See Richard W. Prawat, "The Value of Ideas: The Immersion Approach to the Development of Thinking," *Educational Researcher* 20 (March 1991): 3–10, 30.

I-Thou dialog and are willing to take the risks and accept responsibility for their part in this relationship.

Buber acknowledged that other approaches were possible. But he cautioned that the student-teacher relationship should not include controlling behaviors that lead the teacher to treat students as objects. Buber was concerned about mechanistic trends in education (such as computer technology and the identification of students by social security numbers), and he stressed the importance of avoiding the I-It relationship in the teacher-student dialog.

For Sartre the trap in education lay in the roles that teachers and students *think* they should play—a teacher who tries to be all things to all students or a student who wants to be "perfect." Both may be so intent on avoiding "failure" that their relationship may become unnatural, inauthentic. Since Sartre held that success and failure are human creations, to accept those roles without choosing them would limit an individual's freedom and sidestep the issue of responsibility.

In general, existential educators want to end the controlling, manipulating practices that teachers and schools sometimes employ. They want students to learn to choose their own educational paths and to take responsibility for the choices they make. Existentialists are generally critical of the education system because of its reliance on bureaucracy, which they see as dehumanizing to individuals.

Critics of existential approaches to education argue that they glorify the individual and encourage students to seek ultimately selfish ends. This does not take into account the children whose environments do not permit choices. Those children's situations are real, the critics say, but existentialists provide no way for such students to handle reality. If no choices are possible, how can one be responsible for making them?

PHILOSOPHERS IN THE CLASSROOM

Now let's take a look at how an educational lesson might be approached by each philosophical system. Suppose the lesson is in geography. An idealist educator—especially a Hegelian one—would find the study important as the "actually existing concrete form of the earth, as the habitation of man. It is thus of immediate *practical* significance."[11] The educational significance of the lesson is that the subject is to be studied as a concrete representation of thought (idea). For example, in studying geography, students encounter universal principles, such as the spacial relations of land to water and of the earth to the sun. The educational purpose is an elementary one of orienting students in the "process of conscious self-adjustment to the actual present outer world," which, in turn, is "the concrete expression of Reason."[12]

To a realist educator the study of geography provides an opportunity for students to obtain a lot of empirical information about the earth: its size, the ratio of land to water, the composition of land, the location of mountain ranges and rivers, and so on.

A pragmatist educator sees geography as important because the earth is the habitat of human beings. To understand the earth's physical properties,

[11]William M. Bryant, *Hegel's Educational Ideas* (New York: AMS Press, 1971), 157.

[12]Ibid., 160–161.

students would draw maps and perhaps make a model of a particular area. The goal would be to relate the study of geography to human experience. Climate, natural resources, and crop patterns would be described in terms of their importance to people's survival and way of life.

For an existentialist educator the study of geography would describe the earth's physical properties as an impersonal habitat in which human beings must act. Stories about people who discovered or settled various parts of the earth—and the challenges they faced—might emphasize the I-thou dialog.

EPISTEMOLOGY AND THE NATIONAL TEACHER EXAMINATIONS

Recently, as part of the certification process for teachers, states have begun requiring candidates to complete a battery of tests known as the **National Teacher Examinations**. These tests reflect the epistemology of scientific realism, which assumes that there is a definable body of knowledge. In accepting this paradigm, states require all prospective teachers to master that knowledge before they can be certified. Designed by the Educational Testing Service (ETS), the core battery of tests consists of three selections:

1. *Test of Communication Skills* covers listening, reading, writing comprehension, and a written essay—each lasting 30 minutes.

2. *Test of General Knowledge* covers science, mathematics, social studies, and literature and fine arts (30 minutes each).

3. *Test of Professional Knowledge* comprises four 30-minute tests covering the candidate's comprehension of knowledge and skills needed for effective teaching.

Currently, the ETS is transforming the core battery so that education students will complete a series of more interactive tests over an extended time, beginning as undergraduates and ending after one year of teaching.

Besides the core battery, there is also a set of *Specialty Area Tests* that some states require for candidates who want to teach in specific fields. The specialty areas include Art Education, Biology and General Science, Business Education, Chemistry, Early Childhood Education, Educating the Mentally Handicapped, Education Administration, Elementary Education, English Language and Literature, French, Home Economics Education, Mathematics, Physical Education, School Guidance Counselor, School Psychologist, Social Studies, Spanish, and Special Education.[13]

The National Teacher Examinations are very controversial to educators who have not accepted the epistemological paradigm of scientific realism. For example, existentialists argue that these tests are conceptually based (rather than perceptually based) and have a subject-matter focus; therefore, they do not take individual and situational differences into account. In other words, the battery of tests does not cover knowledge relating to an individual's insights and interpersonal abilities. It also assumes that a teacher is to be an expert in theory and practice, rather than a person who interacts meaningfully with students.[14]

[13]Research & Education Association, *NTE Core Battery* (Piscataway, N.J.: Research & Education Association, 1991).

[14]See, for example, Harriet Morrison, "The Holmes Group Plan vs. a Phenomenological Scenario for Teacher Education: An Epistemological Methodological Comparison" (paper presented at the Annual Convention of the American Educational Research Association, San Francisco, 20–24 April 1992).

AXIOLOGY: WHAT IS "VALUE"?

IDEALISM AND VALUES

For idealists, ethics, or moral philosophy, is absolute and unchanging. What is right behavior today was also right conduct ten, a hundred, or a thousand years ago. In other words, how we ought to behave toward others and how we ought to act in situations like taking a test have a permanency that transcends time and cultures.

Idealists see social values as unchanging because they are part of the universe; they are not culture bound. The aims and laws that regulate human conduct are determined by a superior intellectual being.[15] Moral values form a world order of goodness and perfection. Hence, evil is disorganization and incomplete good.

For Hegel, as the spirit expresses itself, evil and ugliness disappear. Because we each are part of a whole system, we need to participate in society so that our moral natures can be realized. Plato and Hegel agreed that each individual has

RESEARCH SAYS

For Tomorrow's Education . . .

The teaching profession lacks a code of ethics and will fail to develop one as long as collective bargaining is at the core of the employee-employer relationship, according to Myron Lieberman in "Professional Ethics in Public Education," in *Phi Delta Kappan* 70 (October 1988): 159–160.

a special place and function within society, given his or her unique nature and talents. The "good life" is possible only within a highly organized society in which each person has a special niche. Carried to extremes, this view of society—with its submission of the individual to the whole social system—leads to totalitarianism. For Plato an oligarchy of wise men who combined wisdom with power (the philosopher-kings) was the best form of government.

Kant's moral view was less totalitarian. He thought that we should act as though our actions were to become a universal moral law that would be binding on all other people in a similar situation. He termed this idea the **categorical imperative**, and pragmatists also subscribe to it.

Consider an example of ethics in the classroom. Suppose you are teaching a sixth-grade class, and several students have been disruptive all day. It is time for afternoon recess, and you wonder whether you should use this time to deal with the disruptive students in some way. You might tell the class that no one can begin recess until every pupil is sitting quietly and all classroom materials are put away. If you think like an idealist—that the classroom is a microcosm of society and that every individual is part of the whole—you well might decide to detain the entire class, because the other students will put pressure on the few who have been uncooperative.

[15]Morris and Pai, *Philosophy and the American School*, 239–242.

"What is beauty?" That depends on what you think is real and how you know it. For idealists, beauty is timeless, outside an object; for realists, it obeys and reflects nature; for pragmatists, it results from experience; for existentialists, it is a choice. —Mark Antman/The Image Works

In terms of aesthetic values, idealists believe in the permanency of beauty. To them, the most worthy, most beautiful art strives to represent the ideal of human perfection—whatever its subject matter or artistic medium. For Plato satisfaction and efficiency were also important aesthetic qualities. For example, besides being beautiful, a building must be functional and must satisfy its intended purposes. Similarly, the sound of music must demonstrate precision and illuminate the perfect transcendental world.

REALISM AND VALUES

Realists believe that values are permanent and objective; that is, values exist independently of the mind. They are part of the laws of nature and are made available to us through our reasoning abilities. Realists also believe that values may *appear* to change because human beings lack complete knowledge of the universe. In short, we do not always realize that ethical and aesthetic values are constants. But realists say that moral laws (for example, against lying, cheating, stealing, and killing) are just as real as the law of gravity. For Thomas Jefferson and other Enlightenment thinkers, the human rights of "life, liberty and the pursuit of happiness" were also part of natural moral law.

Classical realists believe that there is a universal moral and spiritual law which is available to our reason. Thomists agree, but they add that the law has been established by God, who gave us reason. Although we can understand these laws rationally, we cannot practice them without God's help.

Scientific realists believe that ethical behavior and morality reflect what scientific investigation has shown to be true. For example, disease is evil, and

RESEARCH SAYS

For Tomorrow's Education . . .

In his 1991 presidential address to the American Educational Research Association, Professor Larry Cuban discussed some of the ethical dilemmas and conflicts of overlapping cultural values that educators face: the university culture, which values research, and the professional education school, whose purpose is to apply knowledge. See Larry Cuban, "Managing Dilemmas While Building Professional Communities," *Educational Researcher* 21 (January–February 1992): 4–11.

health is good. In this view, medicine strives toward goodness, because it helps us remain healthy. (Small wonder that the medical profession has such an exalted status, for it helps us attain this particular type of goodness!)

Let's look again at the disruptive classroom situation. If you think like a realist—behavioristically—you might remove the offending students from the room, until they are ready to behave appropriately. Meanwhile, the rest of the class can enjoy the recess period.

Regarding aesthetic values, realists believe that art must reflect nature. Therefore, it must be orderly and functional. An airplane is beautiful to the extent that it represents aerodynamic principles. A painting is a work of art when it accurately represents its subject, and music is pleasing when its sounds are precise and balanced like a mathematical formula. Thomists believe that art is created intuitively and comes from the spiritual realm of God.

PRAGMATISM AND VALUES

As philosophical systems, idealism and realism have focused on metaphysics—on the nature of reality—and their epistemology and axiology have grown out of that. In contrast, pragmatism has evolved in a reverse direction. Pragmatic philosophers have focused primarily on defining and explaining knowledge and values.

With regard to values, pragmatists deny any notion of permanent absolutes that are timeless and unrelated to social contexts. Instead, both ethical and aesthetic values are tied inextricably to the situation. Thus, good moral conduct is identified by the beneficial consequences that it yields for most of the people. If you think like a pragmatist in handling the disruptive sixth-grade students, you will not keep the entire class from recess, because that will not benefit the majority. Instead, like a realist, you let them have recess. But you also will want to see whether you can get to the bottom of the disruptive behavior. Perhaps the offending pupils feel like failures in the class, or perhaps they have personal problems that affect their classroom conduct. A pragmatist would act in favor of the majority but also would try to understand the problem better in order to help the disorderly students change their behavior and, hence, its negative consequences.

To pragmatists, ethical human conduct involves two conditions. First, pub-

Comparative Perspective on Today's Issues . . .

◆ *SHOULD FOOTBALL FANS PAY FOR ARCHERY CLASS?*

The Issue   Is it ethical to funnel money from the most popular high school sports back into those sports when other, less profitable sports programs might be canceled?

YES   This practice of funneling the "gate receipts" back into the programs that generated it, was a common practice and one that school personnel regarded as fair. After all, if a program cannot carry its own weight, it should be canceled. It is not the responsibility of the better fund-raising sports to foot the bill for sports that are less popular.

NO   This is not an issue of a sport's popularity but rather one of student fitness—of learning to do one's best while being part of a team and learning how to accept victory as well as defeat. High school sports are a valuable part of the curriculum, and their merits for individual athletes cannot be measured by their receipts.

Source: Based on Dennis Dempsey, "Ethics and the Principal: Five Vignettes," *NASSP Bulletin* 72 (December 1988): 21–25.

lic consensus dictates what is appropriate conduct. (That is why pragmatists view democracy as the best form of government, because it is based on majority rule.) Second, the situation reveals what is ethical. Although it generally is wrong to take a life, for example, if you are threatened by an armed intruder, your only choice may be to defend yourself by killing the intruder. Thus moral decisions are not absolute; they are determined by the action that brings the best results in a given situation.

Aesthetic values, to a pragmatist, are not determined by some expert or by some objective or transcendental standard. Art is beautiful if most people experience it as such, or if most people gain meaning or feeling from it. From a pragmatic point of view, if the Beatles' music is regarded as enjoyable by a majority of people, it has aesthetic value. Critics who might want to pan the Beatles will have to be ignored. Similarly, although the role of movie critics is to guide and direct public taste, it is box-office results that will tell pragmatists whether or not a particular movie has aesthetic value.[16]

EXISTENTIALISM AND VALUES

Because existentialism rests on the notion that choice is the essence of being and reality, it is often regarded as a value system, as a philosophy that is preoccupied with axiology. In existential terms, an individual's values are revealed by the choices he or she makes; or values *are* the choices an individual makes. There is no attempt to reach consensus, for an existentialist opposes public norms because they subordinate the individual's choices to pre-existing values. Existentialists deny that any values exist until an individual chooses.

[16]Hug, "Are You Philosophically Consistent?" 185–186.

Morality also depends on metaphysics. How would each philosophical system regard Jack Kervorkian, a doctor who assisted ill people in ending their lives? Which philosophy do you think he would espouse? Do you see him as "Doctor Death" or an "Angel of Mercy"?
—Blake Discher/Sygma

For similar reasons existentialists are against most forms of government, including democracy. Admitting that society needs some kind of political framework within which an individual lives and makes choices, existentialists generally submit to the form of government that least restricts personal freedom. In the United States the platform of the Libertarian party might be preferred, since it calls for minimal government involvement in personal affairs.

The English school Summerhill, founded in 1921 by A. S. Neill (1883–1973), is often regarded as fitting the ethical principles of existentialism. Classes at this residential school are conducted normally, but students have the choice of not attending. A student who chooses to attend, however, is expected to participate regularly so that no one slows down the rest of the class. In other words, a student who does not attend class regularly is not exhibiting ethical conduct because that person has not taken responsibility for having chosen to attend class.[17]

Similarly, returning again to the disruptive sixth-graders, they are not acting ethically, because they are not taking responsibility for coming to class. As an existentialist teacher, you might point out to them that, perhaps, they need to act responsibly for the choice they made in coming to class. In a broad sense this position is difficult to support, since the law requires these students to attend school. But their behavior in this instance is the issue, and existential choices are always made only in the present (or they are constantly remade in the present). In addition, of course, you can point out that they have chosen to act unfairly to you and to their classmates.

Aesthetically, an existentialist ultimately stands alone. What an individual

[17]A. S. Neill, *Summerhill: A Radical Approach to Child Rearing* (New York: Hart, 1960).

RESEARCH SAYS

For Tomorrow's Education . . .

Because teaching involves numerous ethical dilemmas, teachers need to know about ethical reasoning—particularly about applying principles to cases and judging the adequacy of those principles. See Kenneth A. Strike, "The Ethics of Teaching," *Phi Delta Kappan* 70 (October 1988): 156–158.

prefers in art is a matter of personal choice. Experts and critics can guide and serve as sources of information in making choices, but no one except the individual is to be regarded as an aesthetic authority. Other people's assessments of art are nothing more than their opinions, their choices. If *I* like the music of Madonna, then her music has beauty.

PHILOSOPHERS IN THE CLASSROOM

Now let's look at two axiological situations—one ethical, and one aesthetic—from the viewpoint of each philosophical system. Suppose that Jenny, a third-grader, has come to school in an angry mood. As she enters the classroom, she pushes Phoebe and shouts, "Get out of my way!" Phoebe pushes Jenny back, yelling, "Stop that!" If Mr. Hill, the teacher, is an idealist, he probably will ask Jenny to correct her behavior, and he also might point out to the rest of the class how dysfunctional both students' conduct is. If Hill is a realist, he might remove Jenny from the classroom until she can behave properly, meanwhile reprimanding Phoebe by saying, "Two wrongs don't make a right." If Hill is a pragmatist, he might let both girls experience the consequences of their behavior. Then he might point out to them that their behavior is socially unacceptable, and he might try to learn what is really bothering Jenny. Finally, if Hill is an existentialist, he would probably remind Jenny that she is responsible for her actions and that nobody likes to be pushed or shouted at, and that such behavior weakens the I-Thou relationship.

Now consider the aesthetic value of some popular musician, say Michael Jackson. An idealist might judge his music as not conforming to higher-order standards of precision and perfection. A realist probably would agree, pointing to experts' opinions that criticize Jackson's music for not conforming to the natural order of things. A pragmatist would note that Jackson has sold more music than just about anyone and would conclude that it has aesthetic value because public consensus has judged it so. And an existentialist would be concerned only with his or her personal opinion of Jackson's music: Do I like it? Do I want to buy it?

Many ethical questions emerge in school settings. One principal—a veteran of twenty-seven years—faced the following ethical challenge. A graduating senior who was an outstanding student had received a college scholarship based on his academic record. But he also had been awarded an American Field Service scholarship for study abroad the following year. The problem was that the college scholarship stipulated that he had to begin study the following fall; he could not defer college entrance for a year. The student's father approached the principal and asked him to "adjust" his son's record to show a false graduation date of one year later. Then the student could accept both scholarships. The principal refused to falsify the school's records, and the student was forced to choose between the two scholarships. But he and his father could never understand why the principal would not change "one little record. . . ."[18]

What would you have done if you were the principal? How would you feel if you were the student? If you were the parent? Which person's attitudes and behavior are most like your own code of ethics?

ANALYTIC PHILOSOPHY

■

A recent approach to the study and practice of philosophy known as **analytic philosophy** holds that all philosophical pursuits are nothing more than a critique of language. It views philosophy as an activity, not as a system with a set of theories and speculating principles.

Two major contributors to this approach were Bertrand Russell (1872–1970) and Ludwig Wittgenstein (1889–1951), who began their philosophical careers as scientific realists but concluded that the systems approach offered no real solutions for human situations. Believing that science was the source and receptacle of all useful knowledge, they held that philosophy could enhance science by logically analyzing the structure and meaning of its language.

Along with Alfred North Whitehead (1861–1947) Russell wrote *Principia Mathematica*, which reduced all mathematical principles to a logical language and set standards for the relationship of statements to one another. Similarly, Wittgenstein put forth a theory of meaning that set standards for the relationship of language to the empirical world of science. Essentially, these theorists thought that there are two types statements and thus two types of knowledge: *empirical assertions*, which contain factual information, and *mathematical propositions*, such as opinions from analytical geometry.

To analytic philosophers, the logical analysis of language can resolve most philosophical problems, because such problems arise from imprecise language. For example, consider the following sentence: "School A needs learning-disability teachers because it is getting more and more children whose parents are on welfare." Analyzing this statement we see that the conclusion ("School A needs learning-disabilities teachers") does not really follow from the premise ("it is getting more and more children whose parents are on welfare"). Instead, the statement *assumes* that children who receive welfare have learning disabilities. But this has not been proved empirically.

[18]"Ethics and the Principal: Five Vignettes," *NASSP Bulletin* 72 (December 1988): 22.

AMERICAN EDUCATIONAL PHILOSOPHY

■

ESSENTIALISM

Educational philosopher G. Max Wingo at the University of Michigan has described three epistemological approaches as being reactions or protests against essentialism, the prevalent philosophy in twentieth-century American education.[19] To understand the reactions, we first need to outline essentialism.

Basically, advocates of **essentialism** believe that American education has properly followed a realist approach by stressing memorization and mastery of "essential" knowledge from the disciplines of English, mathematics, history, science, and foreign languages. Vocational subjects, physical education, and fine arts have been regarded as peripheral, as not being essential to the core of knowledge. Because an essentialist's purpose in education is the transmission of certain cultural elements, this position is regarded as a conservative, disciplined approach to schooling. Essentialists would support the use of the National Teacher Examinations in certifying teachers.

Among the advocates of the essentialist position is a former president of Harvard, James Conant, who has been critical of the other epistemological approaches found in American schools. There have been three major reactions to the essentialist approach.

[19]For an account of these and other educational positions, see G. Max Wingo, *The Philosophy of American Education* (Lexington, Mass.: Heath, 1965).

Did the falling tree make a sound or not? Philosophy enters the classroom all the time —in determining content, curricula, methods, values, and results. For teachers it is never too early or too late to explore the implications of one's educational philosophy. —K. Preuss/The Image Works

REACTIONS AGAINST ESSENTIALISM

PROGRESSIVISM   Growing out of the pragmatic tradition, **progressivism** holds that the child should be at the center of the educational process. Rather than transmitting a defined body of knowledge, progressives believe that education should take students' needs and interests into account. Thus the curriculum should consist of activities that engage the child in the learning process. For example, in learning to write, students should be given assignments that allow them to create stories which are interesting to them and which tie into their experiences. Progressive teachers avoid the essentialist approach of "pouring in" a defined body of factual information that is of little interest or use to the student. Generally, then, a progressive school has a pragmatic purpose—to foster and enhance a student's practical intelligence.

RECONSTRUCTIONISM   Closely associated with progressivism, another reaction to the essentialist approach is **reconstructionism**, which holds that education should be devoted to building a global democratic social order. Philosophically attuned to Marxist theory, reconstructionists view education as being embedded in a particular social and historical context. The learning process, therefore, takes into account the fact that students are experiencing a particular social order at a particular point in time.[20]

PERENNIALISM   Another reaction to essentialism (and progressivism) is **perennialism**, which is rooted in idealism and classical realism; basically, perennialists believe that certain cultural dimensions of education are universal and timeless. They also believe, like idealists, that students have inborn talents and will learn as much as their character and talent will permit.

Mortimer Adler's *Paedeia Proposal*, mentioned earlier, is an example of a perennialist curriculum, and it is organized into three stages. First students acquire an organized body of knowledge (including the fundamentals of language, literature, fine arts, mathematics, natural sciences, geography, history, and social studies). Next they learn skills (in reading, writing, speaking, listening, arithmetic, and empirical observation). Finally, they expand their understanding, appreciation, and creativity through a question-and-answer approach based on great works of literature and art.[21]

TOWARD YOUR OWN EDUCATIONAL PHILOSOPHY

■

Although Americans generally tolerate a broad range of philosophical beliefs, ideologically there is a collective commitment to democracy and to the importance of consensus. It is also commonly assumed that the basic metaphysical tenets of scientific realism are true—that the physical world is real and permanent and follows natural laws. In education we can see this in the "effective

[20]See, for example, Theodore Brameld, *Toward a Reconstructed Philosophy of Education* (New York: Dryden, 1956), 4–19.

[21]Adler, *The Paedeia Proposal*, 23.

schools'' models, which are governed and operated democratically with an emphasis on consensus. We can also observe that the methods and discoveries of science hold an important place in the American curriculum.

To begin developing your own educational philosophy (or to test and refine your philosophy), ask yourself to what extent you approve of the effective-schools models. If you do not approve, which elements bother you, and what objections do you have? Next, consider whether you think that empirical knowledge is all that schools should teach. Can you identify other kinds of knowledge and skills that should be taught? (If you are unsure about these questions, perhaps you need to read and study more about them. But you probably have some ideas about these issues. What are they?)

Next, think about your various classes, and ask yourself how you feel about the different methods they employ. Which classes do you enjoy most? In which do you learn best? Can you identify which philosophical systems underlie the content and methods used? Do you think that most other students like the same classes and methods that you do?

As a teacher, what will you need to know about the subject(s) you teach? What methods do you think you will use? How will you ensure that your students learn? How will you evaluate students' progress, and what will you do if you discover that some students are not learning?

This chapter has outlined a great number of ideas that you will have to think about again and again. How do you define reality? Knowledge? Value? Your answers will help you decide what to teach and how to teach it. It is never too early—or too late—to work on your educational philosophy.

CONCLUSIONS

■

This chapter has described how philosophy fits into education and society as well as its relation to the study of science. We explored four major philosophical systems—idealism, realism, pragmatism, and existentialism—in terms of how they approach three categories of philosophy: metaphysics, or ontology; epistemology; and axiology. We also considered analytic philosophy, not as a system but as a means of thinking clearly about philosophical issues in education. Finally, we described the major philosophical approaches to American education. Essentialism has dominated twentieth-century American schooling, while progressivism, reconstructionism, and perennialism have arisen in reaction to it.

KEY TERMS

■

science	aesthetics
empiricism	philosophical system
empirical verification	idealism

empirical confirmation

paradigm

philosophy

metaphysics

cosmology

ontology

epistemology

logic

syllogism

inductive reasoning

deductive reasoning

axiology

ethics

Cartesian method

classical realism

religious realism

scientific realism

pragmatism

existentialism

National Teacher Examinations

categorical imperative

analytic philosophy

essentialism

progressivism

reconstructionism

perennialism

SUGGESTED READINGS

Harry S. Broudy, *Building a Philosophy of Education* (Englewood Cliffs, N.J.: Prentice-Hall, 1961). In this classic text, Broudy describes his own rational realistic philosophy and takes the reader step by step through the process of building a philosophy.

John Dewey, *How We Think* (Boston: Heath, 1933). Another classic that describes a pragmatic view of the thinking and conceptual process.

Ben Agger, *Critical Theory of Public Life: Knowledge, Discourse and Poltics in an Age of Decline* (Bristol, Penn.: Falmer Press, 1991). This book is part of a series, Critical Perspectives on Literacy and Education, and its essays discuss a variety of contemporary topics and social problems by applying critical theory.

William F. O'Neill, *Educational Ideologies: Contemporary Expressions of Educational Philosophy* (Santa Monica, Calif.: Goodyear, 1981). This book lays out a new approach to thinking about the traditional educational philosophies and is aimed at pre-service and in-service students.

Edward Stevens, Jr., and George H. Wood, *Justice, Ideology, and Education*, 2d ed. (New York: McGraw Hill, 1992). This book combines text and readings to address a variety of educational issues related to the universal theme of the individual and social justice.

Douglas J. Simpson and Michael B. Jackson, *The Teacher as Philosopher* (New York: Metheun, 1984). The intent of this book is to provide teachers with a way to think philosophically about problems that arise from educational concerns in daily classroom life.

Barbara Senkowski Stengel, *Just Education: The Right to Education in Context and Conversation*, Values and Ethics series (Chicago: Loyola University Press, 1991). Through the use of scenarios, Stengel takes a look at the meaning of the phrase "the right to education" in a multidimensional context. She then discusses whether or not the phrase helps or hinders justice in education.

III

TODAY AND TOMORROW

We stand on the brink of the twenty-first century, when some of our most pressing problems will likely continue to be the legal and social issues that bind us now. As in the past, our education system will be one of the stages on which these dramas will be presented. For most of the current century educators have struggled with equity issues relating to civil rights, multiculturalism, and curricular relevancy. Society has pondered what role the schools should play in mediating and educating against social, psychological, and physical ills related to crime, drug abuse, and health. More recently, toward the close of this century, we have also been confronted with global issues—our shrinking planet puts the various peoples of the world into cultural, economic, and ecological interdependency. This last section of the book will take a closer look at such issues and how they currently affect society and our schools. But we also will take a look into the future and consider the educational outlook in the coming century.

Chapter 11—Education and the Courts—examines our legal system in terms of civil rights (especially First Amendment freedoms), church and state issues related to education, segregation issues, and the legal implications of school policies.

Chapter 12—Issues in Education—casts a wider net, pulling in other problems and concerns and seeking new solutions. These include attempts to reform the curriculum to induce a more relevant, educationally sound course of study; provisions for meeting the needs of our culturally diverse society; and efforts to respond to students' changing family and social patterns.

Finally, Chapter 13—Education in the Twenty-first Century—looks at some of the predictions experts have made about the next century's demographic patterns, technological advances, global and environmental trends, and the overall effects of such changes on our educational institutions.

Education and the Courts

People sometimes forget that Americans have always used law to shape public education. They have written constitutions and statutes to build and transform public schooling. The legal system has been used to require that instruction be given only in English as well as to provide bilingual classes, to mandate Bible reading as well as to declare it unconstitutional, to inculcate monocultural Americanism as well as to offer multicultural instruction. . . . In one form or another, government has always been in the classroom.

—David Tyack, Thomas James, and Aaron Benavot, Law and the Shaping of Public Education,
1785–1954 (Madison, Wis.: University of Wisconsin Press, 1987), 4

11

Education
and the
Courts

ADVANCED ORGANIZERS

■

In this chapter you will learn

How the legal system interprets individual rights in our schools

Which legal issues relate to church and state roles in education

What role courts play in desegregating schools

How the legal system affects school management

CHAPTER OUTLINE

■

THE LEGAL SYSTEM AND SOURCES OF LAW

LEGAL ASPECTS OF EDUCATION
   Personal Rights Versus Role Limitations
   Issues of Church and State
   Segregation and the Courts
   School Board Issues

CONCLUSIONS

obert Jackson teaches seventh grade, and it is the first day of a new school year. It begins as other days have for many years in this school district: Everyone stands as "The Star-Spangled Banner" plays over the intercom, and then a student leads the homeroom group in saying the Pledge of Allegiance.

Robert noticed that two students in back of the room had remained seated during the national anthem and the pledge. When the class was seated again, he reminded them that everyone is expected to stand and participate in reciting the pledge. As students filed out of homeroom to attend their first class, several of them were talking about the classmates who had stayed seated. "Did you see those jerks? Boy, are they gonna get it!" is one comment that Robert overheard.

One of the two nonparticipants stopped by Robert's desk and said, "Mr. Jackson, our family doesn't believe in flags and pledges. My father says that I don't have to recite the Pledge of Allegiance." Robert asked the student to come back after school, when he learned that both nonpledgers attend the same Jehovah's Witness church. They believe that saluting a flag is a form of idolatry and, therefore, sinful.

When Robert got home for dinner, there was a message on his answering machine asking him to call Bill Perry, the president of the school board. He dialed Perry right away.

"Bill, it's Bob Jackson. What's up?" (In a town of less than four thousand, most people know each other well. Besides working together, Jackson and Perry are both members of the Lions Club.)

"I heard about the revolt in your class today. Doc Simmons said his daughter told him about it, and he called me as a 'representative of the Citizens for a Better America.' He was pretty agitated. You know I don't always agree with Doc, but I think he's right about this. We all pay a lot of taxes to turn these kids into good American citizens, and we're counting on you to shape 'em up before this thing gets out of hand."

"Bill, I understand how you feel, but I can't make these kids recite the pledge."

"Well, you can at least get them out of the room. The other kids don't need any bad examples."

Robert Jackson hung up after promising, "I'll see what I can do."

What *can* Jackson do? Can he require the two students to recite the pledge? Can he send them to study hall until the national anthem and pledge are over? If you said no to both questions, you are right. The courts have ruled that neither teachers nor students can be forced to recite the Pledge of Allegiance, and students cannot be required to stand or to leave the room.[1]

THE LEGAL SYSTEM AND SOURCES OF LAW

■

The management, governance, and overall operation of schools are complex and are affected by many forces. An increasingly significant source of school

[1]West Virginia State Bd. of Educ. v. Barnette, 319 U.S. 624, 63 S.Ct. 1178, 87 L.Ed. 1628 (1943); Holden v. Board of Educ., Elizabeth, 46 N.J. 281, 216 A.2d 387 (1966); Russo v. Central School Dist. No. 1, Towns of Rush et al., 469 F.2d 623 (2 Cir. 1972), cert. den. 411 U.S. 932 93 S.Ct. 1899, 36 L.Ed.2d 391 (1973).

regulation is the legal system. Courts determine many of the rules affecting students, parents, teachers, administrators, school boards, vendors of school supplies and services, and state and federal legislatures.

Several sources of law affect education. A major one, of course, is the U.S. Constitution. But state constitutions also address education, as do federal and state statutes, local regulations, and executive orders. In addition:

> The original law in the United States was founded on the common law of England. Certain customs became the accepted bases of proper conduct. These customs became crystallized into principles that in specific cases were enunciated by the courts. These judicial pronouncements formed American common law. The courts then tended to follow their earlier decisions and there came into being the doctrine of "stare decisis," "let the decision stand."[2]

As you might guess from this quotation, the largest amount of law today is **common law**, rather than **enacted law**. This means that courts "discover" law in earlier decisions, which have the force of time behind them.

Given the weight of legal interpretation—whether of common law or of enacted law—the rulings of the court system are often critically important to educators. What school boards, administrators, teachers, parents, and pupils must do (may do, must not do)—and under what conditions—is spelled out in **case law**. Although most litigation involving education systems is conducted by specialists, teachers should understand how the legal process works and should be familiar with significant court decisions.

The United States has two basic and parallel systems of courts: federal and state (see Figure 11.1). Cases involving "substantial" federal statutory or constitutional issues may begin in a **U.S. district court**, which is at the lowest federal level. There are ninety courts for the fifty states and the District of Columbia, and four more for Puerto Rico and other territories. The next federal level is an appellate system of thirteen **federal judicial circuit courts**.

Cases that involve no federal issues must begin in the lowest state court, or **municipal court**; those involving federal issues *may* start in state or in federal court systems. States usually have either one or two levels of appeal (court names and appellate procedures vary). All states have a "court of last resort," which often is called the **state supreme court**. Not all cases are appealable to a state supreme court, but many are.

Ultimately, the **U.S. Supreme Court** is the court of last resort for both state and federal systems. Most cases are appealable, but the U.S. Supreme Court is under no obligation to accept an appeal. On the other hand, the Supreme Court may call up for review cases from lower courts—even when no appeal is pending. Once a matter has been judged by the highest court with jurisdiction over it, the matter is considered **res judicata**, ("a matter judged"); it may not be brought back into court for further litigation.

[2]E. Edmund Reutter, *The Law of Public Education*, 3d ed. (Mineola, N.Y.: Foundation Press, 1985), 1.

FIGURE 11.1   The Court System of the United States

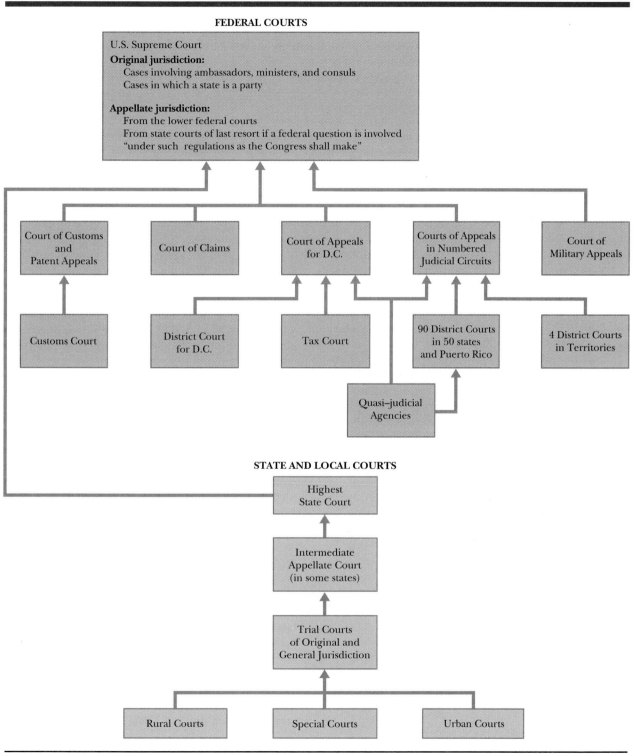

FEDERAL COURTS

U.S. Supreme Court
Original jurisdiction:
  Cases involving ambassadors, ministers, and consuls
  Cases in which a state is a party

Appellate jurisdiction:
  From the lower federal courts
  From state courts of last resort if a federal question is involved
  "under such regulations as the Congress shall make"

Court of Customs and Patent Appeals

Court of Claims

Court of Appeals for D.C.

Courts of Appeals in Numbered Judicial Circuits

Court of Military Appeals

Customs Court

District Court for D.C.

Tax Court

90 District Courts in 50 states and Puerto Rico

4 District Courts in Territories

Quasi–judicial Agencies

STATE AND LOCAL COURTS

Highest State Court

Intermediate Appellate Court (in some states)

Trial Courts of Original and General Jurisdiction

Rural Courts

Special Courts

Urban Courts

LEGAL ASPECTS OF EDUCATION

■

We have already noted several aspects of case law in Chapter 2, in regard to collective bargaining and related issues. Among the other topics of substantial interest to educators—and on which courts have ruled—are (1) personal freedoms and rights versus the obligations or limitations of one's role (such as teacher, parent, pupil, administrator, board member); (2) church and state issues that relate to education; (3) affirmative action issues; and (4) matters concerning school board procedures. Court rulings on these topics are outlined briefly in the following sections. Keep in mind that even "matters judged" may be shaded or changed through future court decisions. Occasionally rulings are even reversed—as in the 1954–1955 *Brown* decisions that overturned the "separate but equal" doctrine of *Plessy v. Ferguson* (see Chapter 4).

PERSONAL RIGHTS VERSUS ROLE LIMITATIONS

Ordinary citizens have rights that are secured both by common law and by the Constitution. Among these rights are freedom of expression, religious liberty, freedom of association, the right to privacy, and protection from arbitrary searches and seizure of property. Are citizens' rights different within educational settings or when they are fulfilling specifically defined educational roles? The answer is sometimes, and to some extent. In considering the following court decisions, remember that a ruling is binding only within the geographic area that is under the jurisdiction of the court rendering a decision; remember as well, however, that rulings are often precedents on which other courts—with other jurisdictions—base decisions.

Ultimately, the U.S. Supreme Court is the court of last resort, and its rulings are of substantial interest to educators. Hardly any aspect of school life goes unnoticed—from searches of students' lockers to how school boards conduct their meetings. —John Elk III/Stock, Boston

FREEDOM OF EXPRESSION   The roles of parent or board member do not usually affect a citizen's right to freedom of expression. But the roles of administrator, teacher, and student do. The primary test concerning school employees is whether or not the exercise of free expression negatively affects the ability to perform one's job. In the case of students, age is sometimes a consideration (is the student nearly an adult or clearly under age?). Nearly always, the extent to which free expression interferes with the orderly conduct of an educational enterprise—or seems likely to interfere with it—is a major element to be balanced.

RESEARCH SAYS

For Tomorrow's Education . . .

Traditionally, courts have treated children under age seven with the presumption that they are without criminal capacity. Youths fourteen or older are presumed to have an adult's criminal capacity. This leaves the interval between ages seven and fourteen, during which courts have presumed that an individual is criminally incapable, although this interpretation can be rebutted. A Maryland appellate court recently ruled that a thirteen-year-old boy was capable of a criminal act (possessing and selling drugs to minors), even though he was below grade level, having twice flunked sixth grade. The court said that the state did not have to prove preciousness for the boy—just that he fell within 98.2 percent of his age group. See Perry A. Zirkel, "De Jure: 'Kidding' Around: The Defense of Youth," *Phi Delta Kappan* 73 (December 1991): 337–338.

Historically, school personnel have been expected to reflect the community's most deeply held values and norms. In cases where a community is divided about some issue, teachers have often found it safer not to be identified prominently with either side. To some extent, whether an individual's action or expression is acceptable or is cause for termination or censure is affected by time, place, gender, and other factors (such as a student's age, a family's standing in the community, or the reputation of the parties in a controversy; even the specific wording of a law or regulation may be a factor). Teachers have lost their jobs for such behaviors as playing cards, dancing, drinking alcohol, smoking cigarettes, homosexuality, swearing, religious proselytizing, using marijuana, getting pregnant, and living with a person of the opposite sex. On the other hand, some teachers have engaged in these behaviors—even controversially—without jeopardizing their jobs. Whatever the variations of a specific case, educators have long been expected to be role models for students, "exerting a subtle but important influence over their perceptions and values," as a 1979 Supreme Court decision stated.[3]

In general, school personnel have little difficulty exercising normal freedom of expression as citizens as long as they keep their religious, political, sexual, and personal beliefs separate from the performance of their job. For example, a chemistry teacher who serves on weekends as a lay minister is not likely to

[3]Ambach v. Norwick, 441 U.S. 68, 99 S.Ct. 1589, 60 L.Ed.2d 49 (1979).

[4]LaRocca v. Board of Educ. of Rye City School Dist., 63 A.D.2d 1019, 406 N.Y.S.2d 348 (1978).

[5]Petrie v. Forest Hills School Dist. Bd. of Educ., 5 Ohio App. 3d 115, 449 N.E.2d 786 (1982).

[6]Cf. Brubaker v. Board of Educ., School Dist. 149, Cook County, Illinois, 502 F.2d 973 (7 Cir. 1974), cert. den. 421 U.S. 965, 95 S.Ct. 1953, 44 L.Ed.2d 451 (1975); Sterzing v. Fort Bend Independent School Dist., 376 F.Supp. 657 (S.D. Tex. 1972), vac. on remedy grounds, 496 F.2d 92 (5 Cir. 1974); Kingsville Independent School Dist. v. Cooper, 611 F.2d 1109 (5 Cir. 1980); Wilson v. Chancellor, 418 F.Supp. 1358 (D. Or. 1976).

[7]Keefe v. Geanakos, 418 F.2d 359 (1 Cir. 1969); State ex rel. Wasilewski v. Board of School Directors of City of Milwaukee, 14 Wis. 2d 243, 111 N.W.2d 198 (1961); Oakland Unified School Dist. v. Olicker, 25 Cal. App. 3d 1098, 102 Cal.Rptr. 421 (1972); DeVito v. Board of Educ., County of Marion, 285 S.E.2d 411 (W.Va. 1981).

[8]Mailoux v. Kiley, 448 F.2d 1242 (1 Cir. 1971).

[9]Penn-Delco School Dist. v. Urso, 33 Pa. Cmwlth. 501, 382 A.2d 162 (1978); Simon v. Jefferson Davis Parish School Bd., 289 So.2d 511 (La. App. 1974); Pryse v. Yakima School Dist. No. 7, 30 Wash. App. 16, 632 P.2d 60 (1981); Shurgin v. Ambach, 56 N.Y.2d 700, 451 N.Y.2d 722, 436 N.E.2d 1324 (1982); Ricci v. Davis, 627 P.2d 1111 (Colo. 1981); Potter v. Kalama Public School Dist. No. 402, 31 Wash. App. 838, 644 P.2d 1229 (1982).

[10]Tinker v. Des Moines Independent Community School Dist., 393 U.S. 503, 89 S.Ct. 733, 21 L.Ed.2d 731 (1969); Bethel School Dist. No. 403 v. Frazier, 1065 S.Ct. 3159 (1986); James v. Board of Educ. of Central School Dist. No. 1, Addison, 461 F.2d 566 (2 Cir. 1972), cert. den. 409 U.S. 1042, 93 S.Ct. 529, 34 L.Ed.2d 491 (1972); Melton v. Young, 465 F.2d 1332 (6 Cir. 1972), cert. den. 411 U.S. 951, 93 S.Ct. 1926, 36 L.Ed.2d 414 (1973).

encounter problems at school if he or she does not confuse the two roles and settings. But if that teacher begins to devote time in chemistry class to discussions of religious matters, protests are likely to arise. If the principal tells the teacher to stop proselytizing in class and the teacher continues to do it, he or she can be dismissed, and courts almost certainly will sustain the teacher's firing.[4]

Whenever a teacher systematically uses instructional time to air personal beliefs that are not related to the subject of the class, there is a basis for complaints by students or parents.[5] If a teacher's "advocacy" of opinions appears aimed at persuading students to accept beliefs that they or their parents disapprove of, courts are unlikely to support the teacher. Less clear are cases in which controversial material is part of the course curriculum and the teacher's "opinion" is based on expert knowledge of the subject. For example, it is one thing for an algebra teacher to spend a half-hour in class explaining why students' parents should vote for a particular candidate in an election; but if a teacher of social studies mounts a mock debate in class to represent all candidates' viewpoints—and then explains why one candidate's platform is preferable—it is another matter entirely. Even though not all students or their parents might agree with the teacher's analysis, the subject is germane to social studies, and there is no good reason for the teacher not to express an opinion.[6]

The use of language that offends some people has been judicially sanctioned in some instances but not others. When a Massachusetts high school teacher assigned an article in *Atlantic Monthly* to his senior class, the Ipswich School Committee objected. The article used, as the court put it, "a vulgar term for an incestuous son," and the Ipswich School Committee required the teacher to promise never to refer to the word in class again—or risk being fired. The teacher would not promise. The court upheld the teacher and scolded the committee on grounds of due process:

> What is to be said or read to students is not to be determined by obscenity standards for adult consumption. At the same time, the issue must be one of degree. A high school senior is not devoid of all discrimination or resistance. Furthermore, as in all other instances, the offensiveness of language and the particular propriety or impropriety is dependent on the circumstances of the utterance.[7]

In a similar case two years later the court upheld a teacher's right to discuss the meaning of a four-letter Anglo-Saxon word for sexual intercourse, but it reasserted that teachers are *not* free to say or write in class whatever they choose.[8] Courts have ruled against teachers when they have introduced sexually suggestive "statements," "materials," or "actions."[9]

Regarding freedom of symbolic expression—such as lapel buttons, black armbands, and T-shirts with signs or symbols—courts have generally upheld the rights of both teachers and students *as long as no substantial disruption in the educational program was likely to be caused by wearing or displaying such items.* In cases where disturbances occurred (or seemed imminent), courts have generally supported an educational authority's prohibitions on such expression.[10]

In 1969 the *Tinker* decision by the U.S. Supreme Court allowed school officials to " 'censor' poor grammar, writing, or research because to reward such expression would 'materially disrupt' the [student] newspaper's curricular purpose"; but it set a high standard generally for extending First Amendment protections to students' freedom of expression. (As the Court put it, public school students "do not shed their constitutional rights to freedom of speech or expression at the school house gate.")

In 1988 a majority of the Supreme Court seemed to back away from *Tinker* in favor of more support for traditional *in loco parentis* power by school authorities.[11] At issue was a St. Louis (Westwood High) principal's decision to delete two pages of an article in the May 13, 1983, issue of *Spectrum*, a newspaper published every three weeks by the school's journalism students. One story to which the principal objected was about the effects of divorce on students, and in the draft version he read it quoted by name a young woman whose comments were "sharply critical of her father." The other story that troubled the principal was about three pregnant students whose anonymity "was not adequately protected . . . given . . . identifying information in the article and the small number of pregnant students at the school."[12] After a telephone conversation with the faculty advisor of *Spectrum*, the principal concluded that there was no time to change the articles, and he decided to kill the two pages on which they appeared. This decision also removed four other articles that were on the suppressed pages.

Members of the *Spectrum* staff brought suit, claiming violation of their First Amendment rights. The U.S. District Court found in favor of the principal, but the Court of Appeals for the Second District overturned this decision, citing the *Tinker* case. In turn, the appellate ruling was reversed by the U.S. Supreme Court,

Do student journalists have the same First Amendment rights in school that adults in other settings have? Not if school authorities can demonstrate a legitimate pedagogical reason to limit students' speech in school-sponsored expressive activities. —Shopper/Stock, Boston

[11]Justice Brennan's dissenting opinion in Hazelwood School Dist. v. Kuhlmeier, 108 S.Ct. 562 (1988).
[12]Hazelwood School Dist. v. Kuhlmeier, 108 S.Ct. 562 (1988).

The U.S. Supreme Court Speaks . . .

◆ CAN *THE PRINCIPAL OF WESTWOOD HIGH CENSOR* SPECTRUM?

YES   MAJORITY OPINION: 5

Students in the public schools cannot be punished merely for expressing their personal views on the school premises—whether "in the cafeteria, or on the playing field, or on the campus during the authorized hours," unless school authorities have reason to believe that such expression will "substantially interfere with the work of the school or impinge upon the rights of other students."

We have nonetheless recognized that the First Amendment rights of students in the public schools "are not automatically coextensive with the rights of adults in other settings," and must be applied in light of the special characteristics of the school environment." A school need not tolerate student speech that is inconsistent with its "basic educational mission," even though the government could not censor similar speech outside the school. . . .

A school must be able to set high standards for the student speech that is disseminated under its auspices—standards that may be higher than those demanded by some newspaper publishers or theatrical producers in the "real" world—and may refuse to disseminate student speech that does not meet those standards. . . .

We hold that educators do not offend the First Amendment by exercising editorial control over the style and content of student speech in school-sponsored expressive activities so long as their actions are reasonably related to legitimate pedagogical concerns. . . .

It is only when the decision to censor a school-sponsored publication, theatrical production, or other vehicle of student expression has no valid educational purpose that the First Amendment is so "directly and sharply implicate[d]," . . . as to require judicial intervention to protect students' constitutional rights.

NO   MINORITY OPINION: 3

Free student expression undoubtedly sometimes interferes with the effectiveness of the school's pedagogical functions. Some brands of student expression do so by directly preventing the school from pursuing its pedagogical mission: The young polemic who stands on a soapbox during calculus class to deliver an eloquent political diatribe interferes with the legitimate teaching of calculus. . . .

Other student speech, however, frustrates the school's legitimate pedagogical purposes merely by expressing a message that conflicts with the school's, without directly interfering with the school's expression of its message. . . .

. . . [T]he student newspaper that, like Spectrum, conveys a moral position at odds with the school's official stance might subvert the administration's legitimate inculcation of its own perception of community values.

If mere incompatibility with the school's pedagogical message were a constitutionally sufficient justification for the suppression of student speech, school officials could censor . . . students or student organizations . . ., converting our public schools into "enclaves of totalitarianism," that "strangle the free mind at its source." The First Amendment permits no such blanket censorship authority.

Just as the public on the street corner must, in the interest of fostering "enlightened opinion," tolerate speech that "tempt[s] [the listener] to throw [the speaker] off the street," public educators must accommodate some student expression even if it offends them or offers views or values that contradict those the school wishes to inculcate. . . .

in a 5-to-3 decision (see the boxed display). The majority opinion held that *Spectrum* did not qualify as a "public forum" and that "school officials retained [the] right to impose reasonable restrictions on student speech." Justices Brennan, Marshall, and Blackmun dissented, saying that the "mere desire to avoid the discomfort and unpleasantness that always accompany an unpopular viewpoint . . . or an unsavory subject . . . does not justify official suppression of student speech in high school."[13]

Courts have generally upheld the right of school districts to set "reasonable" standards of dress and appearance for both teachers and students. But much litigation has centered on these matters, and it is difficult to generalize about them. Circuit courts in the Third, Fifth, Sixth, Ninth, Tenth, and Eleventh federal circuits have supported such regulations more than have courts in the other circuits. A 1972 decision involving a North Carolina school district's policy regulating hair length and sideburns summarized the conflicting decisions up to that point.[14]

FREEDOM OF ASSOCIATION   Students may associate with whomever they (and their parents) wish—outside of school. But courts have generally upheld school authorities' power to regulate students' associations within school, to promote equity and order. School authorities may, for example, bar membership in "secret societies"—including in some cases fraternities and sororities—if orderly operation of the educational enterprise is at stake. Parents' wishes to the contrary have not been sufficient cause for courts to overrule school authorities.[15]

Regarding freedom of association for teachers and administrators, the general rule of being a moral exemplar applies. Membership in religious and union groups has generally been protected by courts, but "subversive" political affiliations has often raised problems for educators. States may require school employees to be fingerprinted, and they may check the prints against police records (at least in states that deny licenses to felons).[16] In 1925 the U.S. Supreme Court ruled that states could require teachers to be "of patriotic disposition" and could bar teachers from anything "manifestly inimical to the public welfare."[17] After World War II many states and local school districts became zealous in establishing "loyalty oaths" for educators. Courts have struck down many of these usually for being too vague or for denying due process.[18] But they have upheld the requiring of oaths that affirm support for the Constitution—while stopping short of supporting the firing of teachers for refusing to sign such statements.[19]

SEXUAL BEHAVIOR   States may outlaw public acts of homosexuality. They may fire teachers and take away their teaching licenses upon conviction.[20] A California teacher lost his teaching license after he was found guilty of homosexual acts on a public beach. The court supported the school board in revoking the teacher's credentials.[21] On the other hand, advocacy of homosexuality and the private practice of homosexuality are not automatic bases for dismissal. Another California teacher won back his license because the court found no connection between his teaching and an admitted homosexual act 2½ years earlier in the apartment of another teacher.[22] The effect on one's teaching is the primary test that courts impose.[23] Engaging in or soliciting sexual activity with minor students

[13]Fraser, 478 U.S. 675, 106 S.Ct. at 3169; and Bethel School Dist. No. 403 et al. v. Fraser, 478 U.S. 675, 106 S.Ct. 3159.

[14]Massie v. Henry, 455 F.2d 779 (4 Cir. 1972); East Hartford Educ. Ass'n v. Board of Educ. of Town of East Hartford, 562 F.2d 838 (2 Cir. 1977).

[15]Hughes v. Caddo Parish School Bd., 57 F.Supp. 508 (W.D. La. 1944), aff. 323 U.S. 685, 65 S.Ct. 562, 89 L.Ed. 554 (1945); Wright v. Board of Educ. of St. Louis, 295 Mo. 466, 246 S.W. 43 (1922); Wilson v. Abilene Independent School Dist., 190 S.W.2d 406 (Tex. Civ. App. 1945); Burkitt v. School Dist. No. 1, Multnomah County, 195 Or. 471, 246 P.2d 566 (1952); Passel v. Fort Worth Independent School Dist., 453 S.W.2d 888 (Tex. Civ. App. 1970), cert. den. 402 U.S. 968, 91 S.Ct. 1667, 29 L.Ed.2d 133 (1971).

[16]Wilson v. Board of Educ. of Montgomery County, 234 Md. 561, 200 A.2d 67 (1964).

[17]Pierce v. Society of the Sisters of the Holy Names of Jesus and Mary, 268 U.S. 510, 45 S.Ct. 571, 69 L.Ed. 1070 (1925).

[18]See, for example, Wieman v. Updegraff, 344 U.S. 183, 73 S.Ct. 216, 97 L.Ed. 216 (1952). Other cases are cited in Reutter, *Law of Public Education*, 530–531.

[19]Biklen v. Board of Educ., 333 F.Supp. 902 (N.D.N.Y. 1971), aff. 406 U.S. 951, 92 S.Ct. 2060, 32 L.Ed.2d 340 (1972).

[20]National Gay Task Force v. Board of Educ. of City of Oklahoma City, 729 F.2d 1270 (10 Cir. 1984), 470 U.S. 903, 105 S.Ct. 1858, 84 L.Ed.2d 776 (1985).

[21]Sarac v. State Bd. of Educ., 249 Cal. App. 2d 58, 57 Cal. Rptr. 69 (1967).

[22]Moser v. State Bd. of Educ., 22 Cal. App. 3d 988, 101 Cal.Rptr. 86 (1972).

[23]Board of Educ. of Long Beach Unified School Dist. of Los Angeles County v. Jack M., 19 Cal. App. 3d 691, 139 Cal.Rptr. 700, 566 P.2d 602 (1977).

is always taboo, regardless of gender issues. Even when student and teacher are both consenting adults, it is professionally risky to engage in a sexual relationship.

In one case, the district court upheld the dismissal of a small-town single female teacher for living out of wedlock with a single man.[24] The same court ruled in a separate case that suspicion of sexual activity of which some members of the community may disapprove is not sufficient grounds for firing a teacher. (In this case a female teacher was fired because some male friends of her adult son had stayed overnight in her house.)[25] But a court did uphold the firing of a teacher for "deviant conduct with a mannequin," even though the activity took place on the teacher's property; widespread knowledge of the activity convinced the court that the teacher's credibility in the classroom was damaged.[26]

RESEARCH SAYS

For Tomorrow's Education . . .

Due process has been interpreted differently in civil and in criminal courts. But recently the criminal interpretation was applied by a New York judge in a case involving a tenured teacher's dismissal. The teacher was charged with incompetence and insubordination, and under New York law she was given a hearing by a three-member panel—one chosen by the school board, one chosen by the teacher, and one chosen by those two panelists from a list of approved arbitrators. The panel found the teacher guilty of insubordination—after a tied vote was broken by the arbitrator, who received $5,700 above the statutory amount. (At the arbitrator's request the board had agreed to pay more to arbitrate this case.) Applying criminal court precedents, the judge ruled that the teacher's right to due process had been violated, using the analogy of a prosecutor's supplementing the income of a criminal court juror. The case is on appeal. See Perry A. Zirkel, "De Jure: The Price of Due Process," *Phi Delta Kappan* 73 (November 1991): 259–260.

WRITTEN EXPRESSION   School officials may regulate student publications and other forms of written expression, but in doing so they may not ignore First Amendment rights. Among the factors that potentially come into play are (1) the likelihood that school disruptions will result from the activity; (2) the age of the students; (3) the extent of the publication's distribution; (4) whether the activity takes place on or off school premises; (5) whether the school has permitted similar expression on other occasions; (6) whether school funds were used in the publication; (7) the nature of the school official's objections ("political expression" tends to get more court protection than "vulgar language" does); and (8) the extent to which any censorship is a result of a timely, clear,

[24]Sullivan v. Meade Independent School Dist. No. 101, 530 F.2d 799 (8 Cir. 1976).

[25]Fisher v. Snyder, 476 F.2d 375 (8 Cir. 1973).

[26]Wisehart v. McDonald, 500 F.2d 1110 (1 Cir. 1974).

consistent review process that includes an effective appeal procedure in case of unresolved differences of opinion.

Courts have protected student expression even when it has reflected "disrespectful and tasteless attitude[s] toward [school] authority."[27] Paid-for student advertising against the Vietnam War was upheld, whereas advertising for drug paraphernalia was not.[28] School officials who prevented the distribution of a questionnaire about sexual attitudes and habits to high school students—which was to be the basis for an article in the school newspaper—were upheld because *some* students might be bothered psychologically by some of the questions.[29] On the other hand, the Fourth Circuit Court of Appeals did not sustain a Virginia school board that had required the removal of some information about birth control from a school newspaper article entitled "Sexually Active Students Fail to Use Contraception."[30]

Administrators decide which banners, posters, signs, and so forth may be displayed in school, and teachers make classroom bulletin boards and sometimes display other items that may "make a statement." Issues surrounding this kind of written expression have not been litigated extensively. It is reasonable to assume that the same tests which are applied in deciding other freedom of speech issues also fit these cases. It is probably safe to display a sign that says "Everyone should vote," but one that says "Everyone should vote Republican" might cause problems—especially if it represents personal advocacy without giving an opportunity to express other viewpoints.

Teachers have experienced difficulties upon writing controversial opinions in the local newspaper, but courts tend to uphold the right of free speech. For example, a teacher in a western state wrote a letter to the local newspaper supporting the position of the American Civil Liberties Union that marijuana should be legalized. This became a matter of controversy in the community. Eventually the school district fired the teacher (who had taught in the district for several years) on the grounds that he was not an effective teacher. Part of the basis for the district's claim was that the teacher had made available to students a pamphlet entitled "The Student as Nigger," which characterized in "unrestrained language" the relationship between teachers and students as that of master and slave. The Ninth Circuit Court of Appeals voided the teacher's dismissal.[31]

In a similar situation an Illinois school board fired a teacher, Marvin Pickering, for criticizing the superintendent and board in a letter to a local newspaper. The board was in the process of trying to pass a referendum to raise money for buildings and equipment, and state courts agreed that Pickering's letter was "detrimental to the efficient operation and administration of the schools." The U.S. Supreme Court acknowledged that "the State has interests as an employer in regulating the speech of its employees that differ significantly from those it possesses in connection with regulating the speech of the citizenry in general." Even if some of Pickering's statements proved incorrect, they all dealt with matters of public debate. "The threat of dismissal from public employment is . . . a potent means of inhibiting speech. . . . Absent proof of false statements knowingly or recklessly made by having a teacher's exercise of his right to speak on issues of public importance may not furnish the basis for his dismissal from public employment."[32]

[27]Scoville v. Board of Educ. of Joliet Tp. High School Dist. 204, 425 F.2d 10 (7 Cir. 1970), cert. den. 400 U.S. 826, 91 S.Ct. 51, 27 L.Ed.2d 55 (1970); Nicholson v. Board of Education Torrance Unified School Dist., 682 F.2d 858 (CA9 1982); Seyfried v. Walton, 668 F.2d 214 (CA3 1981); Trachtman v. Anker, 563 F.2d 512 (CA2 1977), cert. den. 435 U.S. 925, 98 S.Ct. 1491, 55 L.Ed.2d 519 (1978); Frasca v. Andrews, 463 F.Supp. 1043 (EDNY 1979).

[28]Cf. Zucker v. Panitz, 299 F.Supp. 102 (S.D.N.Y. 1969) and Williams v. Spencer, 622 F.2d 1200 (4 Cir. 1980).

[29]Trachtman v. Anker, 563 F.2d 512 (2 Cir. 1977), cert. den. 435 U.S. 925, 98 S.Ct. 1491, 55 L.Ed.2d 519 (1978).

[30]Gambino v. Fairfax County School Bd., 564 F.2d 157 (4 Cir. 1977).

[31]Wagle v. Murray, 560 F.2d 401 (9 Cir. 1977), cert. den. 434 U.S. 1014, 98 S.Ct. 729, 54 L.Ed.2d 758 (1978) and 546 F.2d 1329 (9 Cir. 1976).

[32]Pickering v. Board of Educ. of Tp. High School Dist. 205, Will Country, 391 U.S. 563, 36 Ill.2d 568, 225 N.E.2d 1 (1967).

ISSUES OF CHURCH AND STATE

Issues involving church and state in relation to education have been litigated extensively and are likely to continue receiving court attention. Of the many topics involved, we will review (1) compulsory attendance; (2) prayer, Bible reading, and meditation; (3) tax-supported services for parochial schoolchildren; and (4) the use of public school property by religious groups. In general, although court decisions in these areas are sometimes confusing, the growing recognition that American society is multifaceted and multicultural has resulted in efforts to guarantee basic rights for many different points of view.

COMPULSORY ATTENDANCE   A landmark Supreme Court case in 1925 recognized the right of states to compel attendance at school on pain of fine or other punishment. At the same time the Court ruled that states could not require attendance at a *public* school. Oregon had passed a law to this effect, and it was challenged by a military academy and by a school run by nuns. Oregon's law would put them out of business. The justices unanimously ruled that the law infringed property rights and could not be enforced.[33]

The Supreme Court has also supported challenges by Old Order Amish— that compelling their children to attend state-sponsored schools is an infringement of religious liberty. The Court put emphasis on how well-established the Amish and their beliefs are, in ruling that they must be granted some relief from compulsory attendance, teacher certification, and curriculum guidelines. In 1972 Chief Justice Warren Burger warned that this principle would not be readily applied to other groups "claiming to have recently discovered some 'progressive' or more enlightened process for rearing children for modern life."[34] Objections of several kinds (curricular, methodological, religious) to public schools have led to a growing interest in "home schooling." Most states allow for the education of children at home, but they impose conditions and restrictions of varying complexity and rigor.[35]

PRAYER, BIBLE READING, AND MEDITATION   Throughout much of American history, each community set its own standards about whether (and from what sources) teachers or students prayed, sang hymns, or read scripture in school. Religiously homogeneous communities tended to integrate some religious activity into the classroom. Many communities—especially after about 1750—contained such a mixture of sectarian interests and people with little commitment to organized religion that teachers avoided direct religious observations. Although some children perfected their reading skills using the Bible as a text, this was a matter of family preference and individual student practice; it did not involve other children in the schoolroom.

During this century a substantial amount of litigation has addressed the issue of Bible reading in schools, with contradictory conclusions. A consensus seemed gradually to emerge that Bible reading was allowable as part of opening exercises in schools as long as two provisions were met: (1) the reading should be without comment, and (2) anyone who objected should be excused.[36] In 1963, however, the Supreme Court ruled by a vote of 8 to 1 that this practice violated the First Amendment of the Constitution, which forbids state establishment of

[33]Pierce v. Society of Sisters of the Holy Names of Jesus and Mary, 268 U.S. 510, 45 S.Ct. 571, 69 L.Ed. 1070 (1925).

[34]Wisconsin v. Yoder, 406 U.S. 205, 92 S.Ct. 1526 (1972).

[35]Kirsten Goldberg, "Pressure Pays Off for Home-schooling Families," *Education Week* 30 September 1987, 11.

[36]Reutter, *Law of Public Education,* 30.

The controversies relating to education and the separation of church and state go far beyond school prayer. The recognition that American society is multifaceted and multicultural has spurred efforts to guarantee basic rights for many different points of view. —Bryce Flynn/ Picture Group

religion.[37] The decision elaborated a two-pronged test: If the *purpose* or the *primary effect* of a law, rule, or practice is either to advance or to inhibit religion, then it is unconstitutional. Bible reading and prayer—no matter how generic—fail this test. (A few months before this ruling the Supreme Court had found the following "denominationally neutral" prayer to be unconstitutional: "Almighty God, we acknowledge our dependence upon Thee, and we beg Thy blessings upon us, our parents, our teachers and our country.")[38]

These two decisions raised substantial controversy. The Bible can be studied as literature or history. Religion can be part of the curriculum if it is approached in a balanced, nonpartisan manner. Religious literature may be dis-

---

RESEARCH SAYS

For Tomorrow's Education . . .

Issues of textbook censorship continue to be litigated. Two federal courts of appeals reversed lower-court decisions that ruled in favor of book banning in Alabama and Tennessee schools. These rulings have been regarded as a major defeat for religious fundamentalists. See Richard Lacayo, "Going Back to the Books," *Time* 130 (7 September 1987): 60. On the other side, student expression was severely restricted when the U.S. Supreme Court ruled in favor of school administrators' rights to censor students' freedom of speech. See Nat Hentoff, "Free Speech at Potrero Hill," *Washington Post*, 22 April 1989, sec. A, p. 23; and "In Iowa, Free Speech for Students," *Washington Post*, 28 August 1989, p. 13.

[37]School Dist. of Abington Tp., Pa. v. Schempp, 374 U.S. 203, 83 S.Ct. 1560, 10 L.Ed.2d 844 (1963).
[38]Engel v. Vitale, 370 U.S. 421, 82 S.Ct. 1261, 8 L.Ed.2d 601 (1962).

tributed in schools *if only one distribution point is used, if all groups have an equal opportunity to place material at the distribution point, and if no school personnel comment on the material.*[39] Religious symbols and observances associated with holidays may be displayed on a short-term basis "as examples of the heritage, and integration into the curriculum of music, art, literature, and drama having religious themes if presented 'in a prudent and objective manner and as a traditional part of the cultural and religious heritage of the particular holiday.' "[40]

Individual students may pray whenever they wish, and presumably they may read the Bible in school any time it does not interfere with their required activities. States *may* pass statutes encouraging teachers to "embrace every opportunity to inculcate . . . the practice of every Christian virtue."[41] Public school authorities *may not* set aside time for silent prayer;[42] provide voluntary instruction in Transcendental Meditation;[43] display the Ten Commandments;[44] designate a member of the clergy to give a "nonsectarian invocation or benediction at a graduation ceremony;[45] or create a voluntary religious exercise immediately before school by having a student volunteer read from the *Congressional Record* the chaplain's "remarks."[46] Until recently, public schools could not allow students to meet on school property for religious exercises before, after, or during the school day.[47]

In 1990 the U.S. Supreme Court, in an 8 to 1 decision, upheld an appeals court decision requiring Westside High in Omaha to allow former and current students "to form a Christian club that would have the same privileges and meet on the same terms and conditions as other Westside student groups, except that it would have no faculty sponsor."[48]

TAX-SUPPORTED SERVICES FOR PAROCHIAL SCHOOLCHILDREN

Supporters of parochial schools (primarily Lutherans and Roman Catholics) have long believed that their schools—or, at least, the parents and children who patronize them—are entitled to some tax funds or tax relief. They argue that most of the instruction in parochial schools is in the secular subjects taught by tax-funded schools, and that the existence of the parochial system saves taxpayers a great deal of money they would necessarily spend if all parochial students attended tax-supported schools. Historically, this reasoning has failed to convince a majority of taxpayers in most of the United States. Some states and communities, however, have wanted to provide tax-funded services to parochial schools.

Since 1930 courts have tended to apply the "child benefit" test to these issues. When Louisiana furnished free textbooks to all children of the state, for example, the Supreme Court held that the primary beneficiaries were the individual children, not the parochial schools that some of the children attended.[49] Thirty-eight years later the Court reaffirmed the "child benefit" doctrine.[50] Not all states have wanted to provide free textbooks for parochial students; some state constitutions do not permit it. Courts have not been entirely consistent, but they generally have permitted such aid as free textbooks *if state law does not preclude it*; they have also provided that such aid not constitute something different from what is available to students in tax-supported schools.

In some instances courts have viewed transportation to and from school as

[39]Meltzer v. Board of Public Instr. of Orange County, Florida, 577 F.2d 311 (5 Cir. 1978), cert. den. 439 U.S. 1089, 99 S.Ct. 872, 59 L.Ed.2d 56 (1979).

[40]Reutter, *Law of Public Education*, 39.

[41]Meltzer v. Board of Public Instr. of Orange County, Florida.

[42]Beck v. McElrath, 584 F.Supp. 1161 (M.D. Tenn. 1982); Duffy v. Las Cruces Public Schools, 557 F.Supp. 1013 (N.M. 1983); May v. Cooperman, 572 F.Supp. 1561 (D.N.J. 1983); Wallace v. Jaffree (1985).

[43]Malnak v. Yogi, 592 F.2d 197 (3 Cir. 1979).

[44]Stone v. Graham, 449 U.S. 39, 101 S.Ct. 192, 66 L.Ed.2d 199 (1980).

[45]Lee v. Weisman, 112 S.Ct. 2649, 120 L.Ed.2d 467, 60 USLW 4723 (1992).

[46]State Bd. of Educ. v. Board of Educ. of Netcong, 57 N.J. 172, 270 A.2d 412 (1970), cert. den. 401 U.S. 1013, 91 S.Ct. 1253 (1971).

[47]Brandon v. Board of Educ. of Guilderland Central School Dist., 635 F.2d 971 (2 Cir. 1980), cert. den. 454 U.S. 1123, 102 S.Ct. 970, 71 L.Ed.2d 109 (1981); Lubbock Civil Liberties Union v. Lubbock Independent School Dist., 669 F.2d 1038 (5 Cir. 1982), cert. den. 459 U.S. 1155, 103 S.Ct. 800, 74 L.Ed.2d 1003 (1983); Karen B. v. Treen, 653 F.2d 897 (5 Cir. 1981), aff. 455 U.S. 913, 102 S.Ct. 1267, 71 L.Ed.2d 455 (1982); Bender v. Williamsport Area School Dist., 741 F.2d 538 (1984).

[48]Board of Educ. of the Westside Community Schools, Petitioners v. Bridget C. Mergens, Daniel N. Mergens, et al., 58 LW 1720 (1990).

[49]Cochran v. Louisiana State Bd. of Educ., 281 U.S. 370, 50 S.Ct. 335, 74 L.Ed. 913 (1930).

[50]Board of Educ. v. Allen, 392 U.S. 236, 88 S.Ct. 1923, 20 L.Ed.2d 1060 (1968).

a "child benefit."[51] They have declared unconstitutional several other forms of assistance: the cost of field trips;[52] salary supplements to parochial schoolteachers for teaching secular subjects;[53] tuition reimbursement to parents;[54] maintenance and repair costs of parochial schools;[55] projectors, audio recorders, films, periodicals, laboratory equipment, and recordings;[56] and "auxiliary services" at parochial schools by public school personnel—for example, guidance services, testing, remedial and accelerated instruction, and services for the educationally disadvantaged.[57] Speech, hearing, and psychological diagnostic services may be supplied in parochial schools by public school personnel because "such services . . . have little or no educational content and are not closely associated with the educational mission of the school."[58]

USE OF PUBLIC PROPERTY BY RELIGIOUS GROUPS   If a local religious group finds itself without a place to meet, can it rent the auditorium of the public high school? It depends. If the state's constitution and laws do not forbid such use, and if the school is rented out for a variety of community purposes, there would not likely be a problem. But if the building is rarely used for nonschool purposes, renting it to a religious group would risk the appearance of favoring that group and thus of "promoting" religion. In the case of a tax-funded college that makes its facilities available to a wide variety of student groups, the U.S. Supreme Court ruled that to deny the facilities to a registered student group because it intended to have a religious service was a denial of free speech.[59]

The Supreme Court ruled invalid a practice in Champaign, Illinois, of releasing those students whose parents wanted them to receive religious instruction so that they could attend either Jewish, Roman Catholic, or Protestant classes *at the high school*.[60] The Court believed that the state's compulsory attendance laws were being used to help particular religious groups. The fact that state buildings were being used for the instruction was an additional factor. But four years later the Court sustained a released-time arrangement in New York state; in that case, volunteer participants *left* school to attend religious instruction, and so no state property was involved. The Court argued that parents have a right to choose what their children study and, therefore, may have them leave school for instruction of their choice.[61]

SEGREGATION AND THE COURTS

DE JURE ISSUES   Since the two *Brown* decisions in the mid-1950s (see Chapter 5), courts have applied steady and reasonably consistent pressure to "desegregate" public schools. The U.S. Supreme Court asked school boards to develop plans for ending de jure (legal) segregation "with all deliberate speed."[62] Lower courts had the responsibility of ruling on specific plans when they were challenged. Hundreds of cases resulted—many occasioned by plans that made little movement toward unitary (as opposed to two separate) school systems. In 1964 and again in 1965 the Supreme Court issued rulings that called for speedier and more effective plans for ending segregated schools.[63] In 1968 the Court completely discarded its earlier criterion of "all deliberate speed," because of the

[51]Everson v. Board of Educ., 330 U.S. 1, 67 S.Ct. 504, 91 L.Ed. 711 (1947); Visser v. Nooksack Valley School Dist. No.506, 33 Wash. 2d 699, 207 P.2d 198 (1949); Luetkemeyer v. Kaufmann, 364 F.Supp. 376 (W.D.MO. 1973), aff. 419 U.S. 888, 95 S.Ct. 167, 42 L.Ed.2d 134 (1974); Epeldi v. Engelking, 94 Idaho 390, 488 P.2d 860 (1971), cert. den. 406 U.S. 957, 92 S.Ct. 2058, 32 L.Ed.2d 343 (1972).

[52]Wolman v. Walter, 433 U.S. 229, 97 S.Ct. 2593, 53 L.Ed.2d 714 (1977).

[53]Lemon v. Kurtzman, 403 U.S. 602, 91 S.Ct. 2105, 29 L.Ed.2d 745 (1971).

[54]Lemon v. Sloan, 340 F.Supp. 1356 (E.D. Pa. 1972); Sloan v. Lemon, 413 U.S. 825, 93 S.Ct. 2982, 37 L.Ed.2d 939 (1973); Committee for Public Educ. and Religious Liberty v. Nyquist, 413 U.S. 756, 93 S.Ct. 2955, 37 L.Ed.2d 948 (1973).

[55]Committee for Public Educ. and Religious Liberty v. Nyquist; Levitt v. Committee for Public Educ. and Religious Liberty, 413 U.S. 472, 93 S.Ct. 2814, 37 L.Ed.2d 736 (1973). Cf. Wolman v. Walter, 433 U.S. 229, 97 S.Ct. 2593, 53 L.Ed.2d 714 (1977), which allowed the cost of "such standardized tests and scoring services as are in use in the public schools of the state [Ohio]."

[56]Meek v. Pittenger, 421 U.S. 349, 95 S.Ct. 1753, 44 L.Ed.2d 217 (1975).

[57]Meek v. Pittenger.

[58]Reutter, *Law of Public Education*, 28.

[59]Widmar v. Vincent, 454 U.S. 263, 102 S.Ct. 269, 70 L.Ed.2d 440 (1981).

[60]People of State of Illinois ex rel. McCollum v. Board of Educ. of School Dist. No. 71, Champaign County, 333 U.S. 203, 68 S.Ct. 461, 92 L.Ed. 649 (1948).

[61]Zorach v. Clauson, 343 U.S. 306, 72 S.Ct. 679, 96 L.Ed. 954 (1952).

[62]Brown v. Board of Educ. of Topeka, 349 U.S. 294, 75 S.Ct. 753, 99 L.Ed. 1083 (1955).

[63]Griffin v. County School Bd. of Prince Edward County, 377 U.S. 218, 84 S.Ct. 1226, 12 L.Ed.2d 256 (1964); Rogers v. Paul, 382 U.S. 198, 86 S.Ct. 358, 15 L.Ed.2d 265 (1965).

[64]Green v. County School Bd. of New Kent County, 391 U.S. 430, 88 S.Ct. 1689, 20 L.Ed.2d 716 (1968).

[65]Alexander v. Holmes County Bd. of Educ., 396 U.S. 19, 90 S.Ct. 24 L.Ed.2d 19 (1969).

"denial of fundamental rights to thousands of school children."[64] Shortly thereafter, in *Alexander v. Holmes County Board of Education*, the Court ordered that *all* dual school systems immediately be ended, with disputes to be litigated after new approaches were in place.[65]

Hundreds of desegregation plans grew out of the 1969 *Alexander* decision, and there were also many court evaluations of these plans. A number of oper-

---

Thurgood Marshall
1908–1993

Champion of civil liberties and the first African-American to be appointed to the U.S. Supreme Court (in 1967), Thurgood Marshall was born on July 2, 1908, in Baltimore, Maryland. Originally named Thoroughgood (he changed it to Thurgood later), Marshall attended Baltimore's segregated schools, where his mother taught, and in 1926 he entered Lincoln University, a prestigious African-American school in Philadelphia. To pay for his education he worked in a grocery store, and he graduated *cum laude* in 1930. Then he entered Howard University's law school and graduated first in his class in 1933.

In 1936 Marshall went to work for the National Association for the Advancement of Colored People, and in 1938 he became its chief counsel, beginning his long struggle on behalf of civil rights for all Americans. He frequented many county courthouses in the South, in an effort to support attorneys who were defending clients' civil liberties, and became so familiar a figure in these arenas that he was called "Mr. Civil Rights."

As the NAACP's chief counsel until 1961 Marshall argued thirty-two cases before the Supreme Court. He won twenty-nine of them, including the famous 1954 landmark case of *Brown v. The Board of Education of Topeka, Kansas*, which legally ended segregation in public schools. He also successfully argued the 1950 case that banned separate state law schools for African-Americans.

In 1955 Marshall's wife of twenty-six years, Vivian Burey Marshall, died of lung cancer. The following year

he married Cecilia Suyat, a native Hawaiian and fellow NAACP worker; the couple had two sons, Thurgood and John.

In 1961 President John Kennedy appointed Marshall to the U.S. Court of Appeals in New York, and his reputation for being politically liberal influenced the court's decisions. In 1965 President Lyndon Johnson appointed

Yesterday's Professional

Marshall solicitor general of the U.S. Justice Department, a third-ranking position that is responsible for directing all litigation before federal courts, including the Supreme Court. Then, in 1967, President Johnson nominated him to the U.S. Supreme Court, and the Senate approved by a vote of 69 to 11. Justice Marshall took his seat as the ninety-sixth justice to be appointed, and during his twenty-three years of service he watched the Court change from a liberally active body, under Chief Justice Earl Warren, to an organ against judicial activism and the rights of criminals. As Court decisions grew more conservative, Justice Marshall's voice became the dissenting one.

He suffered his first heart attack in 1976 but continued to serve on the Court until 1991, when he retired. His health continued to fail during the two years of his retirement, and he died on January 24, 1993, of heart failure.

Thurgood Marshall is regarded as one of the most influential Americans of this century. His impact benefited not only African-Americans but also such minority groups as the imprisoned, the disempowered, and the destitute. Noted historian John Hope Franklin said about Justice Marshall that he spoke not "just for black Americans but for Americans of all times."

Source: Based on "Justice Marshall Dies, Leaving Legacy of Equal Rights," *Chicago Tribune, 25 January 1993, pp. 1, 5.*

ating principles emerged from this process: that busing was a legitimate instrument for achieving desegregation; that in instances where court-ordered desegregation had not produced substantial integration in all of a district's schools, the burden of proof was on the local district to show that discrimination was not a factor in how students were assigned to schools;[66] that if a system had too few white students to allow integrated schools, adjacent districts with predominantly white student populations need not be involved in desegregation plans *"unless the state or those surrounding districts were involved in discriminatory acts"*;[67] that the principles under discussion applied equally to segregation of Hispanic students and Native Americans;[68] and that the terms *desegregation* and *integration* have identical legal meanings.[69]

The Court's tests of whether a school district has made or is making appropriate progress toward integration involve activities in six areas: (1) balance in assigning students to attendance centers; (2) transportation parity—most students of one race should not be bused when most students of another race are not; (3) equity in physical facilities; (4) equal access to extracurricular activities; (5) equitable allocation of resources; and (6) personnel placement that puts majority and minority teachers and principals in each building in proportion to their overall numbers in the system. The Court delineated these factors in *Green v. County School Board of New Kent County* (1968); hence, legal writings refer to the six tests as the *Green* categories, or *Green* factors. "Green held that the duty of a former de jure district is to take all necessary steps to convert to a unitary system in which racial discrimination is eliminated . . . and instructed the district courts to fashion remedies that address all these factors"; the term *unitary* has no single fixed meaning "and does not confine the court's discretion in a way that departs from traditional equitable principles."[70]

In the late 1960s the Supreme Court ruled that "all deliberate speed" was still too slow in ending segregated school systems—and that busing was a faster, legitimate way to achieve desegregation. But were teachers to be bused, too? —Spencer Grantill/Stock, Boston

[66]Swann v. Charlotte-Mecklenburg Bd. of Educ., 402 U.S. 1, 91 S.Ct. 1267, 28 L.Ed.2d 554 (1971).

[67]Milliken v. Bradley, 418 U.S. 717, 94 S.Ct. 3112, 41 L.Ed.2d 1069 (1974): "The notion that school district lines may be casually ignored or treated as a mere administrative convenience is contrary to the history of public education in our country."

[68]Cisneros v. Corpus Christi Independent School Dist., 467 F.2d 142 (5 Cir. 1972), cert. den. 413 U.S. 922, 93 S.Ct. 3052, 37 L.Ed.2d 1044 (1973); Arvizu v. Waco Independent School Dist., 495 F.2d 499 (5 Cir. 1974); Morales v. Shannon, 516 F.2d 411 (5 Cir. 1975), cert. den. 423 U.S. 1034, 96 S.Ct. 566, 46 L.Ed.2d 408 (1975); Natonabah v. Board of Educ. of Gallup-McKinley County School Dist., 355 F.Supp. 716 (D.N.M. 1973); Geraud v. Schrader, 531 P.2d 872 (Wyo. 1975).

[69]United States v. Jefferson County Bd. of Educ., 380 F.2d 385 (5 Cir. 1967), cert. den. 389 U.S. 840, 88 S.Ct. 77, 19 L.Ed.2d 103 (1967).

[70]Freeman v. Pitts, 1992 WL 59190 (U.S. Ga.),112 S.Ct. 1430 (1992).

School systems that are under district court supervision need not measure up in all six *Green* categories simultaneously in order to be released from supervision in areas where they have made satisfactory progress. The general principle in deciding how a school system is doing is pragmatic: "The task is to correct, by a balancing of the individual and collective interest, the condition that offends the Constitution."[71] An important measure of compliance is "whether the school district has demonstrated, to the public and to the parents and students of the once disfavored race, its goal-faith commitment to the whole of the decree and to those statutory and constitutional provisions that were the predicate for judicial intervention in the first instance." Finally, "Once racial imbalance traceable to the constitutional violation has been remedied, a school district is under no duty to remedy an imbalance that is caused by demographic [that is, racially segregated housing] factors." Or so, at least, the Court recently ruled.[72]

Of all the *Green* factors, the residual effects of segregation on school faculties has been one of the most persistent issues. During the early years of replacing segregated dual systems by unitary integrated ones, many African-American teachers and administrators lost their jobs. In one North Carolina district, for example, when desegregation occurred, all white teachers who wanted to stay did so, and fourteen new white teachers were hired. But only eight out of twenty-four black faculty members were rehired. The Fourth Circuit Court of Appeals ruled that the black teachers who already were employed were entitled to be rehired before new white teachers were brought in.[73] The Fifth Circuit Court of Appeals went further, saying that "recruitment of a person of a race, color, or national origin different from that of the individual dismissed or demoted [in a situation where getting rid of de jure segregation caused the reduction in force]" will not be allowed "until each displaced staff member who is qualified" rejects an offer to fill the vacancy.[74]

There have been a number of court challenges involving different local or individual situations.[75] In general, courts have tended to address the faculty issue as representing more than the employment rights of teachers. They have held that desegregating the teaching staff is an integral part of ending de jure segregation and that students should "have the opportunity to be taught by an integrated faculty."[76]

DE FACTO ISSUES   It is clear that states and local school districts are expected to actively redress de jure segregation. But are public education authorities equally responsible for remedying segregation that has resulted from housing patterns or from other causes not attributable to governmental action which *intended* to require or encourage segregation? The answer is no, but these authorities do have the power to do so.[77] Intent is not always easy to know or prove, and so there is sometimes extensive disagreement about which aspects of segregation are intended and which are accidental. Several factors affect how courts look at de facto issues, including (1) whether there is a history of discrimination, (2) what the effects of an action are likely to be, (3) what sequence of events leads to an action, (4) whether a practice departs from "normal" procedures, and (5) whether inequalities are "rationally explainable."

Courts found that de facto segregation was not rationally explainable in

[71]Ibid., 13.

[72]Ibid., 203.

[73]Chambers v. Hendersonville City Bd. of Educ., 364 F.2d 189 (4 Cir. 1966); North Carolina Teachers Ass'n v. Asheboro City Bd. of Educ., 393 F.2d 736 (4 Cir. 1968).

[74]Singleton v. Jackson Municipal Separate School Dist., 419 F.2d 1211 (5 Cir. 1970), cert. den. 396 U.S. 1032, 90 S.Ct. 612, 24 L.Ed.2d 530 (1970).

[75]See, for example, Wall v. Stanley County Bd. of Educ., 259 F.Supp. 238 (M.D.N.C. 1966); Wall v. Stanley County Bd. of Educ., 378 F.2d 275 (4 Cir. 1967).

[76]Kromnick v. School District of Philadelphia, 739 F.2d 894 (3 Cir. 1984), cert. den. 469 U.S. 1107, 105 S.Ct. 782, 83 L.Ed.2d 777 (1985); Morgan v. Kerrigan, 509 F.2d 599 (1 Cir. 1975); Morgan v. Kerrigan, 509 F.2d 580 (1 Cir. 1974), cert. den. 421 U.S. 963, 95 S.Ct. 1950, 44 L.Ed.2d 449 (1975).

[77]Bell v. School City of Gary, Indiana, 324 F.2d 209 (7 Cir. 1963), cert. den. 377 U.S. 924, 84 S.Ct. 1223, 12 L.Ed.2d 216 (1964); Downs v. Board of Educ., 336 F.2d 988 (10 Cir. 1964), cert. den. 380 U.S. 914, 85 S.Ct. 898, 13 L.Ed.2d 800 (1965). On authority to correct, see Washington v. Seattle School Dist. No. 1, 458 U.S. 457, 102 S.Ct. 3187, 73 L.Ed.2d 896 (1982).

the ability-grouping (tracking) system in Washington, D.C., and they ordered it dismantled.[78] The District of Columbia Circuit Court of Appeals upheld this decision.[79] The Supreme Court of California ruled that the state constitution mandates all of California's school districts "to take reasonably feasible steps to alleviate school segregation, whether such segregation is de jure or de facto in nature."[80]

COLORBLINDNESS IN REMEDIES   In seeking to correct past discrimination based on skin color or on ethnic heritage, is it permissible to recognize color, race, or ethnicity in plans designed to promote equality? Courts have repeatedly—although warily—ruled in the affirmative. The 1982 Seattle case is a landmark,[81] but many cases recognize that race may (must) be taken into account.[82] A 1978 California case reaffirmed that race may be *one* factor in a medical school's admission decisions, while leaving it unclear whether race may safely be taken as the *only* major criterion.[83] During President Bush's administration (1989–1993) the Department of Education appeared to move away from recognizing race or ethnicity as a legitimate factor in redressing the effects of past discrimination.[84] No doubt the issue will continue to be discussed. In cases where state legislatures have tried to block local efforts at achieving racial or ethnic equity, the U.S. Supreme Court has generally sided with efforts to achieve greater equity.[85]

SCHOOL BOARD ISSUES

AUTHORITY OF BOARD   For two centuries local school boards were the paramount authority over most educational matters in the United States. School boards still tend to have considerable practical discretion in making policy, although courts view them as *extensions of state authority*, not as units with independent or parallel powers. (The development of this arrangement is discussed in Chapter 9.) Technically speaking, local boards have only the power that is delegated to them by the states. They must operate within the context of federal law and state constitutions as defined by the courts.

A significant definitional aspect of board issues is that a local board exists only "as a whole"; that is, an individual board member has no authority to act for the district. Moreover, any action must be taken at a legal meeting of the board. But what is a "legal" meeting? There are several varied and complex considerations, which the following few examples will begin to illustrate.

LEGALITY OF MEETINGS AND ACTIONS   Local school boards may formulate and adopt procedural rules for their meetings. However, if there are no rules—and if the state has not established specific rules—usual parliamentary procedure applies.[86] To be considered legal, a meeting must be announced in advance to all members of the board, unless it is a regularly scheduled meeting set by law, in which case all members are already informed. Courts are vigorous in watching over this matter. To give "notice" of a meeting means that every member must be informed far enough in advance to attend. It does not mean that a member who is out of state must return before any action can take place.[87] If all board members attend a specially called meeting and participate, board actions are

[78]Hobson v. Hansen, 269 F.Supp. 401 (D.D.C. 1967).

[79]Smuck v. Hobson, 408 F.2d 175 (D.C. Cir. 1969).

[80]Crawford v. Board of Educ. of City of Los Angeles, 17 Cal. 3d 280, 130 Cal. Rptr. 724, 551 P.2d 28 (1976).

[81]See note 77.

[82]For example, School Committee of Boston v. Board of Educ., 352 Mass. 693, 227 N.E.2d 729(1967), app. dism. 389 U.S. 572, 88 S.Ct 692, 19 L.Ed.2d 778 (1968); Jenkins v. Township of Morris School Dist., 58 N.J. 483, 279 A.2d 619 (1971); Balaban v. Rubin, 14 N.Y.S.2d 281, 199 N.E.2d 375 (1964).

[83]Regents of Univ. of California v. Bakke, 438 U.S. 265, 98 S.Ct. 2733, 57 L.Ed.2d 750 (1978).

[84]Scott Jaschik, "Scholarships Set Up for Minority Students Are Called Illegal," *Chronicle of Higher Education*, 12 December 1990, A1, A20.

[85]Reutter, *Law of Public Education*, 802–803.

[86]McCormick v. Board of Educ., 58 N.M. 648, 274 P.2d 299 (1954).

[87]Consolidated School Dist. of Glidden v. Griffin, 201 Iowa 63, 206 N.W. 86 (1925).

legal even if a member later claims not to have been notified. But if all members are present and one or more refuses to participate because of not having been adequately notified of the meeting, any action taken may be declared illegal.[88]

To be legal a board meeting must have a quorum present; unless otherwise defined, this usually means a simple majority of the total board membership. Similarly, unless otherwise specified by law or by the board's rules, a simple majority of the quorum is sufficient to adopt a motion. Voting—unless differently specified by the board's rules or by law—may be by any usual method that the board prefers (roll call, voice, show of hands, secret ballot).

Members' knowledge of any laws or board regulations affecting their procedures is important. Courts have ruled that even a well-intended violation of procedures because of ignorance of them can invalidate actions taken by the board. For example, an Arkansas administrator got the approval of each board member to take certain personnel actions but did not present them at a legal board meeting; a teacher who was discharged under this procedure won salary to the end of her contract period in an appeal to the state supreme court.[89]

[88]Knickerbocker v. Redlands High School Dist., 49 Cal. App. 2d 722, 122 P.2d 289 (1942).

[89]Farris v. Stone County School Dist. No. 1, 248 Ark. 19, 450 S.W.2d 279 (1970).

[90]Payne v. Petrie, 419 S.W.2d 761 (Ky. 1967); Edwards v. Mettler, 268 Minn. 472, 129 N.W.2d 805 (1964).

ABSTENTIONS   Courts have generally ruled that board members who are present at a meeting should vote, not abstain, when a matter is properly before the board. Abstentions are not counted but are treated as approval of what the majority of voting members decided.[90] This does not prevent board members from leaving a meeting in order to remove a quorum so that a legal vote cannot be taken. For this strategy to work, however, the members must actually depart; they

Comparative Perspective on Today's Issues . . .

◆ **DO SCHOOL BOARDS HAVE THE RIGHT TO CENSOR STUDENTS' LITERARY AND ARTISTIC EXPRESSIONS?**

The Issue   Free expression in student newspapers and artwork typically comes under scrutiny of school administrators, who usually allow or disallow it according to whether or not they think it might be morally harmful or questionable. Many see this as a violation of basic civil rights.

YES   School boards and their designees—superintendents and administrators—are charged with setting school policy and deciding on the curriculum. When students produce works that fall under the school's jurisdiction, these expressions should be subject to school board policies and, at least, become part of the informal curriculum.

NO   School officials do set policies and determine the curriculum. Yet there is a limit to their power, and that limit is exceeded when their decisions cross into areas of students' civil liberties. Principals do not have the right to practice "unreasonable censorship" when it comes to students' free speech or expression.

Source: Based on Nat Hentoff, "Free Speech at Potrero Hill," *Washington Post*, 22 April 1989, sec. A, p. 23; *Wall Street Journal*, 17 January 1989, sec. C, p. 27, and 11 October 1989, sec. B, p. 1; and "Students' Spicy Artwork Doesn't Please 'Vanilla' Taste," *Washington Post*, 17 May 1990, sec. B, p. 1.

may not simply step to another part of the room and then rejoin the meeting after the matter has failed to be addressed because of the lack of a quorum.[91]

BOARD COMMITTEES   Just as an individual member may not act for the board, a board's committees may not make decisions for it. The board may, of course, appoint individuals or committees to perform specific tasks about which it has voted legally. For example, the board may appoint a committee to gather information and report it at a meeting. The board may even appoint a "hearing examiner" to conduct hearings when no board members are present. The examiner may take evidence, summarize facts, and explain conclusions. But at this point the board must take action.[92]

PUBLIC MEETINGS   Must school board meetings be open to the public? What does it mean, to say that a meeting must be "public"? These are important questions, because most states mandate that school board meetings be public. However, part or all of a particular board meeting may be held in **executive session**, which excludes members of the public (for example, so that the board can discuss personnel actions); but the board's final votes must normally be taken in a meeting which members of the public may attend.[93] Probably, also, meetings should be in a public building, and within the district's geographic boundaries.[94] Unless state or board rules specify otherwise, the board is not required to give advanced publication of its agenda for a meeting.

School boards usually keep minutes of meetings and other records. Generally, members of the public may examine the minutes of open meetings, but they may not necessarily see the handwritten notes taken by the board's secretary, from which the minutes will be constructed.[95] People may make videotapes or audiotapes of public board meetings, but the board may vote not to allow its own members to tape an executive session.[96]

What happens if there are no records of a board meeting? And how extensive must records normally be? Board actions have been invalidated when no records were kept—but not always. It depends partly on the requirements of state law and board rules. In almost all cases, it is expected that at least the results of the board's action will be recorded, and official records of such action is all that courts normally use in deciding these matters. Usually they do not—after the fact—take additional testimony about the "real intent" of a particular action or about any debate leading to the action if these are not reported in the record of the meeting.

CONCLUSIONS

Courts affect educational operations in many ways. Indeed, hardly any aspect of school life has gone completely unnoticed by the courts. From searches of students' lockers, to the conditions for hiring and firing school personnel, to the procedures for electing board members and conducting their meetings—if people can disagree about an educational issue, courts have rendered an opinion. And they will hand down many more.

[91]State v. Vanosdal, 131 Ind. 388, 31 N.E. 79 (1892).

[92]Reutter, *Law of Public Education*, 868–869.

[93]Alva v. Sequoia Union High Dist., 98 Cal. App. 2d 656, 220 P.2d 788 (1950).

[94]Quast v. Knudson, 276 Minn. 340, 150 N.W.2d 199 (1967).

[95]Conover v. Board of Educ. of Nebo School Dist., 1 Utah 2d 375, 267 P.2d 768 (1954).

[96]Belcher v. Mansi, 569 F.Supp. 379 (D.R.I. 1973); Maurice River Tp. Bd. of Educ. v. Maurice River Tp. Teachers Ass'n, 187 N.J.Super. 566, 455 A.2d 563 (1982); Dean v. Guste, 414 So.2d 862 (La. App. 1982).

Courts perform two major functions in education. One is that they provide a forum of final resort in which to settle differences that otherwise cannot be resolved. Perhaps equally important, however, is that courts provide a mass of codified tradition and values which shape how individuals and groups reach decisions about appropriate action without resorting to litigation. Thus the public and educators need not be practicing attorneys to know enough about the legal aspects of education that they can (at least sometimes) cooperate for the benefit of students and society in general.

KEY TERMS

common law

enacted law

case law

U.S. district court

federal judicial circuit court

municipal court

state supreme court

U.S. Supreme Court

res judicata

executive session

SUGGESTED READINGS

For historical and contemporary Supreme Court views on **desegregation** read Plessy v. Ferguson (1896); Brown v. Board of Education of Topeka (1954, 1955); and Freeman v. Pitts (1992). For issues related to **Hispanic education** read Cisneros v. Corpus Christi Independent School District (5 Cir. 1972; and S.Ct. 1973). And for **students' First Amendment rights** read Tinker v. Des Moines Independent Community School District (1969) and Hazelwood School District v. Kuhlmeier (1988).

E. Edmund Reutter, *The Law of Public Education*, 3d ed. (Mineola, N.Y.: Foundation Press, 1985). This book gives a good overview of many topics of interest to educators.

Michael W. LaMorte, *School Law: Cases and Concepts* (Boston: Allyn & Bacon, 1991). This book introduces school law concepts to readers with little background in the topic and includes subjects of interest to students, such as drug testing, freedom of expression, AIDS, and employment discrimination; it also includes teacher-related issues.

Martha M. McCarthy and Nelda H. Cambron-McCabe, *Public School Law: Teachers' and Students' Rights* (Boston: Allyn & Bacon, 1992). This book provides educators and students with an extensive

discussion of the development of laws affecting public education; it also covers current trends.

Julius Menacker, *School Law: Theoretical and Case Perspectives* (Boston: Allyn & Bacon, 1987). This more theoretical approach to legal concepts and issues in educational settings also discusses major policy issues.

Louis Fischer, David Schimmel, and Cynthia Kelly, *Teachers and the Law* (White Plains, N.Y.: Longman, 1991). This book discusses legal issues related to teaching and also describes the expanding body of constitutional law that affects students' and teachers' rights.

A. H. Nothem, *Collective Bargaining in Education: A Casebook* (Boston: Allyn & Bacon, 1992). Using the case-study method, this book synthesizes theory and practice in collective bargaining.

Gary Orfield, *Turning Back the Clock: The Reagan-Bush Retreat from Civil Rights in Higher Education* (Washington, D.C.: University Press of America, 1992). This book studies civil rights policies and changes and practices in enforcement during the 1980s, assessing their effects on higher education for minority students.

Issues in Education

Formal education systems everywhere [are] . . . increasingly obsolete and maladjusted in relation to their rapidly changing societies. . . .

—Philip H. Coombs, The World Crisis in Education: The View from the Eighties
(New York: Oxford University Press, 1985), 21

Addressing educational problems and proposing reforms often bring significant political benefits, while changing educational policies may entail unacceptably large political costs.

—David N. Plank and Don Adams, "Death, Taxes, and School Reform: Educational Policy Change in
Comparative Perspective," Administrator's Notebook *33, no. 1 (1989)*

No significant and enduring improvement in our schools is possible without the leadership and commitment of the nation's teachers.

—Ronald A. Wolk, "Connections: The Power of Ideas," Teacher Magazine *2, no. 1 (September 1990): 3*
[Italics removed from original]

12

Issues in Education

ADVANCED ORGANIZERS

■

In this chapter you will learn

How Americans have viewed their schools in recent years

What some national reports have said about educational reform

Which major issues challenge American educators today, and how those issues relate to social and political factors

armen Valdez has taught math for several years, and in recent weeks she has noticed that Aida Gonzales has missed more second-period algebra classes than she has attended. Aida has quit handing in homework, and she failed the last quiz; when she is in class, she stares into space. Today she has entered the class late, has worn sunglasses throughout the period, and has obviously been copying from a classmate's test paper. Carmen has decided to question Aida about all this, and as the bell rings, she calls out:

"Aida, I need to talk with you. Do you have some time later today?"

"Just at noon. I have to be home by 2:30."

Carmen suggests that they grab a bite together at a nearby fast-food restaurant—teacher's treat, this time—and Aida agrees. During lunch Carmen asks Aida in Spanish about her poor attendance, her missing homework, and her apparent cheating on the test. Aida is vague in her answers, and Carmen presses on: "I know that your family hasn't been in this country long, and I know you are having trouble in some of your classes. But you were doing well in algebra. What's happening?"

Soon Aida pours out her story. The family has lived here less than two years, having left Central America to escape civil war. Aida's grandparents and an older brother died as a result of the fighting. She also has two younger brothers who are ten and seven, and two young sisters, one who is three and one who is only eleven months old. Her parents know little English. Both worked for a cleaning service, but her father was laid off three months ago. He looks for work on days when he feels OK, but he often has migraine headaches, and he has been losing weight and has a persistent cough. A neighbor looks after the two youngest children when Aida's mother is at work, but the neighbor leaves for her job at 2:30 every afternoon—that's why Aida has to rush home. And since her mother comes home exhausted at 7 PM, Aida has to make dinner—which lately has often been just beans and rice because there has been little money. The family hasn't been able to benefit from unemployment compensation and food stamps, because her father has heard that the Immigration and Naturalization Service might deport them if they apply for assistance.

Aida says that she is going to quit school. She reads and understands English fairly well, but she is failing English and social studies and may fail biology, too, since she can't write without making spelling and other errors. She is shy about explaining her language problems to teachers. Finally, she shows Carmen a black eye hidden under makeup and sunglasses: Her father hit her the night before during an argument when she said that she was going to earn some money. "He thought I meant I was going to be a whore on the street," she sobbed.

It is 1:05, and Carmen has to get to her trigonometry class. What should she do about Aida? What *can* she do? What would you do?

EDUCATIONAL REFORM DURING THE 1980s

■

"There are few things in life that one can count on, but one is dissatisfaction with schools," write comparative education experts David Plank and Don Adams of the University of Pittsburgh. "The United States is hardly unique in this respect," they add. "Campaigns to reform national educational systems are launched regularly in countries around the world." Which issues raise the call for reform? These "vary from country to country or from period to period, as do the proposed solutions," they conclude, "but the belief that something is wrong with the schools and that 'reform' will fix it appears to be one of the few reliable features of modern life."[1]

In the United States school reform last became a dominant theme during the 1980s, and many of the issues raised were rooted philosophically in the progressive reform efforts of the 1930s. At the time—in response to the Great Depression—reform educators called for schools to take the lead in transforming American society. One of the most vocal reformers was Columbia University's George S. Counts, who dared schools to build a new social order by taking responsibility for the transmission of (1) ideals that foster a democratic, egalitarian society; (2) the skills and knowledge needed by free citizens living in an advanced technological culture; and (3) attitudes and values that guarantee civil liberties for everyone. However, no concrete reform plans or proposals were developed during the 1930s.

Things were different a half-century later. From 1983 to 1988 more than a dozen commissions and professional organizations published analyses of educational problems, and this time they proposed changes. President Ronald

School reform was politicized during the 1980's, when Secretary of Education William Bennett announced that American schools were terrible. During the 1988 election he advised presidential candidates to make schools a central issue, and George Bush became "the education president." —UPI/Bettmann

[1]Ronald A. Wolk, "Connections: The Power of Ideas," *Teacher Magazine* 2, no. 1 (September 1990): 3.

Reagan's controversial and aggressive U.S. Secretary of Education, William Bennett, announced that American schools were terrible—and that Chicago's schools were worst of all. He advised the presidential candidates to make education a central issue in the 1988 campaign.[2] George Bush followed Bennett's advice, saying that he wanted to be "the education president."

Just how bad were American schools during the 1980s? A few were awful; many others were less effective than their teachers and administrators wanted them to be; but a substantial number of schools were excellent. On balance, more students were completing more years of schooling than at any time in American history—and a high proportion of them were satisfied with what they were getting. For example, a Roper poll asked one thousand students, ages eight to seventeen, if they liked school, and 77 percent said yes; when asked to give their schools a grade, 78 percent said A or B.[3] Similarly, in 1988 a Gallup poll asked parents to grade the school attended by their oldest child: 70 percent said A or B. In the same poll 51 percent of parents who had children in school gave the public schools generally an A or a B; only 37 percent of parents who did not have children in school gave the public schools those two grades.[4] In other words, students and their parents—who had direct knowledge of schools—were much more likely to assess public schools positively than were citizens without children in school, whose impressions were formed primarily by the media. (Indeed, there were twice as many favorable responses from students than from citizens who did not have children in school.)

RESEARCH SAYS

For Tomorrow's Education . . .

High school and college students readily admit to lying, cheating, and stealing in school, at work, and in personal relationships—so reports a two-year study of nine thousand youth questioned during 1991–92 by the Josephson Institute for the Advancement of Ethics, in Los Angeles. See "Unethical Acts Common Among Young, Study Says," *Chicago Tribune*, 15 November 1992, sec. 1, p. 26.

Although the negative impressions of schools were carried by the media, journalists were simply reporting what politicians and policy analysts were saying about U.S. education. Why were political figures so critical of our schools? One reason is that so many seemingly intractable social problems are visible in schools, including teenage pregnancy, substance abuse, AIDS, suicide, teen unemployment, and gang violence—all of which also occur *outside* of schools even more frequently. But other social pressures also had an impact on schools. The 1980s was a period of doubt about American achievements. The automotive and computer industries seemed to be dominated by Japanese companies, and some commentators said that Japan had a superior school system. American technological supremacy was over, claimed some analysts. A comparative assessment of math and science knowledge in twenty-one countries revealed that several in-

[2]Steven Teske, "Bennett Says Presidential Hopefuls Should Support Accountability Measures," *Education Daily* 9 September 1987, 1–2.
[3]Cited in Ben Wattenberg, *The First Universalist Nation* (New York: Free Press, 1990), 88–89.
[4]Alec M. Gallup and Stanley M. Elam, "The 20th Annual Gallup Poll of the Public's Attitudes Toward the Public Schools," *Phi Delta Kappan* 70 (September 1988): 36. Also see "Poll: My School's OK, Yours Isn't," *USA Today*, 28 August 1992, p. 1A.

dustrialized nations appeared to be outdoing the United States.[5] Concern arising from factors like these inevitably found political expression.

Beginning in 1981, then, President Ronald Reagan's administration intended to reverse the thirty-year trend of a growing federal role in funding education. In fact, after adjusting for inflation, federal expenditures for education decreased by 20 percent from 1980 to 1988. But since funding had not been keeping up with the rate of inflation, it was politically risky simply to cut the money spent on schools. However, if it could be shown that schools were so impossibly bad that without "extensive reform" it was a waste to spend money on them, then it would be prudent instead of irresponsible to cut funding.

"A NATION AT RISK"

The U.S. Department of Education created a prestigious **National Commission on Excellence in Education**, which, after deliberation, issued its report in 1983. Entitled *A Nation at Risk: The Imperative for Educational Reform*, the report was blunt:

> Our Nation is at risk. Our once unchallenged preeminence in commerce, industry, science, and technological innovation is being overtaken by competitors throughout the world. This report is concerned with only one of the many causes and dimensions of the problem, but it is the one that undergirds American prosperity, security, and civility. We report to the American people that while we can take justifiable pride in what our schools and colleges have historically accomplished, . . . the educational foundations of our society are presently being eroded by a rising tide of mediocrity that threatens our very future as a nation and a people. What was unimaginable a generation ago has begun to occur—others are matching and surpassing our educational attainments.[6]

Without major educational reform, the commission said, the upcoming generation's skills "will not equal, will not even approach, those of their parents."

Who was to blame for this situation? Basically, the report blamed teachers—and the colleges and universities that had prepared them. The least intelligent college students had chosen teaching; education units had taught them "methods" instead of content; once in schools they lowered graduation standards, gave little homework, and allowed students to avoid academic subjects—especially math, science, and computer courses.

A Nation at Risk set off a flurry of activity in many areas. "The debate . . . produced countless—often conflicting—analyses of the problems and proposals to solve them," noted the editor of *Teacher Magazine*.[7] Some individuals and groups, for their own reasons, joined the finger pointing at schools and those who worked in them. Social critic and author Jonathan Kozol, for example, published a book claiming that one-third of adult Americans are illiterate.[8] The claim was insupportable, but Kozol had made a living for twenty years through books and lectures describing the ills of American schools.

More than a dozen groups advanced their critiques and made suggestions for reform. A number of universities formed themselves into the **Holmes Group**

[5]Alan C. Purves and Daniel U. Levine, eds., *Educational Policy and International Assessment* (Berkeley, Calif.: McCutchan, 1975). Also see Carol Jouzaitis, "American Schools Short-change Students in Science, Study Reveals," *Chicago Tribune*, 27 March 1992, p. 1.

[6]National Commission on Excellence in Education, *A Nation at Risk: The Imperative for Educational Reform* (Washington, D.C.: U.S. Department of Education, 1983), 5.

[7]Wolk, "Connections," 3.

[8]Jonathan Kozol, *Savage Inequalities: Children in America's Schools* (New York: Crown, 1991).

George S. Counts
1889–1974

Known for his down-to-earth midwestern style, George Sylvester Counts was born on a farm near Baldwin, Kansas, situated in the eastern part of the state. He was educated in the local public schools and graduated from high school in 1907; he then entered Baker University, in his home town. After earning a bachelor's degree in 1911, Counts taught math and science for a year at Sumner County High School, in Wellington, Kansas, and then accepted a principalship for the following year in Peabody, Kansas. In 1913 he married Lois Hazel Bailey and entered graduate school at the University of Chicago. He worked under educational scientist Charles Judd at a time when the study of education was preoccupied with intelligence scales and the measurement of achievement and aptitude. Counts also worked with Albion Small, a noted sociologist. Thus, his graduate study combined scientific education—testing and measuring—with sociology.

In 1916 Counts attained his doctorate, having written a dissertation about the arithmetic scales used in a 1915 survey of Cleveland's schools. From 1916 to 1926 he joined faculties at Delaware College, Harris Teachers College (St. Louis), the University of Washington, Yale University, and the University of Chicago. During this decade he turned attention away from educational science and toward philosophical and sociological analysis of schools and society. In 1922 he published a study of high school dropouts in *The Selective Character of American Secondary Education*. His analysis revealed that high schools reinforced racial, ethnic, and social-class inequities and tended to serve the needs and interests of the upper classes while neglecting immigrant and African-American students. He also chastised educators for not taking charge of the curriculum in order to keep pace with the demands of a technological society.

In 1927 Counts became a faculty member at Teachers College, Columbia University, and that same year he published a study of *The Social Composition of Boards of Education*, in which he described American schools boards as being composed of society's elite: bankers, merchants, lawyers, physicians, and business leaders. In 1928 he published a study of the politics of Chicago and its schools, *School and Society in Chicago*.

By the early 1930s Counts had published three other books. Two of them took a more historical view of edu-

Yesterday's Professional

cation, noting that the rise of high schools was related to urbanization and industrialization and that schools had been (and continued to be) isolated from America's social, political, and economic forces. He also visited the Soviet Union and wrote *The Soviet Challenge to America*, in which he blamed the political and social crisis of the Great Depression on the lack of social planning.

In 1932 Counts wrote his most controversial book, *Dare the Schools Build a New Social Order*, in which he lamented the failure of a capitalistic economy and challenged the educational workforce to become the movers and shakers of society: to lead the nation in shaping a just, egalitarian, economically solid society in a technological and industrial era.

Counts was a major figure in the progressive decades of the 1920s and 1930s. During the early 1930s he became one of the editors of the progressive journal *The Social Frontier*, which aimed to interpret education broadly enough to include all forces and influences that serve the individual and promote the wellbeing of all who do the work of society. He was president of many professional organizations, including the American Federation of Teachers.

In 1955 Counts retired from Teachers College and for the next two decades occupied visiting professorships at the University of Pittsburgh, the University of Colorado, Michigan State University, Northwestern University, and Southern Illinois University (where a major John Dewey collection had been formed). He remained active throughout his emeritus years, attending many scholarly and professional meetings until his death in 1974, at age eighty-five.

Source: *Based on Gerald L. Gutek, George S. Counts and American Civilization (Macon, Ga.: Mercer University Press, 1984).*

and advocated making all teacher education programs postbaccalaureate. They thus hoped to identify with the reformers and disassociate themselves from criticism of past teacher education. In any case, these institutions had few undergraduate education majors.

RESEARCH SAYS

For Tomorrow's Education . . .

A summer reading program in Waucanda, Illinois, received less-than-glowing reviews by students who participated. In an attempt to maintain students' reading interests and achievement levels during the summer months, this district instituted a summer reading assignment for all students. Although many complained, about two-thirds completed their assignments and pledged to stick to the program. See Jerry Thomas, "Summertime Reading Still Tees Off Kids," *Chicago Tribune*, 20 September, 1991.

Of the numerous parties with a stake in the outcome of educational reform, no group had a higher stake than governors and state legislators. This was nothing new, for struggles over the control of education date to the mid-nineteenth century (see Chapter 9). "The politics of school reform in rich and poor countries alike revolves around the question of who shall control the schools," write David Plank and Don Adams.[9] Talk of educational reform heightened the issue of control once again. Given the Reagan administration's push for states and local districts to assume a larger share of school financing, many state officials wanted to secure greater control over their schools at the same time.

CONTROL OVER PUBLIC EDUCATION

One tangible consequence of the reform conversations during the 1980s was an increase in state involvement in education. Most states came up with their own **reform package**. Some of the most elaborate—for example, House Bill 72 in Texas—called for more sweeping changes than were ever adopted. Simple economics got in the way. To implement career ladders and salaries commensurate with the performance and skill levels that the plans anticipated would have meant raising taxes far beyond existing rates. As Plank and Adams cautioned:

> Politicians and policy-makers may be more interested in cultivating a public image of leadership than in bringing about significant educational change. The political benefits that accrue to those who propose reforms are often large, but the political costs to be borne by those who seek to disrupt the status quo by putting their proposals into operation may be prohibitive.[10]

Many states that backed away from funding reform nevertheless asserted a new level of authority in regulating education. It was another round in the long arm-wrestling contest between centralized control versus community power. Cen-

[9]David N. Plank and Don Adams, "Death, Taxes, and School Reform: Educational Policy Change in Comparative Perspective," *Administrator's Notebook* 33, no. 1 (1989).
[10]Ibid.

tralization beat out community control, on balance, although it remains to be seen how long state legislators and governors will retain the level of interest in schools that they have shown since the early 1980s. When President Bush chose a new secretary of education in December 1990, he named Lamar Alexander— a man who had run successfully for governor of Tennessee on a platform of educational reform. Similarly, President Clinton's choice for heading the Department of Education, former Governor Richard Riley, was known for his educational accomplishments and reforms in South Carolina.[11]

There were many local examples of the struggle for control that constituted a major feature of the reform movement. Boston's mayor, Raymond Flynn, moved to abolish the elected School Committee and to have his office take over appointing the superintendent of schools.[12] The Illinois state legislature mandated state rather than local certification of teachers and administrators for Chicago's schools. In compensation, the legislature gave parents and teachers more say in school matters by creating eleven-member local school councils for each of the city's 547 public schools. Each council included two teachers (selected by the building's staff), two community representatives (elected by voters), six parents (elected by parents), and the principal. Each council had budgetary authority and selected the school's principal. In 1990 the Illinois Supreme Court ruled that this plan was unconstitutional, and so the law was rewritten, and the councils continued to operate. In 1992 a new suit charged that the method of electing council members was unconstitutional.[13]

At the heart of the struggle for control over schools is the issue of public funding for education. Dissatisfied with the traditional ways that public schools have been financed, some reform politicians—especially in larger metropolitan districts where local tax support is not as great as in wealthier suburban districts— are seeking amendments to state constitutions that would make the states guarantee equal expenditures per pupil.[14] Opponents complain that this type of funding reform would put an additional burden on the state income tax system and also would take property taxes away from wealthier districts and give them to poorer districts—an approach that might lead to educational mediocrity for all. Opponents also point out that other state-funded services (such as mental and public health) would be slighted as a larger portion of the financial pie goes to education. Still others support voucher or tuition plans that can be spent in the school of one's choice. Some Vermont towns, for example, have no local school system; instead, the local tax revenues that would normally be used to support such a system are given directly to students, who can attend the school of their choice—even if the school is outside Vermont.[15]

CULTURAL DIVERSITY

■

Another focus of *A Nation at Risk* was for schools to pay more attention to meeting the needs of disadvantaged students. Several other reports echoed this thought.[16] The idea was not new, but it was stated with renewed emphasis. Why? Because

[11]See, for example, "Clinton Completes His Cabinet," *Chicago Tribune*, 25 December 1992, p. 1.

[12]"Democracy and Schools," *Christian Science Monitor*, 24 December 1990, p. 2.

[13]Scott Pendleton, "Chicago School Reform Takes Root in Community Action," *Christian Science Monitor*, 17 October 1990, p. 9; Jeffrey E. Mirel, "Will Politics Spoil School Reform?" *Chicago Tribune*, 2 December 1990; Karen M. Thomas and Patrick T. Reardon, "Chicago Leaders Scramble to Keep School Reform Plans Alive," *Chicago Tribune*, 2 December 1990, sec. 2, p. 3; and "School Council Elections Illegal, New Suit Charges," *Chicago Sun Times*, 19 April 1992, p. 28.

[14]See, for example, "School Fund Amendment Plan Targeted," *Chicago Tribune*, 11 September 1992, sec. 2, p. 1.

[15]"Time to Get Out of the School Business," *Chicago Tribune*, 25 August 1992, sec. 1, p. 18.

[16]See, for example, the Twentieth Century Fund, *Making the Grade*, and the Carnegie Foundation for the Advancement of Teaching, *The Early Years*.

the needs of business and industry had changed dramatically. In 1918, when the Commission on the Reorganization of Secondary Education named "vocation" as one of seven Cardinal Principles (see Chapter 7), there were many occupational positions for school leavers. The skills needed for many of these positions could be learned easily and quickly on the job. Schooling was not required for many well-paying jobs. A worker could make steel, drill for oil, assemble or repair cars (and thousands of other products), pave roads, or construct buildings with minimal knowledge of the three R's.

Under these circumstances, large numbers of students could leave high school without a diploma—even having poor abilities in reading, writing, and calculating—and create no economic difficulty. The fact that standardized testing, ability-group tracking, and the marking system worked against many working-class students may have been an ethical problem, but it was not an economic one. Vocational preparation in high school meant one of three curricular tracks: (1) college preparation, (2) secretarial and commercial, and (3) general (everyone else). With minor exceptions the only truly vocational aspect of the large "general" track was time away from school for on-the-job training.

BASIC SKILLS AND THE JOB MARKET

By the early 1980s a major transformation in the nature of American jobs was obvious. Assembly-line work was mostly automated and becoming robotic. Even assembly operations that retained the need for human manipulation, such as clothing construction, were relocating to places like Mexico, Korea, and Hong Kong, where labor costs were lower. The American economy was based increasingly on information and services, and so were the jobs.

As assembly-line jobs became automated or moved to countries where labor was cheaper, American workers needed new skills—raising another call for "school reform." People without jobs cannot pay taxes or buy the products of automated industry.
—George Haling/Photo Researchers

As computers became commonplace, symbol-manipulation skills became a universal necessity. Those who could not read, write, and think mathematically—and at rather sophisticated skill levels—were not qualified for most jobs. And people without jobs could not pay taxes or buy the products of automated industry. Thus students who left school without adequate basic skills (including computer literacy) were a liability. This was certainly a problem, and politicians addressed it under the label of "school reform."

The issue of basic skills has had two major, interrelated dimensions—one curricular and one sociopolitical. On the curricular side, most **reform proposals** have called for more homework, improved texts, more computer work, more time on tasks, and a guaranteed minimal performance on *a single national curricular standard.* So far the preoccupation with students' basic skills has been the overriding concern. But rather than acknowledging that schools operated as they did because of historic economic and social conditions, many reformers have blamed the people who worked in schools. Some questioned whether teachers themselves lacked basic skills, and so checks on this possibility became part of many reform proposals. "Blaming the schools' problems on those who work in them may be politically expedient," say Plank and Adams, but it minimizes the likelihood that reform proposals will work.[17] Teachers and administrators resent being blamed, of course, but—more important—such a call for reform misunderstands the reasons for existing conditions and, therefore, misdirects solutions.

RESEARCH SAYS

For Tomorrow's Education . . .

In a national study of science achievement, of twenty-thousand pupils who were tested in grades 4, 8, and 12, a disappointing percentage failed to understand basic science. The study concluded that students were not being taught enough and not being taught properly. Average scores of minority students were substantially lower than those of white students. Females in grade 4 scored about the same as boys, but by grade 12 girls' scores were significantly lower. See "American Schools Shortchange Students in Science, Study Reveals," *Chicago Tribune*, 27 March 1992, sec. 1, p. 4.

The sociopolitical dimension of the basic-skills issue found its expression in reform proposals that called for meeting the needs of **at-risk students**, or disadvantaged students. Because a disproportionate number of African-American, Hispanic-American, and Native American students have come from working-class or underclass families, they historically have dropped out or flunked out at higher rates than white students (see Chapters 4 and 5). Because many at-risk, or disadvantaged, students traditionally come from backgrounds that are culturally different from those of white Anglo-Saxon (Protestant or Roman Catholic) peers, reformers have pointed to the need for educators to value the cultural heritage of each student. Although the call for recognizing the value of cultural

[17]Plank and Adams, "Death, Taxes, and School Reform."

diversity is not new, it has gained a new credence and an urgency—and (most importantly) a much-expanded base of political support—because students' ethnicity, race, or recency of arrival have little impact on which skills they need to acquire. *All* Americans need basic skills, which means that all need to succeed in school. And they are much more likely to do so if their school values rather than downplays their individual cultures and backgrounds. Hence, an emphasis on the appropriateness of cultural diversity is part of the reform movement. (See Figures 12.1 and 12.2.)

Not everyone will get what he or she wants from the reform movement. "Educational policies are the product of interplay and negotiation among interested groups, and cannot be altered to suit one group without discomforting many others," Plank and Adams remind us. "The latent political conflicts in the system impose strict limits on the accomplishments of educational reformers."[18] Yet, in the last decade of this century, the value of cultural diversity and the commitment to a single national standard of academic achievement are likely to remain controversial, raising issues both about the concepts themselves and about their definitions.

In opposition to the value of cultural diversity are those who want **cultural literacy**, a term prominent in the writing of E. D. Hirsch, who advocates "a traditional literate curriculum." By this he seems to mean the curriculum of American elementary schools early in this century; in his view one result of abandoning the "Dick and Jane" reader in grade schools is "the current ignorance explosion among young people."[19] Hirsch has published a list of information

FIGURE 12.1   Scholastic Aptitude Test, Verbal Score Averages

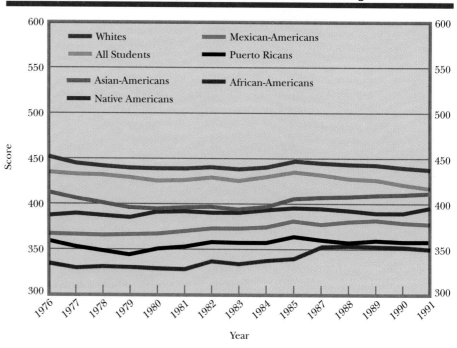

[18]Ibid.
[19]E. D. Hirsch, "Restoring Cultural Literacy in the Early Grades," *Educational Leadership* 45 (December–January 1987–1988): 70.

Source: *Digest of Education Statistics 1992*, National Center for Education Statistics, U.S. Department of Education, Office of Educational Research and Improvement, p. 125.

FIGURE 12.2   Scholastic Aptitude Test, Mathematics Score Averages

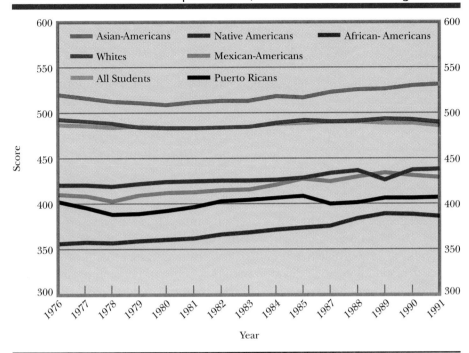

Source: *Digest of Education Statistics 1992*, National Center for Education Statistics, U.S. Department of Education, Office of Educational Research and Improvement, p. 125.

that every American ought to know, and he thinks that many children and adults do not know as much as is desirable.[20] Richard Rodriguez agrees, saying that "education's primary purpose, its distinguishing obligation, is to foster communality. The child learns . . . to put on a public self, apart from family or ethnic community."[21]

Many, like Alba Rosenman, disagree with Rodriguez, saying that the primary purposes of an early education are "to teach students that in school they will learn how to survive in our society and to solidify their feelings of worth." She continues:

> Though I am not brown or Mexican, I am a Hispanic who coped with my own set of differences in growing up. While I succeeded probably as well as most within the assimilationist American system, I don't advocate that schools today do to children what was done to me and many others. Schools should offer acceptance and nurturing. They should be places where students feel free to learn and grow, not places where some must every day make an effort not to let anyone know they're different.[22]

"TRADITIONAL VALUES" AND CURRICULA

People who have felt pessimistic about America's future have expressed concern about "traditional values."[23] Political philosopher Allen Bloom, for example, has indicted "new studies" programs in universities (such as African-American,

[20]E. D. Hirsch, *Cultural Literacy: What Every American Needs to Know* (Boston: Houghton Mifflin, 1987).

[21]Richard Rodriguez, "What Is an American Education?" *Education Week* 9 September 1987.

[22]Alba Rosenman, "The Value of Multicultural Curricula," *Education Week* 11 November 1987.

[23]See, for example, Bob Slosser, "Who Should Control Education?" *Saturday Evening Post* 258 (November 1986): 32, 98.

Latino, Native American, Asian-American, and Women's Studies) as explaining "How Higher Education Has Failed Democracy and Impoverished the Souls of Today's Students" (the subtitle of Bloom's 1987 book *The Closing of the American Mind*). Many who have objected to renewed calls for cultural diversity (because underrepresented groups might gain influence) have found comfort in Bloom's analysis. Some have been more comfortable to blame various minority groups for educational and social problems than they have been to hear the calls for consciousness raising and political action that members of those groups have made. Although new studies originally were treated as peripheral and insignificant to a university's programs, they have provided alternate paradigms for reality and for planning educational and political action.

Issues of how to interpret the past have been a primary focus of each of the new studies. "The central problem in American education . . . is not exclusively academic," writes Floyd W. Hayes, III, professor of African-American Studies at San Diego State University. "Rather, as both Bloom's text and responses to it indicate, that problem is a result of a clash of cultures, a conflict of interests and a struggle for power." Hayes describes a contest "between proponents of tradition and proponents of change, . . . between hegemonic forces and counterhegemonic forces and between historically included groups and historically excluded groups. These developments," he says, "are taking place in the midst of a dramatic transformation of American society."[24]

Two specific points of disagreement between traditionalists and those who advocate new studies illustrate the nature of their conflict. One disagreement is about the efforts to rid textbooks and other school publications of sexist language. Traditionalists see such efforts as distorting reality and damaging the English language.[25] The other dispute involves the explanatory framework for understanding the African-American experience in this country. Professor Hayes explicates this as follows:

> Within the relatively new field of African-American Studies, the **Afrocentric** critical **perspective** is an important intellectual strategy. It seeks the radical critique of the dominant **Eurocentric ideology** [which holds that everything of cultural importance came from European males] and the undoing of Western cultural hegemony, a challenge Bloom seeks to subvert. While maintaining that the Eurocentric tradition is valid within its own context, Afrocentric criticism soundly rejects that tradition's universalist and absolutist self-representation. . . .
>
> The displacement of Western cultural hegemony also demands the development of an emancipatory theory and practice that cultivates and empowers a conception of public life that respects the multicultural and multiracial character of America's emerging postindustrial-managerial society. Critical intellectuals from within historically dispossessed and disenfranchised cultural and racial groups must emerge so that they can be looked to directly for new knowledge and its application. . . . Achieving this goal demands that African-American Studies and the other 'new studies' forge . . . theory and practice . . . that privileges the multicultural and multiracial nature of America's evolving . . . society [emphasis added].[26]

[24]Floyd W. Hayes, III, "Politics and Education in America's Multicultural Society: An African-American Studies' Response to Allen Bloom," *Journal of Ethnic Studies* 17, no. 2 (Summer 1989): 71.

[25]Robert Lerner and Stanley Rothman, "Newspeak, Feminist Style," *Commentary* 89, no. 4 (April 1990): 54–56.

[26]Hayes, "Politics and Education in America's Multicultural Society," 81–83.

Comparative Perspective on Today's Issues . . .

◆ IS BILINGUAL EDUCATION JUSTIFIABLE?

The Issue To amelioriate social and educational disadvantages among non–English-speaking students, the federal government provided funding to local districts that had developed bilingual programs. Research into the efficacy of these programs pointed to mixed results, and eventually the government relaxed its policies, giving local districts greater freedom in the types of programs they could implement. Many districts adopted the English-immersion approach, which mainstreams students into English-speaking classes as soon as possible.

YES Bilingual education policies over the last twenty-five years have not been based consistently on solid research. Instead, decisions have been formulated on insufficient, flawed, or unavailable data. Thus courts have had to rely on ambiguous policy language and research when making legal decisions. This has led to a variety of rulings, some of which have been more favorable to students of "limited English proficiency." Bilingual education policies need to be based on less limited research and more adequate measures of assessing programs and students' achievement.

—Tony Baez, Program Coordinator, and Ricardo Fernandez, Director, of MNODAC (Midwest National Origin Desegregation Assistance Center); Richard Navarro, Senior Researcher, Michigan State University; and Roger L. Rice, Attorney

NO Bilingual educational programs have become politicized because proponents have pressed for them regardless of their effectiveness. Thus public schools have been forced to be the vehicle for political purposes. While biculturalism is a valid goal in a democratic society, it might better be served and implemented in the more private, nonpublic, freely chosen endeavors and activities of various ethnic groups. Also, there is concern whether bilingual education has actually advanced the equality of educational opportunity, since data do not show that minorities are being mainstreamed effectively into American society.

—Diane Ravitch, Adjunct Professor, History of Education, Teachers College, Columbia University

Source: Based on James Wm. Noll, ed., *Taking Sides: Clashing Views on Controversial Educational Issues,* 5th ed. (Guilford, Conn.: Dushkin, 1989), 306–331.

Curricular arguments will doubtless continue. What is different from the past, however, is that—no matter which curriculum one advocates—there is general agreement that all children can and must master basic skills to an extent that never seemed so possible or so necessary. The day is also past when educators can ignore the strengths and perspectives of their students' many cultures.

OTHER EDUCATIONAL ISSUES

■

Whether discussed in the context of reform or not, a number of social issues confront schools and everyone who works in them. These include

■ Health-related matters (teenage pregnancy and prenatal care, AIDS and other sexually transmitted diseases, contraceptive availability, sex education, substance-abuse education, suicide counseling)

■ Issues related to changing family patterns (working parents, latchkey children, child abuse, dropping out)

■ Issues arising from social disruption (drug sales, gangs, delinquency)

SCHOOLS AND HEALTH

Most people agree that schools should help young people understand matters of safety and health. Physical education is usually defended as belonging in the curriculum at least partly on the basis of its contributions to students' health. But how far should schools go in providing health education or health care? Those who work in schools are often on the horns of a dilemma in answering this question.

When teachers, principals, and counselors see a child or a teenager in obvious physical or emotional distress, they want to help. In severe cases, the student can't engage in learning unless the problem is addressed and improved. Educators—and especially teachers in the classroom—feel a strong urge to help when a student is at risk due to behavior that they know will likely lead to emotional or physical damage (sometimes including death). To some extent the decision about how much to intervene is personal. But there are also legal and policy factors to consider, along with the general expectations set by community norms.

School boards and educators have clear permission, even responsibility, to deal with health matters in three broad areas:

1. Safeguarding the school population by requiring certain inoculations (usually as a precondition to attending school) and by barring students who have infectious conditions that might put others at risk.[27]

2. Teaching about health and health-related practices

3. Providing timely and reasonable first aid in emergency situations

Having clear-cut authority in these three areas is one thing; knowing where their boundaries lie is another. For example, a condition like ringworm or lice would be cause for excluding a student from school until treatment could remedy the condition, but AIDS probably would not be cause for exclusion. Similarly, state and common law give school boards the authority to set the curriculum, which means that fairly extensive instruction in health matters is permissible—including sex education—but parental requests for exemption must be given due consideration.[28] Schools may teach students about contraception, but providing condoms or other contraceptive devices approaches the boundary of what courts have typically sustained.[29] Fortunately, most actions by individual principals or teachers don't end up in court; therefore, it is possible to find instances of health services in particular schools or districts that might not be upheld if efforts to provide those services were widespread.

School personnel are expected to arrange for medical attention in emergencies, and failure to do so may result in liability. Suppose, for example, that a

[27]City of Dallas v. Mosey, 286 S.W. 497 (Tex. Civ. App. 1926). Whether or not schools are dealing with these responsibilities is also an issue; see "Study Finds Health-care Crisis in U.S. Classrooms," *Chicago Tribune*, 16 September 1992, p. 22.

[28]Medeiros v. Kiyosaki, 52 Haw. 436, 478 P.2nd 314 (1970); Mercer v. Michigan State Board of Educ., 379 F.Supp. 580 (E.D. Mich. 1974), aff. 419 U.S. 1081, 95 S.Ct. 673, 42 L.Ed.2nd 678 (1974); Cornwell v. State Board of Educ., 428 F.2nd 471 (4 Cir. 1970), cert. den. 400 U.S. 942, 91 S.Ct. 240, 27 L.Ed.2nd 246 (1970).

[29]Recently Baltimore adopted a controversal plan for curtailing teenage pregnancies by providing surgically implanted contraceptives that last five years; see "Baltimore Schools to Offer Norplant," *Chicago Tribune*, 4 December 1992, p. 3.

Schools have authority to teach about health-related matters, but there are boundaries to consider. More than half the nation's schools do not provide sex education, because communities have not decided what role the schools should play. —Michael Newman/PhotoEdit

coach does nothing about an athlete who is suffering from heat stroke, assuming that the athlete will "shake it off." If the athlete is disabled as a result, the coach may be liable for not seeking medical attention.[30] But offering medical treatment in a nonemergency situation—or providing harmful emergency treatment—may also result in liability. Thus two teachers who treated a ten-year-old's infected finger by holding it under boiling water were liable for medical damages.[31]

The health-related issue of greatest concern to parents, students, and the public in general is that of alcohol and drug abuse. Only about half the nation's schools now offer instruction in substance abuse, but most students think that their schools *should* offer it. As Figure 12.3 shows, there seems to be a decline in drug use over the last decade, although the rate of alcohol abuse by students continues to be very high. Even if more schools do not add substance-abuse instruction to the curriculum, the real world seems to be teaching some lessons. Most people know someone whose life has been damaged (or ended) by alcohol or drugs, and they tend to learn from another's misfortune. Most educators certainly try to be conscientious in keeping drugs and alcohol off school grounds and in warning students of the dangers and tragedies of substance abuse. But schools exist within a community, and the community at large must also be conscientious in protecting its young people.

Teenage pregnancy is another perplexing problem for educators, and it, too, reflects society at large. Attitudes about sex have changed greatly over the past two decades. In 1972, for example, 46 percent of Americans thought that sex before marriage was "always" or "almost always" wrong; in 1989 this number had dropped to 35 percent. It is not surprising, then, that sexual activity among teenagers has increased. The fact that more than half of our schools do not provide sex education reveals that communities have not decided what role

[30]Mogabgab v. Orleans Parish School Board, 239 So. 2nd 456 (La. App. 1970).
[31]Guerrieri v. Tyson, 147 Pa.Super. 239, 24 A.2nd 468 (1942).

FIGURE 12.3   Use of Illegal Substances Among High School Seniors

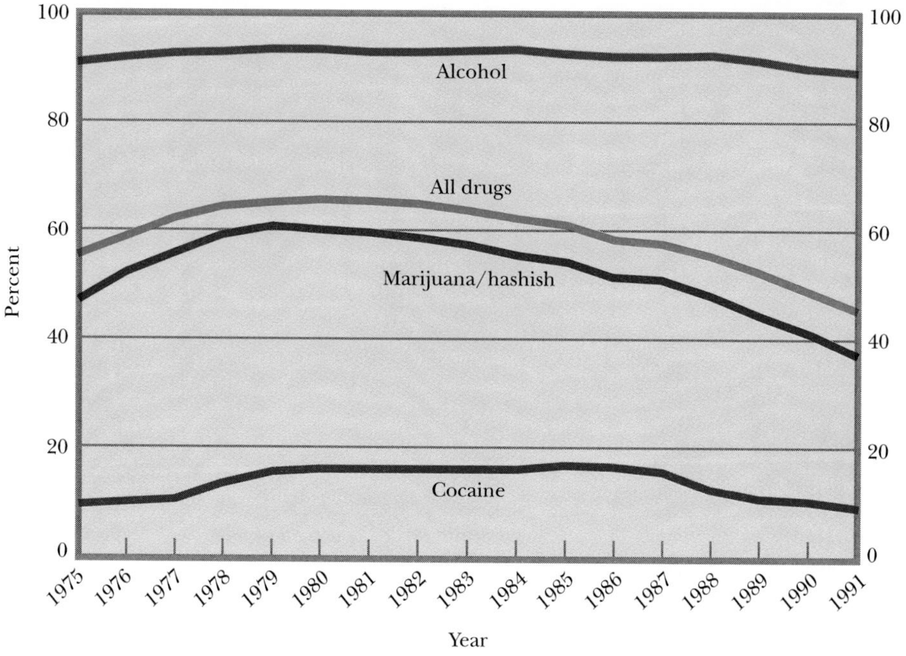

Source: *The Condition of Education 1992*, National Center for Education Statistics, U.S. Department of Education, Office of Educational Research and Improvement, p. 44.

schools should play in these matters. Many high schools—although certainly not all—do attempt to serve the needs of teenage parents. Some even make day care available. As a result, many student parents are able to complete their studies; most aspire to get married and do so.[32]

A small increase in teenage suicide from the 1950s to the 1970s—and widespread publicity about "suicide pacts"—led to concern about this issue, which fortunately seems less urgent in recent years. Suicide is always a trauma for family, friends, and peers, and teenage suicide is especially traumatic. On the positive side, in a recent survey 90 percent of youth aged eight to seventeen said that they were happy, and 93 percent said that they were happy about the amount of love their families showed them.[33]

CHANGING FAMILY PATTERNS

In the ideal world depicted on television programs like "Leave It to Beaver," children come home from school to be greeted by warm cookies, cold milk, and an all-patient mother whose full-time job is taking care of the family. Today, many parents—whether single or with a mate—have to work and cannot be home when their children arrive from school. More and more such **latchkey children** let themselves in and are unsupervised until a parent gets home. The cost of child care is especially hard on single-parent households headed by women, whose income is often below the official poverty line. But there is some encouraging news even here. One recent study found that children of working mothers were

[32]See "Making Room for Baby," *Teacher Magazine* 2 (September 1990): 92; and "Teen Moms Raise Hope with Help of Day Care," *Chicago Tribune*, 29 October 1990, sec. 2, p. 1.

[33]Cited in Wattenberg, *First Universalist Nation*, 88–89.

more self-reliant and had better scores on achievement and communication tests than did children whose mothers did not work. In a survey of young people, 59 percent said that they preferred their mothers to have a job, while 34 percent said that they did not.

RESEARCH SAYS

For Tomorrow's Education . . .

There is a relationship between the number of days a student is absent during the early primary grades and later success in high school. Students who have high absentee rates in the early years tend to have higher dropout rates. See "Dropout Tendency Starts with ABCs: Study," *Chicago Tribune*, 29 October 1990, sec. 2, p. 1.

Human beings have a dismal pattern of child abuse dating back as far as history records. Although we seem to have made some progress in this area, nearly two million cases of child abuse were cited in the United States in the mid-1980s. Some states have tightened laws regarding child abuse, and the media are making people more aware of the problem.

Educators are in a key position to recognize and call official attention to cases of child abuse and neglect. Most teachers see relatively few cases; some encounter more than their share. Aida's story at the beginning of this chapter illustrates that life sometimes deals out more problems than anyone should have to handle. And while it isn't always possible for teachers to solve every student's life problems, sometimes they can and do make the difference.

DROPOUTS

Part of the lament that has accompanied reform discussions has been the refrain that too many students are dropping out of high school, but the issue is not as simple as it may seem. Although it is true that not everyone who starts first grade finishes high school twelve years later, it is also true that the percentage of eighteen-year-olds who finish high school has increased steadily throughout this century. The number of people aged twenty-five to twenty-nine who have high school diplomas is nearly 90 percent of the U.S. population—and climbing. No other country equals this.[34]

A more serious social problem than those who drop out of high school is the lack of good jobs for those who graduate. Consider the example of Marvin Bright, who has had five jobs since graduating from high school in Akron, Ohio: clerk in a sporting-goods store; work in a local car wash; a "stint in the Army Reserve"; work as a part-time cook; and finally a job as a security guard, paying $3.90 per hour. "So now, at 21, Bright lives at home, sleeps in the same room he did as a kid, unable to afford his own place. Bright struggles despite the fact that he did the proper thing. He earned his high school degree."[35] An economy that has the technical capacity to produce more goods and services than there

[34]See "June Is Cruelist Month to Dropouts," *Chicago Tribune*, 14 June 1992, p. 1.
[35]Dennis Kelley, "Making Ends Meet Is an Uphill Battle," *USA Today*, 31 July 1990, pp. D1, D2.

RESEARCH SAYS

For Tomorrow's Education . . .
Research into learning styles may provide a key to reducing the dropout rate. See Janet Perrin, "The Learning Styles Project for Potential Drop-outs," *Educational Leadership* 48 (October 1990): 23.

are people to consume them (and can do so without drawing heavily on workers aged fifteen to thirty) creates political and social problems that go beyond educational issues.

SOCIAL DISRUPTION

The fact that a high school education is not enough to ensure one a decently paid job communicates a powerful message to American youth. Working hard in school for twelve years only to need at least four more in a college that they can't afford is an uninspiring incentive for some. Everyone needs meaningful work, and school will not seem like meaningful work if it cannot lead to the kind of salary that one's parents could earn as eighth-grade dropouts. Given such circumstances, the prospect of getting "big money" by selling drugs is a temptation. Similarly, "being someone" in a teenage gang, as opposed to "being nobody" without the gang, has drawing power. And for teenage girls, creating and nurturing a baby can seem like a tangible and powerful achievement.[36]

The job situation alone does not fully explain why young people discount school and sell drugs, join gangs, act antisocially, or have babies. But economic factors must be addressed if these other problems are to be solved. Educators and schools can be a dynamic partner in creating a future for the young, but the job will not get done if educators are made the scapegoats for social and political conditions.

CONCLUSIONS

■

There are many ways to frame the issues relating to education. Having a developmental context helps us to understand the issues, and so we have examined the history of education. Knowing the important concepts and the language of philosophy lets us apply our analytical power. Being familiar with social factors and forces and being aware of political realities provides an essential framework for considering educational issues. And having exposure to issues and developments in other societies gives us perspective. Everyone who has a stake in education benefits from this knowledge. But for professional educators, context, analysis, realism, and perspective are essential.

[36]See, for example, "More Single Moms Living in Poverty," *USA Today,* 2 August 1990, p. 6A; "Deportation Gaining as Gang-fighting Tool," *Chicago Tribune,* 6 July 1992, p. 1; and "Racism Retains Its Malignant Hold," *Chicago Tribune,* 10 May 1992, p. 1.

KEY TERMS

National Commission on Excellence in Education

Holmes Group

reform package

reform proposals

at-risk students

cultural literacy

Afrocentric perspective

Eurocentric ideology

"latchkey children"

SUGGESTED READINGS

Joel Perlman, *Ethnic Differences* (Cambridge, Mass.: Cambridge University Press, 1988). The author examines ethnic differences in occupational and educational attainment by means of case studies and also offers some theoretical explanations.

B. J. Armento, G. G. Nash, C. L. Salter, and K. K. Wixson, *America Will Be* (Boston: Houghton Mifflin, 1991). This book provides a racially diverse picture of Americans by looking at ethnic heritages from a historical perspective.

Gary G. Wehlage, Robert A. Rutter, Gregory A. Smith, Nancy Lesko, and Ricardo R. Fernandez, *Reducing the Risk: Schools as Communities of Support* (New York: Falmer Press, 1989). The authors describe fourteen dropout prevention programs in detail and then explain their similarities and differences.

Jerry Paquette, *Social Purpose and Schooling* (New York: Falmer Press, 1991). This book presents alternative models of schooling in terms of social and political issues and the assumptions that surround them.

Jack L. Nelson, Kenneth D. Carlson, and Stuart B. Palonsky, *Critical Issues in Education* (New York: McGraw-Hill, 1990). This book examines thirteen topics by presenting opposing viewpoints about each issue.

C. A. Bowers and David J. Flinders, *Responsive Teaching: An Ecological Approach to Classroom Patterns of Language, Culture, and Thought* (New York: Teachers College Press, Columbia University, 1990). This

provides a theoretical framework for viewing the classroom as a composite of linguistic and cultural patterns that need to be part of the professional basis for teachers' decision making.

Lucille G. Natkins, *Our Last Term: A Teacher's Diary* (Washington, D.C.: University Press of America, 1986). This is a personal account of the successes and disasters of a school that went from being one of the best to being mediocre.

Jonathan Kozol, *Savage Inequalities: Children in America's Schools* (New York: Crown, 1991). Kozol examines inner-city and suburban schools in America and concludes that the local funding structure ensures a correlation between affluence and better education.

Larry Martz, *Making Schools Better: How Parents and Teachers Across the Country Are Taking Action— And How You Can, Too* (New York: Time Books, 1992). The author profiles a wide range of communities that have taken action to improve their schools.

Dinesh D'Souza, *Illiberal Education* (New York: Vintage, 1992). The author argues that multiculturalism has created "balklanized tribal enclaves" instead of a truly diverse culture.

Lorene Cary, *Black Ice: An Autobiography* (New York: Vintage, 1992). Cary describes her experiences as an inner-city Philadelphia teenager who was one of the first African-Americans to attend a prestigious New England boarding school.

Education in the Twenty-first Century

There is every indication that the world as known is coming apart and reassembling itself in a new way. . . . The whole thing is breaking loose. What you see on the back of the American dollar bill is what we're getting. "Novus ordo seclorum," that is, "a new order of the ages." It's American. . . . We are the first universal nation. . . . In America, we come from everywhere, becoming one people getting along pretty well with each other, and vastly enriched by our pluralism. We have the world's highest standard of living, and diminishing poverty. . . . We have the best universities and researchers. . . . Around the world, people tap their feet to American music, watch American movies and television, follow American fashions, are enthralled with American culture, speak American, emulate American economic and political ideas. . . . All this influence is increasing exponentially.

—Ben J. Wattenberg, The First Universal Nation (*New York: Free Press, 1990*), *7, 10, 24*

13

Education in the Twenty-first Century

Nathan Martinez is nine years old. He is one of two hundred students who attend a neighborhood learning center. He is not in a particular grade; instead, he enters the school and goes to his learning station, where he works on his daily assignments using a computer. Nathan's learning level was determined by a battery of intelligence tests that assessed his aptitudes and development in a variety of intellectual and social areas. The computer wishes him good morning and reminds him where to begin today's lessons. He will start with reading, writing, and computer literacy, and then he will go on to interdisciplinary programs that include math and science, foreign language, global and political economics, and moral and health education. Most of these subjects will be presented in theory and by application, and the work will emphasize problem solving and critical thinking.

When Nathan finishes today's learning module, he will go to an assigned classroom with several others his age, and—along with a facilitating teacher—they will have a dialog and discussion based on the newly learned material. He also will join a group that will be presented with a problem to solve; together they will practice their critical-thinking and problem-solving skills.

This will be the instructional pattern for all of Nathan's studies. He also will have the opportunity to learn technological skills which the business community makes available through a cooperative partnership with the schools.

Like many of his friends, Nathan has a family of mixed ethnicity. His mother is Jewish, and his father is Hispanic; they are in their early forties and have been married for fifteen years. Nathan's one sister is six years older than he and plans to enter college next year. His mother is in college now, preparing to begin a different career. It is common for people to change careers several times during their work lives. The year is 2020.

Nathan's story reveals a number of things that experts are predicting for the next century in terms of demographic patterns, technological advances, global and environmental trends, and social and educational trends. This chapter will describe all these predictions, and then we will explore some topics that experts think will be most important in the future—challenges that could reach crisis proportions during the next twenty-five years. First, though, it will be both fun and instructive to look back at American society one hundred years ago to see what predictions the experts made about our own century—and to consider why the experts weren't always right.

AMERICA 100 YEARS AGO

AN EMERGING SOCIETY

During the 1890s the United States was just beginning to emerge as a powerful force in the world. The country had won the Spanish-American War and had acquired the Philippine Islands, Cuba, Guam, Puerto Rico, Hawaii, Wake, and part of Samoa.[1] There were mixed feelings about entering into the world and dominating peoples in other lands. The nation was, after all, a rural society, and it did not really become urban until the middle of the twentieth century. Western states were still regarded as part of the frontier, and they were attracting thousands of people to settle their territories. Issues of conservation and environmental pollution were not yet strong concerns.

Transportation was slow—with luck, perhaps 100 miles could be covered in a day. Automobiles were still a novelty, and trains were the fastest, most popular way to travel. Methods of communicating were also slow. For most Americans writing letters was the most common way to "keep in touch," although the telephone was becoming popular with the upper and middle classes. Nevertheless, it was not unusual for mailed messages to take weeks to be delivered.

Homes had floor plans that were similar to those of today: three bedrooms, one bath, a parlor or living room, a dining room, and a kitchen. The common architectural style was colonial, with a front porch. Kitchens were equipped with iceboxes, sinks, cupboards, and cast-iron stoves that were fueled by wood in rural areas and by gas or oil in cities. Central heating was available to the upper classes, as were washing machines, sewing machines, phonographs, and fully equipped bathrooms.

As mentioned in Chapter 2, the medical profession had not yet emerged as knowledgeable, scientific health experts. In fact, health and fitness were not popular topics, although everyone celebrated the development of the smallpox vaccine. Sanitation was just becoming a reality as milk became pasteurized and water systems and sewer systems appeared. Sewers were hidden under newly paved street networks, which developed first in cities.

The effort to make education compulsory was handicapped by ineffective and unenforced child labor laws. In Chicago alone, 16,791 children were enrolled in schools, but truant officers estimated that another 31,593 were not attending. The city was experiencing rapid and unprecedented growth in population as large numbers of European immigrants settled there. Increased numbers of African-Americans had moved to the North during and following the Civil War, even though racial stereotypes flourished and the Ku Klux Klan was starting to organize northern chapters.

As always, there was controversy about schools' curricular offerings. Many educators wanted to concentrate on the three R's, to the exclusion of manual or industrial arts. Others wanted to include vocational subjects but thought that they should be offered in special high schools. Still others thought that manual training should be incorporated into regular high schools. The issue was finally resolved in 1918, when the Commission on the Reorganization of Secondary Education (see Chapter 9) recommended that American high schools have three tracks: an academic college-preparation or "general" track; a commercial or business track; and an industrial or manual track. The commission also recommended that sports, student government, and extracurricular activities be incorporated into schools so that working students and college-bound classmates could interact.

[1] John Center, "Where America Was a Century Ago," *Futurist* 23 (January–February 1990) 1: 22–28.

Sports became an issue at the college level. Athletic personnel were beginning to offer inducements to talented prospective players, and questions of ethics arose. Excessive violence in sports was another issue, along with the practice of advertising a college's winning team as a device to recruit students. Winning teams attracted not only students but also monetary gifts and endowments. Thus, by the turn of the century, today's college sports practices had taken root.

Making money was a preoccupation with many Americans, as second-generation businessmen like Jay Gould, John D. Rockefeller, Phillip Armour, Andrew Mellon, and William Waldorf Astor became millionaires. Their names were as well known in the last century as Lee Iaccoca's, Donald Trump's and Merv Griffin's are today.

PREDICTIONS ABOUT OUR CENTURY

As the experts a hundred years ago looked into the twentieth century, they saw many things—some good, some bad; and they made many forecasts—some accurate, some wrong. They correctly foretold the technological explosion. For example, they said that cooking would be made easy by the invention of kitchen appliances; that the telephone would become a worldwide means of communication; that a device like the telegraph would transmit pictures; and that there would be nonrefillable bottles and inexpensive storage batteries. Forecasters also correctly predicted that cities would develop and grow vertically as well as horizontally, and that the nation would be transformed from a rural to an urban culture. They envisioned the spread of automobiles and the necessary network of freeways with multiple lanes.[2]

The experts made many wrong predictions, too. For instance, because wood was used for fuel, some turn-of-the-century futurists predicted that few trees would be standing by 1920. Some military personnel recognized the importance of the automobile but failed to see its potential as a future form of military transportation. Others thought that the spread of cars would make streets much quieter than during the clamoring horse-and-buggy era. And, based on 1890 rates of population growth, it was predicted that by the end of the twentieth century there would be 60 million African-Americans in the United States, which would constitute a majority.[3]

CHARACTERISTICS OF WRONG FORECASTS

The incorrect predictions about this century have several things in common. First, they sometimes assumed that a current trend would continue at the same rate. This was the problem with the predictions about the growth rate of African-Americans and about the rate at which trees would be cut.

Second, predictions that describe "gloom and doom" are usually off the mark. Such forecasts fail to take into account that people will usually do something about problems that might lead to a doomsday situation. For example, in the 1960s many people were convinced that the country would be overpopulated by the 1980s if people continued to have large families. But people did *not* continue to have large families.

[2]Ibid.
[3]Ibid.

Finally, forecasts about new developments go astray when they are under-generalized (the change will have no affect on society) or overgeneralized (the change will have too much of an impact). The military's inability to see the potential of the automobile as its means of travel was an example of under-generalization, while the fantasy of quiet streets was an example of over-generalization.[4]

As we turn to look toward the twenty-first century, keep in mind these characteristics of wrong forecasts. When considering the various predictions that follow, ask (1) whether they are based on false assumptions, (2) whether they might be altered by actions taken, and (3) whether they are overgeneralized or undergeneralized.

PREDICTIONS ABOUT THE NEXT CENTURY

DEMOGRAPHIC PATTERNS

The face of America is changing once again. Before the middle of this century, 80 percent of immigrants came from Europe; since midcentury, however, 80 percent have come from outside Europe—mainly from Hispanic and Moslem countries, Black Africa, Asia, and the Caribbean. If current rates of population change continue, it is predicted that by the year 2080 ethnic proportions will be as follows: 19 percent Hispanic-Americans (8 percent in 1990); 16 percent African-Americans (currently 12 percent); 55 percent non-Hispanic whites (77 percent in 1990); and 11 percent Asian-Americans and other ethnic groups (now at 3 percent).[5] (See Figure 13.1.)

Although the United States has never been free of ethnic and racial discrimination, evidence indicates that discriminatory attitudes weaken with each passing generation. For example, nonsemitic Americans of our great-grandparents' and grandparents' generations distrusted Jewish immigrants and their heritage, and the 1924 immigration law restricted Jewish immigration. But a recent poll asked Americans whether or not the immigration of certain religious, racial, and ethnic groups had been beneficial to the United States; more specifically, it asked whether the addition of various groups was a good thing or a bad thing. In descending order, the groups were ranked as follows: English (66 percent), Irish (62 percent), Jews (59 percent), Germans (57 percent), Italians (56 percent), Poles (53 percent), Japanese (47 percent), African-Americans (46 percent), Chinese (44 percent), Mexicans (25 percent), Koreans (24 percent), Vietnamese (20 percent), Puerto Ricans (17 percent), Haitians (10 percent), and Cubans (9 percent).[6] Although no one can say whether these attitudes will persist into the future, it seems likely that the contributions of Asians, Hispanics, and African-Americans will be viewed positively.

Early in this century people tended to marry within their own ethnic group. Recently, however, common ethnicity is less important in marriage. Even several

[4]Ibid.
[5]Ben J. Wattenberg, *The First Universal Nation* (New York: Free Press, 1990), 45–48.
[6]Ibid., 47.

FIGURE 13.1   Racial Composition of Twenty Largest Metropolitan Areas, 1990

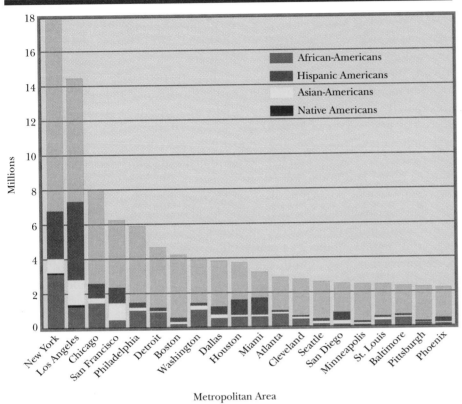

Source: *Statistical Abstract of the United States, 1992*, 112th ed., U.S. Department of Commerce, p. 34.

Kennedys have wed partners who are not Irish Catholics. While Rose and Joseph Kennedy represent the former trend, their granddaughters have married a Jew (Schlossberg), an Austrian (Schwartzenegger), and an Italian (Cuomo).[7] It is predicted that the trend toward multiethnicity will continue and will extend also to interracial marriages. Although futurists do not expect dramatic increases, interracial marriage is likely to become more common.

Another trend that is expected to continue is the later age at which people are marrying. In 1963 the median age of marriage for women was 20.3 years; in 1980 it was 21.8 years; and in 1987 it was 23.6 years. For men the median age for a first marriage was 23 in 1955; in 1988 it was 26.[8]

Related to this are the predictions that marriage and family life are becoming less popular. Forecasters cite the following statistics: two-thirds of first marriages end in divorce; the proportion of unmarried mothers has increased from 5 percent in 1950 to 23 percent in 1988; the percentage of forty-year-olds who have never married has increased from 12 percent in 1960 to 28 percent in 1988; and the number of couples who cohabit without marrying has risen from 0.5 million to 2.5 million.[9]

[7]Ibid., 52–53.
[8]Ibid; and "The Revolution in Family Life," *Futurist* 23 (September–October 1990) 5: 53.
[9]Ibid.

Some fear that marriage and family life—as institutions—may no longer be important to Americans, but other statistics paint a different picture; in fact, the reverse may be true. Polls reveal that family and children are the most important aspects of American life. In a recent survey 90 percent of young women said that they wanted their lives to include marriage and children, while 63 percent said they also wanted a career. The desire for a career among women has recently seemed to peak. In 1974, for example, 60 percent of women preferred to stay home, and 35 percent wanted a career. In 1980 and 1985 the percentages who wanted a career rose (to 46 and 51 percent, respectively), while those wanting to stay home decreased (to 51 and 45 percent, respectively). In 1989, however, only 42 percent of women said that they wanted a career, and 51 percent preferred to stay home. Overall, it seems probable that this statistical vacillation between career and home life reflects temporary attitudes and will level off.[10]

Many gloomy predictions have centered on the increasing number of out-of-wedlock births and on the decrease in traditional families—parents with two children. But other factors need to be considered as well. In the first place, 50 percent of unwed mothers do marry within five years of giving birth, and 70 percent have married within fifteen years. And while the divorce rate is high, 9 out of 10 divorcees try again by entering into other marriages. Finally, the "traditional family" profile does not include those with a single child or more than two children. For all these reasons—and admitting that there are problems—it seems certain that predictions of gloom and doom about marriage and family are inaccurate.[11]

Other predictions and trends probably will affect the nation's future. First of all, the number of elderly Americans will continue to increase before the average life span levels off. By the year 2025 it is predicted that older Americans will outnumber teenagers by a ratio of 2 to 1. More adult children are living at home, and more single men are heading up households. In fact, the number of single nonfamily households headed by men is expected to increase by 72 percent, whereas the number of single nonfamily households headed by women will increase by 42 percent. Finally, throughout the world, more than half the population will probably be living in cities, with the biggest growth occurring in developing countries.[12]

TECHNOLOGICAL ADVANCES

Most predictions put technology at the forefront of forces that will change society. Several areas of development promise dramatic changes. Perhaps the most exciting developments are expected in telecommunications and "telematics"—electronic automated systems. Such information technology will allow people to shop from home and to do most of their personal and professional communications, from banking to work itself. All kinds of products and services will be tailored to fit consumers' ethnic and socioeconomic profiles, so that personal taste and preference will replace mass-market promotion and products. Fiber-optic systems will dominate communication. The merging of video transmission, facsimile machines, handheld computers, and telephones are just the beginning

[10]Ibid., 85–87.

[11]Wattenberg, *First Universal Nation,* 81–91.

[12]Edward Cornish, ed., "Outlook '93," *Futurist* 25 (November–December 1992) 6: 1–8; and United Way Strategic Institute, "Nine Forces Reshaping America," *Futurist* (July–August 1990): 9–16.

Predictions about exciting developments in information technology—such as the merging of computers, television, and telephones—forecast profound effects on every kind of human interaction, including the interaction between teacher and student. —AT&T Photo

of a technological revolution that will profoundly affect every kind of human interaction—including, of course, teaching and learning.[13]

Technology will advance in other areas as well. Robots may carry your luggage, clean your home, mind your children, and feed your pets. Biotechnology is another advancing domain. The unlocking of the genetic code and the ability to map human gene structures will allow medicine to leap forward in treating, curing, and preventing many diseases. Advances in genetics are not all rosy, however, and the field will continue to raise controversy and concern because

RESEARCH SAYS

For Tomorrow's Education . . .

An important new form of education will be distance learning—the use of computers, interactive video, satellites, and other media to link classrooms to students and to other classrooms. See "Long-distance Teaching," *Futurist* 24 (November–December 1990): 48; and Edward Cornish, ed., "Outlook '93," *Futurist* 26 (November–December) 6: 1–8.

[13]Ibid.; and Joseph F. Coates and Jennefer Jarratt, "What Futurists Believe," *Futurist* 23 (November–December 1990) 6: 23–27.

of the potential for abusive and unethical practices. "Test-tube babies," genetically altered foods, life-support systems, and cryonics are just the beginning of biotechnological developments.[14]

The number of small businesses will increase, boosted by technology that lets them compete with large corporations. Futurists predict that small businesses will proliferate and will supply the products created by the technology explosion. Obviously, the labor force will change in response to other changes. Blue-collar workers will be in even less demand as employers seek people who have skills in advanced technology. Traditional skilled laborers will be valued most in underdeveloped countries.

Predictions about science and technology are most likely to fall into the traps that make forecasting inaccurate—especially the tendency to think that current trends will continue at increasing rates. There can be no doubt, however, that technological advances will play a major role in shaping the future, both in the United States and the world.

GLOBAL AND ENVIRONMENTAL TRENDS

Most futurists think that in most societies nationalism will be replaced by **globalism**, or internationalism. This can be seen already in economic areas. Both industrialized and underdeveloped nations have become partners in a multinational economy. Our interdependency on oil reserves and other natural resources requires cooperation within the world economy. Some have predicted global economic collapse unless some national debts are forgiven, alternative energy sources are developed, and world population growth is checked. Nations will have to develop political and social strategies to serve the global interest, not nationalistic competition. The European Economic Community is but the first step in a process that will alter trading agreements around the world. The nations of the Pacific Rim and North America are poised to follow, although an agreement in North America faces formidable opposition in the United States.

Experts disagree about the future position and role of the United States. Most forecasters predict a decline in U.S. economic and military power as the era of "Superpowers" recedes and nations take their world places as equals. Some see the United States as falling into serious decline, while others say we are witnessing the **Americanization of world culture**. For evidence they cited the fact that America is a nation of immigrants of all ethnicities and races, making it a microcosm of the world. In other words, America has become universalized, and it is now exerting a strong influence on other nations. American hotels, fast-food franchises, and information services are found throughout the world. With the longest-running national democracy in modern history, the United States has become a model for other countries' efforts to mix politics and capitalism. Although the U.S. education system has many problems, its ideology of "equal opportunity" has also permeated the world. More than 400,000 foreign students come to study in U.S. universities, whereas only 62,341 Americans study abroad (see Figure 13.2). In a recent poll ranking the best universities in the world,

[14]Cornish, "Outlook '93," 1–8.

FIGURE 13.2   Foreign Students in U.S. Institutions of Higher Education and American Students
                   Studying Abroad

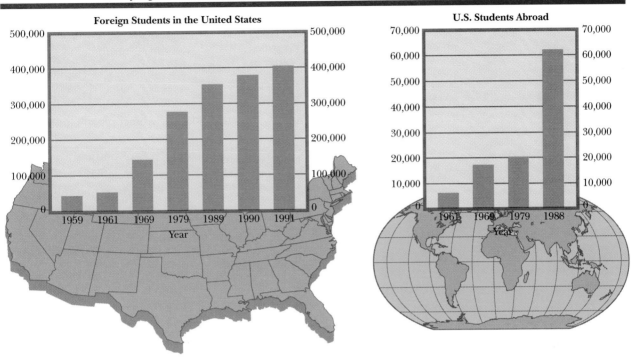

Source: *Digest of Education Statistics 1992*, National Center for Education Statistics, U.S. Department of Education, Office of Educational Research and Improvement, p. 421.

eight of the top twelve were in the United States. These American penetrations
into other cultures are not likely to recede.[15]

Turning to another front, a peaceful international society is seen as our
biggest challenge by many futurists. Military regulation will need to be balanced
with Third World political, social, and economic developments. Although no
one predicts a full-scale nuclear war, access to nuclear weapons is a concern.
Peace-keeping mechanisms will need to be developed and strengthened to
safeguard the future.[16]

Global environmental interdependence is also an important factor for the
next century. Already there is much concern about ozone depletion, global
warming, and tropical deforestation. Solving such problems, however, requires
a national commitment. For example, Americans are becoming more aware of
the benefits of recycling. First, it creates new jobs; paper recycling adds five jobs
to every job needed to harvest trees. Second, recycling saves energy and slows
down global warning. Third, recycling aluminum, steel, and paper helps save
and maintain important natural resources. Consider this: By 1990 Americans
were throwing away "enough aluminum to rebuild the entire American fleet 71
times; enough steel to reconstruct Manhattan; and enough wood and paper to
heat 5 million homes for 200 years."[17]

[15]Wattenberg, *First Universal Nation,*
11–13.

[16]Ibid.; and John Platt, "What We
Must Do," *Futures Research Quarterly*
6 (Summer 1990) 2: 36–52.

[17]*The Participant* (Champaign, Ill.:
State University Retirement System
of Illinois, Winter 1990), 2.

SOCIAL AND EDUCATIONAL TRENDS

The federal government is expected to take a back seat to state and local governments, the private sector, and special interest groups in managing certain social and political matters. For example, although health care will have strong federal components, it also will leave many areas of responsibility to the states; and child care will become the responsibility of business and state and local governments. Regional and private interests are expected to lead the way in cleaning up the environment and in providing treatment and cures for deadly diseases. Drug abuse, community safety, and home protection will also be local and private concerns, not national.

Some predictions are contradictory, mixing doses of optimism with pessimism. On the one hand, for instance, wellness and self-help activities will become more important for Americans; on the other hand, violent crime rates will escalate and will include more family violence and more violence initiated by youth.[18]

Educational forecasts are mixed, too, although there is general agreement about trends that are under way now. First, let's acknowledge that the education system has its share of problems: a too-high dropout rate, coupled with an educational ladder that inhibits females and minority students from reaching its highest rungs; not enough spending on education; math and science scores below those of some industrialized societies; and unnecessary bureaucracy that maintains poorly qualified personnel teaching diluted curricula. Now let's examine the evidence for each of these problems.

First, consider the dropout rate. As shown in Table 13.1, the rate diminished over the past two decades; that is, the percentage of students who graduated increased. The high school graduation rate is still too low—especially for minority students—but at least it is moving in the right direction.[19] (See Chapter 5 for a discussion of minority students and dropout rates.)

Next, consider the percentage of people aged twenty-five to twenty-nine who have had four or more years of college (see Table 13.1). Again, for both white students and minority students, the percentages increased over the past two decades. For African-Americans, however, the 1980s were a decade of leveling off in the rate of college completion.[20] Future educators will need to make a strong commitment to remedying this. Some feel that the decrease in blue-

[18]United Way Strategic Institute, "Nine Forces Reshaping America," 11–16.

[19]U.S. Department of Education, National Center for Education Statistics, *The Condition of Education, 1992* (Washington, D.C.: U.S. Government Printing Office, 1992), 62.

[20]Ibid.

TABLE 13.1   Educational Attainment of 25- to 29-Year-Olds (Percentages)

	High School Graduates			4 + Years of College		
Year	Whites	African-Americans	Hispanic-Americans	Whites	African-Americans	Hispanic-Americans
1971	81.7	53.9	44.8	23.1	12.5	11.3
1981	89.8	76.3	60.4	26.3	15.2	12.4
1991	89.8	80.7	55.9	29.7	13.6	16.4

Source: U.S. Department of Education, National Center for Education Statistics, *The Condition of Education, 1992* (Washington, D.C.: U.S. Government Printing Office, 1992), 62.

TABLE 13.2   National Average Expenditure per Public School Pupil

Year	Average Expenditure per Pupil
1930	$ 623
1940	835
1950	1,188
1960	1,885
1970	3,144
1980	4,188
1990	5,399
1991	5,342

Source: U.S. Department of Education, National Center for Education Statistics, *The Condition of Education, 1992* (Washington, D.C.: U.S. Government Printing Office, 1992), 130.

collar jobs will motivate students to stay in school to develop technological skills, which will be required and valued in an **information-based society** in which the better jobs will demand information-processing skills.[21]

The second problem relates to spending for education. Once again, the picture presented in Table 13.2 is not as bleak as some might think. Over the past sixty years the amount spent on public education has increased from $623 per student in 1930 to $5,399 per student in 1990; in 1991 it dropped slightly to $5,342. Note, however, that these figures are national *averages*; the expenditures in individual school districts vary greatly, and the poorest districts can barely afford the basics of education. In addition, some education experts warn that we cannot expect real improvements in our school system until teachers are paid in amounts that are comparable to what other professionals earn.[22]

Regarding the math and science scores of U.S. students, the data are not encouraging. American nine- and thirteen-year-olds do not compete favorably with students in other industrialized countries (see Table 13.3 and Figure 13.3). Generally, nine- and thirteen-year-olds in Korea, Taiwan, fourteen Russian-speaking countries, Spain, and Canada ranked higher than American students did.

When it comes to the education bureaucracy and diluted curricula, the picture is complicated. Most suburban communities are providing adequate to good schools for their students. Problems are most severe in metropolitan areas, where many minority students seem to be stranded. Public awareness has sparked some reform efforts, which aim to include parents and the community in the administration and operation of schools. Some districts have instituted school-based management in an effort to improve education. Numerous media reports about both the problems in schools and attempts to reform them have raised public awareness, which is usually the first step toward remedy. We can hope that the focus on education will help urban schools to turn around soon.

One encouraging sign is that public attitudes toward schools are again becoming more positive. In 1973, for example, 58 percent of Americans ex-

[21]Wattenberg, *First Universal Nation,* 91.

[22]Ibid.

TABLE 13.3   Math Scores of 9- and 13-Year-Olds (Average Percent Correct)

Country	9-Year-Olds	13-Year-Olds
Korea	74.8	73.4
Taiwan	68.1	72.7
14 Russian-speaking countries	65.9	70.2
France	—	64.2
Spain	61.9	55.4
Canada	59.9	62.0
United States	58.4	55.3

Source: U.S. Department of Education, National Center for Education Statistics, *The Condition of Education, 1992* (Washington, D.C.: U.S. Government Printing Office, 1992), 50.

pressed confidence in public schools, but in 1981 the proportion had fallen to 42 percent; in 1989 the proportion expressing confidence had risen to 51 percent. (The two problems that most bothered Americans were lack of discipline in schools and student use of drugs.)[23]

Another encouraging sign is that the literacy rate worldwide has been rising and is expected to continue to climb throughout the 1990s. In 1990 the literacy

[23]Ibid., 97, 116.

FIGURE 13.3   Science Activities of 13-Year-Olds in Educational Systems Participating in the International Assessment of Education Progress, 1991

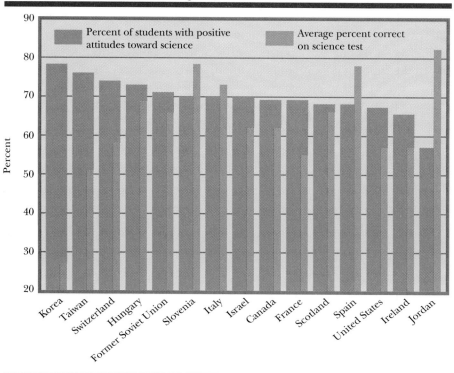

Source: *Digest of Education Statistics 1992*, National Center for Education Statistics, U.S. Department of Education, Office of Educational Research and Improvement, p. 416.

rate was 73.5 percent, and it is expected to increase to 78.2 percent by the year 2000. Even with this gain, however, 948 million people were illiterate in 1990, and the number is expected to be 935 million by 2000. Africa has the lowest literacy rate of the countries surveyed, and the rate is expected to worsen throughout the 1990s.[24]

Those who support the ideas of Brazilian educator and reformer Paulo Freire believe that, for the world's poor, literacy will entail teaching and learning words that have strong personal and social meanings. Freire's methods have been used successfully in teaching Brazil's poorest peasants. Known as **liberating education**, this linguistically based pedagogy includes politically active, consciousness-raising messages. But, as Harvard psychologist Howard Gardner has pointed out, Freire's type of educational intervention can succeed in other countries and settings "only if similar support systems exist in the new 'host' country; or, alternatively, if suitable alterations are made so that the educational program meshes with the dominant values, procedures, and intellectual orientation of the host land."[25]

Another aspect of literacy needs to be considered. During the 1980s some educators—Jonathon Kozol, in particular—have lamented the high levels of **functional illiteracy** in American society, meaning that people are unable to function adequately, even though they have attended school. In *Illiterate America* (1985) Kozol disclaims census figures that report adult Americans as being 99 percent literate. He claims that sixty million Americans are illiterate to some degree. For example, he says that students who have completed only the fifth-grade curriculum in an "excellent and successful" school are "functionally illiterate," and those who have completed the ninth-grade curriculum in the same type of school are "marginally illiterate." Thus, if people cannot read the telephone book or a menu or street signs, they are considered functionally illiterate. Based on these definitions—without sufficient data to support their characteristics or rate of incidence—Kozal has arrived at his sixty-million figure.[26]

Even if we try to credit this argument, it is difficult to believe that young adults cannot read traffic signs well enough to drive or that they cannot recognize familiar foods listed on a menu. Older adults may have a higher illiteracy rate, because more of them dropped out of school. This is not to say that there is no literacy problem, for there is—especially looking into the future, when computer literacy is taken into account. This "new literacy" will require creativity, problem-solving skills, and exercise of judgment. In other words, literacy will depend on thinking abilities, not solely on reading skills. Seventeen states now include efforts to instill this type of literacy as part of their school reform packages.[27]

Overall, most futurists agree that education will be more important than ever in an information-based society. Unfortunately, not all of them are optimistic about the schools' abilities to prepare students for life in the next century. Some think that educational institutions will not be major players in the future; they see corporations as taking over the highly technical and skill-based training that will be needed. In this view, as schools decline, computers and robotics will replace teachers. (This is not the first time that the end of teachers has been predicted. When printing presses became available late in the fifteenth century, some said that teachers would no longer be needed, because people could read

[24]"World Literacy Rate Rises," *Futurist* 24 (September–October 1991) 5: 47.
[25]Howard Gardner, *Frames of Mind* (New York: Basic Books, 1983), 382.
[26]Ibid., 92; citing Jonathan Kozol, *Illiterate America.*
[27]"Toward a Literacy of Thoughtfulness," *Futurist* (November–December 1991): 43.

Paulo Freire
1921–

During the early 1970s a book entitled *Pedagogy of the Oppressed* appeared in the libraries of many educational reformers. It described a type of pedagogy that called for the educator to enter into a learning experience along with the student; a pedagogy that was built on the belief that teachers can provide a productive learning environment only when they understand the social, political, and psychological contexts of their students' lives. The author was Paulo Freire.

Paulo was born in 1921 in Recife, Brazil, one of the poorest regions in the northeastern part of the country, where unemployment, malnutrition, and birthrates are quite high, while literacy and life-expectancy rates are very low. Paulo's family was not as poor as many in this region: His father had received some education and was a low-ranking military officer until he lost his job during the Depression. The family then moved to another poverty area in northeastern Brazil, where Paulo recalled experiencing hunger.

Paulo's father taught him to read, and by age fifteen or so he went to high school in a nearby town. His teachers thought that he was mildly retarded, but he said later that it was hard for him to concentrate when he could not ignore how hungry he felt. He was able, nonetheless, to matriculate at the University of Recife, where he studied law. He was also quickly drawn into a popular reform movement that focused on social change and the con-

ditions of poverty in the northeast region.

In 1943 Freire married his first wife (who died in 1987), and in 1946 he began working for a social agency in one of the Brazilian states. Being responsible for educational programs, he soon became interested in adult literacy and mass-education. In 1954 he resigned to accept a position teaching history and philosophy of edu-

Yesterday's Professional

cation at the University of Recife. He continued to develop his own pedagogy and educational philosophy, and in 1959—with the election of a reform mayor in Recife—Freire became head of a reform movement for adult education and also completed his doctorate at the university.

By 1963 Freire's pedagogy had gained attention and popularity, and he was asked to head up the National Literacy Program of the Brazilian Ministry of Education and Culture. He held the position for only a year, when, through military coup, a new government took office; he was called a traitor and was jailed for seventy-five days. Eventually, he fled to Bolivia and then to Chile, where he helped develop educational programs. From there, he went to Harvard. By the early 1970s his ideas were capturing international attention, and in 1975 *Pedagogy of the Oppressed* was published in English. He traveled, assisted in developing educational programs in various countries, and continued to write. In 1980 he was permitted to return to Brazil, where he once again became active in educational reform. Having remarried after the death of his first wife, Freire continues to conduct an international dialog about the problems of literacy and the politics of education.

and teach themselves.) So far, however, teachers and schools stand solid because they do more than convey information; they socialize children, transmit society's values, and impart social and political roles, to name a few.[28]

Again we need to remind ourselves that forecasts of doom have usually been wrong, and in general those who predict educational doom do not have the loudest voices. They have not drowned out the optimists. Two among these are Marvin J. Cetron and Margaret Evans Gayle, who foresee a renaissance of education. In their formulation of forty-three trends for American schools in the

[28]Coates and Jarratt, "What Futurists Believe," 26.

twenty-first century, they group the trends into the following categories, which we will examine closely:

- Schools, business, and technology
- Families and schools
- Students and teachers
- Curricula and instruction
- School policies, reform, and leadership.[29]

SCHOOLS, BUSINESS, AND TECHNOLOGY   According to Cetron and Gayle, education will be seen by the business world as the key to economic growth. Technology will create jobs that require ''high-tech'' skills. To ensure the supply of such skilled workers, businesses will continue to enter into partnership with schools, so that they will not have to devote employees' work time to training. In restructuring curricula to meet these needs, a mismatch will occur between workers and the new skills. In fact, for the new jobs created over the last twenty years, only 75 percent of applicants will be qualified for only 40 percent of the jobs. By the year 2000 information-based employees will hold 43 percent of the jobs, and 22 percent of all workers will do their work from home. Small businesses will employ most of the work force by the end of this century.

Some eight million jobs requiring high levels of executive, professional, and technical skills will become available, but the employment picture will vary from state to state. Thus, because of the unemployment rate, overqualified workers will still hold lower-skilled types of jobs in some states. Also, the need for two incomes in many families will keep the part-time and moonlighting work force at high levels. By the year 2000 the proportion of two-income families is expected to reach 75 percent.

Education is crucial in an information-based society, and some futurists think technology will replace teachers. But schools do more than convey information; they also socialize, transmit values, and prepare children for social and political roles. —Spencer Grant/Photo Researchers

[29]Marvin J. Cetron and Margaret Evans Gayle, *Educational Renaissance: Our Schools into the Twenty-first Century* (New York: St. Martin's, 1990), 33–40.

RESEARCH SAYS

For Tomorrow's Education . . .
Recent data imply that significant educational upgrading will be needed in
the occupational structure for the future job market. Although such forecasting is limited at best, it seems likely that future occupational issues will
focus on the content of education, not on the amount. See Thomas Bailey,
"Jobs of the Future and the Education They Will Require: Evidence from
Occupational Forecasts," *Educational Researcher* 20 (March 1991): 11–20.

Such a job market will phase out lifelong careers in a single firm, and
people will change jobs and even careers five or more times. Like Nathan's
mother in the introduction to this chapter, many adults will return to schoool
to prepare for new jobs, and education will become a lifelong process. This will
bring further changes to schools, which will have to provide more opportunities
and alternatives for returning adult students.

EDUCATION, FAMILIES, AND VALUES Educational professionals will continue to be involved in helping people to adjust to changing values. They will be
faced with growing concerns about how technology makes society seem less human; and they will have to deal with people whose longer life span brings worries
about the quality of their lives. Educators have already confronted many ethical
dilemmas relating to medical confidentiality and students' exposure to conta-
gious diseases, including AIDS, and this will continue; more ethics committees
and policies will emerge to handle such matters.[30]

Family values will be more visible in the marketplace as consumers become
less concerned about satisfying their personal pleasures and more concerned
about their children's needs and comforts. Even so, today's differences in the
values held by different generations are expected to continue. Table 13.4 shows
the gaps in values across three twentieth-century generations. Based on the predictions in this chapter, how would you fill in a column for the first generation
of the next century?

SCHOOLS, STUDENTS, AND TEACHERS The changing family portrait will
certainly affect educators and schools. With single-parent and two-income families on the rise, schools will be asked to assume more child care roles. By the
turn of the century 75 percent of all three-year-olds will be attending nursery
schools or day-care centers. To accommodate such changes, schools will adopt
more flexible year-round schedules. They will probably remain open for more
hours in the day, although class time is likely to be reduced as schools assume
new roles in adult education and day care.

In the mid-1980s school enrollments dropped to under 40 million pupils,
but since then they have begun to rise. In 1991 enrollments were 41.6 million,
and by the year 2002 they are expected to reach 47 million. Private school en-

[30]Cornish, "Outlook '93," 6–7.

TABLE 13.4   Values and Generation Gaps

Value	World War II (1925–1945)	Baby Boomers (1946–1964)	20-Something (1965–1975)
Personal	allegiance	self-discovery	self-oriented
Political	conservative	liberal	pseudoconservative
Social	law & order	altruistic-humanistic	competitive
Ethical	fundamental	moralistic	situational
Financial	save, pay cash	Buy now, pay later	almost hopeless
Buying	based on necessity	Have it now	Whoever has the most wins
Products	home appliances, tools, homes, cars	Clothes, entertainment, travel	high-tech gadgets for fun & work
Reward	"I earned it"	"You owe me"	"I want it, but may not be able to get it"

Source: Edward Cornish, "Outlook '93," *Futurist* 26 (November–December 1992), 6: 2.

rollments are expected to increase at about the same rate—13 percent (from 5.3 million in 1991 to 5.9 million in 2002). For schools the challenge will be to provide facilities, schedules, and curricula that will meet students' needs. Returning adult students will also have to be accommodated, probably in settings like a community college. Some educators predict that the annual demand for new teachers will rise until the end of the century (see Figure 13.4). Other forecasters think that the demand for new teachers will not be so great, because

FIGURE 13.4   Trends in New Hiring of Classroom Teachers

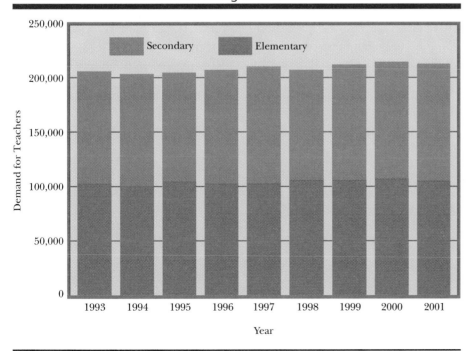

Source: *Projection of Education Statistics to the Year 2001: An Update,* National Center for Education Statistics, U.S. Department of Education (1990), tab. 35, 36.

experienced teachers return to the classroom after a break.[31] The demand for minority teachers—to keep in proportion with minority students—will be particularly high, especially in southern states (where minority students range from 25 to 56 percent but minority teachers fluctuate from 4 to 35 percent).

CURRICULA AND INSTRUCTION   Educators will need to develop and implement flexible, varied delivery systems that accommodate the needs of many kinds of students. New media and communication techniques will make it possible to tailor instruction to individual needs and at the same time to serve a wider range of individuals.

The global perspective that arises from nations' interdependence will mean that foreign languages will return to the curriculum, perhaps even as part of a new core of required studies. This new core will include technological literacies that today are only rudimentary. Critical thinking will also be emphasized in the curriculum. The traditional boundary lines between vocational and academic training may blur as interdisciplinary study becomes a more pragmatic approach to meeting students' lifelong learning needs.

Relating to higher education, only 15 percent of future jobs will require a college degree, but over 50 percent will demand postsecondary training. Community colleges and technical institutes are expectd to offer these new types of education. Teacher education programs will continue to change in response to the demand both for more teachers and for teachers of more kinds. Internationally, a global university is materializing to join students and professors from many countries through telecommunication techniques; such a network is expected to develop important new ways for scholars to collaborate in teaching and in research.[32]

SCHOOL POLICIES, REFORM, AND LEADERSHIP   School reform efforts will continue to be emphasized as community members, business leaders, and parents get involved in the policy-making branches of education. But since laypeople do not have the required professional preparation for such involvement, programs to educate them will be needed.

Control over curricula, training of education professionals, and standardized testing are expected to remain centralized. On the other hand, decentralization through school-based management is likely to continue, and so principals will need to play a larger role in coordinating and facilitating this process. About 50 percent of all principals and 75 percent of all superintendents will retire over

---

[31]U.S. Department of Education, Office of Educational Research and Improvement, National Center for Education Statistics, Projections of Education Statistics to 2000 (Washington, D.C.: U.S. Government Printing Office, 1989); and Cornish "Outlook '93," 3.

[32]Ibid.

RESEARCH SAYS

For Tomorrow's Education . . .

Colleges and universities will need to limit discipline-focused education during the next century. Instead, interdisciplinary programs and networks of resources linked electronically will need to become the norm in order to serve the diversity of educational populations. Resources will include teachers, students, information, and hardware. See "University of the 21st Century," *Futurist* 24 (September–October 1990): 53.

Comparative Perspective on Today's Issues . . .

◆ **ARE THE CARDS STACKED AGAINST PUBLIC SCHOOL REFORM?**

__The Issue__   Faced with reform reports and research that label the public schools as mediocre—and watching students move to private schools and parents seeking alternative forms of schooling—many educators wonder about the future of public education and whether or not the schools can be truly reformed.

YES   School improvement has been a much-discussed topic over a considerable amount of time. Yet the schism between our stated goals and the reality of schooling in terms of implementing those goals remains. "If school improvement continues on its present course, our schools will remain very much as they are."

—*John I. Goodlad, Professor of Policy, Governance, and Administration, University of Washington, and Director of the Center for Educational Renewal*

NO   Student's experiences are the measure of successful or unsuccessful schools. So far, public education has not provided successful experiences in terms of developing thinking skills, transmitting necessary knowledge, and molding character. Increased efforts at state and local levels, however, hold promise for improved public education. These efforts include better preschool experiences for poor children, more work-study opportunities, and greater community involvement in education.

—*Amitai Etzioni, George Washington University, and Director of the Center for Policy Research*

Source: Based on James Wm. Noll, ed., *Taking Sides: Clashing Views on Controversial Educational Issues,* 5th ed. (Guilford, Conn.: Dushkin, 1989), 134–153.

the next few years, and they will need to be replaced—another challenge for schools of education.

America's future education needs will come with an expensive price tag, to be sure, and a commitment to funding will be crucial. Various new approaches will be needed to support our schools. Besides traditional public revenues from taxes, additional income will be needed from vouchers, from private-sector partnerships, and from other sources. Issues of educational equity will relate less to equal access and more to equality of expenditures. The legal system will handle more and more cases relating to equity issues, especially in connection with regional disparities among all types of educational resources.[33]

CHALLENGES FOR THE NEXT CENTURY

The future of education will be exciting in America and throughout the world. In 1986 a poll of thirty-six Nobel laureates asked two questions: (1) In your opinion what are the two or three most compelling challenges confronting

[33]Ibid.

humanity? and (2) Do you have any precise proposals for meeting these challenges?[34]

The top three challenges identified by these Nobelists were world population growth (nineteen votes); defense costs and nuclear/conventional war (eighteen votes); and environmental degradation (ten votes). Other challenges, listed in descending order of votes, were the need for arms control, a revamped United Nations of world government with a world police force, hunger in the Third World, the need for education, and assistance to the Third World.

Answers to the second question—about meeting these challenges—focused on the quality of human existence. One solution proposed a new religion that would incorporate scientific advances and material matters "with the spiritual needs of human beings." This proponent pointed out that the major religions were developed before the revolutions in science and industry and that—unless people's spiritual needs are reconciled with day-to-day material life—

FIGURE 13.5   Student Futurists' Priorities for Next 100 Years

80 Percent	Avoid major nuclear war. Avoid marked deterioration of our planet. Dramatically improve policy-making laws to meet needs of people.

50 Percent	Most children in the world will receive adequate love attention and
	  opportunity to learn.
	Foster and facilitate self-esteem, good mental health, personal growth.
	Achieve a fairly peaceful world.
	Foster the finest human values.
	See a dramatic increase in portion of people who have adequate food,
	  water, shelter, clothing.
	Widespread freedom of speech, assembly, inquiry and political opinion.
	Widespread desire to cooperate and contribute.
	No second class citizens.
	Majority have adequate opportunities and for learning a wide variety of
	  knowledge and skills.
	Keep planet's beautiful wilderness.
	Avoid irretrievable loss of 50% of any part of human civilization and its record.
	Enormously improve the field of future studies, social change and
	  public administration.
	Encourage global and regional interpersonal and intersocial experiences.
	Aim for breakthroughs and advances in humanity's total body of knowledge.
	Achieve low to zero population growth.
	Avoid deterioration of the human gene pool.

	Reduce government debt. Encouage emergence of new subculture. Genetic and biological technology. Space. Study of supernatural and life after death. Computers and robots. Extraterrestrial intelligence.

[34]Howard F. Didsbury, Jr., "Beyond Mere Survival: A Report on a Poll of Nobel Laureates," *Futures Research Quarterly* 6 (Summer 1990) 2: 7–25.

Source: Based on Allen Tough, "Today's Priorities for the Next 100 Years: A Survey of Student Futurists," *Futures Research Quarterly* 6 (Summer 1990) 2: 27–34.

future society may opt to ignore science. The Nobelists regarded this possibility as dangerous.[35]

Education in the classical liberal or rational-realist tradition was seen by some Nobelists to counteract the effects of our materialistic society. (This tradition emphasizes the dignity of humanity and the individual's right to political freedom and happiness.) Another Nobel laureate pointed to the need to teach ethics on a global basis, noting that humanity is experiencing an "ethical Sahara." Another solution called for a world government that can uphold a loftier, more ethical world order. In the quest for a more humane existence, an American Nobelist in chemistry made this proposal:

> Education of the individuals on this earth that imparts both knowledge and character so that the decisions that they make will not only derive from understanding, but also from unimpeachable moral and ethical motivations. A person who has developed dignity and self-respect is likely to respect others and avoid antisocial behavior.[36]

Now consider Figure 13.5, which summarizes a study conducted among students in "Futures" classes. It reveals a strikingly similar picture to the one painted by the Nobel Prize winners. Sixty student futurists were asked to study a list of twenty-six goals and to give a "highest priority" ranking to no more than seven. The top three were (1) avoid major nuclear war; (2) avoid marked deterioration of planet; and (3) "dramatically improve policy-making laws to meet needs of people." As you consider the other goals in Figure 13.5, ask yourself how your own list would compare with the goals of the Nobelists and the student futurists.[37]

CONCLUSIONS

Many of the problems faced a hundred years ago have been solved during this century. In terms of education, controversies over the cirruculum—should it be entirely academic, or should it include industrial training and manual arts plus extracurricular activities and sports—were resolved, although new controversies always arise. Some of the forecasts about our century have also been realized—particularly the technological explosion and how it would ease our lives.

If we look into the crystal ball today, what do we see? First, we see an American society that will change as far as its ethnic and racial composition is concerned. The proportions of Hispanic-Americans and Asian-Americans will increase most dramatically. In addition, the next century will see more interethnic and interracial marriages, as well as more single-parent households—particularly those headed by males.

Schools will face some enormous challenges in the future. New definitions of literacy will emphasize technological skills and even foreign languages, as a global perspective will be needed. Learning centers with flexible schedules, al-

[35]Ibid., 11.
[36]Ibid., 22.
[37]Allen Tough, "Today's Priorities for the Next 100 Years: A Survey of Student Futurists," *Futures Research Quarterly* 6 (Summer 1990) 2: 27–34.

ternative curricula, and multiple delivery systems will be needed to accommodate the variety of students' lifelong learning needs, from infancy to late adulthood. All these changes will require financial solutions that go beyond tax revenues to include vouchers, lotteries, and private-sector partnerships and investment.

Finally, we considered the kinds of challenges that the next century will bring concerning peace, population control, environmental issues, and global education. Since education plays such an important role in society, there can be no doubt that the future will be an exciting time for educational professionals.

KEY TERMS

globalism

Americanization of world culture

information-based society

liberating education

functional illiteracy

SUGGESTED READINGS

Isaac Asimov and Frank White, *The March of the Millenia: A Key to Looking at History* (New York: Walker, 1991). This book looks to the future by assessing the past millennia. It concludes that human beings now hold the key to the planet's future and that human civilization now holds the possibility of being united globally.

Chester E. Finn, *We Must Take Charge: Our Schools and Our Future* (New York: Free Press, 1991). This book calls for radical changes in how we view our schools and run them. Finn challenges Americans to take charge of public schools and not to assume that at-risk students are someone else's concern.

Mark H. Mullin, *Educating for the 21st Century: The Challenge for Parents and Teachers* (Washington, D.C.: University Press of America, 1991). The Reverend Mullin draws upon more than twenty years' experience as headmaster of one of the nation's top-ranking secondary schools to envision how schools ought to be.

Phillip C. Schlechty, *Schools for the 21st Century: Leadership Imperatives for Educational Reform* (San Francisco: Jossey-Bass, 1990). This book discusses

how schools should be structured to accommodate children in the future.

Myron Tuman, *Word Perfect: Prospects for Literacy in the Computer Age* (New York: Falmer Press, 1991). This book examines the ways that computer technology is likely to change the concept of literacy in the future.

Ben J. Wattenberg, *The First Universal Nation* (New York: Free Press, 1990). This provocative book cogently analyzes how America arrived at its current social and political place and where it is likely to be headed during the next decades.

Mervin J. Cetron and Margaret Evans Gayle, *Educational Renaissance: Our Schools into the Twenty-first Century* (New York: St. Martin's, 1990). This book examines trends in education and society in order to paint an enlightening and informative picture of America in the future.

Ira Shor and Paulo Freire, *A Pedagogy for Liberation: Dialogues on Transforming Education* (South Hadley, Mass.: Bergin & Garvey, 1987). These dialogs discuss educational problems and issues and provide a vision for solving them.

Yesterday's Professional Photographs

Francis Wayland Parker, page 12: Chicago Historical Society; **Margaret A. Haley, page 33:** Chicago Historical Society; **Horace Mann, page 74:** National Portrait Gallery/Smithsonian Institution; **Sara Winnemucca, page 92:** Nevada Historical Society; **Mary McCleod Bethune, page 119:** Painted by Betsy Graves Reynau/Fisk University, Special Collections; **Maria Montessori, page 153:** UPI/Bettmann; **Margarethe Meyer Schurz, page 180:** Blackwell History of Education Collection, Northern Illinois University; **Quintilian, page 215:** Giraudon/Art Resource; **W. E. B. Du Bois, page 253:** Bettmann; **Ella Flagg Young, page 278:** UPI/Bettmann; **Thurgood Marshall, page 314:** Theo Westenberger/Gamma Liaison Network; **George S. Counts, page 327:** Special Collections, Morris Library, Southern Illinois University at Carbondale; **Paulo Freire, page 358:** Jorge Jeria.

Additional Acknowledgments

Table 1.1: F. Howard Nelson, *Survey and Analysis of Salary Trends, 1992,* American Federation of Teachers, Washington, D.C., p. 43. Reprinted by permission of F. Howard Nelson; **Table 1.2:** Reprinted by permission of Educational Research Service, Arlington, Virginia; **Table 1.3:** Reprinted by permission of the Phi Delta Kappan, vol. 72, p. 47, September 1990; **Table 1.4:** Reprinted by permission of Robert Knoop; **Figure 1.1** Reprinted with permission of the Phi Delta Kappan, vol. 70, p. 792, June 1989.

GLOSSARY

■

Notes

Following each entry, the number in brackets tells you which chapter covers the concept fully. Within glossary entries, words in *italic type* refer you to other entries you should compare. Also remember to check the indexes to locate additional information about a glossary entry.

ability-to-pay principle   [3]

The idea that people's tax burdens should be related to their financial capabilities and needs. (See *benefit principle.*)

academic freedom   [7]

Nineteenth-century German ideas (1) that it was exclusively a student's right to decide when and where to take the doctorate examination and (2) that professors had the right to say or write whatever they believed to be true.

academy   [8, 9]

(1) Milton's term for a school that stressed a *curriculum* of classics, mathematics, religion, and technical subjects like surveying and bookkeeping. (2) Greek term resurrected during the Renaissance by religious dissenters first in England and then in the colonies. In America the *Great Awakening* and subsequent religious revivalism led to the proliferation of academies, which offered classes in classical grammar and practical schooling—a *curriculum* that today is known as secondary, or college preparatory, education.

accommodation   [6]

Piaget's term for the second of two cognitive functions that help an organism adapt to the environment; accommodation occurs when an individual changes his or her mental structure, or picture of reality, to fit particular assimilated material. (See *assimilation.*)

aesthetics   [10]

The subfield of *axiology* that addresses questions about the nature of beauty. (See *ethics.*)

Afrocentric perspective   [12]

An intellectual position which challenges the notion that all ideas of cultural significance arose from European males. (See *Eurocentric ideology.*)

American Federation of Teachers (AFT)   [2]

Often regarded as more militant than

the *National Education Association*, this rival teacher organization reached the height of its popularity during the 1960s, when it advocated unionism and the use of the strike.

Americanization of world culture   [13]

The idea that American culture is exerting a strong influence on other nations—so strong, that America is being universalized.

analytic philosophy   [10]

An approach to the study and practice of *philosophy* which holds that all philosophical pursuits are nothing more than a critique of language; it views philosophy as an activity, not as a system with a set of theories and speculating principles.

apperception   [6]

According to Herbart, the total process by which an organism associates and stores *mental states*. (See *apperceptive mass* and Figure 6.2.)

apperceptive mass   [6]

Herbart's term for the totality of an individual's *mental states*. (See *apperception* and Figure 6.2.)

aretè   [8]

In ancient Greece, the combined values of virtue and honor as seen in the traditions of Achilles and Ulysses; the focus and goal of a Homeric education.

ascribed status   [1]

The degree of *status*, or prestige, that the public generally grants to a particular occupation or group. Figure 1.1 shows how much status the public ascribes to teaching. (See *earned status*.)

assimilation   [6]

Piaget's term for the first of two cognitive functions that help an organism adapt to the environment; assimilation occurs when an individual takes something from the environment and incorporates it into his or her mental structure, or picture of reality. (See *accommodation*.)

associationism   [6]

Aristotle's theory that ideas are best remembered when they are associated with other, existing ideas (which may be congruous, similar, sequential, or opposite). (Figure 6.2 outlines the evolution of learning theories.)

at-risk students   [12]

Label that arose during the educational reform activities of the 1980s to describe disadvantaged students, the majority of whom are nonwhite and are from working-class or underclass backgrounds.

axiology   [10]

The field of *philosophy* that is concerned with questions of value; its subfields are *ethics* and *aesthetics*.

behaviorally disordered   [7]

Classification for an individual who exhibits socialization difficulties. (See *emotionally disturbed, learning disabled*, and *mentally retarded*.)

benefit principle   [3]

The idea that people should pay taxes only for the government services that they receive. (See *ability-to-pay principle*.)

biculturalism   [5]

Coexistence of two cultures within one community. (See *cultural assimilation* and *multicultural society*.)

block grant [3]
Federal funding for schools that can be used for broadly defined purposes; a common form of funding since the early 1980s. (See *categorical grant.*)

board of education [3]
Group of community members who are responsible for setting educational policies, which the school district's *superintendent* then administers. Table 3.6 presents a demographic profile of school board members.

bureaucracy [3]
Any system characterized by a hierarchy of authority, specialization of functions and responsibilities, and adherence to fixed rules. To counteract the negative effects of educational bureaucracy, some districts have implemented *school-based management.*

Cardinal Principles of Secondary Education [7]
Document formulated by the *Commission on the Reorganization of Secondary Education* that enumerated seven main objectives aimed at training workers for life in a rapidly changing society. The areas identified in Cardinal Principles are health, command of fundamental processes, worthy home membership, vocation, citizenship, worthy use of leisure time, and character.

career-ladder plan [2]
An administrative approach that identifies various levels of expert knowledge and provides evaluative criteria for assessing each level. As teachers climb the rungs of the career ladder, they attain greater compensation and additional ways to use their expertise.

Cartesian method [10]
René Descartes' attempt to discover ideas that are undoubtable by doubting everything; he realized that he could doubt everything except the fact that he was thinking while doubting, leading him to conclude, "I think, therefore I am" (Cogito ergo sum).

Casa dei Bambini [6]
"Children's house" founded in Rome by Italian physician Maria Montessori (see "Yesterday's Professional" in Chapter 6); the site where Montessori made the observations on which she based her educational and developmental theories. (Figure 6.2 outlines the evolution of learning theories.)

case law [11]
Law based on court decisions and rulings. (See *common law* and *enacted law.*)

categorical grant [3]
Federal funding for schools that is designated for a specific purpose; a common form of funding during the 1960s and 1970s. (See *block grant.*)

categorical imperative [10]
Immanuel Kant's term for the ethical idea that we each should act as though our actions were to become a universal moral law that would be binding on all other people in a similar situation.

centering [6]
Seeing oneself as the center of the world, as is typical of children during the *preoperational stage* of cognitive development. (See *egocentrism* and Figure 6.1.)

certification   [1]

"The process by which a government or non governmental agency grants recognition to an individual who has met certain predetermined qualifications set by a credentializing agency." (See *licensing.*)

charity school   [9]

Nineteenth-century *common school* for which the community or a religious group paid some or all of a student's tuition, or "head tax."

child-centered curriculum   [7]

Idea advocated by Francis Wayland Parker that subject matter should be subordinated to the interests and motivations of the child. In other words, the child is the *curriculum,* and school subjects are presented in ways that involve the child actively and practically. (See *project-centered curriculum.*)

choice plan   [3]

Alternative schooling arrangement in which parents can select which of various specialized schools in a system their child will attend. (See *magnet school, tuition tax credit,* and *voucher plan.*)

Civil Rights Act of 1964   [3, 5]

Legislation signed by President Lyndon Johnson which states that all federally funded education programs must be administered without discriminating against *minority groups.*

classical realism   [10]

The *philosophical system* that subscribes to Aristotle and Plato's views about human free will and spiritual realism but does not hold that the spiritual dimension is Divinely created. (See *religious realism* and *scientific realism;* also see Figure 10.1.)

cognitive science   [6]

Field of study that combines cognitive psychology and scientific research into brain processes, drawing from neurosurgery, neuropsychology, developmental psychology, and computer science. (Figure 6.2 outlines the evolution of learning theories.)

Coleman report   [5]

Congressional study of educational inequality completed in 1966 by sociologist James Coleman which implied that school achievement depended more on a student's social class and family background than on "the facilities and the curriculums of the schools."

collective bargaining   [2]

Group negotiations with an employer to secure better economic or better work conditions.

colonialism   [5]

Domination of one group by another in an unequal relationship that benefits the colonizer at the expense of the colonized. Feminist Bonnie Cook Freeman has argued that the concept of colonialism can be applied to women's experiences in their power relations with men.

Commission on the Reorganization of Secondary Education (CRSE)   [7]

Committee of the *National Education Association* that formulated the *Cardinal Principles of Secondary Education* in recognition of the economic need to train teenagers and keep them off the streets.

Committee of Ten   [7]

Group of *National Education Association* intellectuals drawn largely from

U.S. colleges and universities who, in the 1890s, recommended a standard high school *curriculum* (see Table 7.1) concentrating on English language and literature, modern or classical languages, mathematics, and physical and natural sciences.

common law   [11]
Law that courts "discover" in earlier decisions after carefully reading and applying them to the case at hand. (See *case law* and *enacted law*.)

common-person class   [4]
According to some sociologists, a future *social class* that will include Americans who are now in the *lower middle class* as well as those who are now in the *upper working class*.

common school   [3, 9]
(1) From the 1620s to the 1850s a single-teacher school that was directly supervised by the community and usually served ten to twenty families who lived within 5 miles of each other. (2) A school for ordinary, or "common," people, rather than for the wealthy or well-to-do; even so, parents usually paid some tuition or tax for each child's education. (See *charity school*.)

compensatory education   [5]
Programs designed to correct educational deficiencies in the backgrounds and lifestyles of children, who are often members of *minority groups* and come from lower social classes.

concrete operations stage   [6]
Piaget's third stage of cognitive development (from about ages seven to eleven), when children develop a more advanced system of classification and are able to reverse operations. (Figure 6.1 summarizes Piaget's stages of cognitive development, and Figure 6.2 outlines the evolution of learning theories.)

connectionism   [6]
Edward L. Thorndike's theory that every mental unit has a corresponding physical component which acts as a stimulus or as a response and that learning occurs when physical and mental elements are connected; also known as *stimulus-response bond theory*. (Figure 6.2 outlines the evolution of learning theories.)

correlation   [4]
Statistical association between two or more items, which is usually expressed as a two-digit number ranging from +1.00 to −1.00.

cosmology   [10]
A subfield of *metaphysics* that is concerned with the nature of the universe as an orderly system. (See *ontology*.)

cultural assimilation   [5]
Blending of minority cultures into the dominant, majority culture, as in the "melting pot" concept. Around the 1970s *biculturalism* became an equally important concept in America, which is now considered a *multicultural society*.

cultural deprivation theory   [5]
Explanation for the learning problems of minority students which claims that the culture of poverty into which minority students are socialized accounts for their lack of academic success. (Table 5.1 compares the scores of various racial groups in the early 1980s.)

cultural literacy [12]
A phrase prominent in the writings of E. D. Hirsh, among others, who advocates "a traditional literate curriculum" and questions the value of multiculturalism.

cuneiform [8]
Sumerian symbols made by pressing a wedge-shaped stylus into a soft clay tablet; first used for business records but by 2700 B.C. also used for literature.

curriculum [7]
Defined course of study (from Latin word meaning "path" or "course"). Table 7.1 shows a typical high school curriculum of the 1890s, as recommended by the *Committee of Ten.*

cytharist [8]
Musician in ancient Athens who taught young boys to play the lyre as an accompaniment to poetry and other songs. (See *grammartist* and *paidotribe.*)

dame school [1, 8, 9]
(1) In colonial America, a school in which a housewife earned extra money (or crops) by taking youngsters into her home and teaching them reading and writing. (2) In post-Reformation England, a private *elementary school* in which a neighborhood housewife taught children for a fee.

Dartmouth College case [9]
Decision by the U.S. Supreme Court in 1819 that made it extremely difficult to tamper with educational charters.

deductive reasoning [10]
The form of *logic* that concludes something specific from a general proposition. (See *inductive reasoning.*)

de facto segregation [5]
The separation of racial groups "in fact." (See *de jure segregation.*)

de jure segregation [5]
The separation of racial groups "under the law." (See *de facto segregation.*)

didactic material [6]
Something that gives instruction in a specific learning concept, such as spacial relations (a puzzle) or sequential organization (stacking blocks); Montessori schools use objects and toys as didactic materials. (Figure 6.2 outlines the evolution of learning theories.)

diploma mill [7]
Institution that offers a college diploma in exchange for money; in the flurry of institution building at the turn of the century, diploma mills were prevalent in the fields of medicine and dentistry.

dissatisfier [1]
A factor that is perceived negatively by the person experiencing it; an aspect of a job that makes the job dissatisfying to a person. (Compare *satisfier.*)

district school [9]
In Massachusetts and Connecticut after 1700, the name for a community school with a single teacher and pupils of all ages. In the 1600s many other names were used, including *common school, free school, grammar school,* and *public school.*

earned status [1]
Status, or prestige, that is granted for

one's performance. (See *ascribed status.*)

eduba　[8]
A Sumerian temple school taught by a priest (*ummia*).

egocentrism　[6]
Being unable to consider any point of view expect one's own, as is typical of children during the *preoperational stage* of cognitive development. (See *centering* and Figure 6.1.)

Elementary and Secondary Education Act of 1965 (ESEA)　[3, 5]
Part of President Lyndon Johnson's "War on Poverty," this act aimed to equalize educational opportunity by making money available to support a variety of public and parochial school programs.

elementary school　[7]
Post-Reformation English vernacular school attended by peasant and working-class students who were not preparing for university study. (See *secondary school.*)

emerging profession　[2]
An occupation, like teaching, that confers less status than, say, medicine and law, and that exhibits fewer professional characteristics to the same degree that medicine and law do. (See *profession.*)

emotionally disturbed　[7]
Classification for an individual who exhibits maladaptive behaviors and has aberrant feelings about the self. (Compare *behaviorally disordered*, *learning disabled*, and *mentally retarded.*)

empirical confirmation　[10]
Experimental method in which an expert places a high degree of probability on what occurred in the experiment. (See *empirical verification.*)

empirical verification　[10]
Experimental method in which the scrutinized variable or set of variables is observed directly. (See *empirical confirmation.*)

empiricism　[6, 10]
The idea that all knowledge is derived from observation and sensory experience, through the process of *empirical confirmation* or *empirical verification.*

enacted law　[11]
Law that is established by constitution, code, or other forms legislation. (See *case law* and *common law.*)

endowment　[9]
A continuing income to support a school. The term first was used in connection with a school founded in 1379 at Winchester Cathedral in England, where the bishop supported the instruction of a small number of boys who were talented but poor. (See *free school.*)

epistemology　[10]
The field of philosophy that is concerned with the nature of human knowledge and its limits. (See *logic.*)

Equal Pay Act of 1963　[5]
Beginning of legal developments aimed at ensuring economic and workplace equity between the sexes, so that women with the same educational background and training as men would receive equal pay for equal work.

essentialism　**[10]**

The prevalent educational philosophy in twentieth-century America, which follows the realist approach by stressing memorization and mastery of "essential" knowledge from the disciplines of English, mathematics, history, science, and foreign languages. (See *perennialism, progressivism,* and *reconstructionism.*)

ethics　**[10]**

The subfield of *axiology* that seeks to answer questions about what is right or wrong, good or bad, both personally and socially. (See *aesthetics.*)

Eurocentric ideology　**[12]**

Label for the dominant society's notion that everything of cultural importance came from European males. (See *Afrocentric perspective.*)

executive session　**[11]**

A school board meeting that excludes members of the public; a board's final votes on a matter must usually be taken in a meeting that is open to the public.

existentialism　**[10]**

The *philosophical system* which holds that human beings live in a meaningless and purposeless world; existentialists consider the material nature of the universe to be real, but the see its existence as absurd. (See Figure 10.1.)

faculty psychology　**[6]**

The nineteenth-century idea, rooted in ancient Greek thought, that the mind possesses specialized compartmental structures which must be exercised. (See *mental discipline* and Figure 6.2.)

federal judicial circuit court　**[11]**

One of thirteen appellate courts in the federal judicial system. (See Figure 11.1.)

feeder school　**[8]**

Medieval English *grammar school* located in London and other urban centers whose graduates often went to Oxford and Cambridge, which were located in rural areas.

formal operations stage　**[6]**

Piaget's fourth and final stage of cognitive development (from about ages eleven to fifteen), when adolescents can understand the form of symbolic operations, such as metaphors, equations, logical propositions, and scientific constructs. (Figure 6.1 summarizes Piaget's stages of cognitive development, and Figure 6.2 outlines the evolution of learning theories.)

free school　**[9]**

Sometimes called "free public schools," these schools in fact charged tuition, but they also made a few endowed, or scholarship, places available. (See *endowment.*)

Freedmen's Bureau　**[9]**

Government agency formed in 1865 to assist four million freed slaves; it was supposed to provide land, economic support, and schools, but during its brief existence it mostly provided schools.

friends of education　**[9]**

In the mid-nineteenth century, those who supported *state action*, or social control over education (rather than personal or local control). Although "friends" were found in every state, they were concentrated in New England. (See the Name Index for references to Henry Barnard, James Carter, and Horace Mann.)

functional illiteracy   [13]

Being unable to function adequately in society even though one has attended school. In *Illiterate America* (1985) Jonathan Kozol claims that sixty million Americans are functionally illiterate to some degree, but his definitions and data are questionable.

gifted education   [7]

Education for children who ''give evidence of high performance capability in areas such as intellectual, creative, artistic, leadership capacity, or specific academic fields and who require services or activities not ordinarily provided by the school in order to fully develop such capabilities.''

gifts   [7]

Six sets of movable geometric shapes used by Froebel in teaching young children in *kindergarten*; the shapes can be manipulated but do not change, thus teaching children about the universal nature of things. (See *occupations.*)

globalism   [13]

Internationalism; having an international outlook rather than a nationalistic perspective.

graded school   [9]

A school that groups pupils by every year of age and gives a different *curriculum* to each group. Although this practice began in the last half of the nineteenth century, it did not become standard until well into this century.

grammartist   [8]

In ancient Athens a teacher of writing, which included reading and arithmetic. (See *cytharist* and *paidotribe.*)

Great Awakening   [9]

First major wave of religious revivalism in colonial America, between about 1720 and 1740. By 1830 the splintering of Protestant groups into new denominations and sects—each wanting its own schools—spurred the evolution and variety of education in America. (See *academy.*)

gymnasium   [8]

In ancient Athens a municipal school for freeborn teenaged males who had completed study at the *palestra.*

hegemony   [5]

Dominance, or authority; in the United States the dominance of European culture over other cultures.

hieroglyphics   [8]

Ancient Egyptian pictographic symbols used for reading and writing.

higher faculties   [8]

Three of the four faculties in the organizational structure of the *universitas*; these advanced faculties taught theology, law, and medicine. (See *lesser faculty.*)

Holmes Group   [12]

An organization including a number of American universities that advocated making all teacher education programs postbaccalaureate, thus identifying themselves with the call for educational reform that was set off in 1983 by a report issued by the *National Commission on Excellence in Teaching.*

humanism [8]
Renaissance "new learning" that focused on the art and literature of classical Greece and Rome and emphasized the study of human feelings, senses, and physical characteristics.

idealism [10]
The oldest *philosophical system* in Western culture; idealists distrust the constantly changing, unstable world and hold that ideas are the source of reality. (See Figure 10.1.)

Indian Reorganization Act of 1934 [5]
Federal legislation that increased the power and self-governing responsibilities of Native American tribal councils.

inductive reasoning [10]
A form of *logic* that makes a generalization on the basis of a specific proposition. (See *deductive reasoning*.)

information-based society [13]
A society in which the better jobs demand information-processing skills.

intelligence [4]
Traditionally, "the ability to learn or understand or to deal with new or trying situations"; early in this century, however, the term came to be synonymous with performance on a few scholastic aptitude tests, which reflect what *most* students have learned or achieved by certain ages.

intelligence quotient (IQ) [4]
Numerical expression of an individual's intelligence as determined by testing to obtain the person's "mental age," or *mental level*, and then dividing that number by the person's chronological age; that result is then multiplied by 100 to eliminate the decimal places.

Kalamazoo case [3, 9]
Decision by the Michigan Supreme Court in 1874 that, based on the Tenth Amendment of the U.S. Constitution, established the primacy of state control over local schools. The Kalamazoo case led to a new definition of the *common school*—as proposed by the *friends of education*—and thus led to tax-supported, state-controlled *public schools*.

kindergarten [7]
"Children's garden," a type of school developed in the nineteenth century by Friedrich Froebel in which young children were taught through the use of *gifts* and *occupations*—shapes and materials that can be transformed through a variety of self-activities.

latchkey children [12]
A term that arose during the 1980s to refer to children who must let themselves in to an empty home after school because their parents are at work.

Latin grammar school [8]
Type of Roman school that followed the *ludus* and taught the *seven liberal arts*, although the Romans placed less emphasis on arithmetic, geometry, music, and astronomy than the Greeks did.

learning disabilities theory [5]
The claim that minority students have different cognitive styles which need to be diagnosed and treated and that *compensatory education* had failed because it sought to bring minority students up to some "mythical norm" of

achievement. (Table 5.1 compares the scores of various racial groups in the early 1980s.)

learning disabled   [7]
Classification for an individual who has a disorder that "may manifest itself in an imperfect ability to listen, think, speak, read, write, spell or to do mathematical calculations." (Compare *behaviorally disordered, mentally retarded,* and *emotionally disturbed.*)

lesser faculty   [8]
One of four faculties in the organizational structure of the *universitas*; the lesser faculty of the arts was preparatory. (See *higher faculties.*)

liberating education   [13]
Paulo Freire's linguistically based pedagogy, which includes politically active, consciousness-raising messages.

licensing   [1]
The "process by which an agency or government grants permission to an individual to engage in a given occupation upon finding that the applicant has attained the minimal degree of competency required to ensure that the public health, safety, and welfare will be reasonably well protected." (See *certification.*)

litterator   [8]
Teacher of young Roman boys between about ages seven through fourteen; also known as a *ludus magister.*

local school councils   [5]
Bodies composed of parents, community members, and teachers and charged with setting and implementing educational policies for their own particular school.

logic   [10]
The subfield of *epistemology* that deals with the rules and principles of reasoning. (See *deductive reasoning* and *inductive reasoning.*)

lower middle class   [4]
Third of five levels of *socioeconomic status* in the United States, including about 32 percent of the population. These people can be characterized as economically independent but thrifty, having incomes at or near the national average, and their leisure activities are those which are the most popular. (See *upper middle class* and *upper working class.*)

lower working class   [4]
Fifth of five levels of *socioeconomic status* in the United states, including about 18 percent of the population. These people are poor and live in tenements and housing projects; they have few skills and have difficulty finding jobs. (See *upper working class* and *underclass.*)

ludus   [8]
Roman school where boys of about seven through fourteen learned reading, writing, and arithmetic; girls were admitted to the ludus during the third century B.C.

ludus magister   [8]
Teacher of young Roman boys between about ages seven through fourteen; also known as a *litterator.*

magnet school   [5]
In large cities a specialized school that provides programs and materials not usually available in neighborhood schools, thus attracting a diverse student body and helping to achieve voluntary integration. (See *choice plan.*)

mental discipline [6]

In Greek education the idea that a student's mind had to be trained or exercised in order to think well, reflecting the belief that an infant's mind at birth was endowed with innate ideas, or inborn potentials. (Figure 6.2 outlines the evolution of learning theories.)

mental level [4]

A person's "mental age" as determined by testing in order to derive the person's *intelligence quotient*, or I.Q. One's mental level may not coincide with one's chronological age.

mentally retarded [7]

Classification for an individual who is significantly below average in general *intelligence* (having an IQ below 65–69) and who is also deficient in adapting appropriately to a particular environment. (Compare *behaviorally disordered, emotionally disturbed,* and *learning disabled.*)

mental states [6]

Sensory impressions that are recognized and accepted by the mind and remain in consciousness. According to eighteenth-century German philosopher Johann Friedrich Herbart, the mind is a "battleground" where sensory ideas compete to become mental states, which, in the aggregate, are the contents of the mind. (See *apperception, apperceptive mass,* and Figure 6.2.)

mentoring program [1]

A supervised classroom experience in which a first-year teacher, or intern, is assigned to an experienced teacher who guides and counsels the intern.

merit pay [2]

Monetary bonus for a job well done.

metaphysics [10]

The field of *philosophy* that is concerned with the nature of reality; as such, its subfields include *cosmology* and *ontology*.

minority groups [5]

Populations whose racial or ethnic characteristics differ from the dominant, majority population's. In the United States any group that is not descended from white Europeans is considered a minority group, and any group that is not Protestant, male, and heterosexual may have minority status—even if its numbers actually constitute a majority.

monitorial system [7]

Quaker John Lancaster's nineteenth-century procedures and routines for running a school efficiently by using older, more accomplished pupils to help younger, less skilled ones; "groups of ten or twelve gathered around their monitors in semi-circles to compete"; the groups were arranged according to skill, and pupils could be promoted to a higher group any time their skills justified it.

Morrill Act of 1862 [7]

Also known as the Land Grant College Act, this legislation set aside 30,000 acres of public land for each member of Congress in each state; income from these land grants was used for collegiate study (both the liberal arts and more practical subjects, like engineering and agriculture). The Morrill Act thus expanded the college curriculum and subsidized tuition costs so that more young people could afford to attend college.

multicultural (pluralistic) society [5]

Society composed of many racial and ethnic groups that voluntarily live and work together while acknowledging and recognizing their original cultures. (See *biculturalism* and *cultural assimilation*.)

municipal court [11]

A court on the first level of a state's court system. (See Figure 11.1.)

National Board for Professional Teaching Standards [2]

A body created in 1987 to implement a teacher assessment process that goes beyond state certification to confirm a high level of competency in one's specialty. Specialty certification can be used in awarding privileges, more benefits, or increased compensation to a teacher.

National Commission on Excellence in Education [12]

A prestigious committee created by the U.S. Department of Education that is best known for its 1983 report entitled *A Nation at Risk: The Imperative for Educational Reform*. The report basically blamed teachers and their training institutions for "a rising tide of mediocrity that threatens our very future as a nation and a people," setting off a flurry of educational reform activity.

National Education Association (NEA) [2]

A popular teacher organization that received its congressional charter in 1906, after many years of development and the merger of several similar organizations. Most teachers belong to a state or local affiliate of the NEA that deals with such issues as sal-

ary, class size, school administration, parents, and various problems in the profession. (See *American Federation of Teachers*.)

National Teacher Examinations [10]

A battery of tests that teachers are required to complete as part of their *certification* process; the core battery covers three areas (communication skills, general knowledge, and professional knowledge), and there is also a set of specialty-area tests.

negative reinforcer [6]

In *operant conditioning*, a stimulus that weakens a response and makes it less probable. (See *positive reinforcer*.)

new method [8]

The scientific method, as set forth by Sir Francis Bacon in *Novum Organum*. Scientists should proceed inductively by first observing facts in nature, then building from such empirical observations an extensive collection of facts, then finding commonalities among them, and finally generalizing from these to form comprehensive formulas and principles.

normal curve [4]

Charted representation of a mathematical formula showing the frequency distribution of a variable within a population (theoretically, a bell-shaped curve).

normal school [1, 8]

(1) An institution to train teachers. A typical program consists of common elementary school subjects followed by psychology, philosophy, history of education, methods of teaching, observation in the classroom, and practice teaching. The first tax-supported

normal school in America was founded in Lexington, Massachusetts, in 1839. (2) During the Enlightenment, concern for educating the masses led to the training of lay teachers in schools that emphasized reading, writing, arithmetic, and character development.

object teaching   [7]
Techniques that involve students' senses in learning (such as using movable letters to teach reading and spelling; counting pebbles and beans to teach arithmetic; and drawing pictures as a first step toward reading). Although Johann Heinrich Pestalozzi received international credit for "The Method," much of it was developed by three younger men at a teacher training institute that Pestalozzi joined.

occupations   [7]
Activities and materials used by Froebel in teaching young children in *kindergarten*; the materials can be transformed into new objects through self-activities such as sewing, weaving, and drawing. (See *gifts*.)

Old Deluder-Satan Law   [9]
A law passed in Massachusetts in 1647 that set aside a portion of each township for a church and usually an equal amount of land for a school; the law was so named because colonial settlers were convinced that, with education, people would not be "deluded" by Satan.

ontology   [10]
A subfield of *metaphysics* that is concerned with the nature of being. (See *cosmology*.)

operant conditioning   [6]
According to B. F. Skinner, the process by which learning occurs. In Skinner's view, learning is a change in the probability that a particular response will occur again—and that probability is influenced by the type and timing of activities which reinforce the appropriate behavior in the learner. (See *positive reinforcer, negative reinforcer,* and *Skinner box.*)

paidogogos   [8]
In ancient Athens a "boy's slave" who accompanied his master to the *palestra*. (See *pedagogue*.)

paidotribe   [8]
A masseuse in ancient Athens who taught young boys gymnastics, which included running, swimming, wrestling, and the use of bow and sling. (See *cytharist* and *grammartist*).

palestra   [8]
A private school in ancient Athens where freeborn males of about ages six to twelve studied such subjects as gymnastics, music, reading, writing, and arithmetic.

paradigm   [10]
A carefully delineated model or template that guides research and allows us to add our own knowledge.

pedagogue   [8]
A slave who accompanied a Roman boy to the *ludus*. (See *paidogogos*.)

pedagogy   [6]
The art of teaching.

perennialism   [10]
A reaction against *essentialism* and *progressivism*, this educational philosophy holds that certain cultural dimensions of education are universal and timeless and that students have in-

born talents and will learn as much as their character and talent will permit. (See *essentialism, progressivism,* and *reconstructionism.*)

petty school   [8]
A department within a post-reformation English grammar school (*public school*) that offered elementary or preparatory education.

philosopher   [8]
In ancient Athens a teacher of such subjects as geometry, astronomy, *logic,* and rhetoric who recruited students at the *gymnasium.* (See *Sophists.*)

philosopher-king   [8]
Plato's name for the intellectually gifted, politically powerful leaders of an ideal society.

philosophical system   [10]
A distinctive way of speculating about *metaphysics, epistemology,* and *axiology.* The text compares how four systems investigate questions about reality, knowledge, and value (see Figure 10.1).

philosophy   [10]
The speculative "pursuit of wisdom" that is concerned with meaning and understanding, with discovery and description; traditional *philosophical systems* include the fields of *metaphysics* (*ontology* and *cosmology*), *epistemology,* and *axiology* (*ethics* and *aesthetics*).

political action committee (PAC)   [2]
A group that lobbies politicians and the public in an effort to influence legislation and public opinion. The *National Education Association* and the *American Federation of Teachers* and their state-level affiliate organizations

have formed PACs to influence educational legislation.

pragmatism   [10]
The *philosophical system* that emphasizes the individual's experiences or interactions with the environment as the main source of reality; pragmatists are concerned with finding processes and solutions that attain agreeable and appropriate results. (See Figure 10.1.)

preoperational stage   [6]
Piaget's second stage of cognitive development (from about ages two to seven), when children extend the scope of their activities in order to bring more meaning and order to the environment; they also expand the *schemes* they began to develop toward the end of the *sensorimotor stage.* (Figure 6.1 summarizes Piaget's stages of cognitive development, and Figure 6.2 outlines the evolution of learning theories.)

private school   [9]
Label used by the *friends of education* to refer to a *common school* that charged tuition, thus separating private schools from the kind of township organization they supported in connection with *state action.*

profession   [2]
An "occupation with a crucial social function, requiring a high degree of skill and drawing on a systematic body of knowledge." Certain characteristics make an occupation a profession: an exclusive body of knowledge, applying that expert knowledge for clients' welfare, a high level of autonomy in decision making and controlling standards, and a sense of collegial identity within a formal

structure. Since teaching in some ways falls short of these criteria, it is often regarded as an *emerging profession.*

progressivism   [10]

A reaction against *essentialism*, this educational philosophy holds that the child should be at the center of the educational process; rather than transmitting a defined body of knowledge, progressives believe that educators should take students' needs and interests into account. (See *essentialism, perennialism,* and *reconstructionism.*)

project-centered curriculum   [7]

A *curriculum* advocated by John Dewey and William Heard Kilpatrick in which each child—after a grounding in *object teaching* and a *child-centered curriculum*—works cooperatively on a major project that involves both manipulative and conceptual skills.

public school   [8, 9]

(1) Post-Reformation English secondary school for upper-class and middle-class students who could afford to pay for education; such schools were neither free nor available to lower-class students. In England today public schools are still few in number, selective, and usually expensive. (2) Based on its Latin derivation, *public* refers to "the people," and it describes schools that in some sense are available to anyone who can meet entry requirements and afford tuition; such schooling generally involves group instruction rather than private, tutorial arrangements. (3) America's public schools today offer group instruction, are tax-supported, and are available to all.

Pygmalion effect   [4]

Rosenthal's hypothesis (also called "the experimenter effect") that students' school performance is affected by the basic attitudes, expectations, and fundamental perceptions that teachers have of them. (In Shaw's play *Pygmalion*—the basis of the musical *My Fair Lady*—the uneducated "flower girl" Eliza Doolittle is "turned into" a lady because Professor Higgins treats her like a lady and expects her to act like one).

quadrivium   [7]

The Christian Church's classification of the last four of the *seven liberal arts* (astronomy, arithmetic, music, and geometry); also see *trivium.*

reconstructionism   [10]

A reaction to *essentialism*, this educational philosophy is closely associated with *progressivism*; it holds that education should be devoted to building a global democratic social order. (See *essentialism, perennialism,* and *progressivism.*)

reform package   [12]

Popular approach taken by many states during the 1980s to institute sweeping, elaborate educational reforms in response to the criticism leveled by the *National Commission on Excellence in Education.*

reform proposals   [12]

The ideas for improving public education that arose during the 1980s in response to criticism leveled by the *National Commission on Excellence in Education.*

regional accreditation associations   [7]

Organizations formed at the turn of

the century to establish minimal standards for high school and college curricula by applying concepts devised by such groups as the *Committee of Ten* and the *Commission on the Reorganization of Secondary Education*. (Also see *Cardinal Principles of Secondary Education*.)

regular education initiative [7]
Method of implementing Public Law 94–142, which calls for "inclusive education" or "least restrictive environments" that give all students the right to free, appropriate education.

religious realism [10]
The philosophical tradition that is compatible with *classical realism* except that it includes a Divine dimension. (See *scientific realism*; also see Figure 10.1.)

res judicata [11]
Literally, "a matter judged"; this means that the highest court with jurisdiction over the matter has decided the issue, and there is no further basis for an appeal.

satisfier [1]
A factor that is perceived positively by the person experiencing it; an aspect of a job that makes the job satisfying to a person. (Compare *dissatisfier*.)

scheme [6]
According to Piaget, the general properties that an individual needs in order to interact with a particular part of the environment. (Figure 6.2 outlines the evolution of learning theories.)

scholasticism [8]
Intellectual efforts to reconcile theological and philosophical ideas about how the physical world relates to the spiritual world; scholasticism dominated intellectual pursuits during the Middle Ages and early Renaissance.

scholasticus [8]
A Roman Catholic Church official who was authorized by a bishop to run a cathedral school.

school-based management (SBM) [3, 5]
To offset the negative effects of *bureaucracy* in education, the central district delegates authority to local schools and shares decision making with their representatives, who might include both staff and community members. SBM gives teachers, parents, and students a greater voice in decisions affecting their school.

science [10]
Knowledge that is connected with the physical world and all its phenomena.

scientific realism [10]
The philosophical tradition which holds that the physical world is real and permanent and that changes take place in accordance with natural laws. (See *classical realism, religious realism*, and Figure 10.1.)

scribes [8]
Learned officials and teachers who lived in ancient Egypt.

secondary school [7]
Tuition-supported institution that developed after the Reformation to prepare aristocratic and upper-class students for university study. (Most peasants and working-class students attended a vernacular *elementary school*; Europeans went either to one

or another type of school, not first to one and then to the other.)

selectmen   [3]
Seventeenth-century colonial officials in Massachusetts and Connecticut who oversaw school matters, such as ensuring that townships with more than fifty families had teachers who were proficient in basic reading, writing, and mathematics and determining which families were too poor to pay for their children's schooling. (See *trustees.*)

sensorimotor stage   [6]
Piaget's first stage of cognitive development (from infancy to about age two), when babies develop schemes to coordinate their motor skills and begin to learn (through *assimilation* and *accommodation*) to find meaning in signals and symbols. (Figure 6.1 summarizes Piaget's stages of cognitive development, and Figure 6.2 outlines the evolution of learning theories.)

***Serrano* v. *Priest*   [3]**
Decision by the California Supreme Court in 1971 which held that a funding scheme which makes the quality of a child's education dependent on the wealth of the school district unfairly discriminates against the poor. This led to a U.S. Supreme Court ruling in 1973 that the U.S. Constitution does not guarantee a right to be educated—thus blunting the movement toward equalizing funding to improve education.

seven liberal arts   [7]
Seven "academic" subjects pioneered by the Egyptians and spread by the Romans throughout their empire (and so throughout the Western world); but it was the Greeks who made these subjects the core of their *curriculum,* believing that they increased human potential by liberating people from irrational passions. The Christian Church divided the seven liberal arts into the *trivium* (grammar, rhetoric, and *logic*) and the *quadrivium* (astronomy, arithmetic, music, and geometry).

Skinner box   [6]
Mechanism used by B. F. Skinner to perform experiments in *operant conditioning.* An animal in the box was presented with a lever that released food when it was pressed (*positive reinforcer*); the box was devoid of any other stimulus, since Skinner's goal was to control the environment and predict behavior. (See *negative reinforcer.*)

Smith-Hughes Act of 1917   [7]
Federal legislation that funded the training of high school teachers of agriculture and home economics.

social bifurcation   [4]
Predicted division or splitting of the U.S. social structure into two increasingly large groupspeople in higher classes and people in lower classes. Middleclass segments are expected to shrink as technology advances; people will need higher job skills or will go unemployed.

social class   [4]
Group of people who have similar values, habits, and lifestyles as well as "common political and economic goals and interests related to their position in the social structure."

socioeconomic status (SES)   [4]
Relative position within society based

on five variables: family background, economic level, occupational status, parents' educational attainment, and living patterns.

Sophists [8]

Another name for philosophers in ancient Athens. Sophists developed a questionable reputation because they sold their knowledge and because many people thought they engaged in deceptive, self-serving reasoning.

state action [9]

Legal term for social control over education (such as township, state, or national government), as opposed to personal, family, or local control over schools. In the mid-nineteenth century those who favored state action began to refer to themselves as *friends of education*—implying that those who supported local control must be foes; in this way education was framed in a political context.

state supreme court [11]

The court of last resort in a state's judicial system; in some states this court has a different name. (See Figure 11.1.)

status [1]

Relative rank in a hierarchy of prestige; one way that social scientists compare occupations or professions. Figure 1.1 shows how the public ranks teaching and ten other occupations.

stimulus-response (S-R) bond theory [6]

Edward L. Thorndike's theory that every mental unit has a corresponding physical component which acts as a stimulus or as a response and that learning occurs when physical and mental elements are connected; also

known as *connectionism*. (Figure 6.2 outlines the evolution of learning theories.)

studium generale [8]

Medieval study center or system of university and its colleges that offered a general array of studies; such systems developed throughout Europe by the fourteenth century and eventually came to be called universities. (See *studium particular*.)

studium particular [8]

Medieval study center that offered only one *higher faculty* in addition to the *lesser faculty* of the arts. (See *studium generale*.)

superintendent [3]

Chief executive officer for a school district. See Table 3.4 for a demographic profile of superintendents and Table 3.5 for a list of superintendents' duties.

swaddling [8]

Tightly wrapping infants and small children in cloth bands to restrict their movement, a practice that continued in the Western world until the seventeenth century.

syllogism [10]

One of the most common forms of *deductive reasoning*; it proceeds as follows: If A is equal to B and B is equal to C, then A is equal to C.

tabula rasa [6]

The idea of seventeenth-century English philosopher John Locke that an infant's mind at birth is a "blank tablet" which accumulates, in an organized way, the impressions of sensory experiences. Thus Locke differed with the ancient Greeks in saying that an infant's mind was empty, rather than filled with inborn potentials. (See *mental discipline* and Figure 6.2.)

tenure [2]

Guaranteed term of office after completion of a probationary period; tenure protects teachers from dismissal without cause.

town-gown disputes [8]

Conflicts between townspeople and the large number of students (dressed in clerical gowns) who attended medieval universities; by the thirteenth century such disputes had spurred the development of residential colleges.

trivium [7]

The Christian Church's classification of the first three of the *seven liberal arts* (grammar, rhetoric, and *logic*); also see *quadrivium*.

tracking [4]

The practice of separating high school students into different classrooms and *curricula* according to their achievement levels. Traditional tracks have been college preparatory, vocational, and general.

trustees [3]

Eighteenth-century property owners who replaced *selectmen* as formal supervisors of township schools; trustees were chosen by general consent or were elected.

tuition tax credit [3]

Alternative schooling arrangement in which parents' income taxes are reduced by some or all of the amount they pay for a child's tuition at a private school. (See *choice plan* and *voucher plan*.)

ummia [8]

A Sumerian priest who taught in a temple school (*eduba*).

underclass [4]

People at the bottom of the social hierarchy, with little hope of escaping their conditions. Often found in larger cities, most of the underclass are members of *minority groups* whose household (if they have one) is headed by a female; their lives are disorganized and dysfunctional, and they cope with high levels of crime.

universitas [8]

Eleventh-century masters guild for teachers of higher education who were supposed to be licensed by the *scholasticus* at Notre Dame before opening a school; by the twelfth century many teachers were being licensed without first becoming members of the universitas.

upper class [4]

Highest of five levels of *socioeconomic status* in the United States, including about 2 percent of the population. These people enjoy inherited wealth and have prominent social standing that can be traced back several generations. (See *upper middle class*.)

upper middle class [4]

Second-highest of five levels of *socioeconomic status* in the United States, including about 16 percent of the population. These people have not inherited wealth but most likely have attained it through hard work; they typically value formal education, are active in their communities, and enjoy some luxuries. (See *upper class* and *lower middle class*.)

upper working class [4]

Fourth of five levels of *socioeconomic*

status in the United States, including about 32 percent of the population. These people are bluecollar, not white-collar, workers, and they may be slightly less educated than the *lower middle class*; they nonetheless have upwardly mobile ambitions (including high school graduation for their children), and they enjoy modern conveniences and leisure time. (See *common-person class, lower middle class,* and *lower working class.*)

U.S. district court   [11]
One of ninety courts at the lowest federal level of jurisdiction, for cases involving substantial federal statutory or constitutional issues. (See Figure 11.1.)

U.S. Supreme Court   [11]
The highest court in America, and therefore the court of last resort for both state and federal legal systems. (See Figure 11.1.)

voucher plan   [3]
Alternative schooling arrangement in which all parents receive vouchers worth a specified amount of money that they can spend at the school of their choice. (See *choice plan* and *tuition tax credit.*)

Woman's Rights Convention of 1848   [5]
Meeting held in Seneca Falls, New York, to secure for women "an equal participation with men in the various trades, professions, and commerce"; one of the earliest efforts by women in the United States to take political action.

INDEX OF NAMES

SUBJECT INDEX

A

Ability testing, 103–104
  reasons for use of, 103–104
Ability-to-pay method, taxation, 78
Academic freedom, 184
Academy, use of term, 225–226,
  243–244
Accommodation, Piagetian, 155
Accreditation
  history of, 185–186
  regional accreditation associa-
    tions, 185
Achievement
  minority students, 126–127
  Pygmalion effect, 106
  and teacher expectations,
    106–107
Administrators
  principal, 53–58
  specialized functions, historical
    view, 73, 75
  superintendents, 60–64
  women and minorities as, 58–59
Aesthetics
  existential beliefs, 287–288
  idealist beliefs, 284
  nature of, 266
  pragmatist beliefs, 286
  realist beliefs, 285
African-Americans
  education of, 252–254
  Freedmen's Bureau, 252, 254
Afrocentric perspective, 334
Alcohol and drug use, 337
*Alexander v. Holmes County Board of
  Education*, 314

Alphabet, development of, 207–208
American education, history of
  academy, 244
  accreditation and licensure,
    185–186
  African-Americans education,
    252–254
  child-centered curriculum, 180
  colonial era, 234–242
  common schools, 250
  diploma mills, 186–187
  friends of education, 249–250
  grammar school, 248
  during Great Awakening, 242–243
  higher education, 255–256
  politicizing of education, 249–255
  private school, 250
  progressive education, 257
  project-centered curriculum, 181
  religious splintering, effects of,
    242–245
  secondary schools, 255
  state action, 249
  state educational systems,
    251–252
  vocational education, 181–183
American Federation of Teachers
  (AFT), origins of, 34–35
American Journal of Education, 251
Analytic philosophy, 289
Ancient cultures and education
  Egyptian education, 206–207
  Greeks, 207–211
  Roman education, 211–215
  Sumerian education, 205–206
Apperception, 148
Apperceptive mass, 148

397

duties and responsibilities of,
62–63
as managers, 63–64
relationship with school boards,
64
Supreme Court, 300
Swaddling, 208–209
Syllogism, 265–266
Symbols, freedom of expression
issue, 304

T

Tablet houses, 204
Tabula rasa, 145–146
Taxation
ability-to-pay method, 78
benefit principle, 78
Teacher expectations
and achievement, 106–107
and performance of minority
students, 129–131
Teacher preparation programs, 6–9
advanced degrees, 73
competency tests, 8
historical view of, 11–14
mentoring programs, 9
Teachers
autonomy of, 43–45
career-ladder plan, 45
certification of, 6, 8, 9
dissatisfactions about profession,
25
education majors versus noneducation majors, 5–6
future demand for, 361–362
licensing of, 6
professionalism, 41–46
pros and cons of profession,
17–20
salaries, 13, 14–15
satisfactions about profession,
20–25
shortages, 9
status of, 15–17

tests of knowledge, 8
Teenage pregnancy, 337–338
Tenth Amendment, 72
Textbooks, 193–196
Texas approved list, 194–195
textbook review committee, 195
traditionalist view, 334
Thoughts on the Education of Daughters
(Wollstonecraft), 228
*Tinker v. Des Moines Independent Com-
munity School District*, 304–305
Total quality education, 79–80
Town-gown disputes, 219
Tracking
criticisms of, 102
and socioeconomic status, 93–94
Trustees, 67
Tuition tax credit, 80
Twin studies, intelligence, 97–98,
105

U

Ummia, 205
Underclass, characteristics of, 90–91
Union College, 182
Unions, 31–40
American Federation of Teachers
(AFT), 34–35
collective bargaining, 35–39
historical development, 31–34
political action committees, 39
teachers' strikes, 35–36
United Federation of Teachers
(UFT), 34–35
United Federation of Teachers
(UFT), origins of, 34–35
United States Department of Educa-
tion, creation of, 70–71, 251
Universal education, 220
Universitas, 217
Universities. *See* Higher education
Upper class, characteristics of, 87
Upper middle class, characteristics
of, 87–88

Some Questions for Our Readers

Your evaluation of *Education Today: The Foundations of a Profession* is very important to us, and will help in the preparation of future editions of the text. Please complete this form and mail it to College Marketing Department, St. Martin's Press, Inc., 175 Fifth Avenue, New York, NY 10010.

1. Please rate *Education Today* in each of the following areas:

	Excellent	Good	Adequate	Poor
a. General interest:	_____	____	_____	____
b. Usefulness:	_____	____	_____	____
c. Selection of topics:	_____	____	_____	____
d. Detail of coverage:	_____	____	_____	____
e. Order of topics:	_____	____	_____	____
f. Writing style	_____	____	_____	____
g. Explanation of concepts:	_____	____	_____	____
h. Study aids:				
Advanced organizers	_____	____	_____	____
Chapter opening vignettes	_____	____	_____	____
Contemporary Perspectives	_____	____	_____	____
Research Says . . .	_____	____	_____	____
Yesterday's Professional	_____	____	_____	____
i. Text design/use of color	_____	____	_____	____

2. Please cite specific examples that illustrate any of the above points: _____

_____

_____

_____

3. What do you find to be the strongest feature(s) of the book? _____

_____

_____

_____

4. What do you find to be the weakest feature(s) of the book? _____

_____

_____

_____

5. What other topics do you think should be included in the next edition of this book? _____

_____

_____